THE 100 GREATEST SCENES IN MOTION PICTURE HISTORY

Anthony G. Puzzilla

For permission requests, please contact Canoe Tree Press.
Published 2020
Printed in the United States of America
ISBN 9781734550429 (print)
ISBN 9781734550436 (ebook)

Canoe Tree Press
4697 Main Street
Manchester, VT 05255
www.CanoeTreePress.com

TABLE OF CONTENTS

ACKNOWLEDGMENTS

To my friend and colleague Martin Gostanian, I express my sincere appreciation for sharing his insight and lifelong love of the cinema with me.

I freely acknowledge my extensive use of the AMC Film site "A Tribute to the 100 Greatest Scenes Film Scenes" written by Tim Dirks (https://www.filmsite.org/scenesD.html). This site provided me with an excellent source of background information concerning many of these scenes, which was a wonderful foundation in which to build my own discussion and analysis.

In addition, the wonderful Turner Classic Movies (TCM) site (http://www.tcm.com/) provided invaluable information, trivia, and insight concerning many of these memorable scenes.

INTRODUCTION

In the history of motion pictures, from the silent era to modern times, there are literally hundreds of thousands of memorable scenes which seem to have achieved a life of their own as they often transcend the movie itself and become a symbol of human intolerance, horror, struggle, salvation, endurance, vindication, joy, and hope. In other words, all aspects of human existence and experience. In most cases, they are the culmination of a movie, the embodiment and essence of the film, or they stand alone and are fondly remembered, either with fondness, hope, laughter, or even utter fear. The scene may also be the prelude to a subsequent sequence of events in the movie, but they set the stage for that series of developments. Whatever the case, they remain the defining film moments and iconic images that will endure for as long as motion pictures are remembered.

The book will not only discuss the intrinsic essence of the one hundred greatest scenes in motion picture history themselves, but also the mechanics and thought processes that created each of these scenes.

Sometimes a particular scene is like a two-sided coin; that is, the scene is shown as well as the associated flip side. For instance, if the scene shows a person is speaking, then we see who the person is speaking to, as well. In this particular case, only one scene is counted in our list of one hundred greatest scenes. Sometimes, other scenes are shown from the same movie. They are included only as a further enhancement to the overall discussion. They are also not counted as one of the one hundred greatest scenes.

In the end, the scene should transcend its existence in the film itself and have meaning and relevance for us even today. Without this, the scene loses its real significance over time and becomes just a memory without substance and form in the continuum of cinematic existence and conscious awareness. I will attempt to address this "relevance" in each of the scenes I discuss in my book.

Because each scene is unique and priceless on its own merit and importance to the film, of which it is an integral part, it would be unfair to try to rank them in any manner except in chronological order beginning with the Silent Era. However, at the end of the book, I will present my own personal top five scenes just as a matter of interest to the readers. I will let each reader decide their favorites among the scenes presented in this book. I hope I included your favorite scenes.

Obviously, my selection of scenes is purely biased, clearly reflecting the era in which I grew up and my innate prejudice for the older vintage movies of the past. If I was born thirty years later than I was, the list of these movies would probably be more biased toward the movies of the 1980s to the present.

CHAPTER 1

THE SILENT ERA

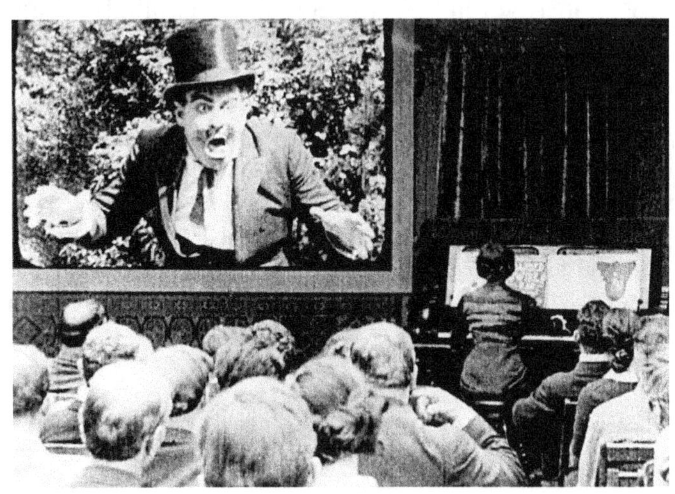

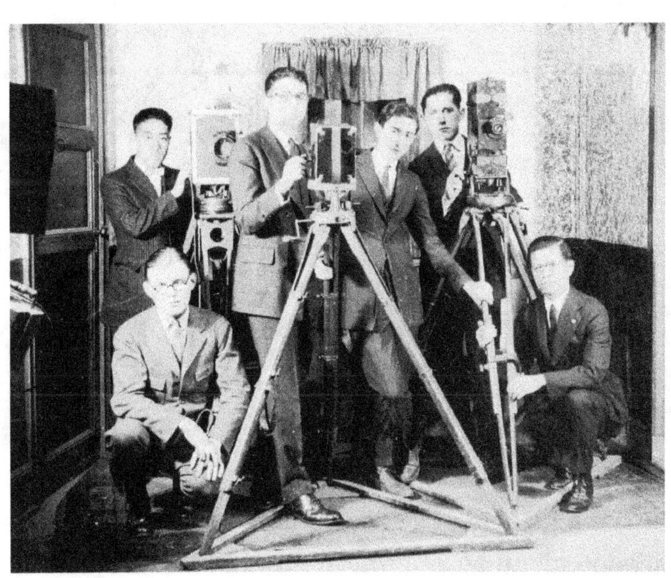

The Birth of a Nation (1915)

A truly controversial, reprehensible, explicitly racist but ground-breaking, landmark American epic film masterpiece—these all describe producer/director D. W. Griffith's cinematic work, *The Birth of a Nation*. Although its themes are considered today to be insensitive, vile, and historically inaccurate, we need to judge it for its innovative approach to movie-making and theatrics. In particular, it is remarkable for its cinematic feel and spectacle of splendidly staged Civil War battle scenes with historical costuming and hundreds of extras.

Scene: The Desperate Charge

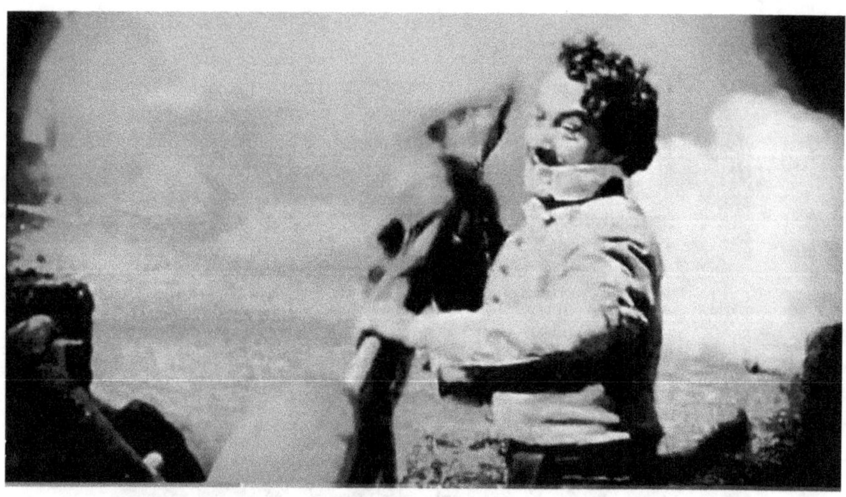

On the battlefield, the eldest son of the Piedmont Virginia Cameron family, Benjamin Cameron (Henry B. Wathall), known as "the Little Colonel," leads a final desperate assault against the Union command of Captain Phil Stoneman (Elmer Clifton), charging down a road leading his troops, in a dramatic moving-camera shot, which was taken from a high angle. Cameron is wounded in action when he leads a final assault carrying the Confederate flag against the Union entrenchment line and defiantly jams it into the barrel of a Union cannon before his prostrate body collapses in front of the entrenchment. This scene is a culmination of many various-range camera shots, both close-up and long-range, that precede it. The close-up shows violent and bloody hand-to-hand combat intermixed with long-range camera shots of the entrenchments of the North and South showing their respective batteries. Interlaced with the violence shown on the screen, the director shows scenes of compassion and humanity. One scene shows the Cameron family tenderly praying for him and redemption in two battlefield scenes. The first battlefield scene shows Cameron stopping to give water and comfort to a dying Union soldier. This act of spontaneous compassion is wildly cheered by the Union soldiers. The other scene shows a momentarily pause in the battle when Stoneman rescues the wounded Cameron from danger.

The brilliantly realistically filmed long-range shots of the battle are probably the first time movie audiences saw how the Civil War, our nation's bloodiest conflict, was actually fought just over fifty years prior (1861–1865). The recreation of a Civil War battle in this film, with all its horror and violence, is gripping and masterfully choreographed by Griffith. It was filmed in the San Fernando Valley of Southern California near Los Angeles.

Scene: The Homecoming

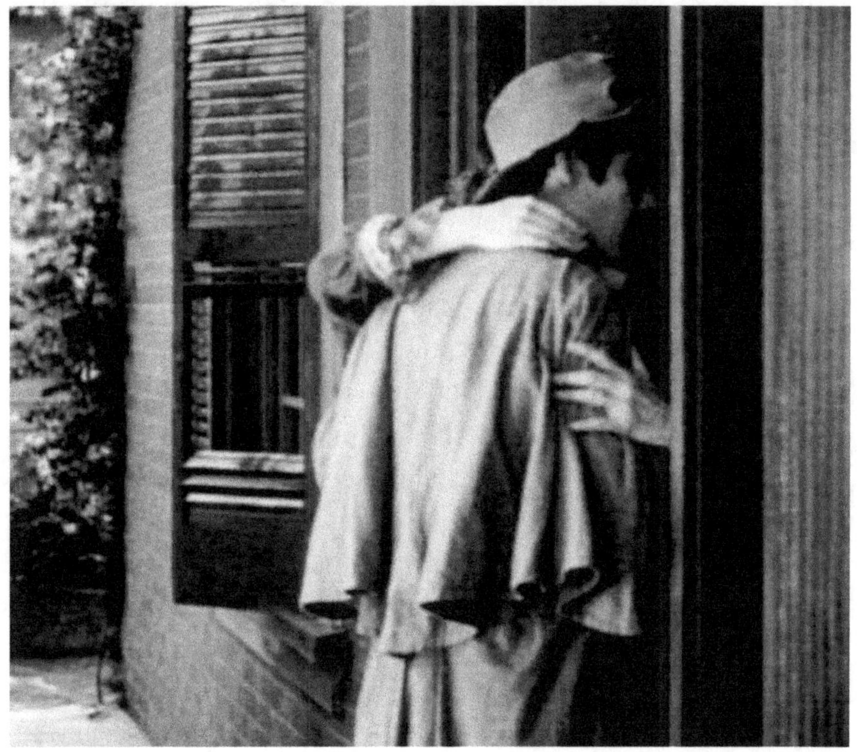

When *The Birth of a Nation* begins, the Camerons are anything but poor, but they hum with close-knit affection, which, as war and reconstruction afford them little but death and poverty, allows them to survive. The survival of families, through whatever storm or strife, is one of Griffith's great themes. Whenever the filmmaker explores it, he's generous with detail and nuance. His most touching and serene moments are when the audience is witness to the enduring love and affection that binds the members of the Cameron family through the best and worst of times.

When Ben Cameron returns from the war tattered, fragile, and weak from his wounds and a long recuperation in a northern hospital, he approaches the homestead with what appears to be fear and trepidation. Weary, Ben approaches the front fence of his home, pausing to notice its disrepair. As he stands there, "Little Sister" Flora (Mae Marsh) and other family members expectantly await his arrival inside. Ben slowly enters the fence gate and approaches the front porch. We see him, in a medium shot, on the sidewalk in the midday sun with the street empty and no life stirring from the house. As he reaches the porch, however, Flora suddenly emerges, greeting him alone because the family, fully aware he's just outside, has planned it that way. They don't want to overwhelm him. Confronting each other, brother and sister are reserved and tentative. Flora grins, but Ben just stares. It's been a full four years since he's seen his kid sister, who has since grown to nubile maturity, and he appears abashed at the development.

The siblings are reduced to commenting on the poor state of each other's wardrobe. Ben distractedly fingers the tufts of cotton Flora has, at the last minute, decorated her homespun dress with (the best of her clothes having already been donated to The Cause), while she points to the holes in his dilapidated (bullet-hole-ridden?) officer's hat. Finally, there's a rush of feeling between them and the two melt into a loving embrace. Then, as Flora leads him to the front door and enters it first, Griffith carefully composes a shot from within the porch but down its length, so that, as Ben reaches the door and hesitates before it, we see Flora's arms and those of his mother, her body and face unseen, extend outward from within, gather him up, and draw him into the house.

Like much of what we see of the Cameron's domestic life, the entire scene is delicately underplayed, but here Griffith's direction provides the emotional realism of a returning, battle-scarred veteran who feels disoriented and weirdly detached at the long-dreamt moment of homecoming. The Little Colonel's mind and body still inhabit the pain and horror of war; it's up to his family to pull him into the warmth of hearth and home. With the camera keeping its medium distance, we see, not faces contorted with joy and streaming tears, but just this simple gesture of welcome and familial restoration. The economy of the image, what it leaves out—and the visual mastery of its conception—is the key to its power and why it's the crowning moment in the film, and possibly the finest in Griffith's entire career.

What *Birth of a Nation* offers, even more than a vision of history, is a template for the vast, world-embracing capabilities of the cinema. It provided extraordinarily powerful tools for its own refutation. The real crime was not totally Griffith's, but the world's: the fact that most viewers knew little about slavery and little about reconstruction and little about Jim Crow and little about the Klan, and were all too ready to swallow the very worst of the movie without question. They saw only what Griffith wanted to say, but not what the movie showed, and, upon seeing what Griffith showed, were ready to take up arms in anger. It would have to be up to other directors to set the history straight concerning the role of African-Americans during this era in our history, such as in *Glory* (1989), but we can't ignore the innovative, creative, and revolutionary cinematic tools and techniques that Griffith brought to the cinema still used today.

Griffith's art offers humanly profound moments, whether graceful and delicate or grand and rhetorical, that detach themselves from their context to probe nearly universal circumstances, such as the wonderfully staged battle showing Cameron's charge, showing the ravages of war delicately interlaced with scenes of mercy on the battlefield and a family in solemn prayer, or the blend of shame and pride in the face of a returning Confederate soldier when he comes home in tatters and finds his sister in tatters as well.

Intolerance (1916)

Intolerance is an epic silent film directed by D. W. Griffith. The lavish three-hour-and-fifteen-minute film used settings varying from ancient Babylon to modern America to dramatize the title theme. Although one form of intolerance it noticeably, and probably deliberately, failed to address was anti-black racism. *Intolerance* is most interesting mainly because its advanced style in storytelling is still very popular in today's cinema. It also started the popular movie theme of depicting such intolerance and its consequences, in such movies as *To Kill a Mockingbird* (1963) and *In the Heat of the Night* (1967).

Scene: The Babylon Set

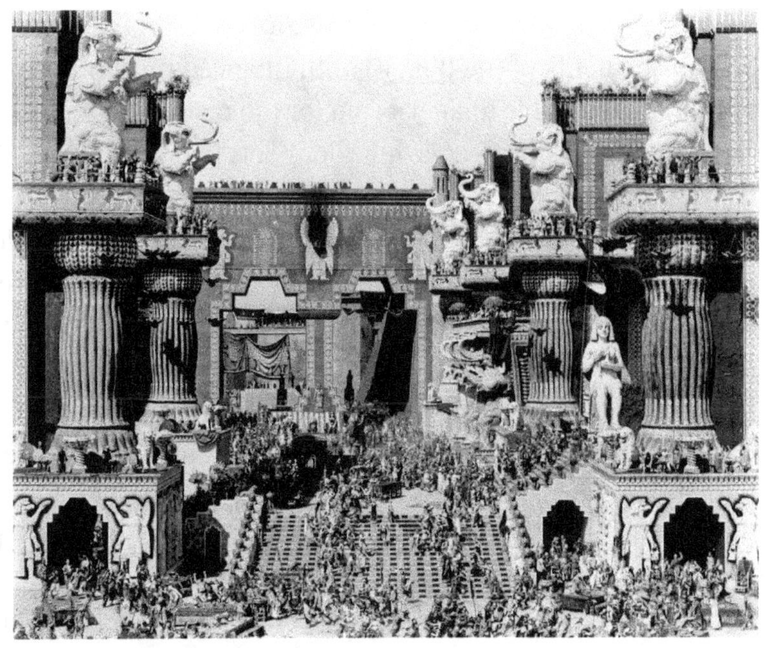

This Babylon set scene is just a "snapshot" of the entire opening sequence of the film. The scene is only a portion of the entire Babylon set, which still takes one's breath away even today.

TCM provided many of the following factoids regarding this remarkable and fascinating film.

The film consists of four distinct but parallel stories—intercut with increasing frequency as the film builds to a climax—that demonstrate humankind's persistent intolerance throughout the ages. The timeline covers approximately 2,500 years. The first episode, the ancient "Babylonian" story (539 BC), depicts the conflict between Prince Belshazzar of Babylon and Cyrus the Great of Persia. The fall of Babylon is a result of intolerance arising from a conflict between devotees of two rival Babylonian gods: Bel-Marduk and Ishtar.

The total cost of producing *Intolerance* was reported to be close to $2 million including $250,000 for the Belshazzar feast scene alone, an astronomical sum in 1916, but accounts for the film show the exact cost to be $385,906.77. One-third of the budget went into making the Babylonian segments of the film. Griffith financed most of the film, which contributed to his financial ruin for the rest of his life.

The epic, three-eighths-of-a-mile-long sets that were created for the Babylonian sequence towered above the streets of Hollywood, but probably not as high as its reputation in Hollywood legend. It is hard to imagine now how the set must have appeared to the citizens of Los Angeles. In the age before skyscrapers dotted the Los Angeles horizon, the Babylon set, towering 165 feet above the Hollywood bungalows, and by far the most expensive set ever made by that time, looked like an ancient city springing up from beneath Los Angeles itself. Griffith's conception of the grandeur of the Babylon sequence was inspired by *Quo Vadis* (1912) and *Cabiria* (1914), both made in Italy.

The undisputed hero of the construction of the Babylon set, as well as other sets in *Intolerance*, was Frank "Huck" Wortman, the chief carpenter, set builder, and stage mechanic. A rough, down-to-earth man who chewed tobacco and spat out of the side of his mouth, it was Wortman who saved Griffith thousands of dollars in production costs by imagining and improvising new ways of making huge sets look the part. The beautiful archways in the Jerusalem set, for example, were ingeniously created by bending thin boards and coating them in plaster. Overall, Griffith depended heavily on Wortman to raise the Babylon set to newer, more stupendous heights. Every day, the sets kept growing larger and higher than the original plans called for. There was a very real fear that they would collapse, so whenever a nighttime windstorm fell upon the city, Wortman and several other crewmen would jump into their cars and race to the set in order to reinforce the cable supports. While the publicity for *Intolerance* greatly exaggerated the sets as reaching five hundred feet high, the truth behind the legendary sets placed the bar for future epic movies in terms of grandiosity and workmanship.

The Babylonian orgy sequence alone cost $200,000 when it was shot. That's near twice the overall budget of *The Birth of a Nation* (1915), another D.W. Griffith film, and, at the time, the record holder for most expensive picture ever made.

The extras in the Babylonian scenes were supposedly paid two dollars a day, per head, an astronomically generous sum at the time. They were also each given a box lunch and had temporary latrine facilities built for them.

The massive life-size set of the Great Wall of Babylon, seen in the fourth story, was placed at the corner of Sunset Boulevard and Hollywood Boulevard (in Hollywood, California) when the movie was completed. It became a notable landmark for many years during Hollywood's golden era. It actually stood on the lot of the studio on Prospect Avenue near the Sunset and Hollywood Boulevard junctions in the eastern end of the city. It was the first such exterior set ever built in Hollywood. Falling into disrepair and ruin, it was eventually torn down.

Many sources claim that the walls of Babylon were actually life-size, at three hundred feet—more than twenty-five stories—high. However, assistant director Joseph Henabery said that the walls, which were made of lath and plaster with a lumber frame, were only one hundred feet high, as three-hundred-foot-high walls of that material would have blown over with just a light wind. In fact, even at one hundred feet high, the walls were guyed with steel cables because a fairly stiff breeze would have blown them down.

The staging and art direction of the Babylonian scenes were largely inspired by the works of nineteenth-century painter Lawrence Alma-Tadema.

The Hollywood and Highland Center is a shopping mall and entertainment complex located at Hollywood Boulevard and Highland Avenue in the Hollywood district in Los Angeles. The 387,000-square-foot (36,000m2) center also includes the TCL Chinese Theatre (formerly Grauman's Chinese Theatre, and Mann's Chinese Theatre) and the Dolby Theater (formerly known as the Kodak Theatre), home to the Academy Awards. The historic site was once the home of the famed Hollywood Hotel. Located in the heart of Hollywood, along the Hollywood Walk of Fame, it is among the most visited tourist destinations in Los Angeles.

The centerpiece of the complex is a massive three-story courtyard inspired by the Babylon scene from the film *Intolerance*, elephants and all. The developer of the shopping center built parts of the archway and two pillars with elephant sculptures on the capitals, just as seen in the film, to the same full scale. It gives visitors an idea of how large the original set must have been.

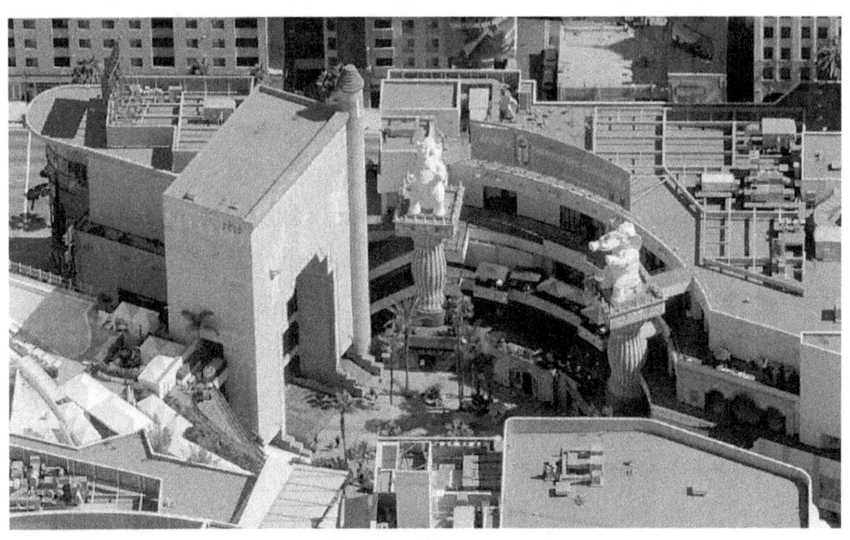

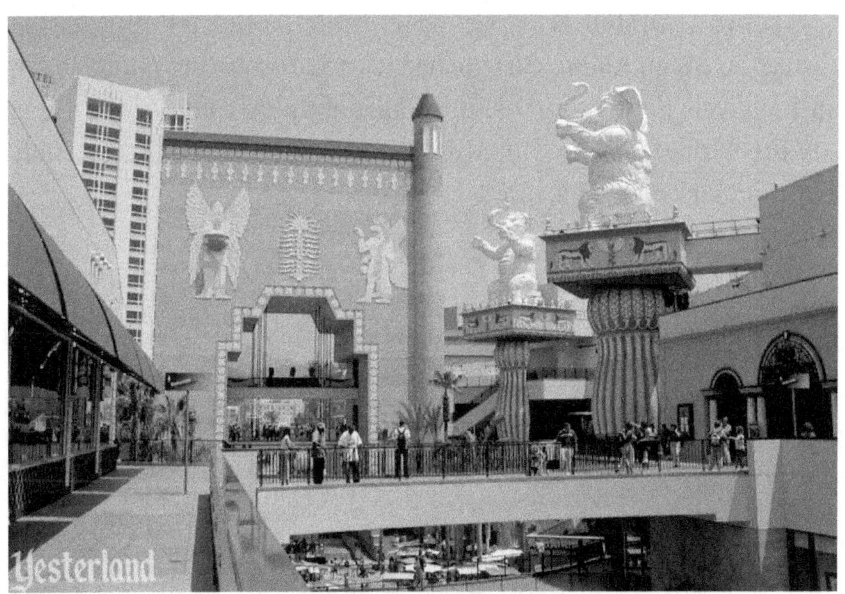
Yesterland

Way Down East (1920)

Way Down East is a silent romantic drama film directed by D. W. Griffith and starring Lillian Gish. It is one of four film adaptations of the melodramatic nineteenth-century play *Way Down East* by Lottie Blair Parker. There were two earlier silent versions and one sound version in 1935 starring Henry Fonda. A naive country girl is tricked into a sham marriage by a wealthy womanizer and then must try to rebuild her life despite the taint of having borne a child out of wedlock. Before she finds redemption and closure, she is nearly killed in a severe winter storm, but is bravely rescued by her future husband in the end. Today's popular movie theme of "love conquers all" got its start in movies such as this classic produced so many years ago.

Griffith's version is particularly remembered for its exciting climax in which Lillian Gish's character is rescued from doom on an icy river. Some sources, quoting newspaper ads of the time, say the sequence was filmed in an early color process, possibly Technicolor or Prismacolor.

Scene: The Perilous Ice Rescue

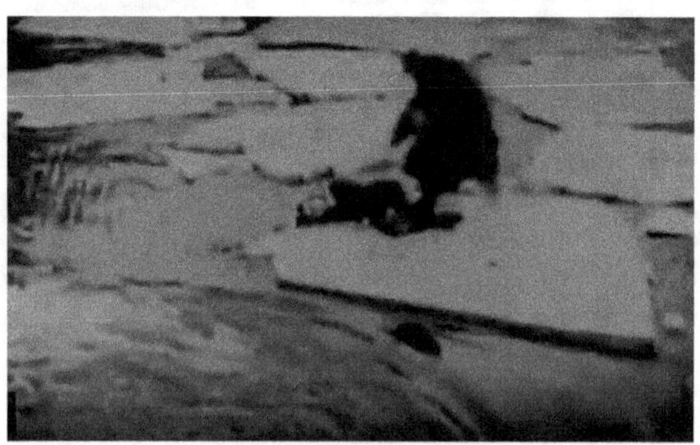

The most stunning and realistic sequence ever filmed was completely real and extremely dangerous is its finale. This is the scene of Anna Moore's (Lillian Gish) daring, last-second rescue from a moving ice floe. The young woman is ejected from the rural Bartlett home during a raging blizzard when her secret past (an unmarried pregnancy) is revealed. Delirious from the cold and blinded by the snow, she falls down and faints on a slab of ice in the middle of an icy river.

Lying on the ice block, her hand trails into the freezing water. As the ice thaws the next morning and breaks apart, her lifeless form is caught unconscious on moving ice floes and is swept downstream toward a precipitous waterfall. The farmer's son David Bartlett (Richard Barthelmess) sees her floating toward the falls. Without a moment to lose, in an exciting, tense "last-minute rescue scene," he dashes out onto the wobbly ice cakes and nimbly jumps from one moving, bobbing ice block to another to try to reach her before the ice jam gives way—rushing to the falls toward her death.

Despite its serial-like melodrama, it was so expertly and convincingly handled by director D.W. Griffith that even today it has audiences on the edges of their seats, bursting into enthusiastic and relieved applause when the rescue is finally affected. Barthelmess, in pursuit, runs across the treacherous ice-packed river, jumping from floe to floe, reaching Lillian ultimately at the very brink of the falls, picking her up and beginning the mad dash back to safety, even as the floe on which they were standing begins to plummet over the falls toward its utter destruction. In the end, she is saved and finds love and vindication after her ordeal.

The famous ice floe sequence was filmed in White River Junction, Vermont. An actual waterfall was used, though it was only a few feet high—the long shot where a large drop is shown was filmed at Niagara Falls. So expertly were these scenes cut in with one or two later studio shots, and with previously filmed scenes of Niagara Falls, that it was impossible to tell the studio version from the actual live footage.

The ice needed to be sawed or dynamited before filming could be done. During filming, a small fire had to be kept burning beneath the camera to keep the oil from freezing. At one point, Griffith was frostbitten on one side of his face. No stunt doubles were used at the time, so Gish and Barthelmess performed the stunts themselves. Lilian, lying freezing on the ice, thinly clad, was revived periodically (how nice) with cups of steaming tea. Gish's hair froze, and she lost feeling in her hand from the cold. It was her idea to put her hand and hair in the water, an image that would become iconic. Her right hand would be somewhat impaired for the remainder of her life.

The shot where the ice floes are filmed going over the waterfall was filmed out of season, so those ice floes are actually wooden. Cinematographically, the ice floe scene is an early example of parallel action.

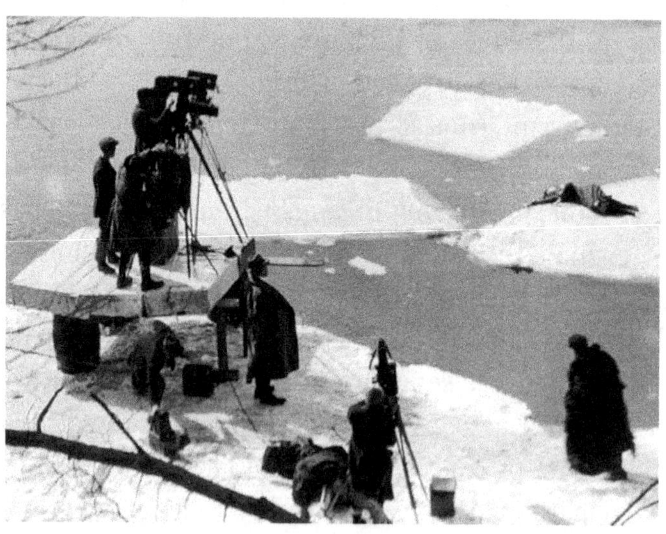

This is a photograph of Griffith and his great and long-time cameraman Billy Bitzer shooting the climactic scenes of the film.

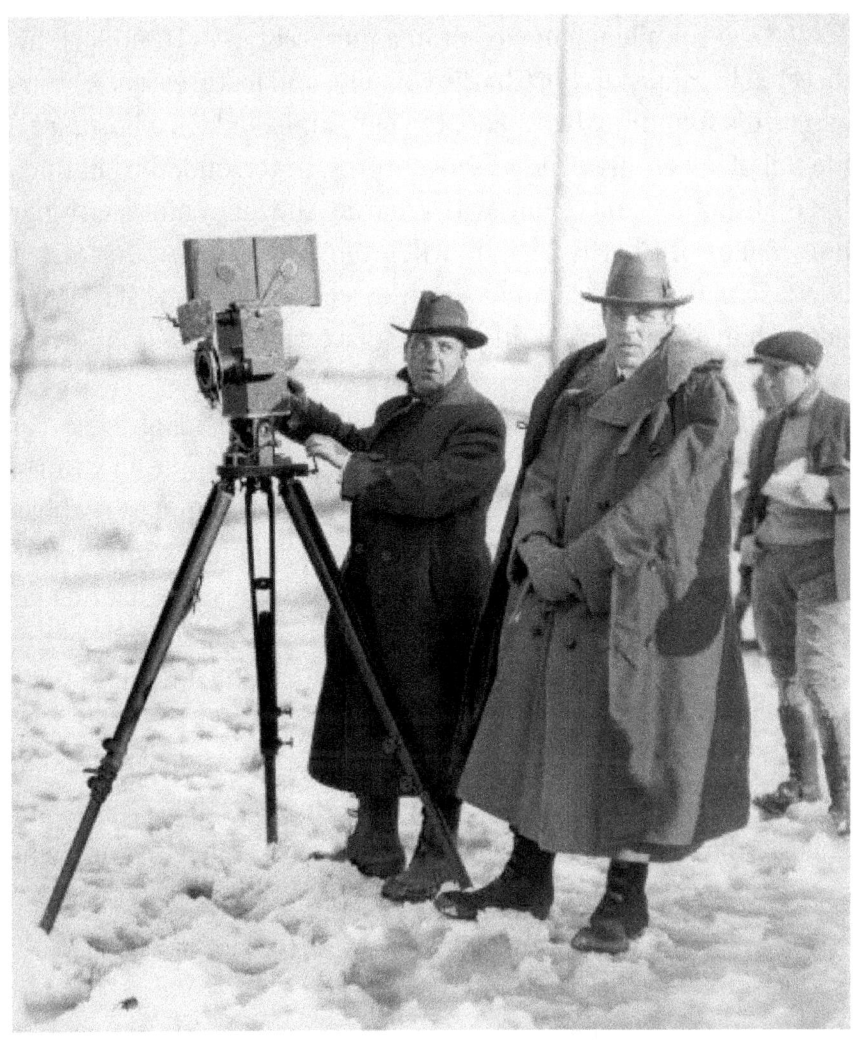

The Kid (1921)

The Kid is a silent comedy-drama film written by, produced by, directed by, and starring Charlie Chaplin, and features Jackie Coogan as his foundling baby, adopted son, and sidekick who share a life full of adventures and misadventures. In the end, the kid finds his real mother and, along with Charlie, they all embrace in her home. Fans of Charlie Chaplin will love *Chaplin Today: The Kid*. It is a fascinating documentary from director Alain Bergala, which takes an in-depth look at this classic masterpiece and its enduring worldwide appeal.

Additionally, the documentary looks at the lasting legacy of Chaplin's work, which has managed to touch people the world over. An interview with contemporary Iranian filmmaker Abbas Kiarostami is featured, who weighs in on Chaplin's strong influence over his own work through the years. He claims that he and Chaplin share "a philosophy of life rather than a philosophy of the cinema," which brings pure human emotion and feelings into their respective films.

In this scene, Coogan has been taken by the authorities while Charlie is refrained from rescuing him. However, he escapes and makes a daring rescue of his adopted ward after a harrowing flight over a series of rooftops.

Scene: Two Hearts Reunited

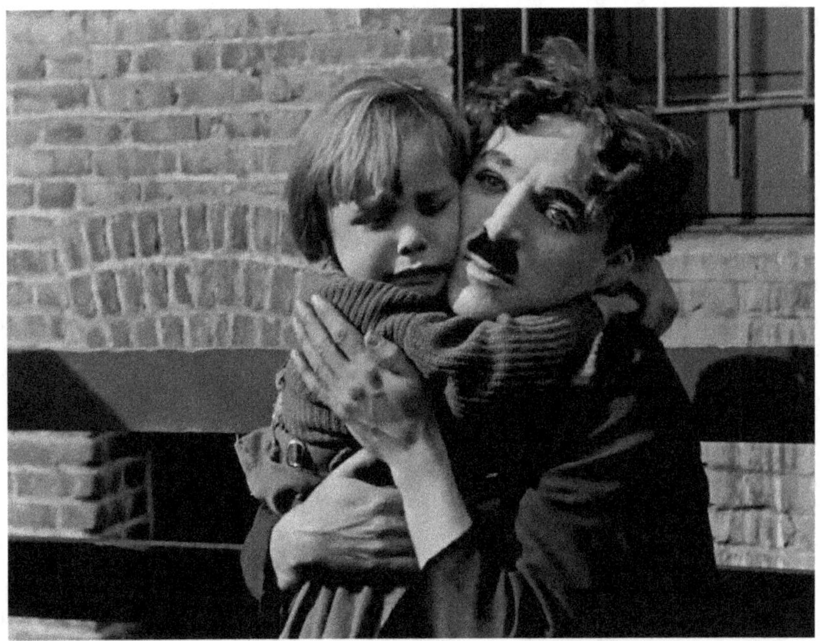

This is probably the most poignant and touching moment in motion picture history, mostly because the love between the two actors was real.

The film was truly a labor of love that took over a year to complete and came in the midst of a difficult divorce from first wife Mildred Harris following the death of their newborn child only ten days before production began.

The film made Coogan, then a vaudeville performer, into the first major child star of the movies. Many of the Chaplin biographers have attributed the relationship portrayed in the film to have resulted because of Chaplin's horrid state of mind at the time of the filming.

The film's ability to combine genuine warmth, pathos, and humor would later become a Chaplin trademark. No moment better illustrated that sublime combination than when the Tramp escapes the grim circumstances of his lot in the slums by imagining the place transformed into heaven and its residents dressed in angels' wings.

Even the story behind Chaplin's making of the film contained an element of melodrama. Severely depressed after the death of his newborn son from birth defects, Chaplin, one night, attended a vaudeville performance in which comedian Jack Coogan performed with his young son. Chaplin was captivated by the dynamic, talented son Jackie, and began writing a story around the charismatic child who had been coached as a performer by his father from the age of three.

The elder Coogan essentially put his career on hold to coach little Jackie Coogan through *The Kid*. Chaplin, in turn, rewarded Jack Senior's role in coaching the boy and assuaged his performer's ego by paying Jack $125 a week, almost double the seventy-five dollars a week Jackie was getting to costar. Jack Coogan Senior also played several roles in the film: as a bum who picks the Tramp's pocket, as the devil in the heaven sequence, and as a party guest.

The off-screen chemistry between Chaplin and Jackie Coogan was just as strong as their onscreen relationship in *The Kid* (initially titled *The Waif*). Every Sunday, during the first few weeks of filming, Chaplin would take Jackie to amusement parks and pony rides and other activities. Some have seen Chaplin's relationship with Coogan as an attempt for Chaplin to reclaim his own unhappy childhood, while others have interpreted Chaplin's attention toward the boy as recasting Coogan into the child he had just lost. The pair remained friends for the rest of their lives, and Coogan eventually went on to enjoy a second career as Uncle Fester on the cult TV comedy *The Addams Family* (1964–1966).

Jackie Coogan was a natural mimic and delighted Chaplin with his abilities on and off the set. Chaplin cast him in a small role in *A Day's Pleasure* (1919). In this candid photograph, one can see Chaplin delighting in the antics of Coogan during a break in filming.

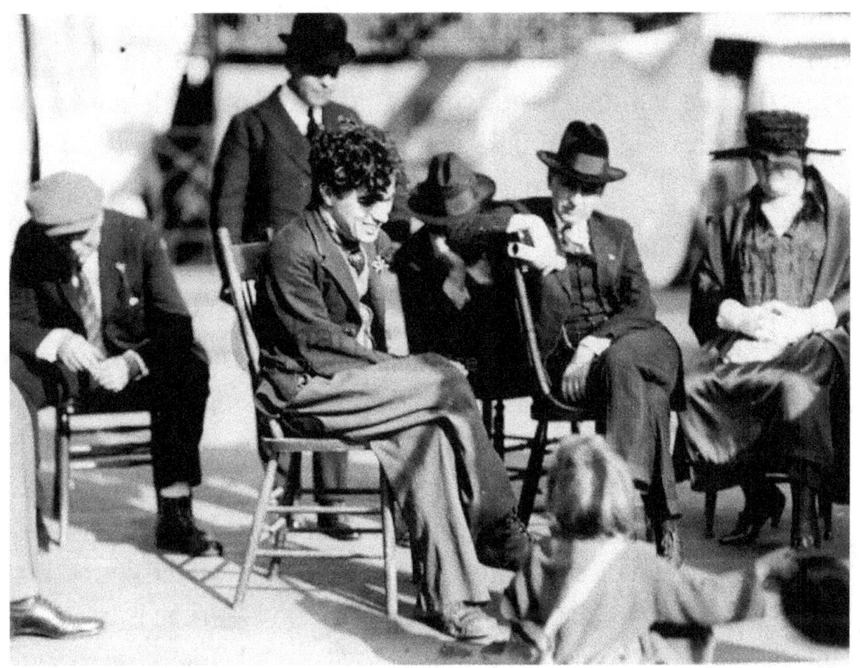

Nosferatu (1922)

Nosferatu is a silent German expressionist film. It was directed by F.W. Murnau with cinematography by Fritz Arno Wagner and Günther Krampf, starring Max Schreck as Count Orlok and Gustav von Wangenheim as Thomas Hutter. It is based on Bram Stoker's book *Dracula*, although the names and a few other details were changed because the studio was unable to obtain the rights to the novel. This particular film is considered by some to be the greatest adaptation of *Dracula* and tells the story of the count's departure from his homeland in Transylvania by schooner (killing everyone on board in the process) to his new home in Germany where begins a reign of terror among the populace, including Hutter's wife until he is "tricked" by her and is destroyed by the rising sun.

The photography in *Nosferatu* is highly influenced by the German Expressionist Movement and is very symbolic and stylized. This is what makes it one of the creepiest of the genre. The photography, for the most part, enhances the story. For instance, almost the entire film is shot in low-key, which adds to the eerie mood Murnau is trying to convey. Many shots are also in high contrast. Count Orlok is often shot in high contrast, which emphasizes his pale hideous face and long, claw-like hands against the shadows and his dark clothing. This might also be used to symbolize the relationship between light and dark.

In this scene at Orlok's castle, Nosferatu seems to materialize in the open door of Hutter's room. Nosferatu's haunting image slowly fills the doorway in the exact shape of the door itself. His ominous and foreboding figure blocks any manner of escape.

Scene: At Hutter's Door

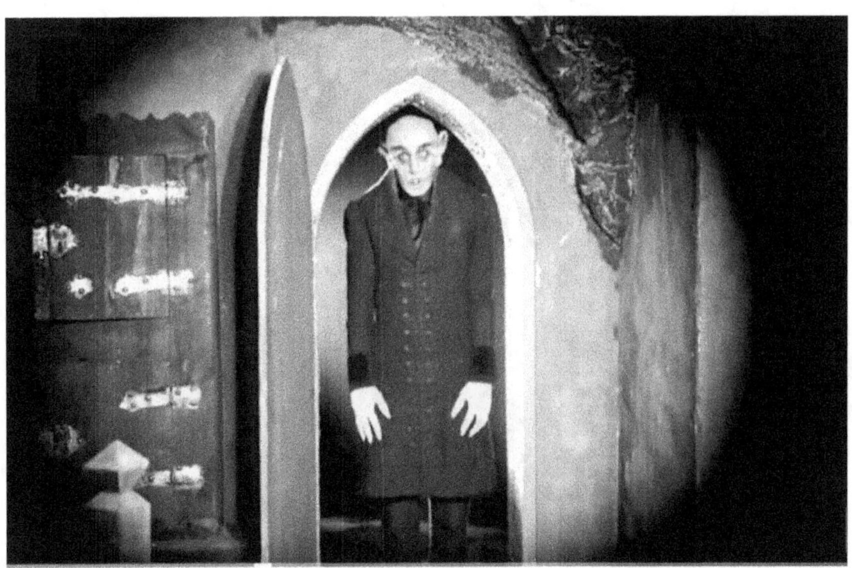

Another thing I noticed was that Murnau barely uses any camera movement in the entire film; in fact, the shots are rather simple, with most being full shots. There are some long shots and establishing shots that give the setting, but few close-ups. He does use some point-of-view shots when characters are looking out of windows. However, he uses a low-angle shot on the ship where we see Orlok walking on the mast.

In this shot, Orlok has risen from the bowels of the ship in search of blood from the few remaining crew members. His imposing figure strikes terror in the men who are unable to escape the horrible death that awaits them.

Scene: On the Mast

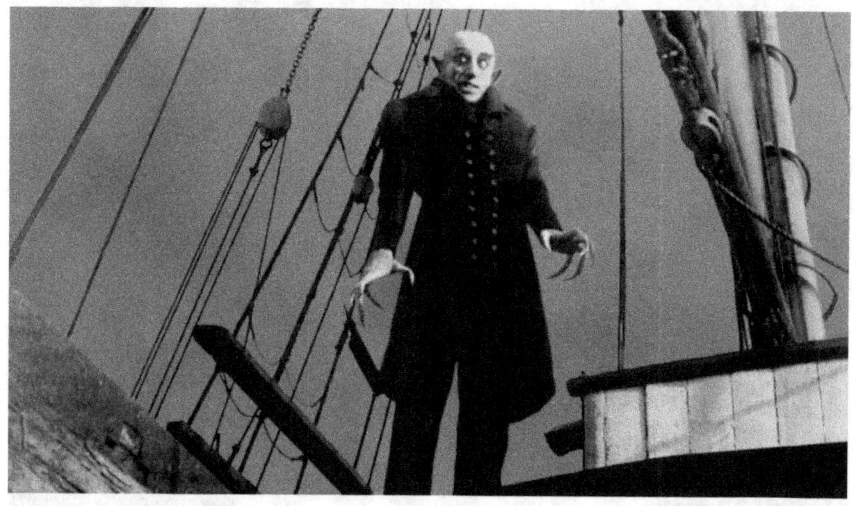

All of these effects and shots enhance the film, but the shots that stand out most to me are the silhouetted ones of Count Orlok preying upon his victims in the night. The shadow of the twisted, stiff, and distorted figure of Orlok with those long, skeleton-like claws is a really powerful image.

In this scene, Count Orlok is seen hauntingly climbing the stair of Hutter's home as he approaches Hutter's wife's room. She is frantically aware of his ominous approach and is unable to escape.

Scene: Lurking up the Stairs

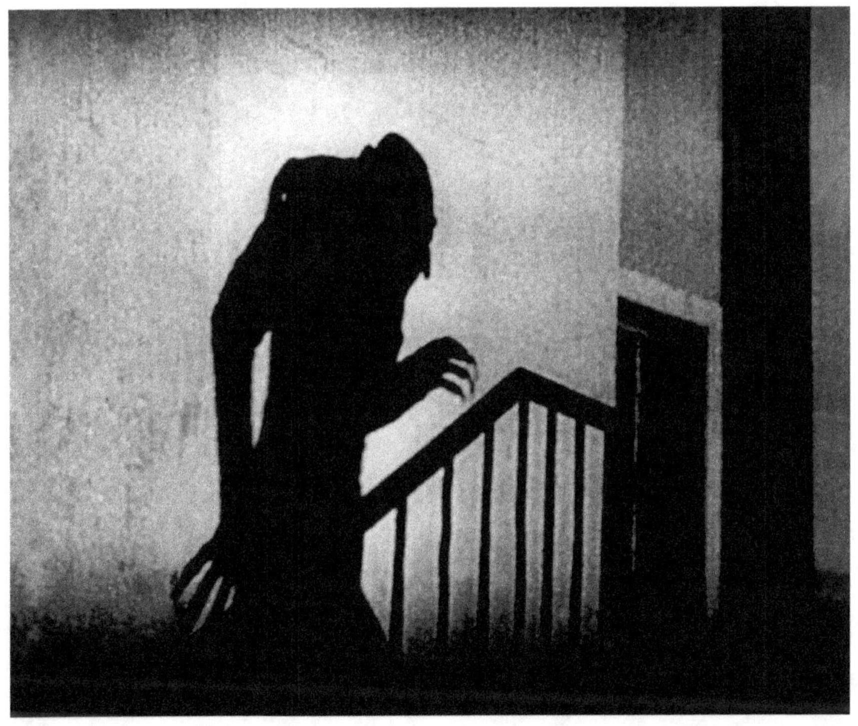

Max Schreck, who plays the lead role as the vampire Count Orlok in this film, was born in Berlin. He worked in an apprenticeship until his father's death before enrolling in a school for acting. He toured the country with his peers and was a member of several theaters until he became a part of Max Reinhardt's group of innovative German actors. He played mostly out of the norm characters, the elderly and the grotesque, because of his talent and passion for makeup and costume fabrication.

Probably the most memorable and chilling aspect of *Nosferatu* is Schreck as the monster. An actor whose own name is German for "terror," Schreck is certainly a nightmarish apparition with his bulbous head, pointed bat-like ears and long, talon-like fingers and fangs. His rat-like facial features also associate him with the rodents who spread the plague across Europe. And Scheck's eerie, stammering, zombielike walk has since become a feature of numerous screen monsters.

His anthological interpretation and perfect characterization as Earl Orlok, a role in which he condenses evil and repugnance, many thought that Max Schreck was, in fact, a vampire who had been hired by F.W. Murnau to give greater veracity to the character and thus produce a timeless masterpiece.

Why is *Nosferatu* still relevant even today? It influenced pretty much everything vampire-related in cinema since 1922. The famous Bela Lugosi Dracula, from 1931, gets most of the credit for directly influencing modern movie bloodsuckers, and rightly so. But it was producer Carl Laemmle Jr.'s love of *Nosferatu* that made him buy the rights to the *Dracula* novel and spearhead a big-screen adaptation. Granted, it was fairly likely that someone would make a successful Dracula movie at some point (there was a Russian one in 1920, now lost), even without *Nosferatu*. But Murano's film got the ball rolling, perhaps sooner than might have happened otherwise. More recently, in 2000, the film *Shadow of the Vampire* cast John Malkovich as Murnau and Willem Defoe as Orlok actor Max Schreck. The film perpetuated the idea that Murnau had hired the actor for the lead role in *Nosferatu* because he actually was a vampire.

Here is a candid photograph of Max Schreck relaxing or lounging on the set of *Nosferatu*. Even in a relaxed state, Max looks foreboding and menacing.

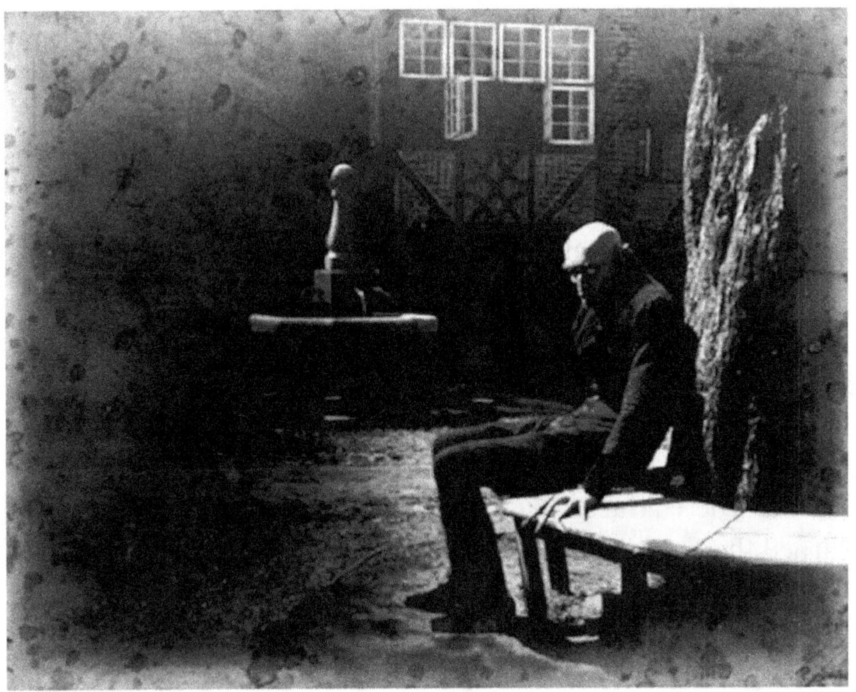

Safety Last! (1923)

Safety Last! is a silent romantic comedy film starring Harold Lloyd. It includes one of the most famous images from the silent film era: Lloyd clutching the hands of a large clock as he dangles from the outside of a skyscraper above moving traffic. The film was highly successful and critically hailed, and it cemented Lloyd's status as a major figure in early motion pictures. The downtrodden character, named "The Boy," finally does reach the top of the building, lands in his girl's arms on the roof, and they go off, arm in arm. The character has proved his worth, become a success, earned the one-thousand-dollar publicity stunt prize money, and won the girl. It is still popular at revivals, and it is viewed today as one of the great film comedies. After Charlie Chaplin and Buster Keaton, the silent film era's "third genius" was Harold Lloyd, who stars in this Horatio Alger-style story of an average country boy trying to make good in the big city.

Scene: Hanging from a Skyscraper Clock

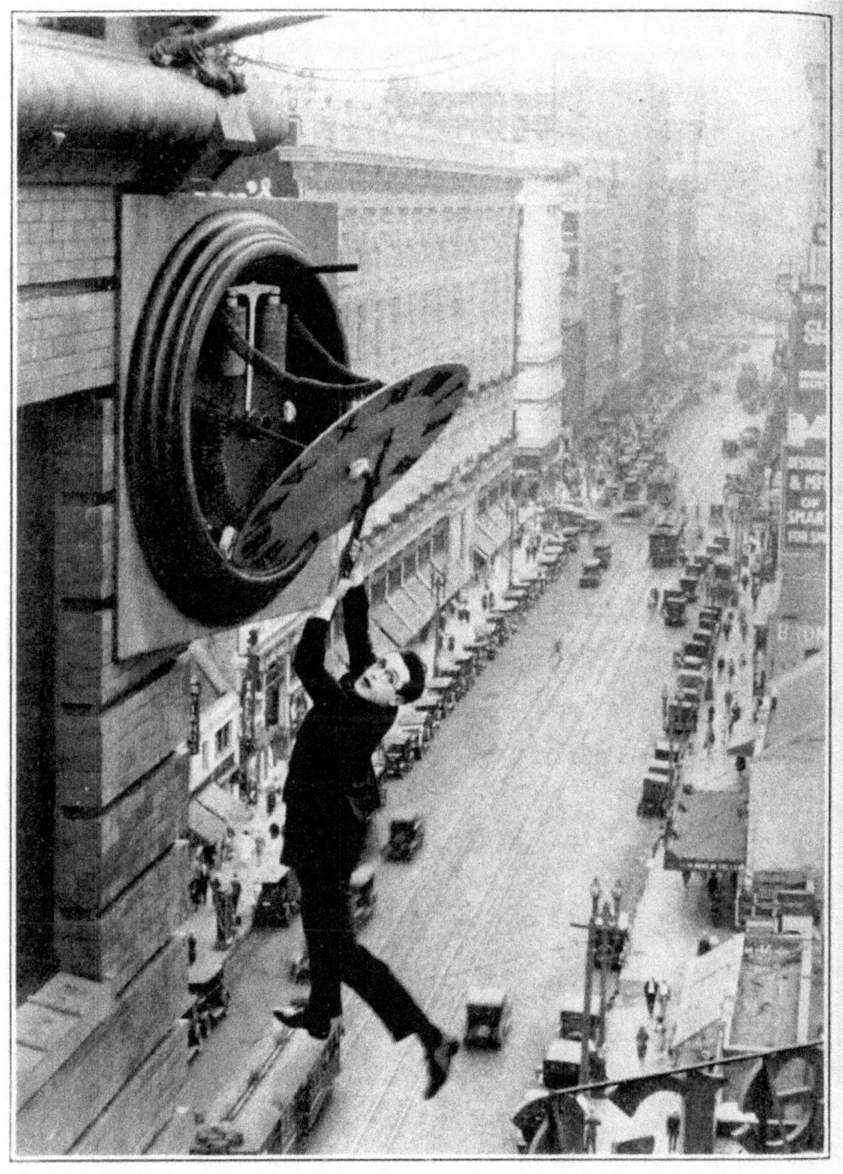

This film earned Harold Lloyd, the bookish, horn-rimmed glasses-wearing comedian, his nickname "the King of Daredevil Comedy." The film is best remembered for its thrilling, hair-raising climax—a reckless, "safety last," humorous stunt on the side of a twelve-story skyscraper above busy city streets. The scary sequence was deliberately shot with most of the camera compositions, including views of the perilous drop behind him.

The film's title is a play on the common expression, "safety first," which places safety as the priority to avoid accidents, especially at workplaces. Lloyd performed some of the climbing stunts himself, despite having lost a thumb and forefinger four years earlier in a film accident.

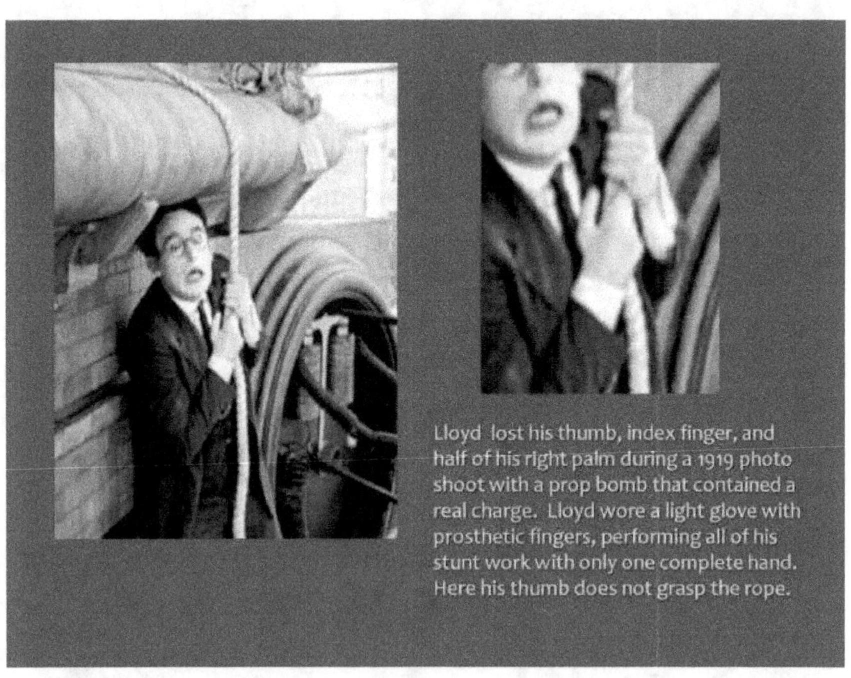

Lloyd lost his thumb, index finger, and half of his right palm during a 1919 photo shoot with a prop bomb that contained a real charge. Lloyd wore a light glove with prosthetic fingers, performing all of his stunt work with only one complete hand. Here his thumb does not grasp the rope.

Lloyd hanging from a giant clock on the corner of a building became an iconic image for him, but it was achieved with a certain amount of film trickery.

Some other interesting factoids from Turner Classic Movies (TCM):

Harold Lloyd first tested the safety precautions for the clock stunt by dropping a dummy onto the mattress below. The dummy bounced off and plummeted to the street below.

In 1919, Harold Lloyd was handed what he thought was a prop bomb, which he lit with his cigarette. The bomb turned out to be real. It exploded, blowing off Lloyd's right thumb, index finger, and putting him in the hospital for months. When he recovered, Lloyd went back to making movies, wearing a white glove while on screen to hide his damaged right hand. He did his stunts in *Safety Last!* and *Feet First*—dangling from ledges, clocks, and windows—using only eight fingers.

Harold Lloyd got the idea for the film when he saw Bill Struthers climbing the Brockman Building in Los Angeles as a stunt one day. Lloyd—who had a difficult time watching anyone else performing a dangerous stunt because he had no control over that situation—hid behind a corner, peeking to check on Stretcher's progress every few moments. After Struthers reached the roof, Lloyd went up and introduced himself.

During the famous clock tower stunt, Lloyd is not as far from the ground as he appears. The building on which he climbs was actually a fake wall constructed on the top of a genuine skyscraper and skillfully photographed to maintain the illusion.

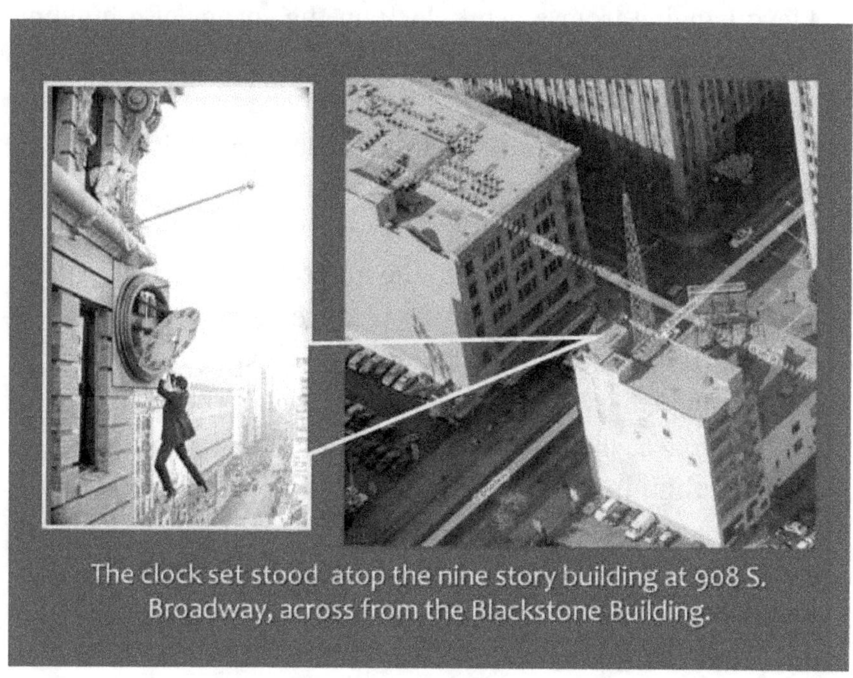

The clock set stood atop the nine story building at 908 S. Broadway, across from the Blackstone Building.

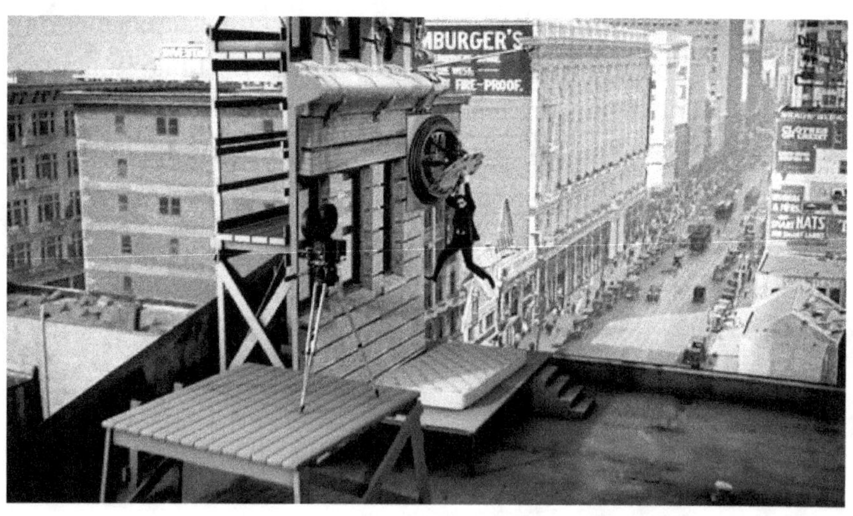

A behind-the-scenes picture from *Safety Last!* showing how the famous clock sequence was shot is shown. Note the location of the camera, facing down, captured the moving traffic in the street below, as well as poor Lloyd hanging precariously from the clock. One can also see a mattress below the comic just in case.

The image of a man dangling from a clock face is so indelibly linked with *Safety Last!* There are a number of examples of how future films paid tribute to Lloyd's famous scene:

In 1962, the "dangling from the skyscraper" scene was included in Harold Lloyd's *World of Comedy*, a compilation movie produced by Harold Lloyd himself. The film premiered at the Cannes Film Festival and created a renewal of interest in the comedian by introducing him to a new generation.

The 1972 *Dad's Army* episode "Time on My Hands" features men hanging precariously from the hands of a clock tower.

The 1978 film version of the John Buchan story *The Thirty-nine Steps* features Richard Hannay (Robert Powell) hanging from the minute hand on the clock face of Big Ben.

In the 1983 martial arts film *Project A*, Jackie Chan also paid homage to Lloyd (whom he has frequently cited as an influence on his work) by falling from a clock tower.

The 1985 film *Back to the Future* pays homage to Harold Lloyd "dangling from the skyscraper" by having one of the film's stars Christopher Lloyd (no relation to Harold) hang from a clock tower as part of the plot. In addition, a meta-reference appears in the opening scene of *Back to the Future* in the form of a physical table clock, which depicts the *Safety Last!* scene.

The 1991 comedy film *Oscar* paid direct homage to the scene, recreating it on its poster, where the main character (played by Sylvester Stallone) hangs from a clock.

In Marin Scorsese's 2011 film *Hugo*, a portion of the scene with Lloyd hanging from the clock is shown when the main characters sneak into a movie theater. Later, the title character Hugo similarly hangs from the hands of a large clock on a clock tower to escape a pursuer.

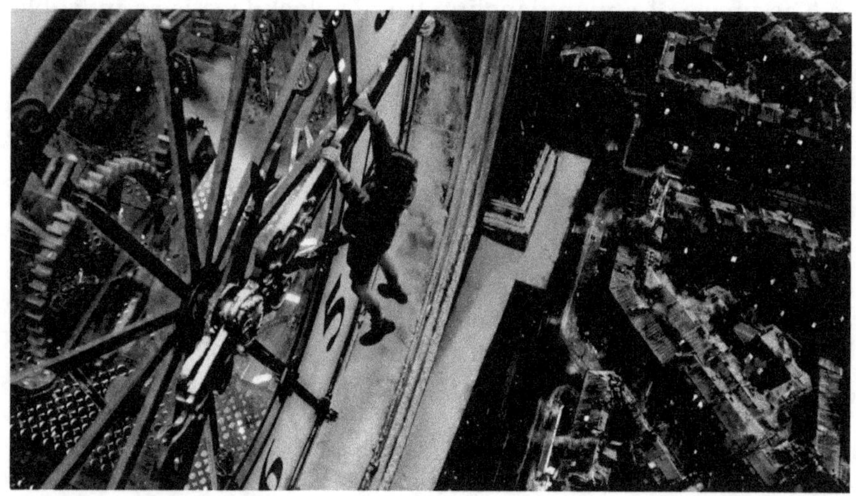

The Ten Commandments (1923)

The film legend Cecil D. DeMille produced and directed two movies entitled *The Ten Commandments*. The first movie, made in 1923, is silent and divided into two parts: a prologue recreating the biblical story of the Exodus and a modern story concerning two brothers and their respective views of the Ten Commandments. It was lauded for its "immense and stupendous" scenes, the use of Technicolor process 2, and the parting of the Red Sea sequence. Roy Pomeroy, the Technical Director, was responsible for the special effects which produced the parting of the Red Sea sequence. It was reported that special effects wizard Roy Pomeroy discovered the secret of parting the Red Sea by watching a child splashing a spoon into a dish of pudding.

Scene: The Parting of the Red Sea

The early Cecil B. DeMille epic used primitive special effects techniques—the parting of the Red Sea was accomplished by filming water as it poured down two sides of a large U-shaped tank, set up in the studio backlot, and then running the film backward—to make the water appear to divide.

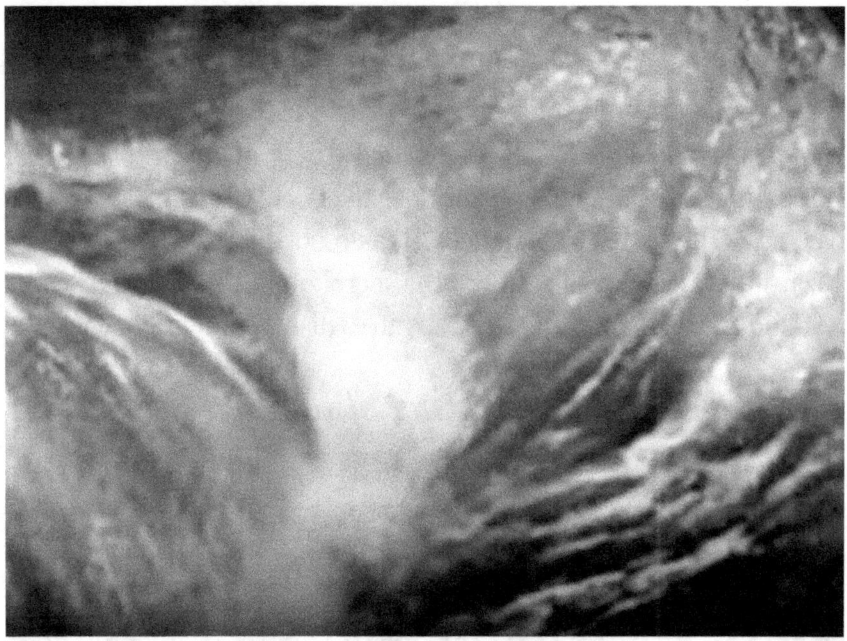

The illusion of keeping the walls of water separated was accomplished by slicing a slab of gelatin in two, running some water over it, and filming it in close-up—and then combining (or double-exposing) it with live-action footage of the Israelites walking into the abyss with the Egyptian chariots in pursuit. Supposedly, the two gelatin molds were jiggled on camera to enhance the effect of cascading walls of water. The separate live-action footage of the escaping slaves was shot using a large group of actors walking on a secluded beach in Seal Beach, California.

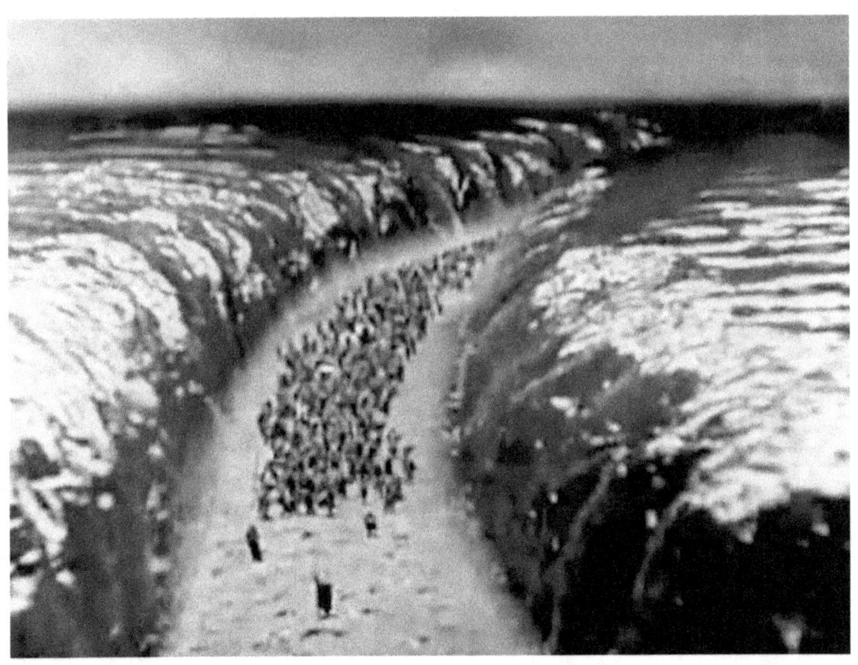

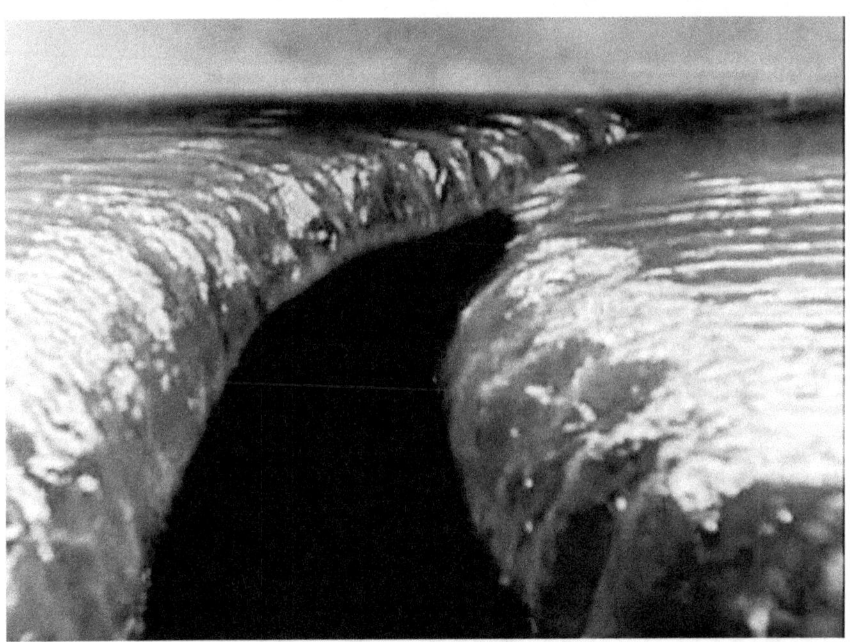

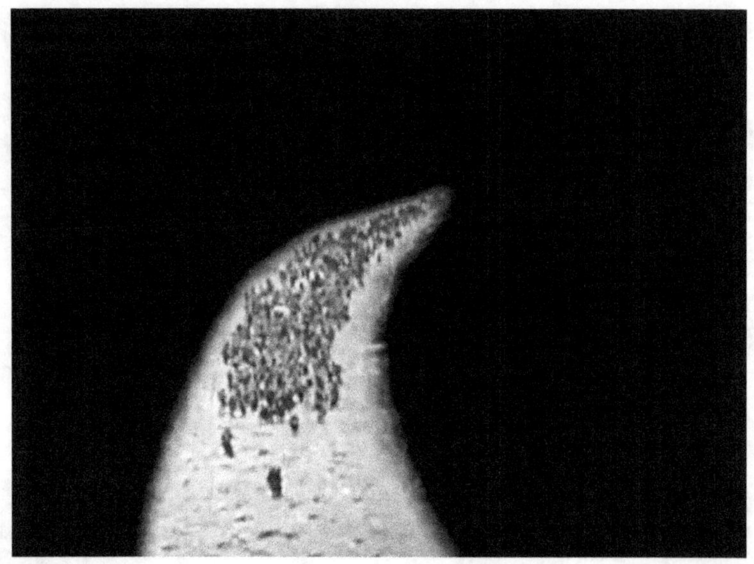

The scene of the Red Sea flooding the Egyptians was done by just flooding the set with water without reversing the film.

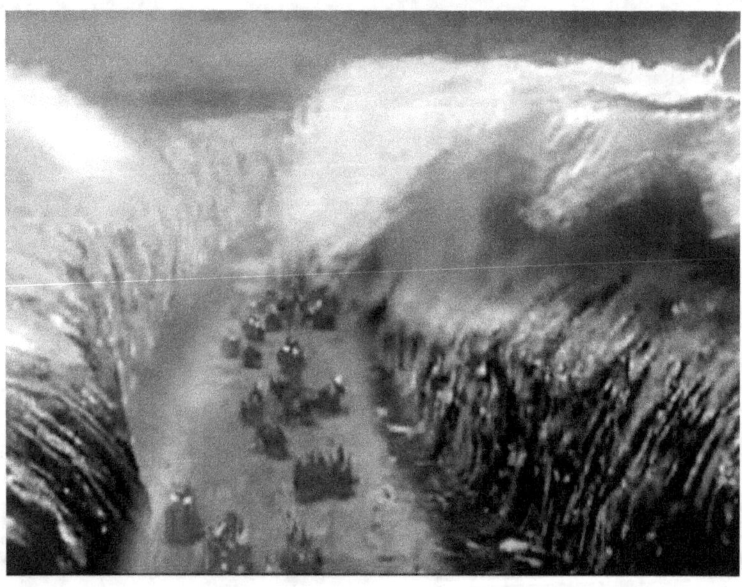

The parting of the Red Sea in movies originated with this particular film. However, since then, there have been at least five more films in which this feat was performed in various degrees of success.

In 1956, Cecil B. DeMille did it again in his film *The Ten Commandments* with Charlton Heston as Moses. We'll talk more about this particular film later.

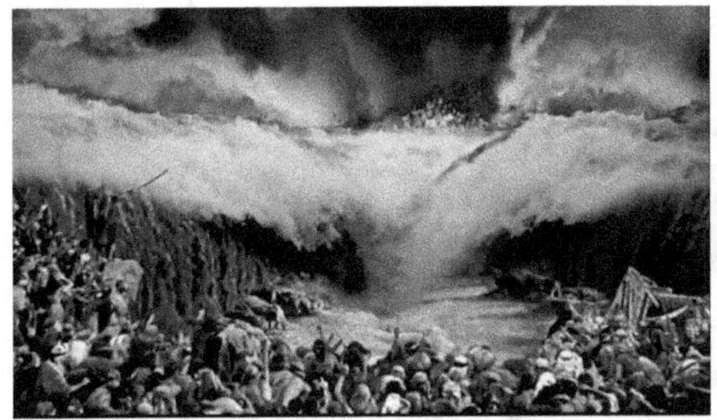

In 1974, the film *Moses, The Law Giver* with Burt Lancaster as Moses, used the reverse rushing water technique resulting in a somewhat feeble special effect.

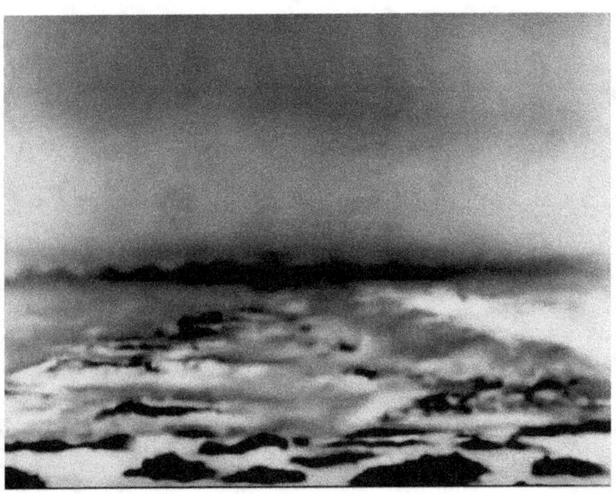

In 1995, the TNT *Bible* series produced with Ben Kingsley as Moses affected the parting of the Red Sea using CGI (computer-generated imagery) to create the walls of the water effect.

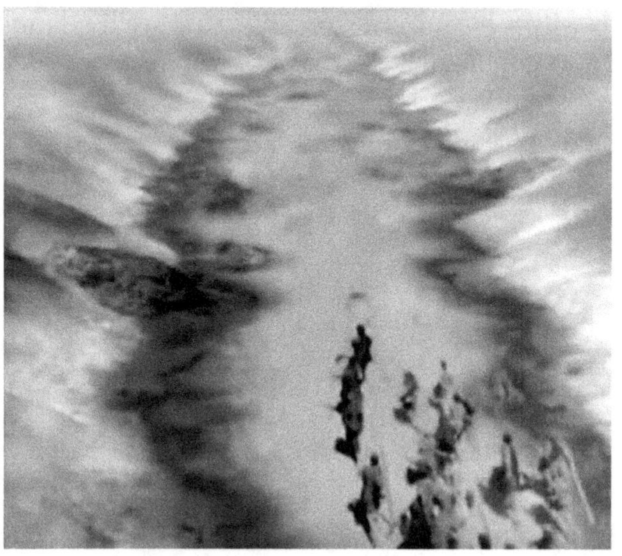

In 1998, the animated film *The Prince of Egypt* used both 2D and 3D animation in order to produce a very nice special effect.

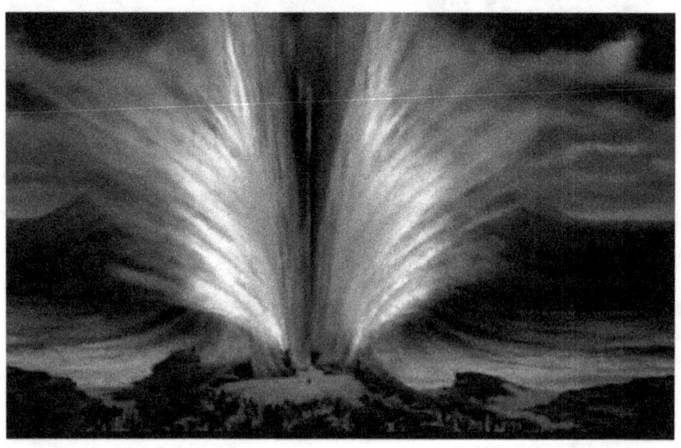

In 2003, in the film *Bruce Almighty*, actor Jim Carrey, imitating "Moses," performs his parting of the Red Sea effect using a simple cup of coffee.

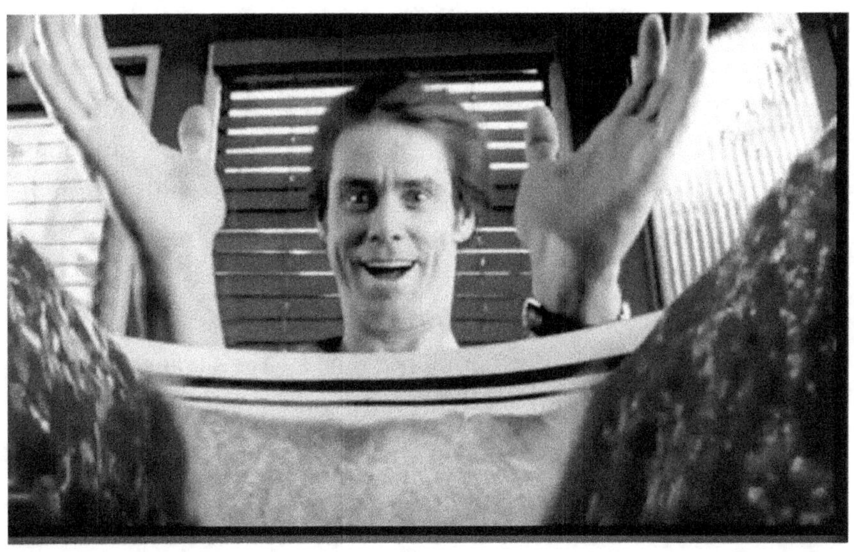

Finally, in 2014, Ridley Scott, in his film *Exodus: Gods and King*, with Christian Bale as Moses, used CGI in order to produce this special effect.

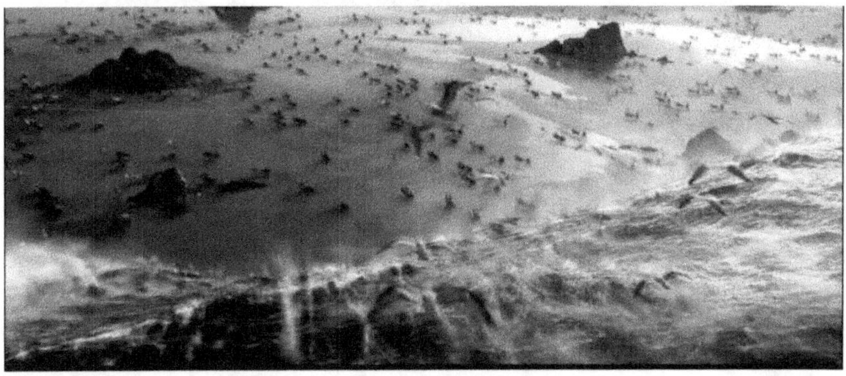

Greed (1924)

The epic film *Greed* was directed by Erich von Stroheim. The film is based on Frank Norris' powerful 1899 novel *McTeague*. The theme of *McTeague* was that greed degrades man until he is little more than a human beast or animal. It is a strange story of a dentist, his marriage to a grasping shrewish wife whose greed and hoarding for gold (originally obtained by winning a lottery) finally forces him to sheer desperation, driving out any humanity, love, and kindness he once possessed, leading him ultimately to the savage murder of his wife and his former best friend. The characters in the movie are cast in what appears to be a Greek tragedy. During the course of the film, they are literally reduced to their "base instincts," which was their greed for gold.

Scene: Human Beast in a Living Hell

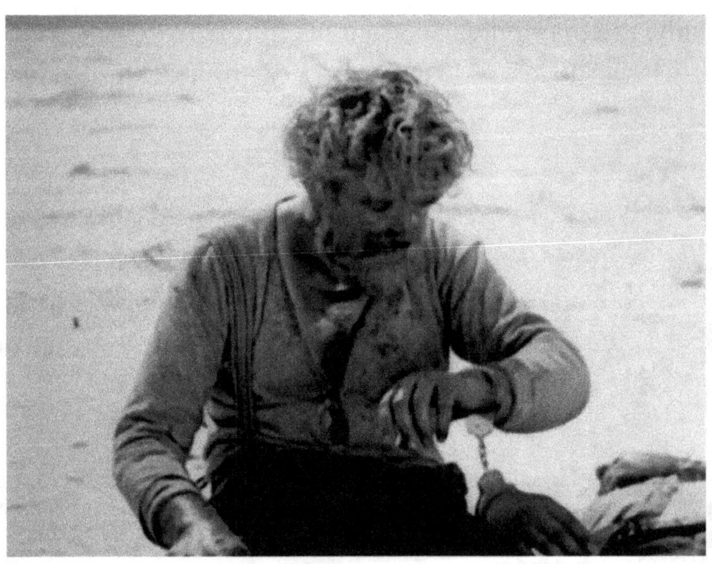

The tragic ending in the great salt flats of Death Valley, in Erich von Stroheim's masterpiece, is absolutely remarkable. Marcus (Jean Hersholt) joins a posse and pursues his old friend/dentist McTeague (Gibson Gowland), greedy for the one-hundred-dollar reward offered following the suspicious murder and burglary of Trina McTeague (Zasu Pitts)—and for the wife's gold coins.

"McTeague was headed for the very heart of Death Valley ... that horrible wilderness of which even beasts were afraid."

In the closing sequence, McTeague flees with Trina's money into the stifling heat and wasteland of Death Valley—a literal hell and a symbolic representation of the expansive, desolate terrain of McTeague's inner world.

In a protracted fight to the death in the middle of the parched desert covered with caked ground and cracked alkaline, the two men face each other and grapple together for the gold as they wrestle for control of the gun. They struggle on the white ground until McTeague overpowers Marcus and strikes with the revolver—he clubs his one-time friend to death with the gun. Marcus lies still and bloody on the ground—yet in the midst of the life-and-death struggle, McTeague's left wrist has become attached to Marcus' right wrist by handcuffs.

He turns and looks at the canvas bag (with its glissading gold coins) on the saddle of the dead mule, looks at the empty canteen, and sinks to his knees. He sits there, anchored in the deadly, pitiless heat of Death Valley, chained to the corpse of his once close friend that he just slew. He has the gold, but no water. There is only vast emptiness around him as he awaits his own death.

Stroheim's uncompromising insistence on realism and accuracy of detail in his films is legendary and is documented in the 2018 film *Greed: The Story of the 1924 Masterpiece.* There was no studio shooting, but thirty-seven days on location filming in the salt flats of Death Valley, for instance. A day and a half ninety-mile trek to film the film's finale was taken on by thirty-nine men and one woman over a hot, sweltering sun, which literally baked the crew and actors with 128-degree temperatures.

The crew and cast trek to their film location sites in Death Valley, carrying much of their own equipment with the assist of a few mules carrying supplies and precious water.

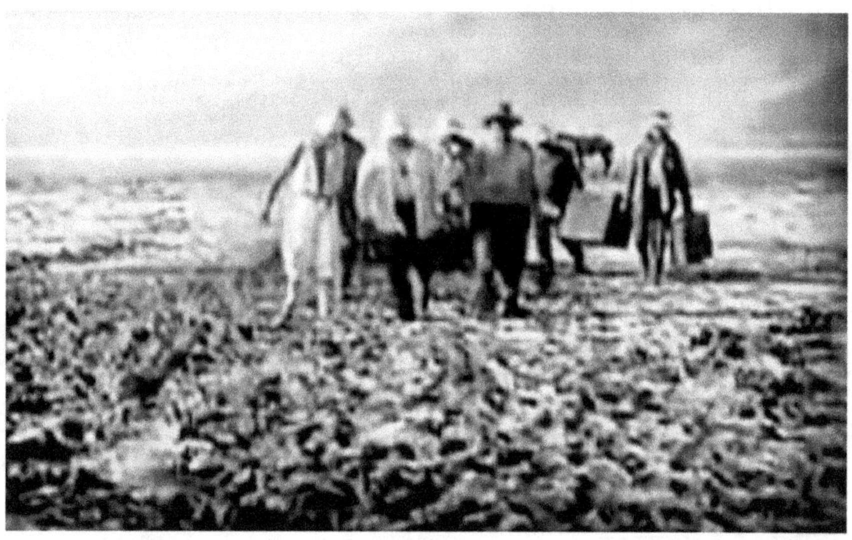

There were no shade or creature comforts to be found. Most of the crew got sick at one time or another during the filming. They ran low on drinkable water and had to resort to daily rationing. Actor Jean Hersholt developed painful heat blisters and had to eventually be hospitalized for months. Stroheim drove everybody mercilessly, and whether it was from loyalty, admiration of his unquestioned genius, or sheer hatred and a determination to show him that they couldn't be licked, he drew performances from his players and work from his cameramen that they never equaled under any other director.

Greed, or avarice, is an inordinate or insatiable longing for material gain, be it food, money, status, or power has been portrayed in a number of different ways since this 1924 groundbreaking film got the ball rolling for future Hollywood productions.

Here are but of few of these features:

Wall Street (1987): A young and impatient stockbroker is willing to do anything to get to the top, including trading on illegal inside information taken through a ruthless and greedy corporate raider who takes the youth under his wing.

Scarface (1993): In 1980, in Miami, a determined Cuban immigrant takes over a drug cartel and succumbs to greed.

Casino (1995): A tale of greed, deception, money, power, and murder occur between two best friends: a mafia enforcer and a casino executive compete against each other over a gambling empire, and over a fast living and fast loving socialite.

There Will Be Blood (2007): This is a story of family, religion, creed, hatred, and madness focusing on a turn-of-the-century prospector during the early days of the oil business.

The Wolf of Wall Street (2013): This film is based on the true story of Jordan Belfort, from his rise to a wealthy stockbroker living the high life to his fall involving crime, greed, corruption, and the federal government.

Greed (2019) is a satire about the avarice world of the super-rich. It is a fictional story of a retail billionaire, set in the glamorous and celebrity-filled world of luxury fashion, which is centered on the buildup to a spectacular sixtieth birthday party in an exclusive hotel on the Greek island of Mykonos. The film was directed by Michael Winterbottom and starred Steve Coogan as Sir Richard McCreadie.

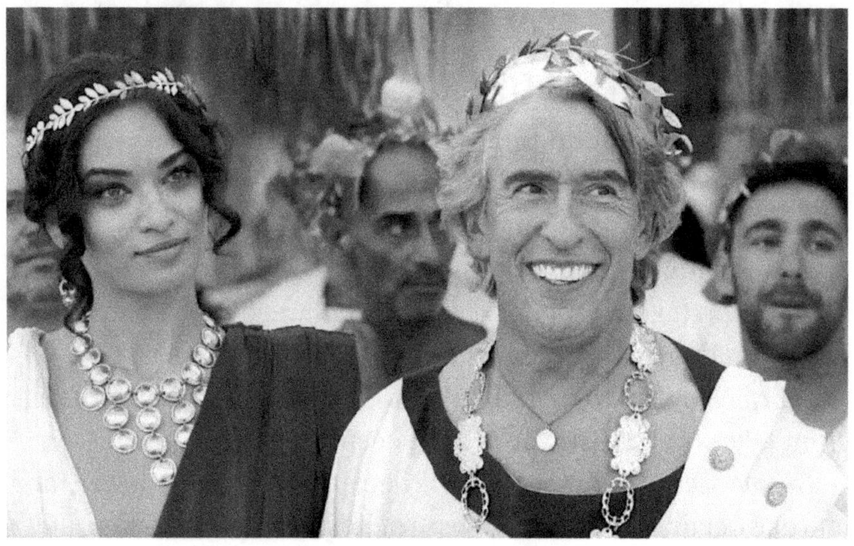

The Big Parade (1925)

The Big Parade is a silent war drama film directed by King Vidor, starring John Gilbert and Renée Adorée. *The Big Parade*, with its poignant love story and realistic battle scenes, was reportedly the highest-grossing film of the entire silent era. Although other anti-war films preceded it, *The Big Parade* is an early film which neither glorified the war nor ignored its human costs. It heavily influenced a great many subsequent war films, especially *All Quiet on the Western Front* (1930). Its simple love story of an American World War I soldier and a French peasant girl transcends the horrors of war as they both survive the war.

Scene: Parting is Such Sweet Sorrow

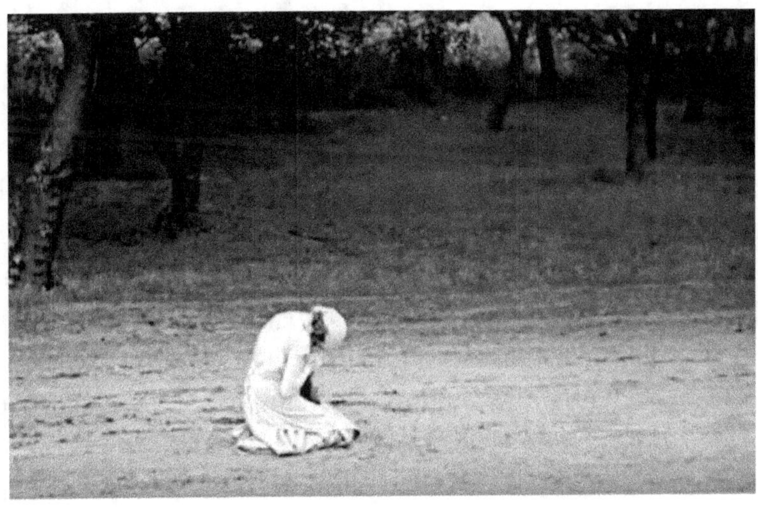

The scene of the parting of the American troops from a French village in King Vidor's *The Big Parade* is one of the most famous and memorable in cinematic history. Four years after making this film, King Vidor re-staged one of its most famous scenes—Jimmy going off to battle and leaving Melisande behind—in *Show People* (1928), a comedy starring Marion Davies as an actress trying to become a Hollywood star. In *Show People*, Davies and William Haines played the parts originally played in *The Big Parade* by Renée Adorée and John Gilbert.

American doughboy Jim (John Gilbert) calls out for French peasant girl Melisande (Renee Adoree) but cannot locate her. She too hears the bugle call and sees the dust of the trucks, the horse-drawn caissons, and the running men assembling for the pull-out. Her distress rises with the suddenness of their leaving. Suddenly, she decides that she is desperately in love with Jim. She pushes her way through the massed ranks of soldiers—looking and calling out for him in the ensuing chaos and rising dust. Her frenzied search becomes more frantic and emotional as she searches for a glimpse of him to bid him a lasting farewell. Two other passing soldiers grab at her—one touches her breast, the other tries to steal a kiss.

Jim climbs into the back of a transport truck, one in a long line of battle trucks. When he finally catches sight of her, he jumps off the truck and races back—they wildly embrace and pepper each other with kisses—framed close-up. Earnestly, he vows to return to her in the touching scene: "I'm coming back!—Remember—I'm coming back!" An officer pulls on Jim and then rips them apart. The agonized, feisty French village girl hits back at anyone who would tear them from each other. As Jim is dragged into the tail end of a truck, Melisande holds on firmly to his left leg, refusing to let go. She runs along for a moment as the truck pulls away. She desperately hangs onto a chain dangling off the vehicle, trying to halt the inevitable and defy both time and fate. When she doesn't let go, she is dragged alongside the procession until she can't hold on any longer.

He tosses her mementos to remember him: his wristwatch, his dog tags, and one shoe and then sprays her with two-handed kisses. She stands and watches the truck disappear—holding his shoe to her bosom. The passing vehicles and clouds of dust envelope her and then subside. In the middle of the road, she sinks to her knees with her head bowed, wondering in her heart if she will ever see him again.

Scene: Reunited at Last

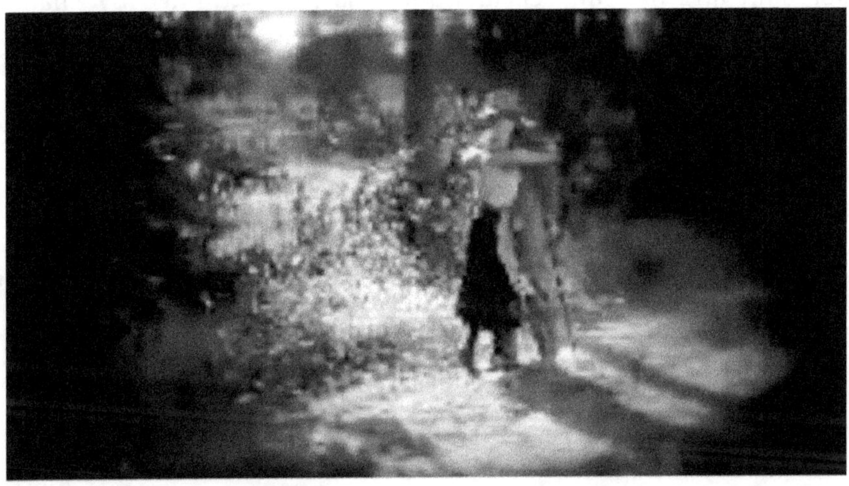

Jim is wounded in battle and loses a leg. After the war has ended, he returns home only to find that his old girlfriend has fallen in love with another. Later, Jim tells his mother about Melisande; she tells him to go back and find her. When he returns to her farm, Melisande is working in the field, chewing on a stick of gum like when they were together. She spots Jim on a hill and rushes toward him. He tries to run, but can't because of his condition. They finally meet and embrace in one of the most touching and heart-wrenching scenes of the silent era.

It was the first realistic war drama and has served ever since as an archetypal model for all other war films. It was the first big box-office success of the newly formed MGM Studios—and possibly the most profitable silent film of all time—it helped bring back the popularity of war films in the late-twenties. Vidor, often compared to the end of the century's director Steven Spielberg, brought his own epic, sweeping style to his intimate yet massive work about love and war. A movie entitled *The Big Parade* was a 1986 Chinese film directed by Chen Kaige. It is the story of a tough Chinese drill sergeant and his raw recruits and was photographed by Zhang Yimou. The soldiers in this film are getting ready to participate in a Beijing celebration of China's National Day. At first, the diverse assortment of recruits find they have one thing in common: their hatred of their harsh leader, but in time, they come to respect him and realize that his strictness is a form of genuine caring and that he is not about to let anyone be denied the great honor of participating in the parade. Still, it is not an easy road for anyone as they all are forced to reexamine their notions of individuality and of working in a group in contemporary China.

The Battleship Potemkin (1925)

The Russian Revolution of 1905 was a wave of mass political and social unrest that spread through vast areas of the Russian Empire, some of which was directed at the government. It included worker strikes, peasant unrest, and military mutinies. The 1905 revolution was spurred by the Russian defeat in the Russo-Japanese war (1904–1905), but also by the growing realization by the people of the need for reform after politicians such as Sergei Witte failed to accomplish this. While the tsar managed to keep his rule, the events foreshadowed those of the Russian revolutions in 1917, which resulted in the overthrow of the monarchy, execution of the imperial family, and creation of the Soviet Union by the Bolsheviks.

In 1925, Sergei Eisenstein produced *The Battleship Potemkin* and made cinematic history. His revolutionary use of jump cuts and montages was shocking at the time, but unequivocally influential. The camera work is stunning for a film of its era, and the tools and techniques that Eisenstein recruited to help him make his masterpiece were well chosen.

Scene: The Odessa Steps

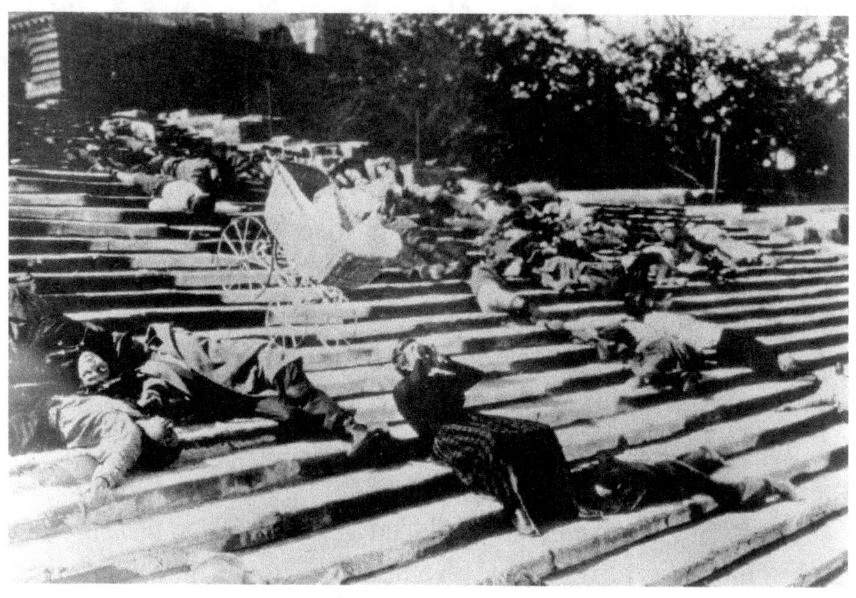

The setting for the scene: While Eisenstein was always interested more in creating an effective and well-constructed film than in being literally faithful to the historical record, many of the key images in the script were in fact inspired by actual events associated with the Potemkin mutiny: the sailors' refusal to eat borsch made from maggot-infested meat; the revolutionary activists Matyushenko and Vakulenchuk (spelled Vakulinchuk in the film) using that incident as a pretext to incite the other sailors to mutiny; the arrival of the battleship into the Odessa port with a red flag; the throngs of townspeople lining up to view Vakulenchuk's corpse; and the Potemkin being greeted by cheering sailors on another ship. Eventually, the revolt was ended by a crackdown by the police and Cossacks.

The most celebrated scene in the film is the probably fictional massacre of civilians on the Odessa Steps (also known as the Primorsky or Potemkin Stairs) on June 14, 1905. It has been assessed as a "classic" and one of the most influential in the history of cinema. In the scene, the tsar's soldiers, in their white summer tunics, march down a seemingly endless flight of steps in a rhythmic, machine-like fashion, firing volleys into a crowd. A separate detachment of mounted Cossacks charges the crowd at the bottom of the stairs. The victims include an older woman wearing pincenez, a young boy with his mother, a student in uniform, and a teenage schoolgirl. A mother pushing an infant in a baby carriage falls to the ground dying after being shot, and the carriage rolls down the steps amidst the fleeing crowd. The way Eisenstein aims and shoots his camera in this famous scene is just incredible. He heightens the suspense by making the cuts increasingly faster and more desperate as the people run around in utter confusion and chaos. It is truly effective and almost nightmarish. For a film without sound to achieve such a thing is even more impressive.

Paraphrasing what Roger Corman observed in a documentary film regarding the Odessa steps sequence: It is primarily a sequence of movement, of different camera angles, and of editing techniques to bring great emotion and excitement to that movement. Eisenstein accomplishes this by using traditional long shots to establish geography with the soldiers standing on the top of the stairs and then slowly and methodically moving downward, killing people in the crowd as they vainly try to escape. Eisenstein intercuts this movement using long shots with medium shots of the crowd and the soldiers and then close-ups of the people's feet as they run down the steps. The camera suddenly stops its downward focus and shifts to a single woman carrying her dead child up the stairs. She seemingly cries out in pain, agonizing over her dead child, showing the soldiers what they have done. She represents a single moment of humanity, in this downward thrust of mass killings, before she herself is brutally shot in the eye in a close-up shot. The scene shifts back to the top of the stairs where a baby carriage, with a poor baby in it, runs helplessly down the chairs, when its mother is shot, as onlookers look at it rolling downward without being able to help because of their wounds. The sequence of scenes ends with repeated shots of the stone lions situated at the base of the stairs. The camera takes various shots of them at different angles, at a very fast pace, giving the impression that they are rising from their pedestal and are, in fact, lamenting the horrible scene they have to witness. However, they also relay a sense of hope that redemption, for these wrenched people, will someday be achieved, The mutiny that occurred in 1905 is brutally ended by the government and the Cossacks, but redemption is finally achieved in 1917 with the Russian Revolution.

The scene is perhaps the best example of Eisenstein's theory on montage, and many films pay homage to the scene, including Brian De Palma's *The Untouchables* (1987) in the Chicago Union Station. Two grand stairways from the "Great Hall" lead passengers down to the rail platforms. In one scene, at the Chicago Union Station on one of the two grand staircases, De Palma filmed one of the most famous crime movie scenes.

De Palma masterfully filmed the scene which showed Elliot Ness (Kevin Costner) embroiled in a slow-motion shootout with Al Capone's men, while at the same time trying to save a baby in a runaway pram down a flight of stairs with wounded onlookers unable to stop it, just like the Odessa steps scene in *The Battleship Potemkin*. In both scenes, the babies are surrounded by bullets and helpless onlookers. The baby in De Palma's film survives, but unfortunately, the baby in Potemkin is stabbed by one of the soldiers.

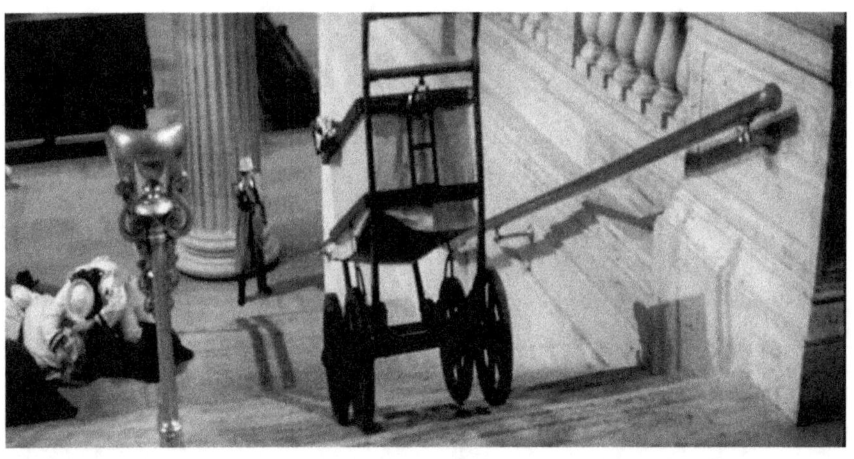

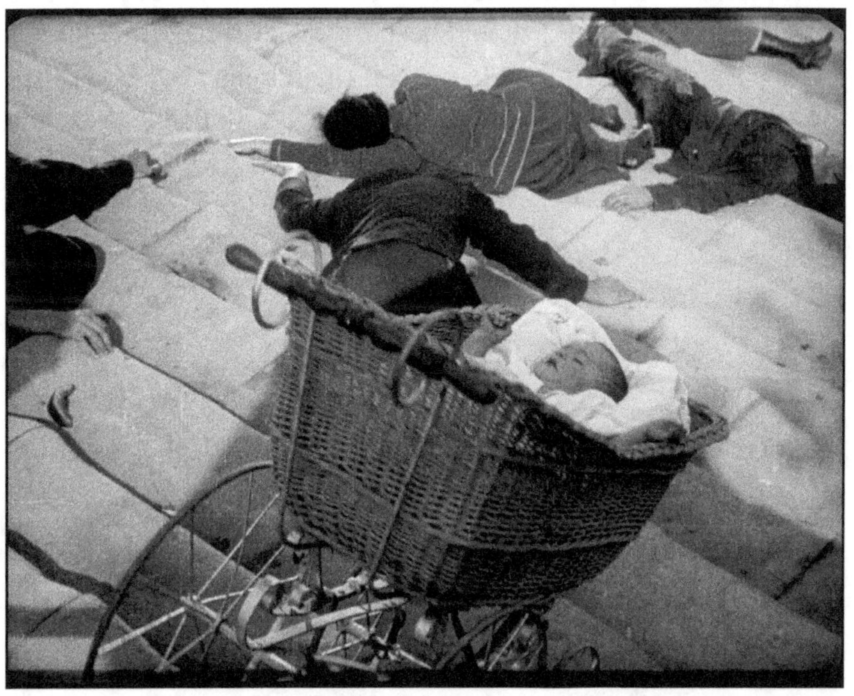

The Gold Rush (1925)

The Gold Rush is a comedy film written, produced, and directed by Charlie Chaplin. The film also stars Chaplin in his Little Tramp persona, Georgia Hale, Mack Swain, Tom Murray, Henry Bergman, and Malcolm Waite.

Chaplin drew inspiration from photos of the Klondike Gold Rush as well as from the story of the Donner Party who, when snowbound in the Sierra Nevada, were driven to cannibalism or eating leather from their shoes. Chaplin, who believed tragedies and comics were not far from each other, decided to combine these stories of deprivation and horror in comedy. He decided that his famous rogue figure should become a gold-digger who joins a brave optimist determined to face all the pitfalls associated with the search for gold, such as sickness, hunger, loneliness, or the possibility that he may at any time be attacked by a grizzly.

Scene: The Gourmet Boot

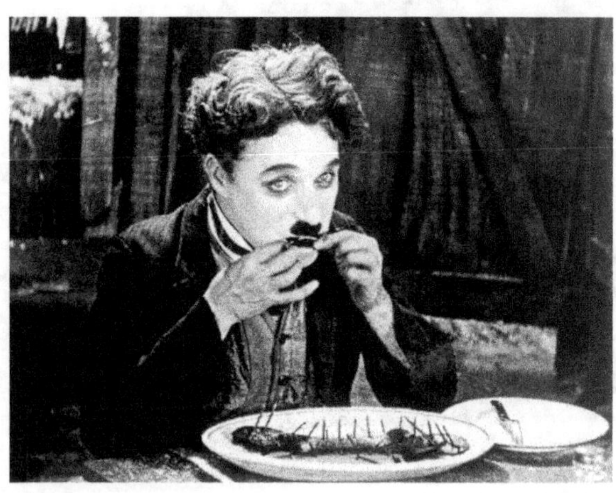

One legendary scene from the movie shows the two famished fortune-seekers during the Alaskan Klondike gold rush celebrate Thanksgiving Day dinner. In their isolated cabin, the starving prospector (Charlie Chaplin) cooks his own boot in a large pot. He takes on airs as a French gourmet at a feast.

When he serves the shoe, he splits the sole, cutting it like a filet, and sets the smaller portion before his large companion Big Jim McKay (Mack Swain). Big Jim greedily switches the plates to get the upper portion of the shoe. The prospector delicately chews on the lower sole part, treating it like a delicacy as he picks his way through the leather—he treats the laces like spaghetti, coiling them about his fork. He daintily sucks the nails, like they were the bones of a game bird.

One of the typically inventive, whimsical films of Charlie Chaplin's long, prolific career in Hollywood, *The Gold Rush* wrests comedy from the struggles of this often helpless waif in the brutal American wilds. The Tramp is so slight, each time Larson opens the door to his cabin, a chilly blast blows him across the room, and out the back door. In one hilarious vignette, the starving tramp and McKay boil a shoe (which was actually made of licorice with rock candy nails for the scene) for dinner, consuming the shoelaces like spaghetti, and licking each tack clean like a scrumptious bone. The scene reportedly took three shooting days and sixty-three takes, and the licorice prop's laxative effect momentarily incapacitated Chaplin and Swan. As the boot was made of licorice, with the many takes, Chaplin was once rushed to hospital suffering insulin shock. The scene where the lone prospector and Big Jim have a boot for supper took three days and sixty-three takes to suit director Charles Chaplin. Just as amusing as that brilliant gag was its comic echo in the film, for the rest of the film, the Tramp wears a burlap cloth wrapped around his shoeless right foot to reiterate his pathetic predicament.

In *My Autobiography*, Chaplin states that the story of *The Gold Rush* was inspired by the tale of the Donner Party, emigrants who, in 1846, split off from a larger wagon train traveling to California through the Sierra Nevada mountains, only to meet with a blizzard that resulted in the death of half the party. The scene in which the "lone prospector" eats his shoe was inspired by tales that the Donner Party members were forced to eat their moccasins (the members also resorted to cannibalism in order to stay alive).

This scene most likely inspired a similar scene in the 1940 Stan Laurel and Oliver Hardy comedy *Saps at Sea*. In this particular scene, the boys have no food onboard. The boys hope to subdue their captor (Nick) by making him a "synthetic meal:" string for spaghetti, soap for cheese, sponge for meatball, lamp wick for bacon, and so on. Unfortunately, Nick spies on them and catches on to their scheme and forces Stan and Ollie to eat the ersatz meal themselves.

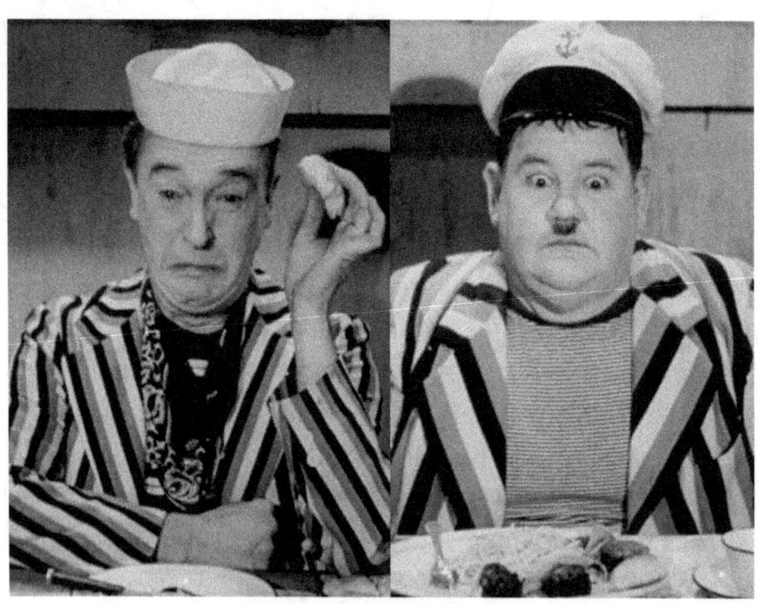

Unfortunately, the boys don't seem to be enjoying their meal as much as Charlie did in *The Gold Rush.*

Scene: The Dancing Dinner Rolls

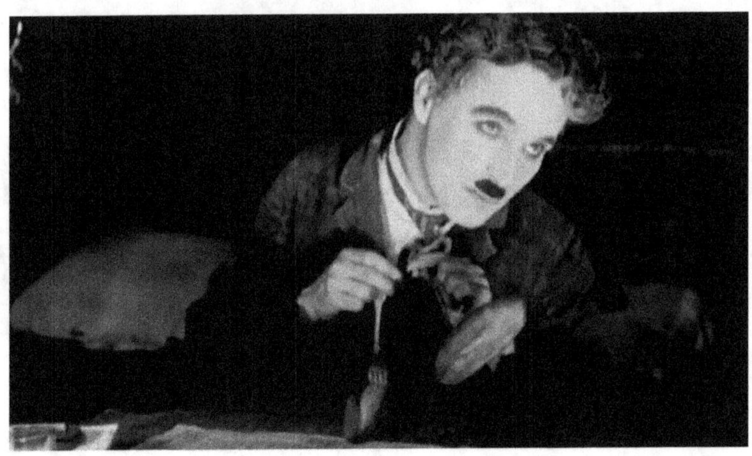

On New Year's Eve, while waiting for Georgia, a dance hall girl to arrive at his elaborate dinner party, along with her girlfriends, the prospector imagines entertaining her and her girlfriends with a dance of bread rolls on forks. Unfortunately, they all fail to make it to his party, after preparing a chicken dinner, elaborate place settings, gifts, and decorations all for naught. We have all felt the pain and sadness of being stood-up at least one in our lifetimes.

Chaplin wonderfully captures the pathos of the moment in a subsequent scene as the little tramp looks over his empty table with its unattended guests. He even fantasizes that they have actually arrived and are having a wonderful time.

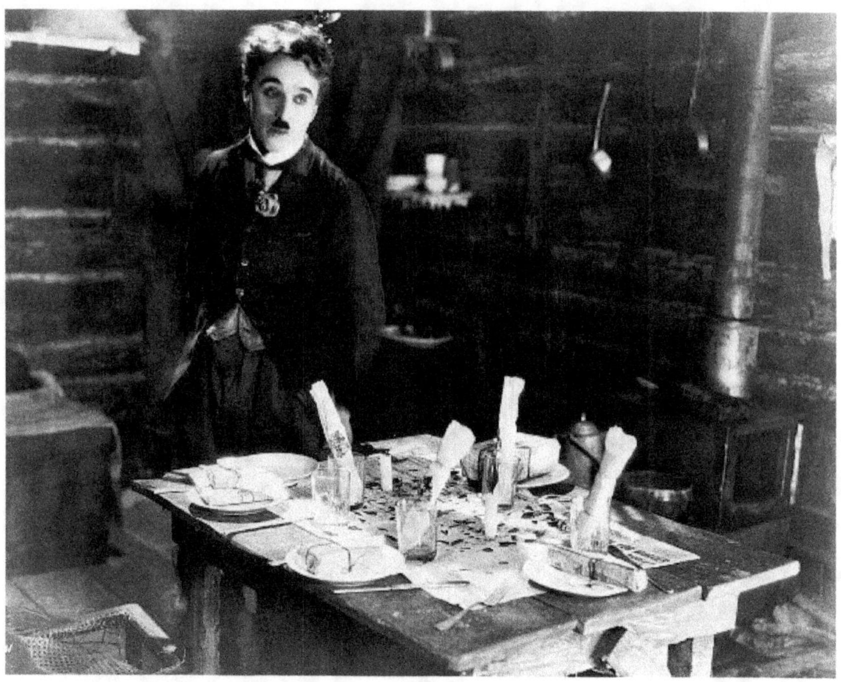

But look at what is happening in this sequence: in his mind, he is not only amusing the girls in his capacity as the little tramp, but he is also living out the fantasy that he is loved and appreciated by the girl of his dreams and her cohort of friends. His food, drink, gifts, and amusing way of entertaining them make them all his fans; but when the fantasy fades away, and we come to, realizing that what we have just seen is a dream, we are left with the prospector asleep in his plate, the candlesticks drooping, the house otherwise empty, the atmosphere pathetic. This scene is not only an excellent embodiment of the Tramp's personality traits (he is shy, devoted, and wistful) but also a great example of Chaplin's universal human appeal. When juxtaposed with the character's reality, the dream not only makes us feel for the disappointed, solitary tramp, but also register a moment of self-recognition. It is a perfect depiction of how sad our little dreams of ourselves can be.

Both of these scenes were filmed on the backlot and stages at Chaplin's Hollywood studio, where elaborate Klondike sets were constructed.

The "roll dance" that the little tramp character performs in the film is considered one of the most memorable scenes in film history, although Roscoe Arbuckle did something similar in the 1917 movie *The Rough House*, which co-starred Buster Keaton. The bit was briefly homaged by Curly Howard in the 1935 Three Stooges film *Pardon My Scotch*.

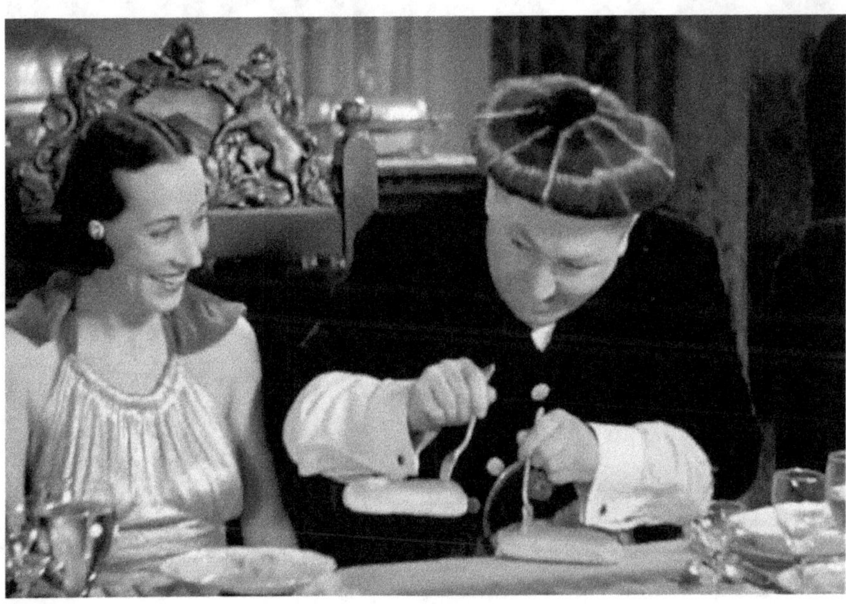

In more recent times, it was replicated by Robert Downey Jr. in his lead role as Charles Chaplin in the 1992 *Chaplin*. Johnny Depp's character in the 1993 film *Benny and Joon* also does the "roll dance" in tribute to Chaplin.

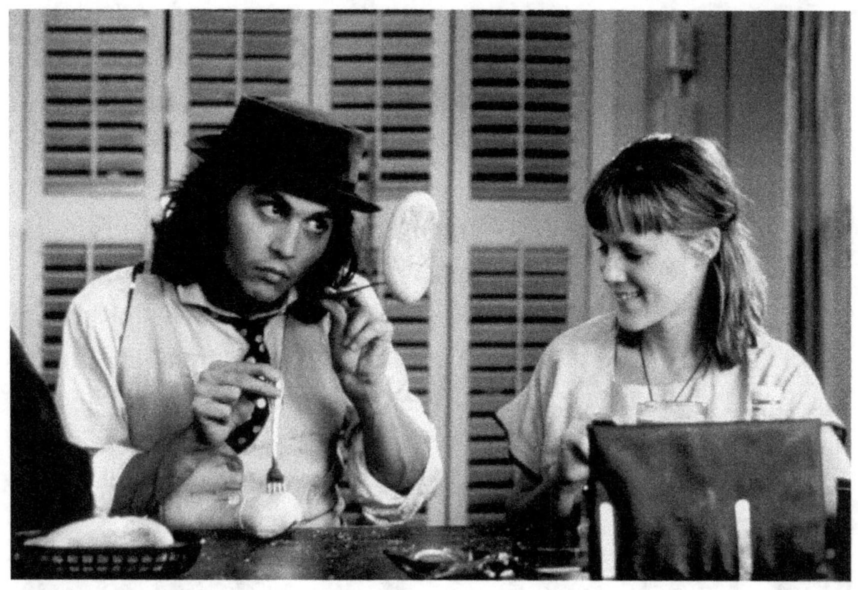

The Phantom of the Opera (1925)

The Phantom of the Opera is a silent horror film adaptation of Gaston Leroux's 1910 novel *Le Fantôme de l'Opéra*, directed by Rupert Julian and starring Lon Chaney in the title role of the deformed phantom who haunts the Paris Opera House, causing murder and mayhem in an attempt to make the woman he loves a star.

Scene: The Unmasking

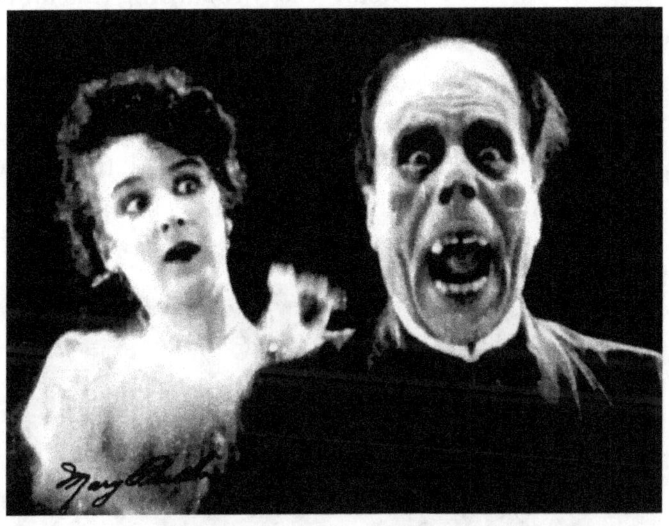

The frightening, eerie moment that the mad Erik (Lon Chaney, Sr.), the horribly disfigured phantom of the opera, is unmasked, reveals his grotesque face—artfully-applied makeup shows round, darkened eyes, jagged decayed teeth, flaring nostrils, and a corpse-like visage. It is Universal's definitive silent horror classic scene. The unmasking scene was said to have made theater patrons scream and faint in 1925.

This scene is from the epic film *The Phantom of the Opera* adaptation of Gaston Leroux's 1910 novel L*e Fantôme de l'Opéra*, directed by Rupert Julian. It is literally is the culmination of a series of sequences in which Mary Philbin (Christine Daae) unmasks Erik, the Phantom. The scene established some of the most iconic and essential ingredients of the horror genre, old and new; the dynamic tension between the woman and the monster, the victim and the villain, beauty and the beast; the lure and the disgust offered by horror; the "attraction" and "repulsion;" and the act of voyeurism (the looker and the looked) so essential to the whole genre.

Donato Totaro wrote a brilliant essay regarding this unmasking scene for *OFF SCREEN* in May 2012. Here is a segment of the essay:

> Another aspect a close analysis of the editing reveals
> is something that no other writer has noted: that there
> are in fact multiple "unmaskings" in this scene.

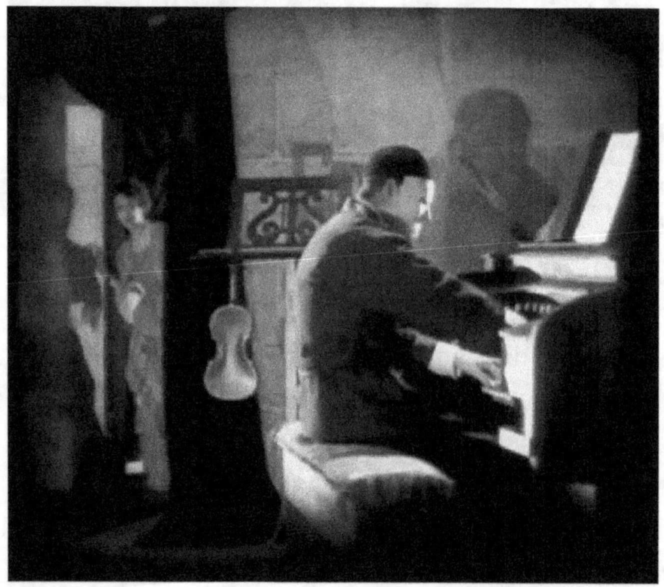

The scene, which lasts approximately five minutes, starting at around the 48 minute mark in the film, begins with Christine entering Erik's room from the door behind the organ where he is seated playing. She walks up to him, as he plays on unaware of her presence. This establishes the sense of this being an invasion of Erik's privacy, and the idea that Christine, a victim, is at this moment, the voyeur and the aggressor: she is sneaking up on Erik. She looks over his shoulder and sees the sheet music, "Don Juan Triumphant." This foreshadows the theme of "triumph" that will be played out in Chaney's performance, notably in the way he raises his arms way above his head in a defiant gesture of celebration. After they briefly acknowledge each other, the camera focuses on Christine's face, as she comes to the decision to unmask him. Again, her face is visible only to us, not Erik, whose back is turned to her. Hence we become complicit with Christine's decision to "unmask" Erik, who has already warned Christine against doing so (which establishes yet another horror cliché: the damsel who treads where she should not). Her decision to unmask Erik is plain to see for the audience, it is in her performance, the way her brain can be seen churning, her seductive eye movements, which again puts us in her mind but perhaps makes us feel sympathy for Erik because he is unaware of what is to occur. Her gesture increases the act as one of violation of his space and privacy. The excitement and sense of anticipation on Christine's face as she slowly moves her hands toward his mask is palpable. It reflects a sense of empowerment, as she is in full control of her destiny and has made the clear decision to break Erik's trust.

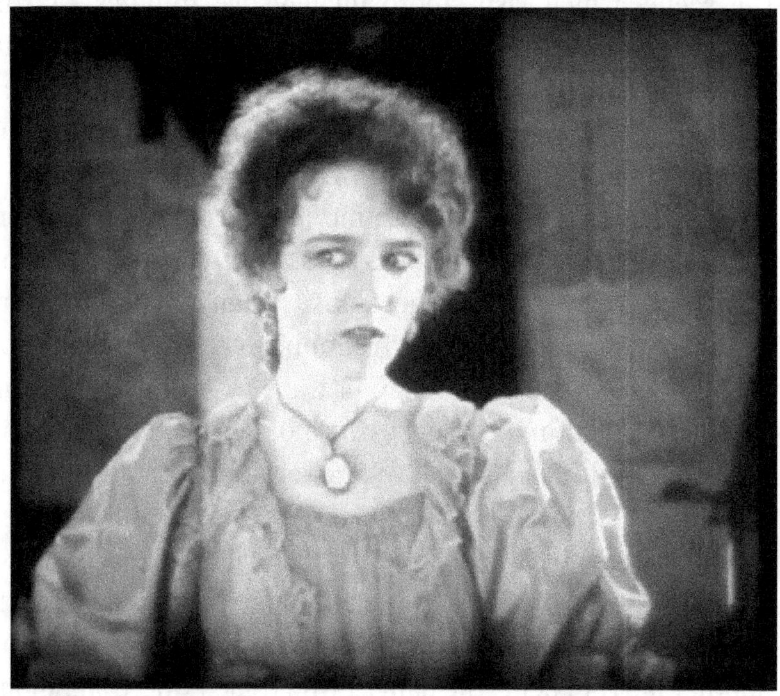

The desire to look is overwhelming. Her curiosity is stronger than any sense of propriety or honor. The way she advances and then recoils her hands is also a reflection of one of the greatest theoretical complexes of horror, as elaborated by Noel Carroll in his book The Philosophy of Horror. The way horror fiction works on our simultaneous attraction to and repulsion of the horrible sight, the "push-pull" effect, what Carroll sees as one of the two great "paradoxes of art-horror," the latter defined as fictional horror: Why would anyone be interested in something unpleasant? And, why are we afraid of something that we know does not exist?

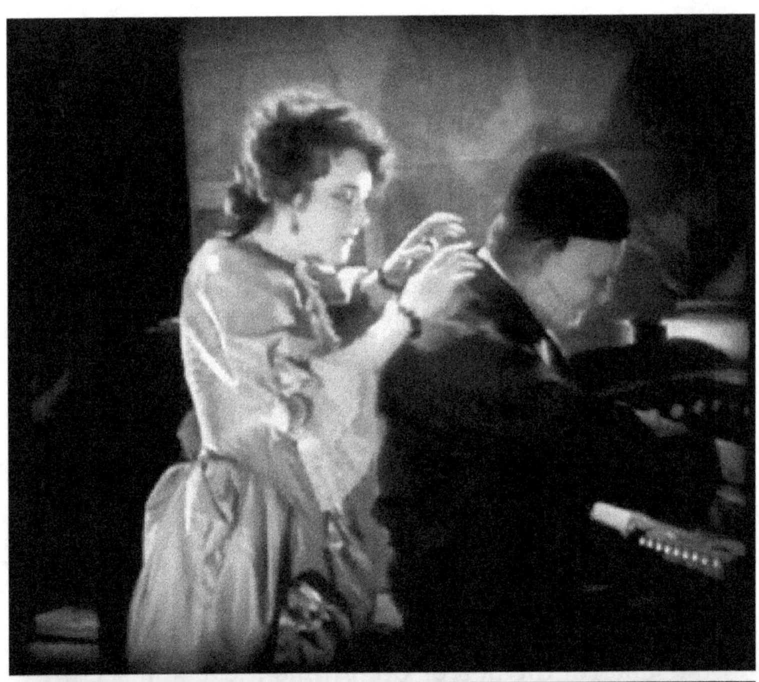

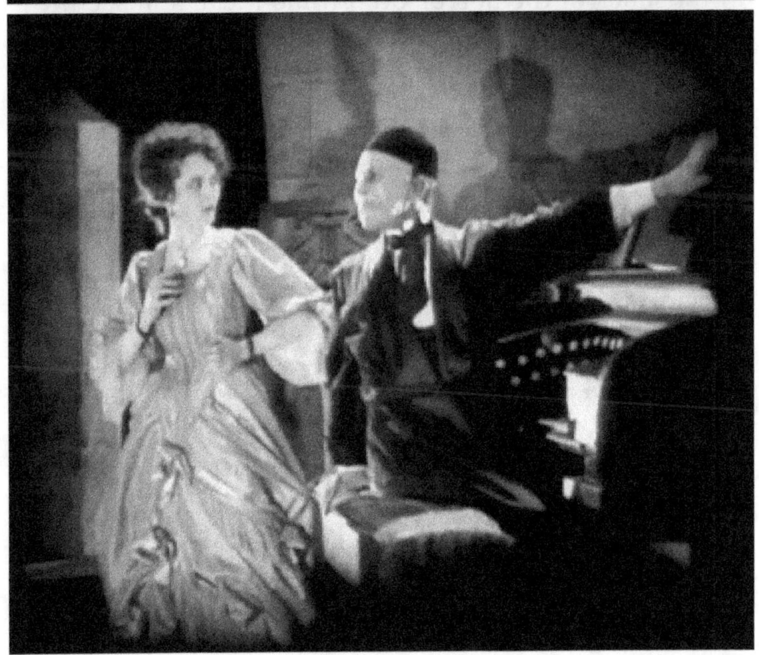

The "push-pull" complex is adroitly used in this sequence. After a slow buildup where she draws her hands to him then away, in medium-shot profile, the unmasking occurs, but abruptly, across a shock edit to an objective point of view looking at both Erik's hideous face and Christine behind him. We actually don't see her remove the mask, but already see her hand, with the mask in it, drawn away from Erik's face. It is a wonderful edit that leaves us with the impression of having seen more than we actually have. What is surprising is that we see Erik's face before she does. As Linda Williams observes in When the Woman Looks, in Re Vision: Essays in Feminist Film Criticism, "In the famous unmasking scene ... we ... see the Phantom's face, this time unmasked before Christine does. The audience thus receives the first shock of the horror even while it can still see the curiosity and desire to see on Christine's face."

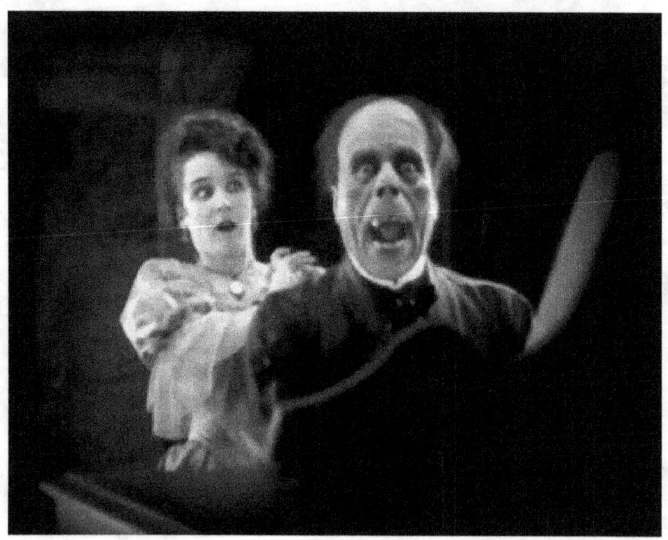

Following the success of *The Hunchback of Notre Dame* in 1923, Chaney was once again given the freedom to create his own make-up, a practice that became almost as famous as the films he starred in. *The Phantom of the Opera* remains most famous for Chaney's ghastly, self-devised makeup, which was kept a studio secret until the film's premiere. The film was released on November 25, 1925.

He is regarded as one of the most versatile and powerful actors of early cinema, renowned for his characterizations of tortured, often grotesque and afflicted characters, and his groundbreaking artistry with makeup. It is suggested that he may have modeled some of his makeup images after seeing some of the real-life horrors of war inflicted on the bodies of wounded soldiers following World War I.

Chaney commented,

> "In *The Phantom of the Opera*, people exclaimed at my weird makeup. I achieved the death's head of that role without wearing a mask. It was the use of paints in the right shades and the right places—not the obvious parts of the face—which gave the complete illusion of horror.... It is all a matter of combining paints and lights to form the right illusion."

Chaney used a color illustration based on the novel written by Andre Castaigne as his model for the Phantom's appearance. He raised the contours of his cheekbones by stuffing wadding inside his cheeks. He used a skullcap to raise his forehead height several inches and accentuate the bald dome of the Phantom's skull. Pencil lines masked the join of the skullcap and exaggerated his brow lines. Chaney then glued his ears to his head and painted his eye sockets black, adding white highlights under his eyes for a skeletal effect. He created a skeletal smile by attaching prongs to a set of rotted false teeth and coating his lips with greasepaint. To transform his nose, Chaney applied putty to sharpen its angle and inserted two loops of wire into his nostrils. Guide-wires hidden under the putty pulled his nostrils upward. According to cinematographer Charles Van Enger, Chaney suffered from his makeup, especially the wires, which sometimes made him "bleed like hell."

When audiences first saw *The Phantom of the Opera*, they were said to have screamed or fainted during the scene where Christine pulls the concealing mask away, revealing his skull-like features to the audience.

Chaney's appearance as the Phantom in the film has been the most accurate depiction of the title character based on the description given in the novel, where the Phantom is described as having a skull-like face with a few wisps of black hair on top of his head. As in the novel, Chaney's phantom has been deformed since birth, rather than having been disfigured by acid or fire, as in later adaptations of *The Phantom of the Opera*.

The infamous unmasking scene in the original *Phantom* is masterfully staged and crafted in order to maximize its effect on the viewing audience. Subsequent movies that depicted this scene are all good, but they don't match the sheer horror and drama of the original Chaney version.

The 1943 movie of the same name starred noted screen actor Claude Rains as Erik and Susanna Foster as Christine.

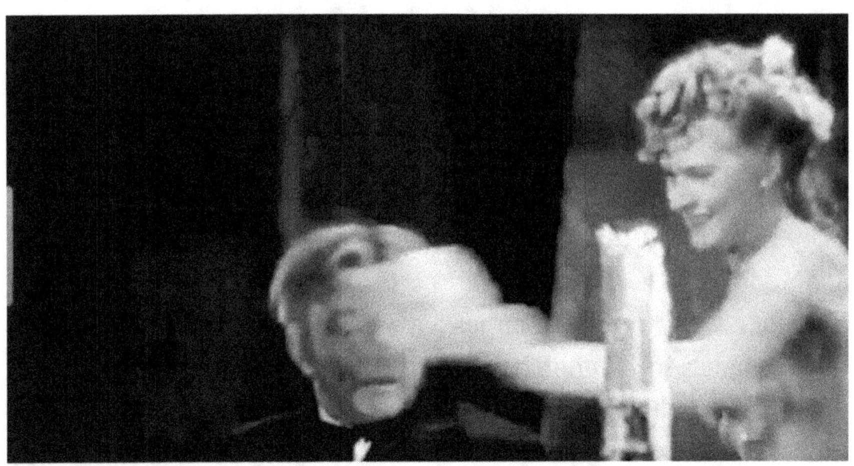

The wonderful 2004 film, again of the same name, starred Gerard Butler and Amy Rossum as the main characters.

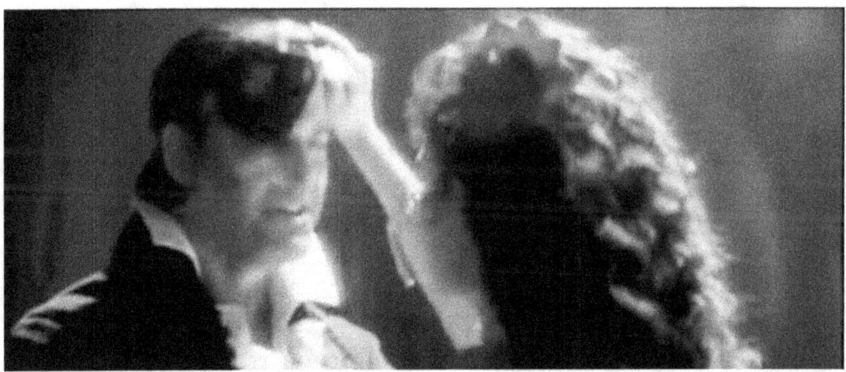

The General (1927)

The General is a silent comedy film released by United Artists. It was inspired by the April 12, 1862 Great Locomotive Chase, a true story of an event that occurred during the Civil War. The story was adapted from the memoir *The Great Locomotive Chase* by William Pittenger, who was one of James J. Andrews Union Raiders who stole the Confederate locomotive *The General*, consisting of rail cars at Big Shanty, Georgia en route to Chattanooga, Tennessee. The film stars Buster Keaton, who co-directed it with Clyde Bruckman. Keaton was a huge fan of train history and had read the book. Although it was written from the Union Army perspective, Keaton did not believe that the audience would accept Confederates as villains and changed the story's point of view. Keaton attempted to rent the real-life General for the film. At that time, the locomotive was on display at a Chattanooga rail station, but the train's owners denied Keaton's request when they realized that the film was going to be a comedy.

The cast and crew arrived in Cottage Grove, Oregon, on May 27, 1926, with eighteen freight cars full of Civil War-era cannons, rebuilt passenger cars, stagecoaches, horses, wagons, and laborers. The crew stayed at the Bartell Hotel in nearby Eugene and brought three 35mm cameras with them from Los Angeles. On May 31, set construction began with the materials, and regular train service in Cottage Grove ceased until the end of production. One-third of the film's budget was spent in Cottage Grove, and 1,500 locals were hired. Keaton brought eighteen freight cars of props and set materials to Oregon.

Scene: The Collapse of the Rock Creek Bridge

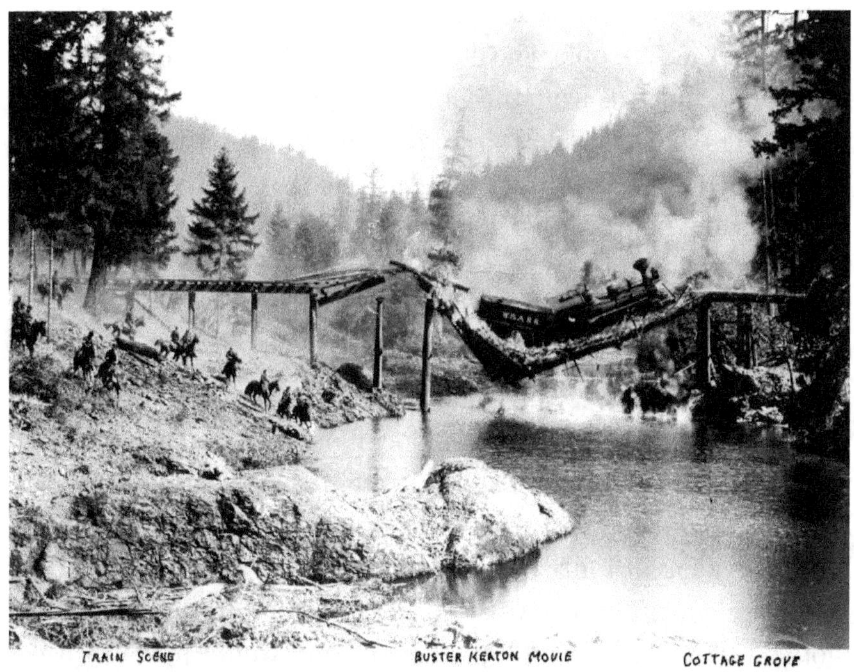

The most spectacular scene in *The General* depicts a train plunging to destruction when a burning bridge collapses. The actual scene was filmed on July 23, 1926, in the conifer forest near Cottage Grove, Oregon. The scene was shot full-scale, in long-shot, using one of two real trains he purchased from the Oregon, Pacific, and Eastern Railways for the production. Later he bought a third locomotive in Oregon to portray *The Texas*, which would be used in the train wreck itself. He also built a three-hundred-foot-long railroad trestle so he could burn it and collapse it with a real train. This meant, however, that they had to get it in one take. Crew members spent hours setting up the stunt just right, with six cameras positioned to get the scene from the best possible angles. They couldn't risk putting actors on the train, so they had a lifelike dummy to stand in for the engineer. When they finally shot the scene, the dummy was so convincing that the three- to four-thousand local townspeople who'd come to watch screamed in horror. Five hundred extras from the Oregon National Guard were "hired" to play the soldiers. They all dressed up in Union uniforms and were filmed going left to right before changing into Confederate uniforms and being filmed going right to left. The sequence began four hours late and required several lengthy simulated trial runs. The shot went off without a hitch, but cost forty-two thousand dollars (almost two million in contemporary terms), making it the most expensive single shot in silent film history. The production company left the wreckage of the locomotive in the riverbed after the scene. It would remain at the location until it was salvaged for scrap metal during World War II. Prior to the time it was salvaged, it became a minor tourist attraction for nearly twenty years.

It is indeed an unbelievable sequence. The throttle of the locomotive was pre-set so that the entire train would move forward onto the already feeble, burned-through bridge. When the train is halfway across, the bridge weakens, sways, and then gives way. The belly of the train droops and falls down through the burning portion of the bridge as it opens wide under its weight. Both the train and collapsing bridge plunge into the river, a mass of hurtling metal, exhaling/hissing smokestack steam, burning bridge logs, spraying water and a geyser of belching smoke.

While all of this activity is developing on the bridge, General Parker's Union army, on foot, and the two Union pursuit locomotives (with their cargos of munitions and troops) all converge at the merrily-blazing bridge. *The Texas*'s engineer hesitates to go farther until Parker on horseback boldly and sternly orders Captain

Anderson and *The Texas* to cross the slightly damaged bridge: "That bridge is not burned enough to stop you, and my men will ford the river. The Union cavalry on horseback and foot soldiers will descend the bank to the water's edge and cross the river beneath the bridge."

The next quick-cut is a medium, close-up reaction shot of the stolid General Parker still astride his horse—his stunned, bewildered face reveals his disbelief, annoyance, and frustration that he was wrong as he looks on at the painful doom of the ruined, fallen train. As the Union general turns back to his men, his officers stare back accusingly, acknowledging that their General has made a complete ass of himself, which was probably not the first time.

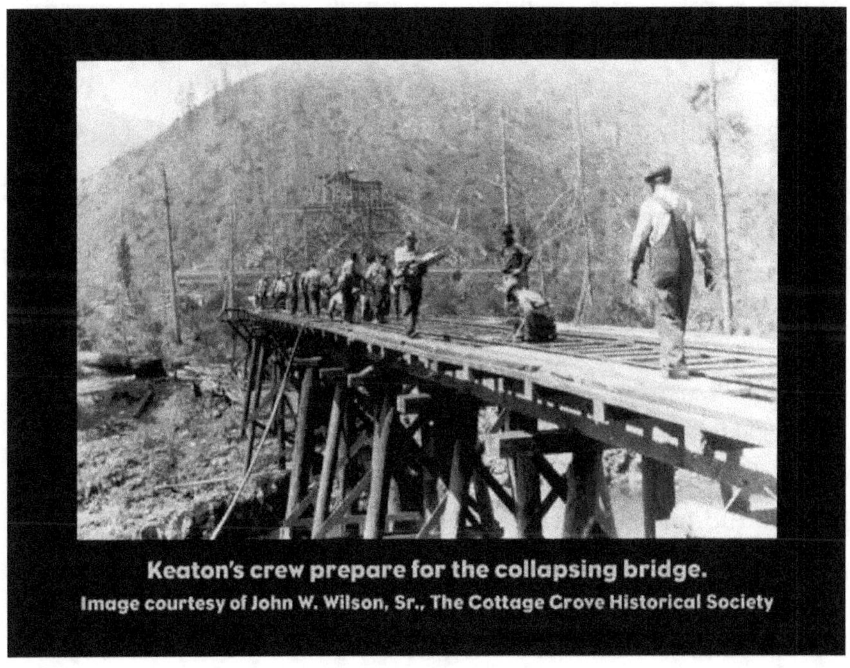

Keaton's crew prepare for the collapsing bridge.
Image courtesy of John W. Wilson, Sr., The Cottage Grove Historical Society

The Great Locomotive Chase is a 1956 Walt Disney Productions CinemaScope adventure film based on the same scenario depicted in *The General* (1927). The film stars Fess Parker as James J. Andrews, the leader of a group of Union soldiers from various Ohio regiments who volunteered to go behind Confederate lines in civilian clothes, steal a Confederate train north of Atlanta, and drive it back to Union lines in Tennessee, tearing up railroad tracks and destroying bridges and telegraph lines along the way.

As far as movies, which mimic the infamous train crash on a collapsing bridge depicted in *The General*, the very best one has to be the truly wonderful scene in the 1957 classic *The Bridge on the River Kwai* where British commandos destroy a bridge just completed by British prisoners of war in Japanese-controlled Burma.

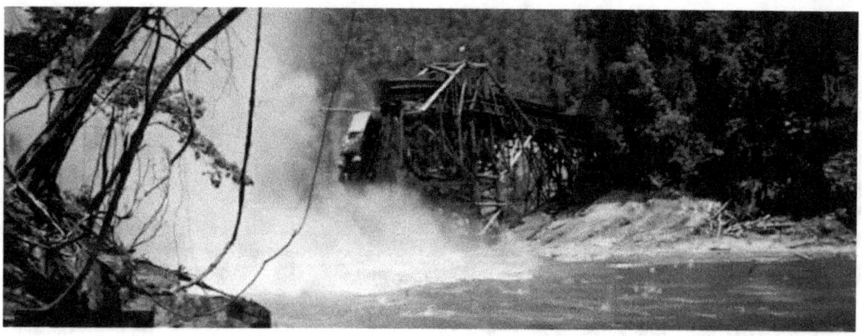

A 1976 disaster movie that throws a plague virus and a crumbling bridge at its protagonists, *The Cassandra Crossing* saw its starry cast stuck on a train headed for disaster as the plague-ridden train crosses the unstable bridge of the title. The catastrophe that follows is depicted using some of the worst model effects I've ever seen in a mainstream film, with tiny toy trains bouncing off the miniature bridge's matchstick girders.

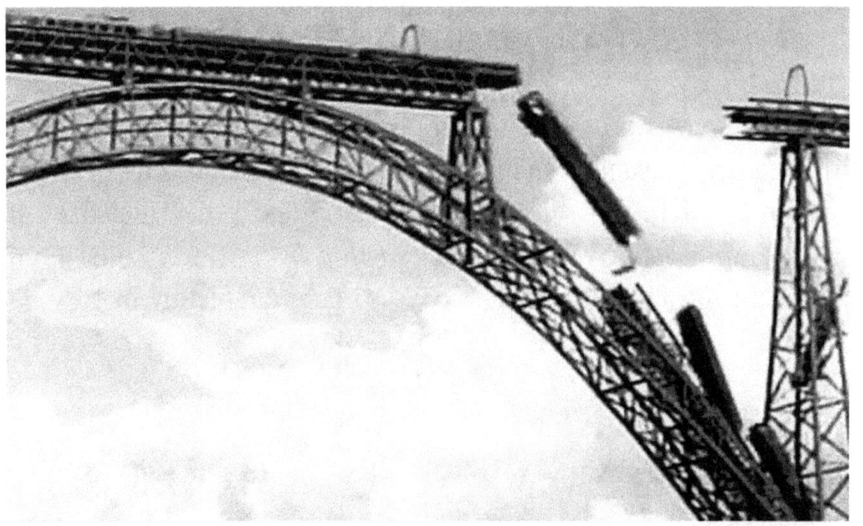

Metropolis (1927)

Fritz Lang's expressionistic, utopian view of the twenty-first-century future, visually-cinematic images foreshadowed the development of future science-fiction films and other diatribes of dehumanized labor versus capital. *Metropolis* is widely considered one of the most iconic and classic films in motion picture history.

Scene: The Futuristic City

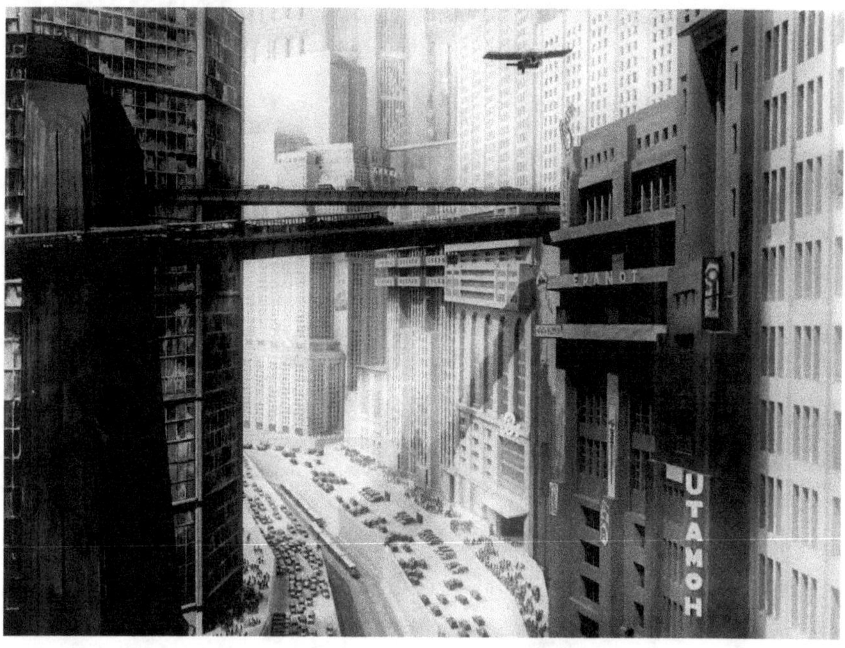

The Art Deco motif of the futuristic city in *Metropolis* reminds me of the city landscape depicted in the 1936 movie *Things to Come*. I am sure the Fritz Lang film was well known to director William Cameron Menzies.

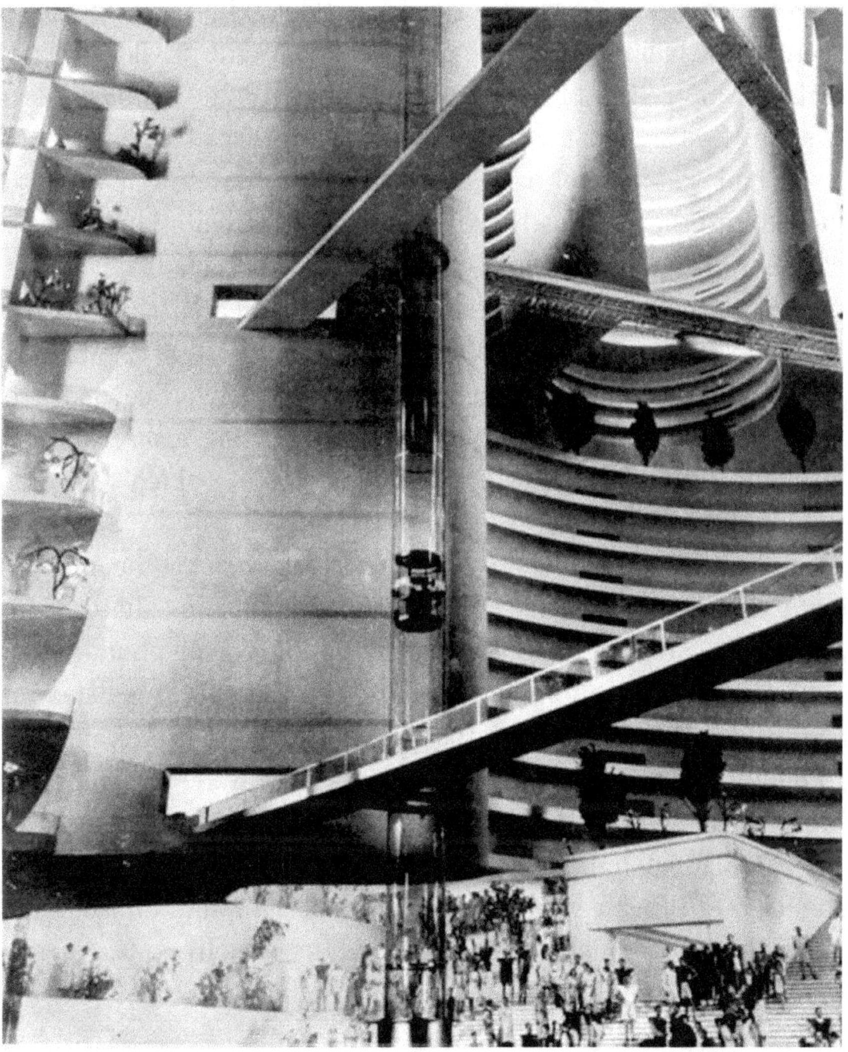

It is the year 2026—a Dickensian "best of times, worst of times."
In the extraordinary Gothic skyscrapers of a corporate city-state,
is the city of Metropolis. Here live the wealthy industrialists and
business magnates who reign from high-rise towers. They are the
planners or deep thinkers who bathe in care-free luxury, serviced

by modern modes of transportation, state-of-the-art technology, recreational facilities—in sort, all the benefits of the privileged class.

In an interview, Fritz Lang reported that "the film was born from my first sight of the skyscrapers in New York in October 1924."

He had visited New York City for the first time and remarked, "I looked into the streets—the glaring lights and the tall buildings—and there I conceived *Metropolis*."

Describing his first impressions of the city, Lang said that "the buildings seemed to be a vertical sail, scintillating and very light, a luxurious backdrop, suspended in the dark sky to dazzle, distract, and hypnotize." The appearance of the city in *Metropolis* was also strongly informed by the Art Deco movement, which was very popular at the time.

In this production shot, we see the crew preparing the magnificent set for the opening sequence. The establishing shots of the city—with cars, planes, and elevated trains moving about—were shot using stop-motion photography. The cars were modeled on the newest taxicabs driving the streets of Berlin. It took months to build the city model and several days to film the few short sequences. Then the lab ruined the first shots. The backgrounds in the shot had been dimly lit to create a greater sense of depth, but the head of the lab, who actually developed the film himself, decided that was a mistake and lightened the backgrounds, thereby destroying the sense of forced perspective.

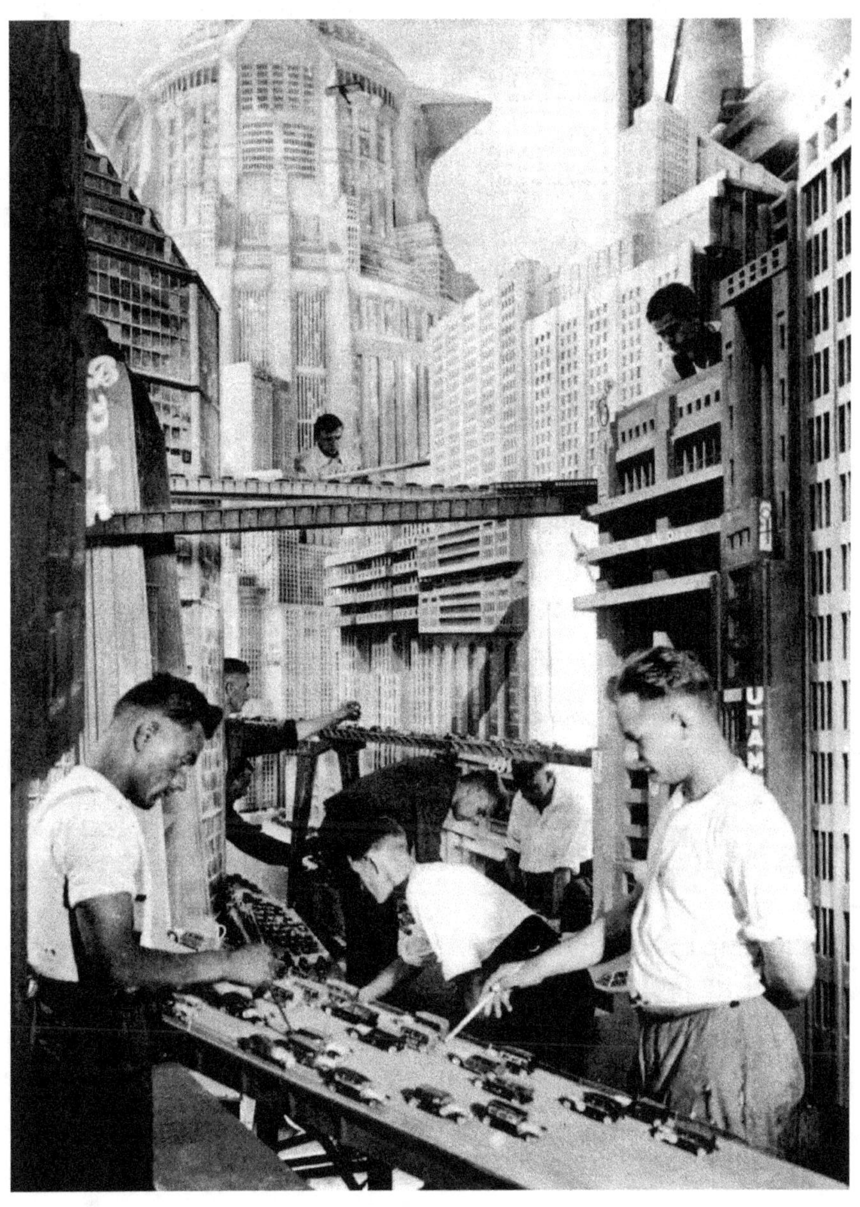

While underground-dwelling workers toil to operate the Heart Machine, which powers the city, all the luxuries of the rich are dependent on the Heart Machine that must be continuously serviced and maintained in order to sustain the lives the privileged class living above who are totally oblivious to their downtrodden and their mixable life.

Scene: The Heart Machine

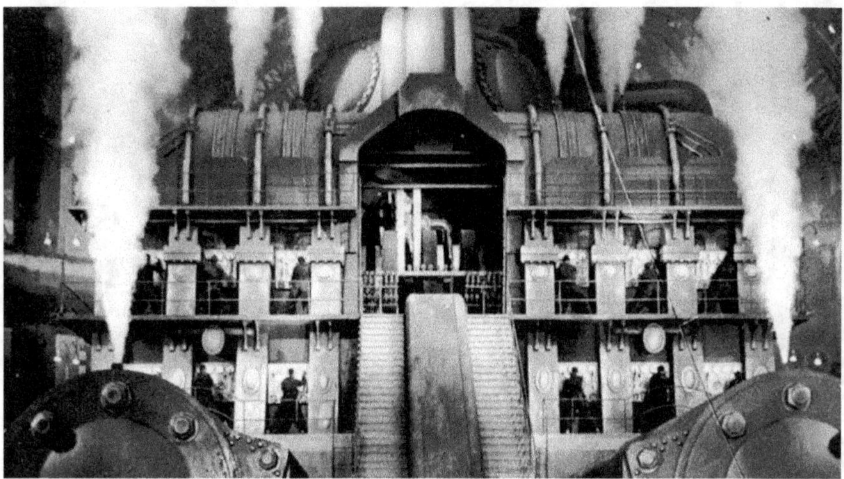

On a trip to New York City for Christmas, my son and I attended the 2019 Radio City Christmas Specular featuring the Rockettes. There on stage, in the opening number, was a structure that immediately reminded me of the infamous Heart Machine, even with people operating controls on each side of the machine. Of course, the machine here is a lot more benevolent.

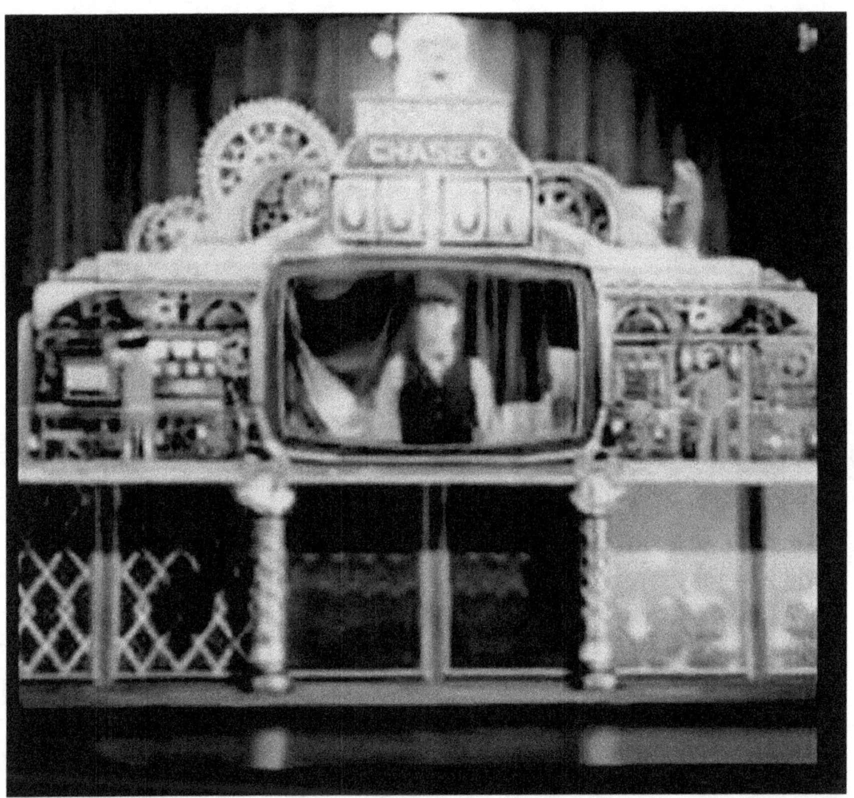

Back to the movie *Metropolis*. A close-up of just one of the poor workers who must sustain the gigantic Heart Machine consisting of enormous pounding pistons of machinery, moving/rotating gears, power stations, gauges and dials, and valves and levers.

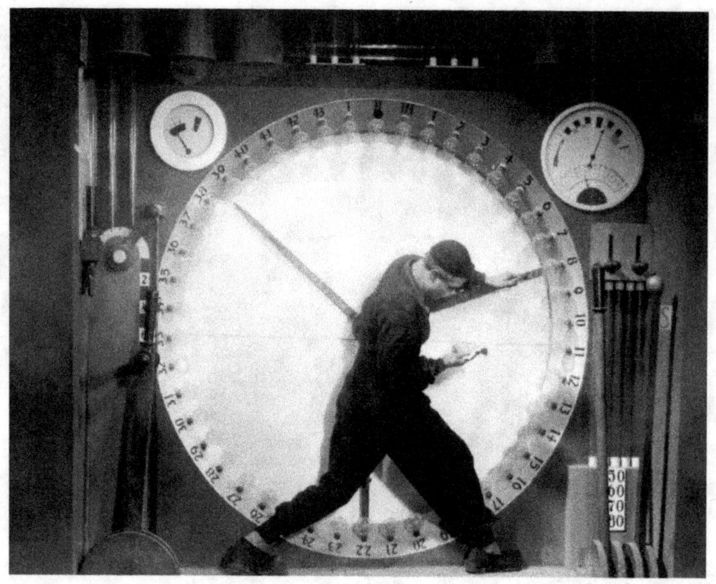

In the world of *Metropolis*, total oppression and manipulation of the masses are wielded by the unquestionable power of the leisurely few. Nameless, amorphous, exploited battalions of uniformed, underground workers are viewed in stylized shots. Black-garbed and unidentifiable, they trudge sullenly to their laborious tasks and alternate their work shifts, day after day, in mechanical routines. The workers entering the factory that houses the Heart Machine have the same defeated attitude as those who are leaving the factory. The will and spirit of the modernized working-class men, who operate the technology that sustains the privileged class, has been destroyed. The work shift (divided into day and night of ten hours each, in the twenty-hour day) changes at the end of ten hours, signaled by steam whistles blowing. In one of the most profound scenes in the movie, two parallel corridors of two groups of uniformed workers (in dark work suits) are lined up in rows of six. The sullen workers leaving the subterranean machine area after their ten-hour shift are totally exhausted, marching forward in unison, only half as fast as the new shift of entering workers. One cage-elevator is used to take one shift up to the Workers' City, after the completion of their shift, while the other cage-elevator takes the relief workers down to the Heart Machine day after day, month after month, and year after year, ad infinitum.

This scene is beautifully "orchestrated" in the film by composer Gottfried Huppertz who used repetitive frantic sounds of the high woodwinds in order to create beat-like and dissonant chords. In recent years, the use of synthesized music, composed by Kevin Weingartner, has been used to accompany this particular scene in the movie using several different styles of twentieth-century composers, including Igor Stravinsky, Arnold Schoenberg, Paul Hindemith, and Bela Bartok.

Scene: The Shift Change

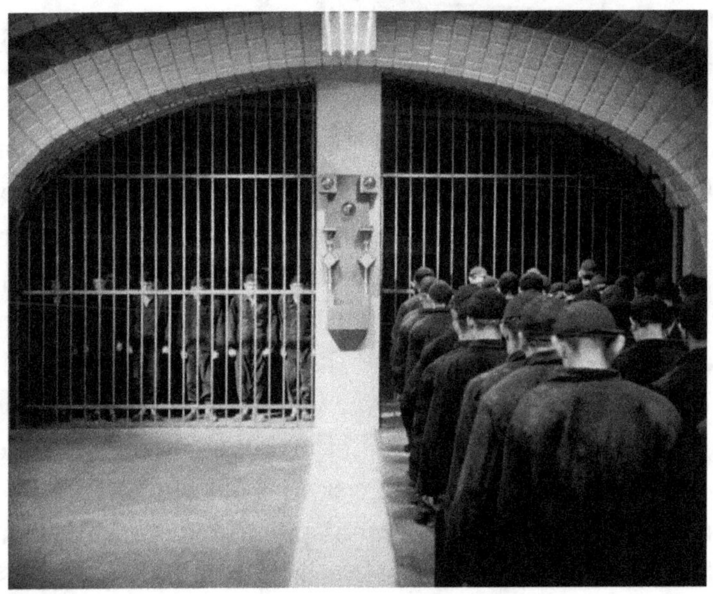

In 1984, Apple produced one of the best Super Bowl commercials ever made. The procession of disheartened citizens of an Orwellian world solemnly marching in unison is very reminiscent of the scene from *Metropolis*.

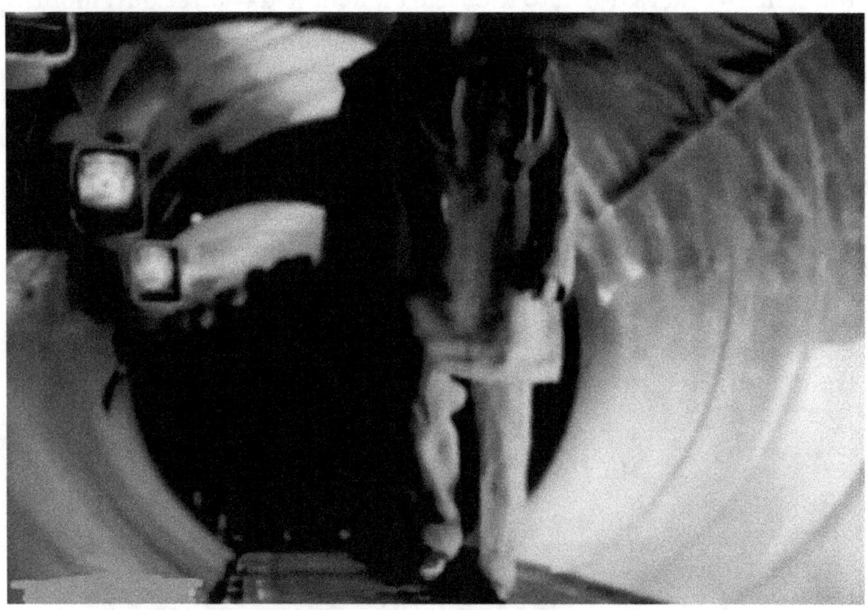

The scene in *Metropolis* of the life-like vitalization-transformation of an android female robot by mad scientist/inventor Rotwang (Rudolf Klein-Rogge) is stunning. Maria (Brigitte Helm) is pursued in the catacombs by Rotwang's glaring flashlight, kidnapped, made captive, and brought to his alchemist laboratory so that he can give the false, evil robotic duplicate the "girl's likeness." Luminous rings circumscribe and travel vertically over the robotic figure, spreading Maria's life and circulatory system into the machine and replacing the robot's inhuman mask with her human face.

Cinematographer Gunther Rittau created the whirling bands of light for the creation of the robot Maria by filming a spinning silver ball in front of a black velvet curtain. The rings' movement was created by raising and lowering the camera.

Scene: The Robot

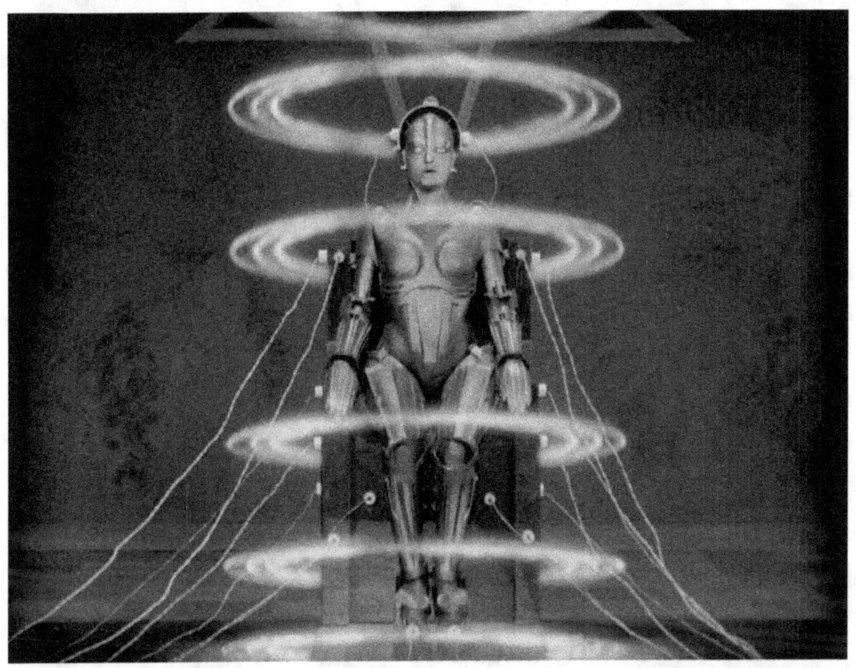

The robot in *Metropolis* reminds me of the threatening robot that appeared in the 1991 film *Terminator 2: Judgment Day*.

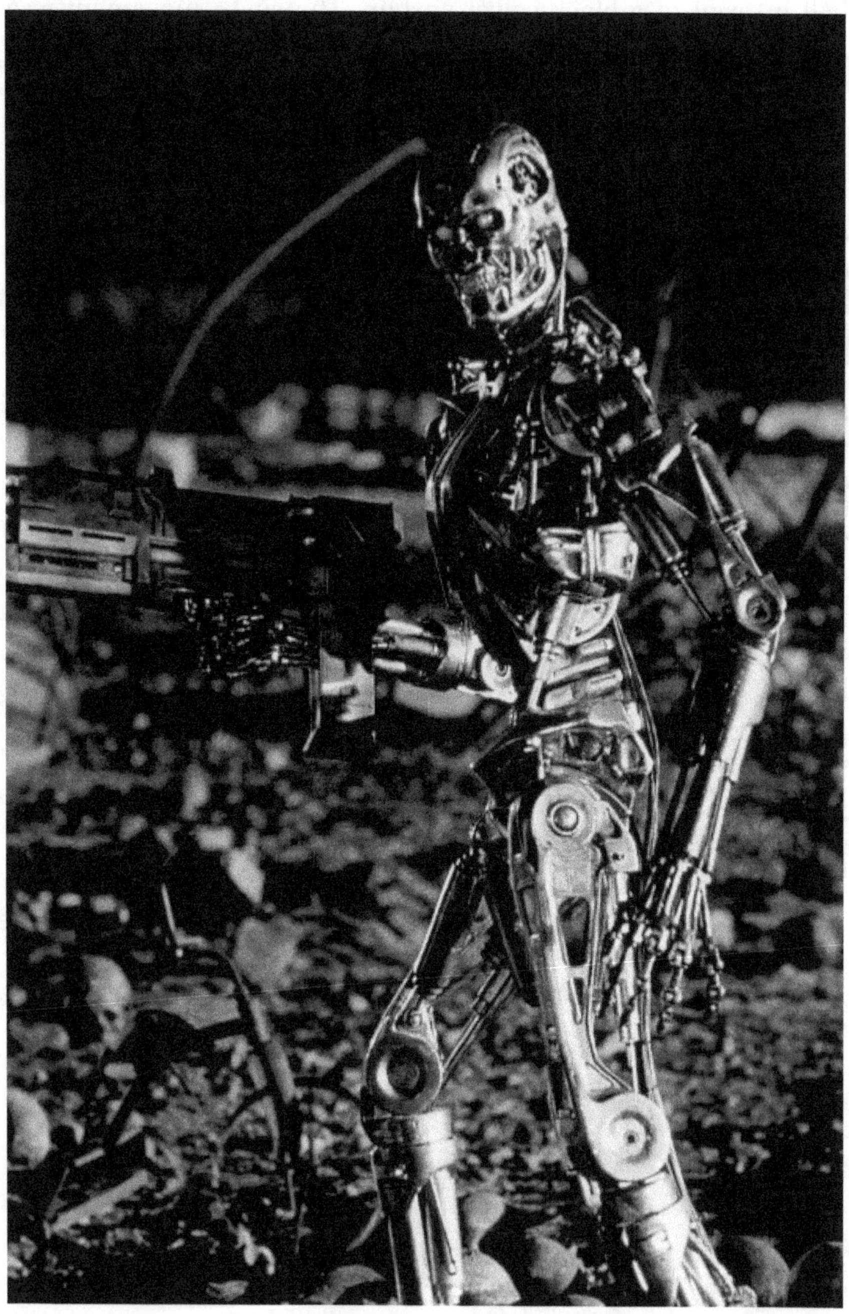

This is a montage of the sequence in *Metropolis* in which the mad Professor Rotwang uses Maria's likeness to create the robot "Hel," so that it can ruin her reputation among the workers to prevent any rebellion.

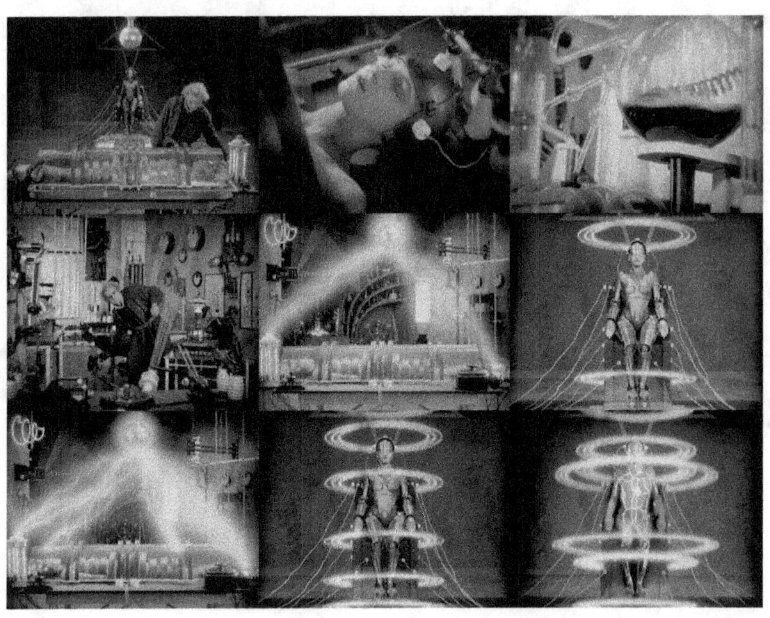

The Maschinenmensch—the robot built by Rotwang to resurrect his lost love Hel—was created by sculptor Walter Schulze-Mittendorff. A whole-body plaster cast was taken of actress Brigitte Helm, and the costume was then constructed around it. A chance discovery of a sample of "plastic wood" (a pliable substance designed as wood-filler) allowed Schulze-Mittendorff to build a costume that would appear metallic and allow a small amount of free movement. Helm sustained cuts and bruises while in character as the robot as the costume was rigid and uncomfortable. Here is a unique production shot in which Helm, portraying the newly created Maria, is given some refreshment while a technician puts some finishing touches on her outfit.

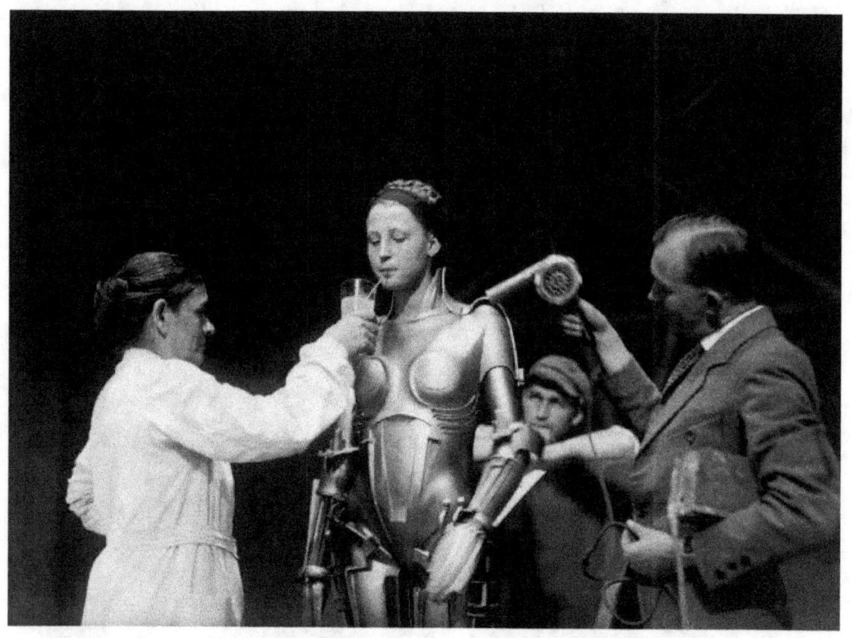

Steamboat Bill, Jr. (1928)

Steamboat Bill, Jr. is a silent comedy film starring Buster Keaton. It tells the story of the adventures and misadventures of a recently graduated college lad who returns home much to the dismay of his father William "Steamboat Bill" Canfield, the owner and captain of a paddle steamer that has seen better days. However, an unexpected cyclone provides the backdrop to prove his worth to his father and win his lady.

Scene: The House Falling

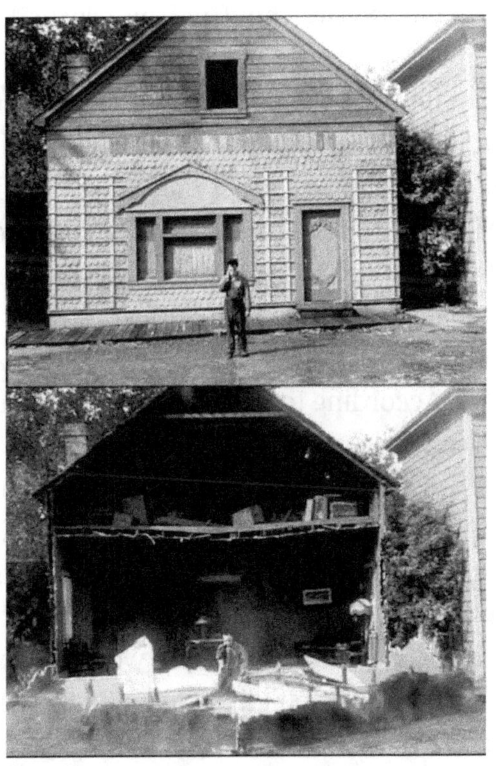

Silent movie comedy was all about slapstick and sight gags. Slipping on banana peels, falling from moving cars, teetering on high window ledges—audiences loved to see comedians testing the boundaries of gravity. And in an era long before CGI, these amazing feats were performed in real-time, the result of careful planning, physical skill, and immense courage. Buster Keaton was certainly a risk-taker in a number of his movies, including *Steamboat Bill, Jr.*, where he incurred a number of bruises and abrasions during the course of the filming. For a performer who had built a cinematic career on dangerous stunts, this scene would perhaps be his most dangerous.

Before shooting, the crew had to be exact in marking off where the two-ton structure would be falling, and the exact spot for "Old Stone Face" to stand so he would not be crushed. According to Hollywood legend, Keaton's shoes were nailed down to the spot so that he would not be tempted to move even slightly off cue and risk his life. Though Buster Keaton had done many stunts before, in the shooting of this scene for *Steamboat Bill Jr.*, his head was far from the right place. His alcoholism had been increasing, coinciding with his marriage falling apart. While battling these personal demons, he had learned that his business partner Joseph M. Schenk had sold their production company to MGM, in effect taking away all of his creative freedom. According to those who knew Buster at this time, in his heart of hearts, he went along with this dangerous feat because he had just given up and did not care what happened to him. In short, Keaton put his life on the line with this particular stunt.

This does not diminish Keaton's creative range and comic inventiveness in tackling everything from subdued, facial comedy to stumbling pratfalls, as with a sequence where a hurricane races through the town, toppling buildings like matchsticks. The hurricane causes an entire side of a building to fall straight toward Buster, who avoids death when his body passes harmlessly through an open window on the building facade. Stories of the filming of this gag are apparently *not* apocryphal—clearly, the structure was weighted and solid, and obviously, it misses hitting Keaton by inches. A carefully placed window in the façade of the structure was just big enough to give him two inches of clearance on either side. To achieve the stunt, a house was dangled on the end of a huge mechanical arm that could be lowered onto Keaton at the proper moment to achieve the hilariously "impromptu" effect. The gag was worked out mathematically, and no doubt, attempted many times with inanimate stand-ins. Nevertheless, many crew members left the premises rather than nervously watch the filming of the shot with Keaton. They certainly knew that if the calculation regarding where the façade was going to fall was off by only a few inches, Keaton would have been killed by the four-thousand-pound house façade falling on top of him.

The gag appeared in two other Keaton films, *Back Stage* (1919) and *One Week* (1920), with smaller buildings, but the *Steamboat Bill, Jr.* version was the ultimate stunt, posing a great deal of danger for Keaton if he in any way miscalculated the complex gag. The comedian remarked later in his career, "I was mad at the time, or I would never have done the thing."

The famous falling house stunt has been re-created several times on film and television (although with lighter materials and more contemporary safety measures in place), including the 1991 *MacGyver* episode "Deadly Silents;" Jackie Chan's *Project A Part II*; the 2004 *Arrested Development* episode "The One Where They Build a House" (performed by the show's character named Buster); *Deadpan*, a 1997 work by English film artist and director Steve McQueen, was also inspired by *Steamboat Bill, Jr.* McQueen stands in Keaton's place as a house facade falls over him. This film was shot from multiple angles, and the scene repeats over and over again while McQueen stands seemingly unaffected. The original Keaton scene is seen on the left, and the McQueen version is on the right.

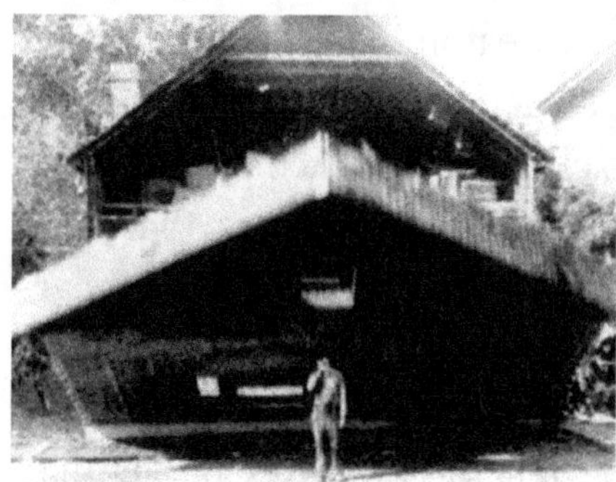 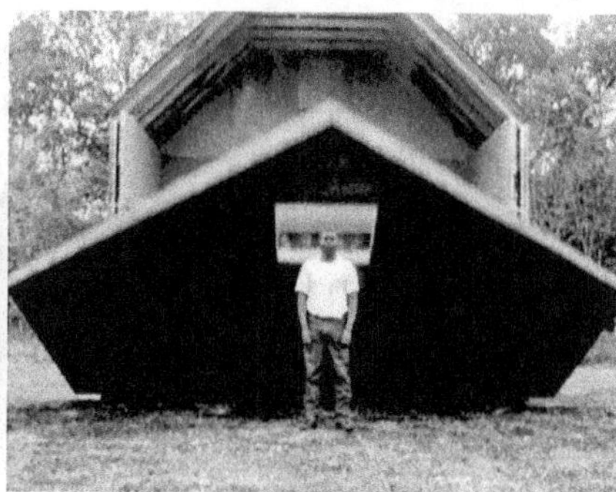

The Circus (1928)

The Circus is a silent film written, produced, and directed by Charlie Chaplin. The film stars Chaplin, Al Ernest Garcia, Merna Kennedy, Harry Crocker, George Davis, and Henry Bergman. The ringmaster of an impoverished circus hires Chaplin's Little Tramp as a clown but discovers that he can only be funny unintentionally.

The production of the film was the most difficult experience in Chaplin's career. Numerous problems and delays occurred, including a studio fire, the death of Chaplin's mother, as well as Chaplin's bitter divorce from his second wife Lita Grey, and the Internal Revenue Service's claims of Chaplin's owed back taxes, all of which culminated in filming being stalled for eight months. *The Circus* was the seventh highest-grossing silent film in cinema history, taking in more than $3.8 million in 1928.

Scene: The Tightrope

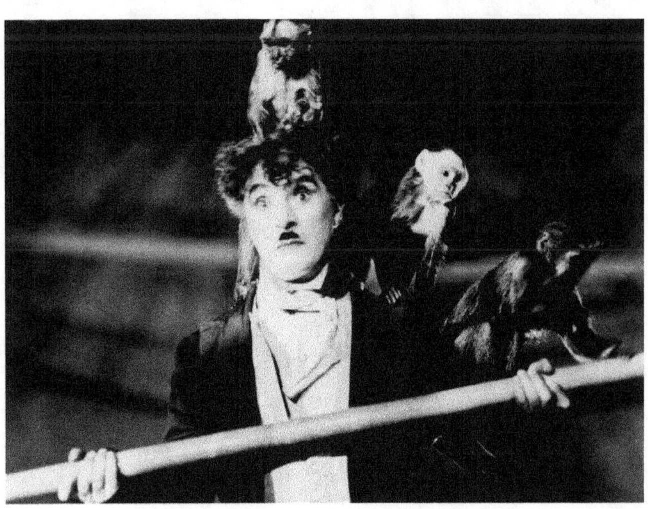

The piece de resistance is the extended tightrope scene. It is a hilarious sequence with a safety wire doing more harm than good and escaped monkeys determined to tear off his clothes as they valiantly try to cause him to fall from the already precarious tightrope.

As the prelude to this scene, the Tramp watches morosely as Rex, King of the Air (Harry Crocker), performs on the high wire, and Merna (Kennedy) sighs and bats her eyes. Later, Rex misses a performance, and the Tramp seizes the chance to go on the wire himself to win back her admiration. With the device of a secret safety wire supposedly manned by a prop man, he performs stunts that are extraordinary because of their difficulty; he uses the wire as a means of making the performance much harder than ordinary tightrope walking would be. Chaplin desperately negotiates the wire while three small monkeys crawl on him and rip off his pants to reveal that he had forgotten to put on his tights.

Chaplin actually learned to walk the wire for this scene, spending two months doing so. No trick photography was used to create the illusion of height, and, luckily, he never fell.

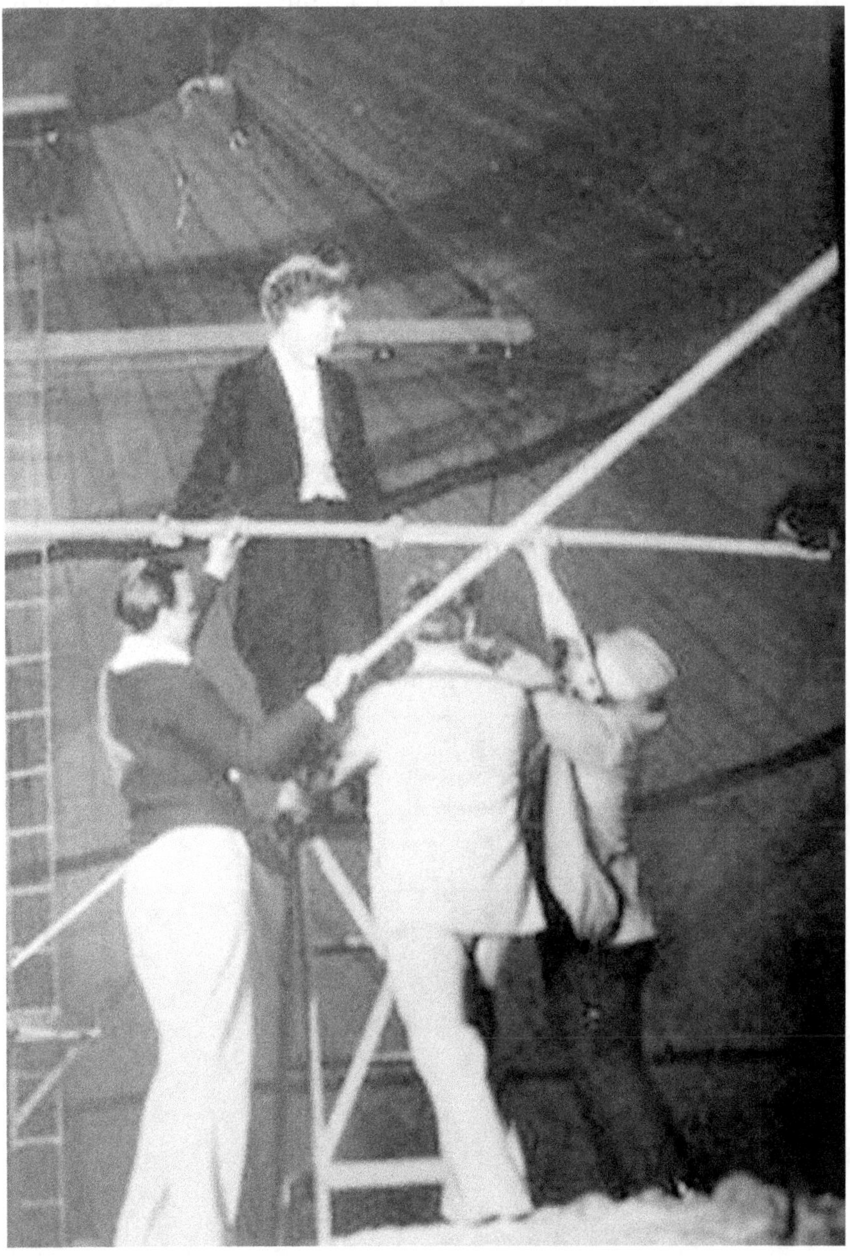

At the end of the movie, Charlie is the odd man out. Merna and Rex have fallen in love and are married. As the circus train leaves, Charlie is relegated to one of the circus wagons. However, he decides to leave the circus and sits dejectedly alone on a box alone. However, the resilient Tramp quickly picks himself up, and once again, with hope and determination, starts walking first a bit slowly and hesitantly, but then with the familiar spring in his step as the movie ends.

Chaplin's films often end with an uncertain future. Yet no one would call Chaplin's work pessimistic. His great sensibility is that, no matter what, the little Tramp will still carry on. Strange, quiet, gentle, and gentlemanly, he might be poor, he might be starving, but he will still pick himself up and walk onward into the sunset. At the end of *The Circus*, alone in the circle of the big top, he collects himself and wanders off. Where he goes is anyone's guess, but you still have the sense that he's out there, always ready to help the innocent child, the frightened young woman, and always ready to make us laugh, even if he feels a bit like crying.

Scene: The Resilient Tramp

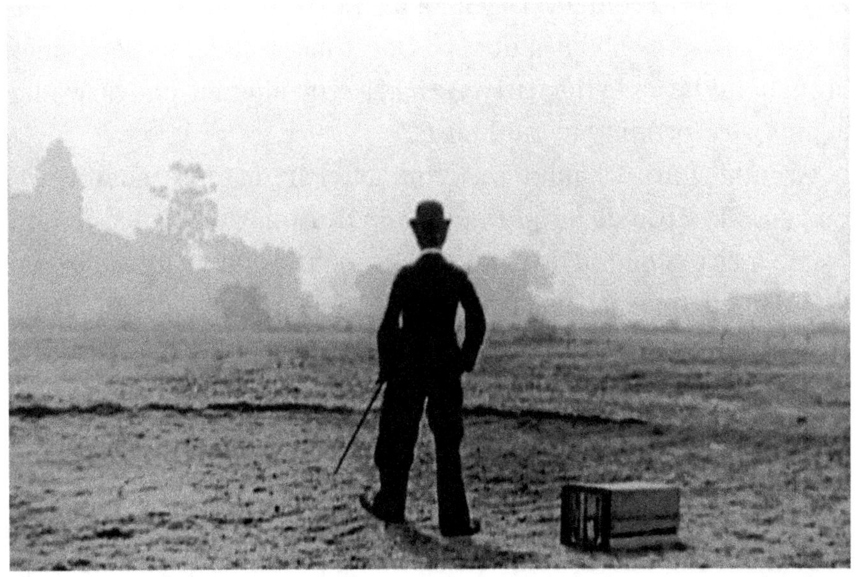

Author Vivica Gardiner wrote an article in the January 13, 2015 edition of *Circus Talk* entitled "Eugene Chaplin: Continuing a Circus Legacy." In the article, she describes how the legendary clown Charlie Chaplin's son Eugene inherited his father's love of the circus and founded the first international circus festival in Canada.

Eugene Chaplin has been a successful stage manager for opera and ballet, a recording engineer for famous rock and roll bands including the Rolling Stones and Queen, a documentary filmmaker, and president of Switzerland's International Comedy Film Festival, but, he says, "My real love is traditional circus."

The child of legendary clown Charlie Chaplin (and the grandson of Nobel-prize winning playwright Eugene O'Neill) says he inherited his love of circus from his father. Growing up in Switzerland, the family lived near a Circus Knie tour stop. When the circus came to town, his father would invite the Knie family and all the circus artists back to the house for late-night drinks and a party. Chaplin was inspired: "From a very young age, I got to see these amazing artists. Circus is about a dream. One time, a Russian performer brought his bears to the party. He had a crocodile act, and he would hypnotize crocodiles in our house."

Around 2010, Chaplin was contacted by a representative of Canada's Festival de cirque Vaudreuil-Dorion who wanted him to create a circus competition to add to their existing circus festival in the small town of Vaudreuil-Dorion, outside of Montreal. Chaplin was delighted: "The thing I love is that the people really wanted it. It was so nice to be able to help them out."

The competition, which does not impose an age limit, provided Canadian circus school graduates a format in which to compete against other talents from around the world. Chaplin's goal is to make the competition as international as possible so that attendees can discover fresh new acts from around the world. Since its inception four years ago, the competition has grown markedly. In 2014, eight thousand people attended the four-day event, which included live music, interactive workshops, a parade, and fireworks in addition to the competition.

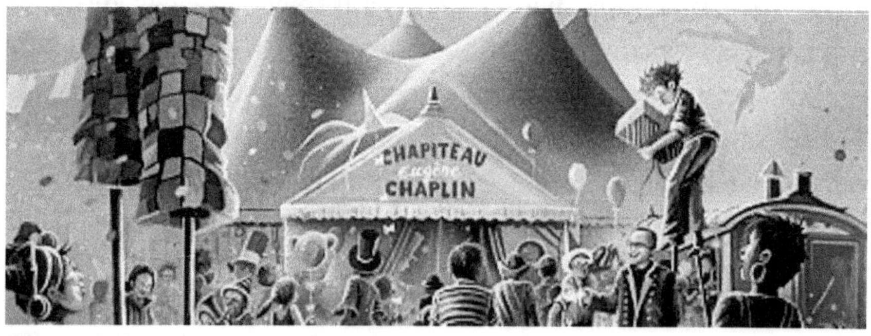

Speaking of family, Chaplin isn't the only member of his family in the industry. His older sister Victoria and her husband Jean-Baptiste Thierrée founded a series of circus companies in France in the 1970s that have been credited with spearheading the contemporary circus movement. "My sister Victoria and her husband were among the first ones renewing circus arts and presenting them on stage instead of in a tent. All of her shows have a story. They were the first ones to have this concept of how their show should be, which had nothing to do with traditional circus. It has jugglers, transformation, and trapeze, but not in the same way as other circuses."

City Lights (1931)

City Lights, subtitled "A Comedy Romance in Pantomime," is generally viewed as Charlie Chaplin's greatest film—a "silent film" released three years after the start of the talkies era of sound. The melodramatic film, a combination of pathos, slapstick, and comedy, was a tribute to the art of body language and pantomime—a lone hold-out against the assault of the talking film. Although it was filmed in 1931, it will be our final entry in the realm of silent films.

It was well known that Chaplin preferred the silent art form to the advent of sound films. Chaplin was responsible for the film's production, direction, editing, music, and screenplay.

The film's theme concerns the consequences (and suffering) resulting from the Tramp's attachment and efforts to aid a blind girl (and restore her sight with money for an operation) and a millionaire, as he persuades both of them that life is worth living. Both characters cannot "see" nor recognize him for what he is. However, the Tramp functions as a savior and wish-fulfiller for the blind flower girl while masquerading as a wealthy duke. For the drunken millionaire, the Tramp repeatedly saves the man's life and provides a congenial friend.

Scene: The Recognition

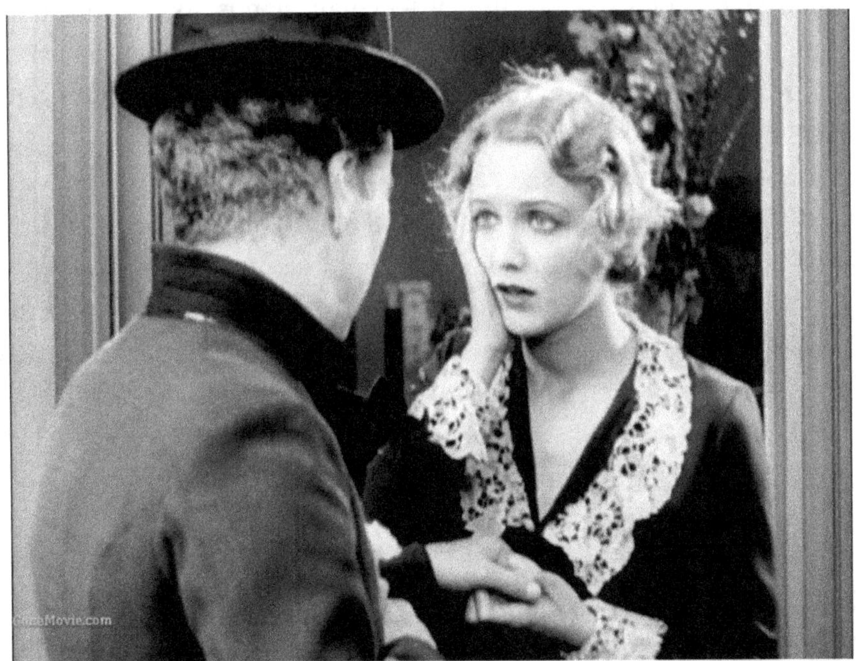

"You?"

The tearful, sentimental ending in this memorable film is brilliantly conceived and acted. A blind flower girl (Virginia Cherrill) with restored sight recognizes and realizes that her benefactor is the vagabond, funny-looking Little Tramp (Charlie Chaplin).

The film's most simple, moving, eloquent, and poignant finale is filled with melancholy and pathos. Although the Tramp tries to walk away and evade her, she stops laughing and pities him. Determined to help him, she calls him back and outside the shop, in a sympathetic act of charity, offers him a fresh white rose to replace the tattered, wilting one he picked up from the gutter. She also offers him a coin that she has just taken from the flower shop register. When she takes his hand and puts the coin in the palm of his hand, it suddenly dawns on her who he actually is. With her acute, sensitive sense of touch, she recognizes the familiar feel of his hands. As she runs her hand up the ragged fellow's coat from his shoulder to his face, she realizes that he is her mysterious benefactor, the shabbily-dressed vagabond who raised the money for her operation.

They recognize and see each other for the first time, reunited, face-to-face, the Tramp feeling many emotions at once—shame, fear, bravery, pain, tentativeness, love, bliss, and joy. At first, she appears slightly dismayed—he looks so completely different from what she expected—and then she is moved. The Tramp smiles and his eyes light up when she recognizes and accepts him for who he is.

The Flower Girl asks: "You?"

The Tramp nods in assent and smiles shyly, and then points to his eyes: "You can see now?"

The Flower Girl nods, and her smile widens: "Yes, I can see now." She grasps his hand to her breast.

The Tramp, anguished and ecstatic at the same time, stands frozen as he holds his finger to his mouth and places the gift of the flower between his teeth and clenches the stem with his teeth—it is a simple, meaningful gesture. The truth is revealed—she can "see now" through his pretense—nothing more can be said. Their social roles are now reversed in this face-to-face encounter—his identity has changed from a benevolent millionaire to a vagabond, impoverished Tramp.

She has turned from a poor, blind girl into a prosperous, beautiful woman. With one of the most staggering shots ever filmed—a close-up of the Tramp's face and smile, she identifies him. The ethereal close-up of his radiant, smiling face fades to black.

In September 1930, Chaplin finished the shooting of the iconic final scene, which took six days. Although Chaplin had a rather rocky association with actress Virginia Cherrill during the filming, in the end, she realized how he wanted the final scene to be filmed and her role in it.

The popularity of *City Lights* has endured, with the film's re-release in 1950, again positively received by audiences and critics. In 1949, the film critic James Agee wrote in *Life* magazine that the final scene was the "greatest single piece of acting ever committed to celluloid." In the 2003 documentary *Charlie: The Life and Art of Charles Chaplin*, Woody Allen said it was Chaplin's best picture. Allen is said to have based the touching final scene of his 1979 film *Manhattan* on the final scene in *City Lights*.

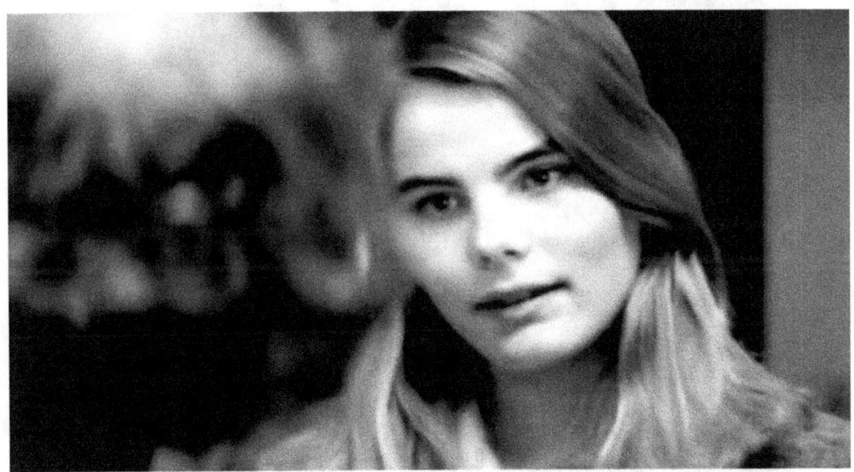

THE 1930s

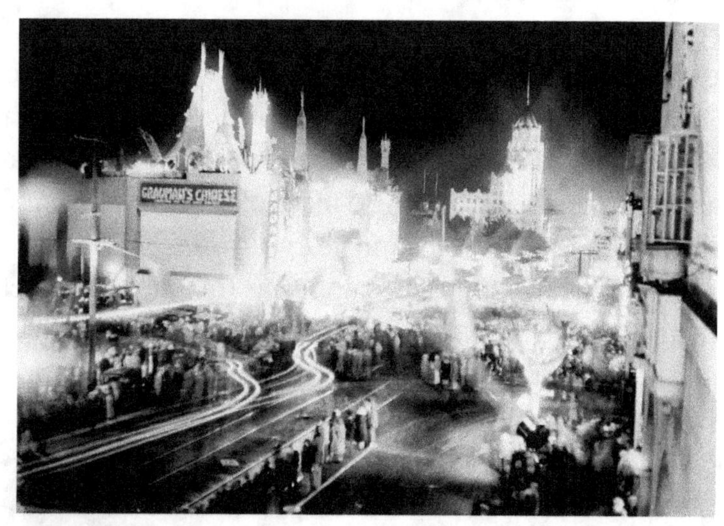

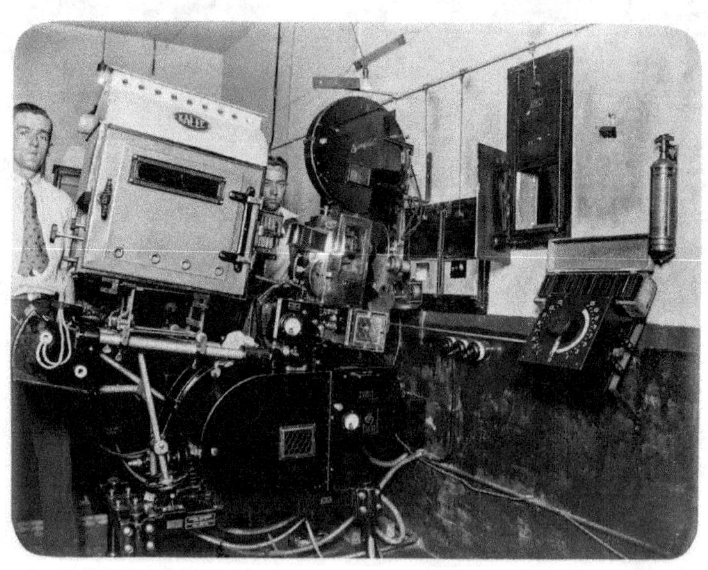

All Quiet on the Western Front (1930)

All Quiet on the Western Front is an epic anti-war film based on the Erich Maria Remarque novel of the same name. It was directed by Lewis Milestone.

It tells the story of a German soldier who becomes disillusioned over the merits of war as a matter of solving human conflict and political differences. The film is a clear indictment of the senselessness of the war, and this film, in particular, was Hollywood's most profane screen statement.

Scene: The Butterfly

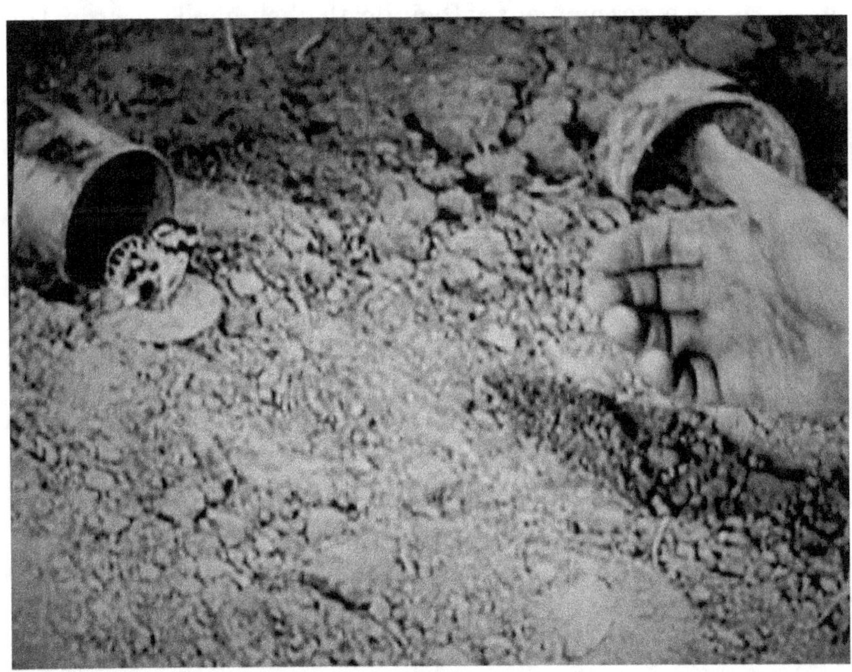

The death of Paul Baumer (Lew Ayers) in this movie has a lot of similarities and traits with the death of William Wallace (Mel Gibson) in the 1995 film *Braveheart.* In both cases, they die violently near the very end of the movie at the hands of their army. Both men fought in a war in which they lost. In the case of Baumer, it was World War I against the allied forces of England, France, and the United States, and for Wallace, it was the First War of Scottish Independence against King Edward I of England. In both cases, the last thing they see before they die is something they deeply loved in the past. For Baumer, it sees a beautiful butterfly near a can recalling his love for butterflies as a youth, and for Wallace, it is the face of his slain wife in the crowd who was brutally killed earlier in the movie by the English. The last word uttered by Wallace on the block is "freedom." Perhaps, as Baumer dies, he finally finds redemption and peace from a war-stricken world in which he can no longer endure. And finally, at the exact moment of their death, their hands go limp. For Baumer, from a bullet fired by a French soldier's rifle, and for Wallace, it is the deadly downward stroke of an ax brutally beheads him.

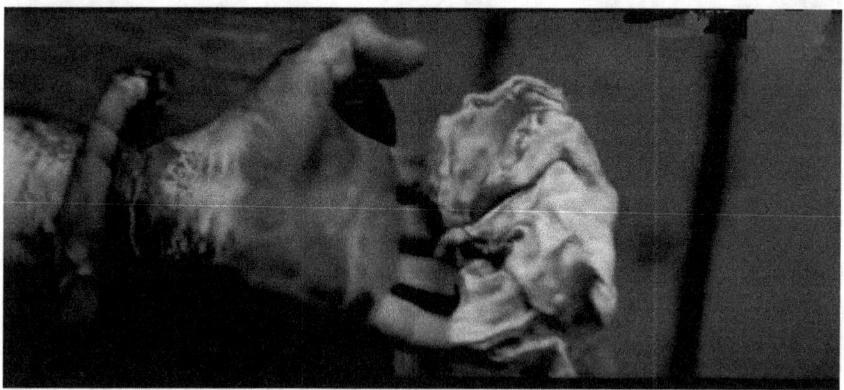

Paul Baumer (Lew Ayers), a young German soldier, is given a furlough during World War I and visits his family at home. He is shocked by how uninformed everyone is about the actual situation of the war; everyone is convinced that a final "push for Paris" is soon to occur. When Paul visits the schoolroom where he was originally recruited, he finds Professor Kantorek reciting the same patriotic fervor to a class of even younger students. Professor Kantorek asks Paul to detail his experience, at which the latter reveals that war was not at all like he had envisioned and mentioned the deaths of his partners.

This revelation upsets the professor, as well as the young students who promptly call Paul a "coward." Disillusioned and angry, Paul returns to the war zone and comes upon another 2nd Company that is filled with new young recruits who are now disillusioned. He goes to find Kat (Stanislaud Katczinsky played by Louis Wolheim), and they discuss the inability of the people to comprehend the futility of the war. Kat's shin is broken when a bomb dropped by an aircraft falls nearby, so Paul carries him back to a field hospital, only to find that Kat has been killed by a second explosion. Crushed by the loss of his mentor, Paul leaves.

In the final scene, Paul is back on the front line. In the unforgettable final moments of this film, just before the "all quiet on the western front" armistice and with all of his comrades gone, soldiers are bailing water out of a dilapidated trench. The faint sound of a harmonica can be heard.

Paul is sitting alone, daydreaming inside the trench on a seemingly peaceful, bright day. He is exhausted, disillusioned, saddened by horrible realities of war.

Through the gun hole of his trench, he sees a beautiful lone butterfly that has alighted just beyond his reach next to a discarded tin can outside the parapet. He begins to carefully reach out over the protection of his bunker with his hand to grasp it, momentarily forgetting the danger that is ever-present.

As he stretches his hand out yearning for its beauty, a distant

French sniper prepares to take careful aim through a scope on a rifle. As he leans out closer to the fragile butterfly and extends his hand, suddenly, the sharp whining sound of a shot is heard. Paul's hand jerks back, twitches for a moment, and then goes limp in death. All is silent and quiet. The harmonica tune stops.

Ayres' death was the last scene shot. Neither the film producer Carl Laemmle, Jr. nor director Lewis Milestone was satisfied with the ending of the film. Originally, they had written an ending in which he died heroically in battle, but neither was happy with that. The front office had already booked a premiere. The book had ended as follows with Paul's death on the field of battle: "He fell in October 1918, on a day that was so quiet and still on the whole front, that the army report confined itself to the single sentence: All quiet on the Western Front. He had fallen forward and lay on the earth as though sleeping. Turning him over, one saw that he could not have suffered long; his face had an expression of calm, as though almost glad the end had come" (Erich Maria Remarque, *All Quiet on the Western Front*).

The director and the producer wished to end the film as simple and as poetically relevant as the book. Production had gone so far over schedule that cinematographer Arthur Edeson had been forced to leave for another picture. His replacement, pioneering German cameraman Karl Freund, suggested the ending they filmed, in which Paul is shot by a sniper while reaching for a butterfly he sees just beyond his trench. He felt that the finish of the picture should be as simple as a butterfly (schmetterling), given Paul's love for that tiny delicate creature during his youth. During editing, Milestone decided he needed a close-up of Paul's hand. With the actors gone to other projects, he served as Ayres' hand double for the iconic shot. In the closing scene, director Lewis Milestone's hand is used for that of Ayres when he reaches for a butterfly.

The ending is a summation of what the movie has been saying its entire runtime: war isn't glorious—it destroys and kills.

Shmoop University did an interesting essay on the significance of the final scene with the butterfly:

The viewer already knew that Paul collected butterflies when he was a youth and that's all the information we get to connect Paul with the imagery of the butterfly, and it leaves the viewer a lot of interpretive blank space to get creative with.

For example, the butterfly could symbolize the home Paul remembers, and his reaching for it an attempt to reconnect with the world he left behind for the Front. Or could the butterfly simply represent Paul's attempt to obtain something beautiful in his life again, beyond the muck and mire of the trenches.

Then again, maybe the butterfly represents metamorphosis and Paul's reaching for it symbolizes his desire to change himself. He remembers when his training instructor Corporal Himmelstoss said, "You're going to be soldiers, and that's all!" Maybe Paul's trying to change into something more than the soldier the war has required him to become.

Frankenstein (1931)

Frankenstein is a horror film from Universal Pictures. It is about a scientist and his assistant who dig up corpses to build a man animated by electricity. The project goes awry when Frankenstein's assistant accidentally gives the Creature an abnormal murderer's brain. The film was directed by James Whale and adapted from the play by Peggy Webling, which in turn was based on Mary Shelley's 1818 novel *Frankenstein; or, The Modern Prometheus*. The created "monster" is portrayed by Boris Karloff in the film. An immediate hit with audiences and critics, the film was followed by multiple sequels and has become one of the most famous horror films in history. Much of the filming was done on Stage 12 of Universal Studios.

Though Karloff's performance went unappreciated by the Universal Studios executives, who even excluded the actor from the movie's premiere, Karloff sufficiently impressed his movie audiences. Many viewers were reportedly so terrified by his appearance they fled from the theater in fear. Karloff called the Monster his favorite film role, and film history has tended to agree with him—the actor was identified with the part until the day he died.

Scene: The Creation

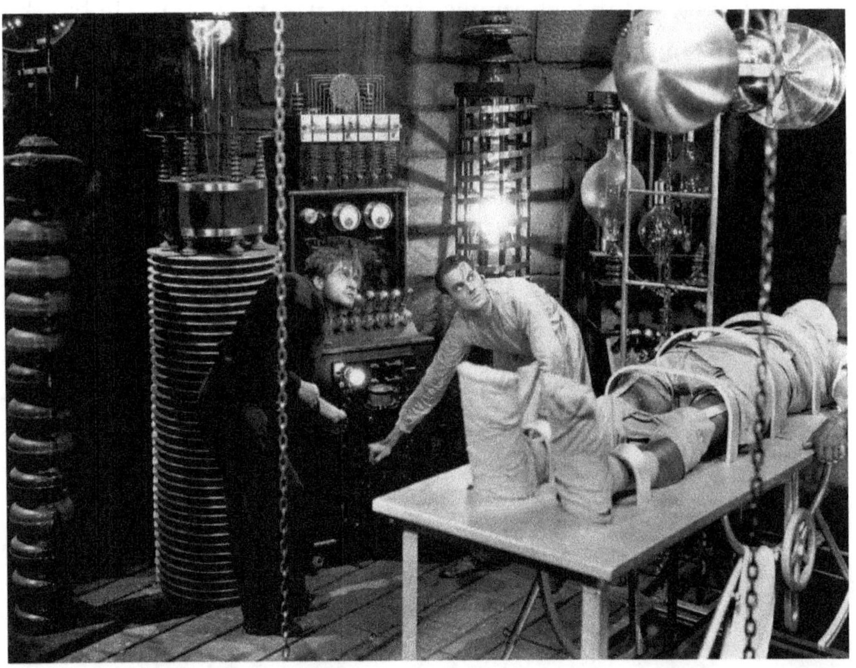

Frankenstein stars Colin Clive (Henry Frankenstein), Mae Clarke (Elizabeth Lavenza), John Boles (Victor Moritz), and Karloff, and features Dwight Frye (Fritz) and Edward van Sloan (Dr. Waldman). The story: Elizabeth and Victor have convinced Dr. Waldman to accompany them to Henry's mountaintop lab to persuade him to leave his experiment and come home. The three are finally admitted to the lab as Henry and Fritz begin the creation sequence, probably the most famous scene in the film, and one of the iconic scenes in horror. You see the monumental three-story vertical set for the lab, including the amazing electrical equipment.

The electrical equipment, for the "creation scene," was designed and built by electrical engineer and photographer Kenneth Strickfaden. Born in 1896, he maintained and tinkered with electrical equipment for the movie studios starting in the 1920s. As a hobby, he created new machines that looked impressive, made a lot of noise, but did absolutely nothing. He said, "It was just a matter of experimentation. I'd put something together and then sit back and marvel at it. The styling all depended on what kind of junk I had on hand."

He gave his creations imaginative and meaningless names such as "Lightning Bridge" and "Nucleus Analyzer." He also created the electrical arc machine for the 1931 film, *The Mask of Fu Manchu,* and stood in for Boris Karloff, who refused to be near the equipment when it was running. Karloff was afraid of being burned by sparks being thrown off the arcing electrical equipment simulating lightning. Although he was partially covered by a surgical drape, Karloff's abdomen was otherwise exposed during the scene, and the high-voltage arc "scissors" threw white-hot bits of metal when they were used to create flashes.

Universal spent ten thousand dollars on the electrical effects for *Frankenstein* but gave Strickfaden no acknowledgment in the credits. The electrical effects in this film were so successful that such effects came to be considered an essential part of every subsequent Universal film involving Frankenstein's Monster. Accordingly, the equipment used to produce them has come to be referred to in fan circles as "Strickfadens." The equipment was used again in *Bride of Frankenstein* (1935), *Son of Frankenstein* (1939), and in 1974, Mel Brooks finally gave Strickfaden credit when the equipment was used in *Young Frankenstein*.

At the end of the creation scene, Henry Frankenstein utters the line, "In the name of God, now I know what it feels like to be God," which was to give censors fits, though not at first. That particular blasphemy was okay until the film's 1938 re-release. By that time, the production code was in full and fulsome effect, so the hammer came down on anything remotely controversial, adult, or even thoughtful. The line was cut and replaced by a thunderclap.

Scene: The Drowning

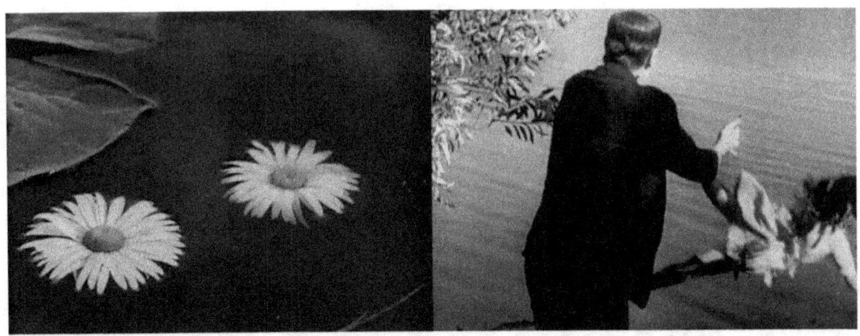

The notorious drowning scene in *Frankenstein* is perhaps the second most famous scene in the film.

Radiating innocence, the child Maria stops the Monster in his errant tracks and forces the only smile ever to cross his hideous face. He is thrilled by a simple game of floating daisies, and, when he runs out of flowers, he innocently reaches for the girl. What follows was censored after only the first showing until the 1980s.

Young Marilyn Harris (1924–1999) would encounter the Monster again, appearing briefly in *Bride of Frankenstein* (1935) among a group of schoolgirls sent squealing in fright when the Monster stumbles across their path. Director James Whale was fond of Marilyn as she also plays small roles in *Show Boat* (1936) and *The Road Back* (1937). Sadly, Marilyn Harris's childhood was an unhappy one, due to parental discord and a domineering stage mother. Marilyn's short film career consisted of playing bit parts and uncredited roles. It petered out in 1944.

While the Creature is roaming the countryside, he comes upon

Little Maria—a small girl playing by the lake waiting for her father to come home. This is probably the third most famous scene in the film, and the most heavily censored, right from the start this time. Maria shows no fear of the Creature and takes his hand to lead him to the lakeside to play a game of throwing flowers into the water. It is two innocent souls sharing a fleeting moment of joy, and we see the Creature smile for the first and last time.

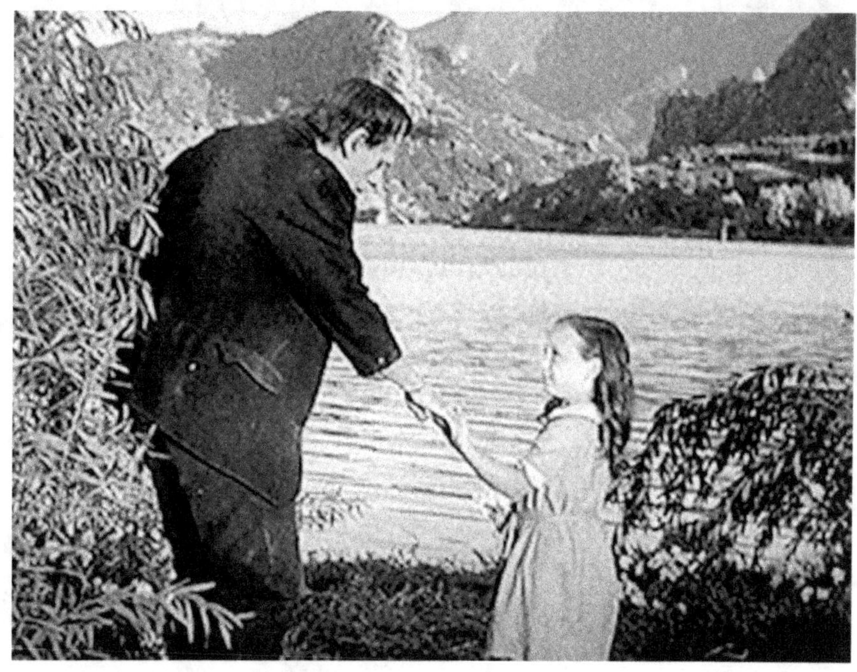

When he runs out of flowers to throw, he gets the idea that the little girl will probably float just as well, so he throws her into the water, drowning her. He runs away in mad confusion, fear, and panic, realizing that he has done something terribly wrong, but not fully realizing it.

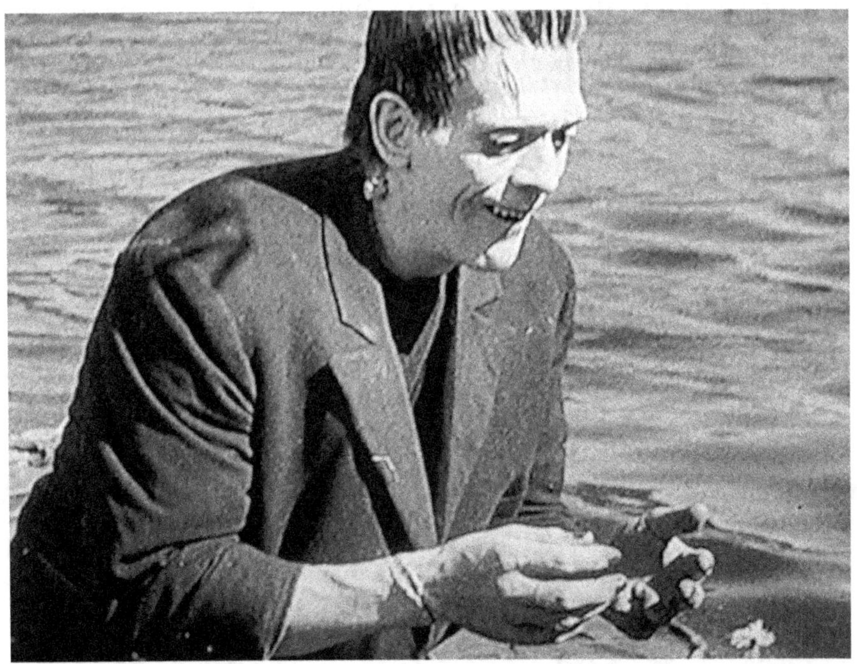

At the first preview of the film, the audience was shocked and confounded by this, and there was some laughter that ruined the mood. Universal founder, Papa Carl Laemmle, Sr., was also shocked, and exclaimed, "No little girl is going to drown in one of my pictures!" The scene was cut at the point the Creature is reaching for Maria. Upon its original 1931 release, the second part of this scene where the Monster throws Maria into the water was cut by state censorship boards in Massachusetts, Pennsylvania, and New York. Unfortunately, this led to a much more disturbing and sinister outcome in the minds of many who watched the movie over the years. Did the Creature molest Maria and then kill her? That was not answered until 1987 when the scene was restored to its original form.

Seven-year-old Marilyn Harris plays Little Maria with great naturalness. She remembered later that she was able to watch Karloff being made up as the Creature, so she never had any fear of him. The first take of her drowning didn't work, as she did not sink into the water as required. Harris had to be taken out, dried, and her hair was redone for a second take. Whale recalled that he got her to do the whole thing over again with a bribe. Harris was kept on a constant diet by her stage mother, and so when Whale asked her what she would like to have if anything at all, her reply was for a dozen hard-boiled eggs. The second take was perfect, and she got her eggs as promised.

Where did Universal shoot the famous Maria-meets-the-Monster scene in the classic 1931 *Frankenstein*?

The definitive answer was uncovered by the following researcher:

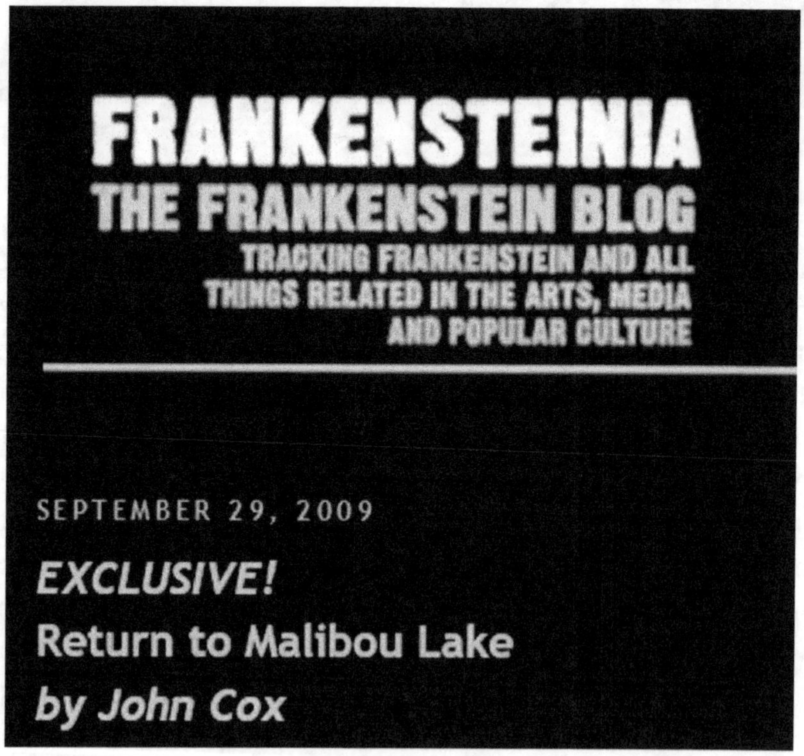

But then one Sunday morning, while browsing the Internet, I stumbled on the Frankensteinia blog and the article The Lake of Frankenstein. Here at last was an authoritative answer (sourced to an article by Gregory Mank in Midnight Marquee, No. 60). The scene was shot at Malibou Lake on September 28, 1931. (Malibou Lake is a small reservoir surrounded by a residential development in the Santa Monica Mountains near Agoura Hills, California.)

As I pulled into Malibou Lake, I was surprised to find such an idyllic setting, a true mountain hideaway resort. Expensive homes and boat slips rimmed a central lake with a small island sitting in the center. Pretty, yes, but nothing looked familiar. This was hardly the rugged "Bavarian" mountain lake of the film.

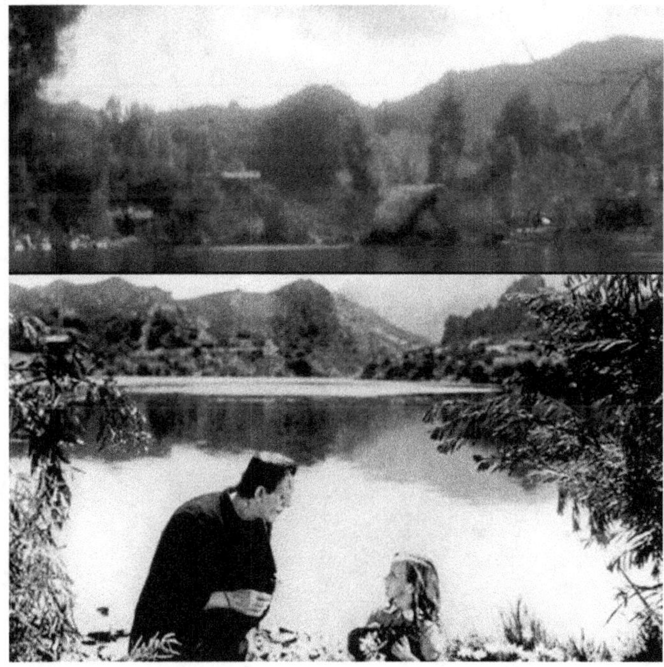

I raised my photo printout to the horizon and everything lined up perfectly. While tree growth has changed the look of the shoreline quite a bit, the silhouette of the mountains was unmistakable. I was standing on the spot where Boris Karloff and Marilyn Harris, with director James Whales and a full Universal crew, filmed one of the most famous scenes in horror movie history.

In *Young Frankenstein*, Brooks takes a more comical approach in this scene where the monster meets the little girl. The Monster comes across a girl named Helga throwing flowers in a well. The Monster joins in until they run out of flowers. When the little girl asks what else can they can throw in the well, the Monster just looks up and gives a devilish grin, but that's as far as it goes. The girl is never harmed. In fact, the Monster actually catapults her into her own bed when he sits on a seesaw.

The Public Enemy (1931)

The Public Enemy is an all-talking pre-code gangster film produced and distributed by Warner Bros. The film was directed by William A. Wellman and starred James Cagney, Jean Harlow, Edward Woods, Donald Cook, and Joan Blondell. The supporting players include Beryl Mercer, Murray Kinnell, and Mae Clarke, who also appeared in Frankenstein that same year. The screenplay is based on an unpublished novel, *Beer and Blood*, by two former newspapermen, John Bright and Kubec Glasmon, who had witnessed some of Al Capone's murderous gang rivalries in Chicago.

The film follows the lives of two kids from the tenements of Chicago's South Side, Powers and Doyle, who find a way out of desperate circumstances through a life of crime, ending with their violent deaths—not at the hands of police (who are rarely seen) but by rival criminals. Along with Warner Bros.' earlier hit *Little Caesar* (1930), this movie set the tone for the popular gangster dramas of the Depression period, gritty and brutally realistic, and Cagney's performance established him as the essence of the ruthless, hair-trigger hoodlum. That image was indelibly stamped on him in a scene that is remembered and imitated even today—the shocking grapefruit-in-the-face moment that stunned audiences and had women's groups protesting the treatment of the hard-luck moll played by Mae Clarke.

Scene: The Grapefruit

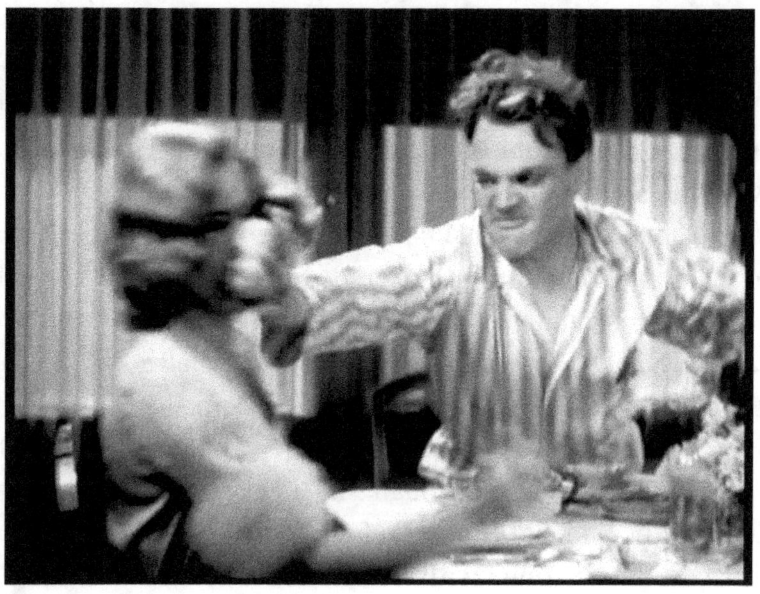

One of the most vividly remembered, misogynistic, demeaning, and vicious scenes in film history is the breakfast scene in this definitive and early gangster film. It is one of the single-most cruel acts ever depicted in a film. A life of crime has made the character cruel and hardened.

In this scene, we are in cocky gangster Tom Powers's (James Cagney) apartment. He walks sleepily to the breakfast table in his striped pajamas. He is in a foul mood, bored, grouchy, and irritable after a demanding phone conversation. Tom has grown tired of his relationship with moll girlfriend Kitty (Mae Clarke). At the table, she greets him without a smile. When he asks her for a beer for breakfast, she talks back.

Tom: Ain't you got a drink in the house?
Kitty: Well, not before breakfast, dear.
Tom: I didn't ask you for any lip. I asked you if you had
a drink.
Kitty: I know Tom, but I . . . I wish that . . .
Tom: There you go with that wishin' stuff again. I wish
you was a wishing well so that I could tie a bucket to ya
and sink ya.
Kitty (provokingly): Maybe you've found someone you
like better.

He looks down, makes a nasty grimace, and then impulsively picks up a grapefruit half from his plate and contemptuously pushes it into her face to end their relationship. She looks down, physically and painfully hurt, and emotionally embarrassed by his crudeness. The iconic grapefruit he shoves into Mae Clarke's face during the famous breakfast scene is the direct result of her having dreams and wishes of normalcy. Tom doesn't want normal. He wants more money, more power, and more instant gratification.

Bright and Glasmon based the scene on a real-life incident. The two learned that Chicago gangster Earl "Hymie" Weiss had once slammed an omelet into the face of his jabbering girlfriend. Wellman liked the idea but thought the omelet would be too messy, so he came up with the notion of using half a grapefruit. What happened next depends on who tells the story. Clarke said Cagney was only supposed to yell at her in the scene and that the actor surprised her with his impulsive use of the breakfast food. Cagney claimed the grapefruit had been decided on beforehand but that it was supposed to brush past her at an angle that would only appear to be a bona fide attack. In a 1973 interview featured in the Turner Classic Movies documentary *The Men Who Made The*

Movies: William Wellman, Wellman said he added the grapefruit "hitting" to the scene because when he and his wife at the time would get into fights, she would never talk or give any expression. Since she always had a grapefruit for breakfast, he always wanted to put the grapefruit into her face just to get a reaction out of her, so she would show some emotion; he felt that this scene gave him the opportunity to rid himself of that temptation.

Some, such as film critic Ben Mankiewicz, have asserted that Mae Clarke's surprised and seemingly somewhat angry reaction to the grapefruit was genuine, as she hadn't been told to expect the unscripted action. However, in her autobiography, Clarke stated that Cagney had told her prior to that take what he planned to do. She said that her only genuine surprise came later when she saw the grapefruit take of the scene appear in the final film, as it had been her understanding that they were shooting it only as a joke to amuse the crew.

Whatever the truth, when the time came to get the shot, Cagney smashed the grapefruit directly (and painfully, the actress said) into her face, and Clarke's very real look of horror and surprise was recorded for posterity.

According to Cagney, Clarke's ex-husband had the grapefruit scene timed and would buy a ticket just before that scene went on-screen, go enjoy the scene, leave, then come back during the next show just in time to see only that scene again.

The grapefruit-to-the-face incident from *The Public Enemy* is parodied years later in the 1961 Cagney movie *One, Two, Three*, when Cagney threatens Otto (Horst Buchholz) with a half grapefruit but then decides against doing so.

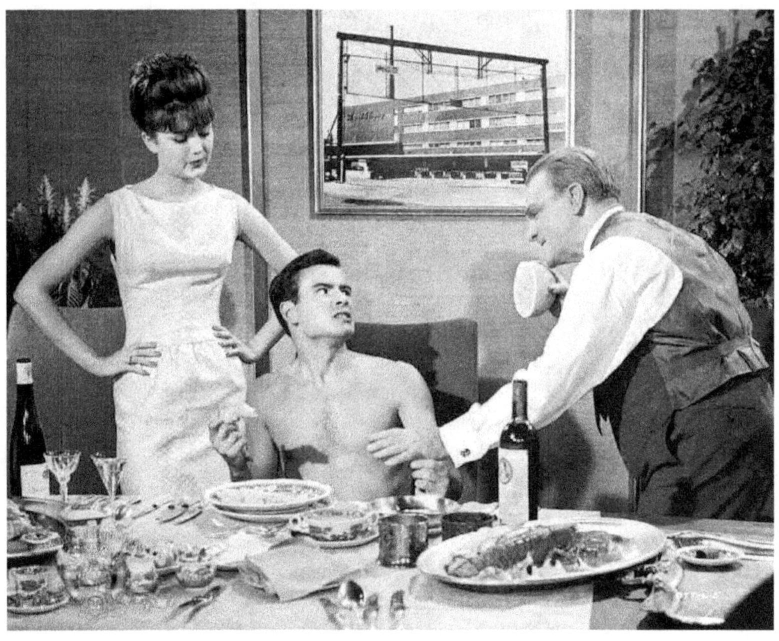

While it certainly stamped him with an unforgettable image, Cagney later came to regret the action recognizing it as a demeaning, humiliating, and cruel scene. For years after, whenever the actor dined out somewhere, fans would have waiters bring him half a grapefruit with his meal. Clarke became equally weary of references to the scene, although she must have gotten a bit of satisfaction from a similar shot that caught Cagney on the receiving end of some violence. Donald Cook, who played Tom Powers's war-shattered brother in the film, was supposed to explode in a fury with a hard sock to Cagney's jaw. In his autobiography, Cagney said he was sure Wellman had urged Cook to let his co-star really have it. Instead of faking it for the camera, Cook hauled off and belted Cagney right in the face, sending him flying across the set and breaking a tooth. Fortunately, no such mishaps took place during the film's most dangerous scenes: the use of real bullets in some of the shooting sequences.

The Public Enemy is extraordinary in a number of ways, but if anything, its success lies in creating a story that is, at first, rooted in history and nostalgia and gradually shifts focus to a contemporary social issue gangster picture.

King Kong (1933)

King Kong is a monster adventure film directed and produced by Merian C. Cooper and Ernest B. Schoedsack. The screenplay by James Ashmore Creelman and Ruth Rose was developed from an idea conceived by Cooper and Edgar Wallace. It stars Fay Wray, Bruce Cabot, and Robert Armstrong, and opened in New York City on March 2, 1933, to rave reviews. The film portrays the story of a huge, gorilla-like creature dubbed Kong who perishes in an attempt to possess a beautiful young woman (Wray). *King Kong* contains stop-motion animation by Willis O'Brien and a music score by Max Steiner.

Scene: Kong on top - of the Empire State Building

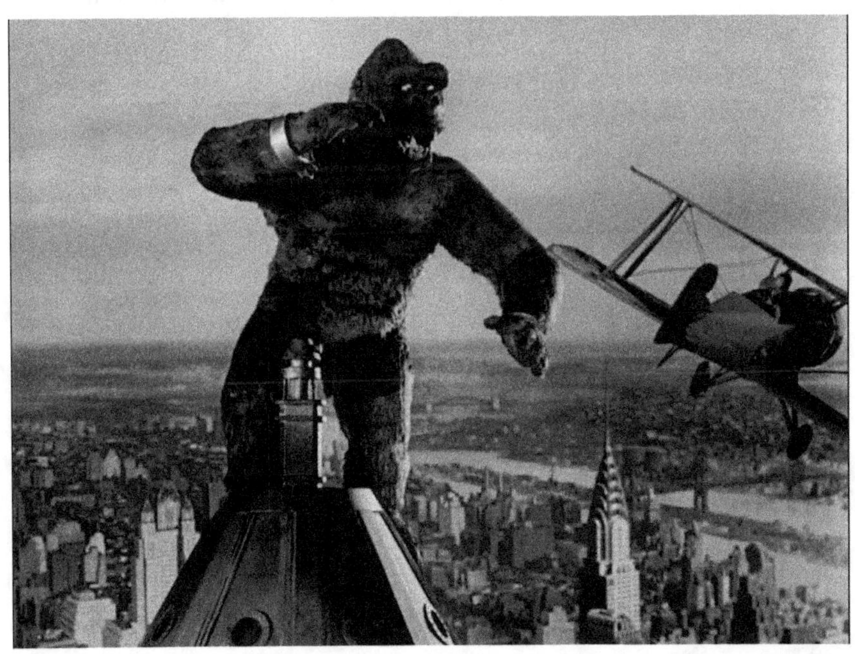

Producer/director Merian C. Cooper had such a holistic under-standing of what made cinema so effective. He knew how the story could motivate the action; he knew how music could heighten the action; and he knew how to shoot action. In addition to directing movies, Cooper was head of RKO and pioneered the Cinemascope and color film processes. More than knowing just how to make a picture, he understood the business side, the technical side, and knew the ingredients required to move his audience, both emo-tionally and to the box office, even in the midst of the Great De-pression. You see this mastery, not just of storytelling but of the medium itself, through every frame of *King Kong*.

Each model of Kong built for the island scenes were only eigh-teen inches high. When decided Kong needed to look bigger while in New York, a new twenty-four-inch armature was constructed, thus changing Kong's film height from eighteen feet on the island to twenty-four feet while in New York. Kong was a mechanically flexible armature covered with foam rubber and rabbit fur.

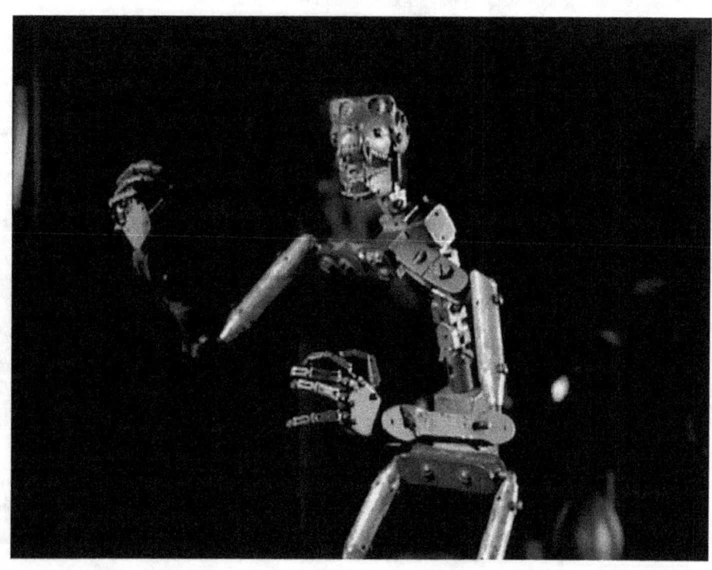

According to the 1975 book *The Making of King Kong* by Orville Goldner and George E. Turner:

> Ernest B. Schoedsack and photographer Eddie Linden went to New York City went to film views of the Empire State Building and action involving the Navy aircraft. The exciting scenes of the airplanes and King Kong in mortal combat, on top of the Empire State Building, would be the product of the live-action shots filmed by Schoedsack and Linden and the miniature wizardry skills of the production company located back in Los Angeles.
>
> The four Navy biplanes and their pilots were obtained from the Floyd Bennett Field, the Naval Air Station located in Brooklyn, New York. Schoedsack contributed $100 to the officers' Mess fund and the pilots were detailed. Before filming, he personally met with the flight commander in the field and planned the "attack" on the Empire State Building. The biplanes were basic training craft, Curtis o2C-2 and Navy NY models. They were photographed flying in formation, peeling off and diving at their imaginary target, then looping and attacking from the other direction. Twenty-eight scenes of the genuine aircraft were intercut with scenes filmed in miniature.
>
> The cityscapes seen behind Kong as he perches on the miniature mooring mast were painted in three planes of depth by the Larrinaga Brothers and Art Tech Bryon L. Crabbe. The illusion is far superior to those achieved in some preliminary test shots wherein a projected photographic background was used. The glass paintings and backing were unusually large, being about

twelve feet wide. This was necessary for the staging of an unusual effect in which Kong is seen through the eyes of the pilots of the attacking aircraft. The camera was made to "dive" toward the monster by being animated down a long wooden ramp. The tracking ramp was about twenty-four feet long, making possible the effect of a diving approach.

The illusion of aircraft swooping around the building itself was difficult to achieve because of the forced perspective of the set. This made the use of model aircraft of various sizes necessary, each scale being chosen to represent a different distance from the model of Kong perched on the studio mockup. The aircraft ranged from four inches to fifteen inches in wingspan. The large models used for the close-up shots while the smaller models were used for the more distant ones.

The model airplanes were suspended on a hair-thin piano wire stretched tightly between pulleys situated outside of the camera range.

The scene in which an airplane crashes down the face of the building is a composite. Art-Tech "Gus" White dropped the burning model from a scaffold on a blue backing; the falling craft was combined in the camera with a previously made shot of the actual building.

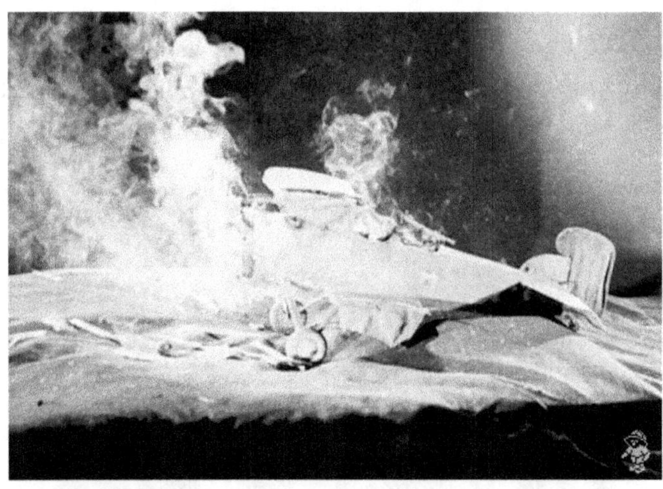

During his New York City trip, Schoedsack obtained details and measurements of the pinnacle of the Empire State Building in order to guide the art department in constructing the actual-size replica. The large prop was built on a sound stage and was ready for use by mid-summer of 1932.

According to the 2005 film documentary *RKO Production 601: The Making of 'Kong, The Eighth Wonder of the World'*, the large-scale model planes were used for close-up shots and the smaller models used for the more distant shots. In some instances, a combination of the live-action footage and the different size plane models were used.

The Making of Kong observes that the close-shots of the pilots and gunners were made at the studio with mockup aircraft and the composite backgrounds filmed in New York City. And guess who makes a somewhat unorthodox appearance in the film? Director-producer Merian Cooper is seen sitting in the backseat of a plane as the pilot of the plane that finally kills King Kong. Ernest Schoedsack is seen in the front seat as the gunner firing the fatal round of bullets that actually kills the beast. Cooper was a World War I fighter pilot, and both men served in the Polish Air Force during the Polish–Soviet War (February 14, 1919–October 18, 1920). This highly unusual bit of casting was the result of Cooper's remark that "we created him, so we should kill the sonofabitch ourselves."

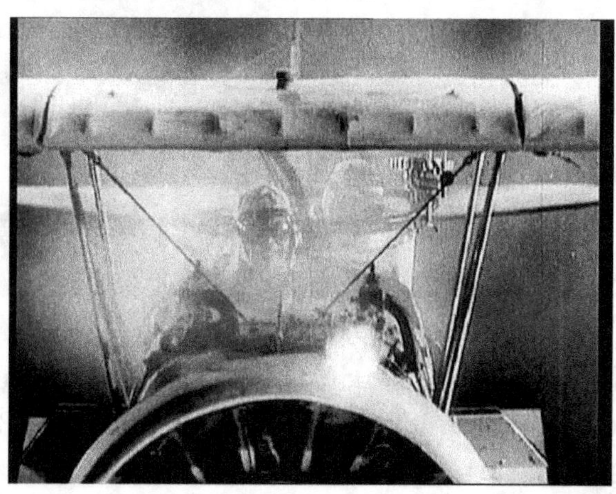

Fay Wray would appear on a ledge of the mooring mast via miniature projection.

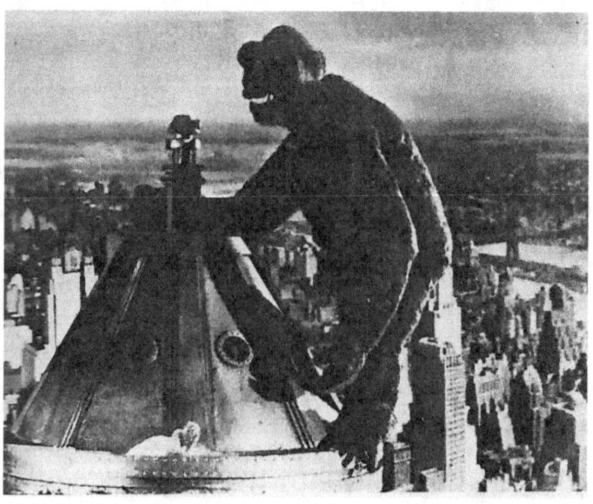

An animated dummy would substitute for Wray when King holds her in his hand.

Close-up footage of the Empire State Building was added to the film when it was re-issued in 1952, for the scene where Kong grabs the first plane and tosses it off the side of the building. We see a pristine picture of the Empire State Building as it existed in the 1950s, with its television antenna. In the other scenes, the landmark building was part of the "Hollywood set" with archival aerial footage of the New York City skyline added. Consequently, the only actual on-location filming was done nineteen years after the film's first release. Film processing had improved by that time, and the difference in clarity between the 1933 footage and the added 1952 shot is quite evident.

Following the death of Fay Wray at age ninety-six from natural causes in Manhattan on August 8, 2004, the lights at the top of the Empire State Building were dimmed in her honor as a final loving tribute to her acting artistry and memorable "screaming" as King Kong relentlessly pursued her to the bitter end. As Carl Denham says at the end of the movie, it was not the planes that got him (Kong), "It was beauty killed the beast."

An inflatable version of King Kong was attached to the Empire State Building on April 14, 1983, in order to celebrate the fiftieth anniversary of the release of this epic movie. Long live Kong!

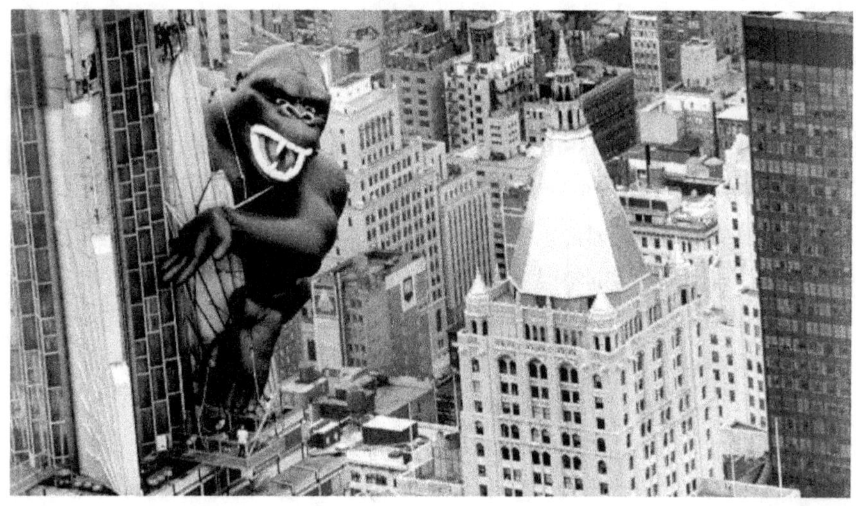

King Kong reappeared again on the Empire State Building in the 2005 film version co-written, produced, and directed by Peter Jackson. It is the second remake of the original 1933 film of the same title. The screen version of *King Kong* released in 1976 used the New York City Twin Towers in which to do battle with the airplanes. That film was produced by Dino de Laurentis and was directed by John Guillermin. The 2005 film stars Naomi Watts, Jack Black, and Adrien Brody. Jackson's treatment of Kong is much more delicate than the previous movie version of this classic, with the lead actress actually showing warmth and kindness to Kong up to the very end of the movie. In this clip from the film, we see Kong actually jumping up from the building in order to destroy a pesky airplane.

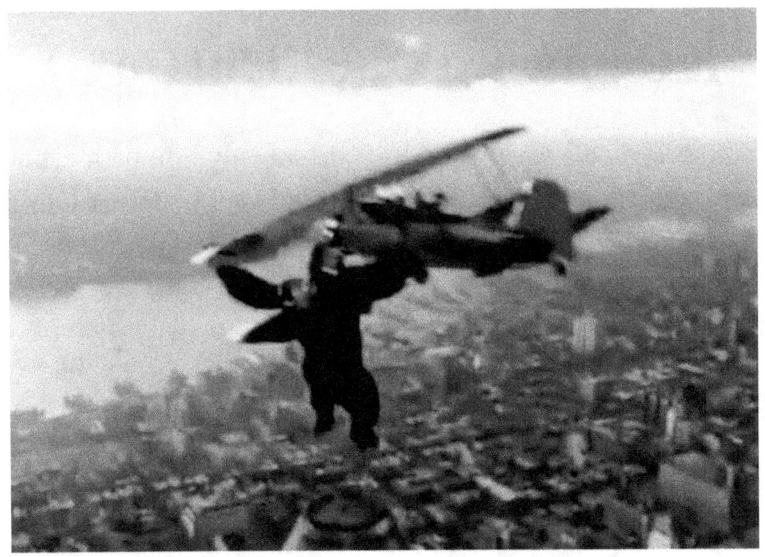

It Happened One Night (1934)

It Happened One Night is a romantic comedy film with elements of screwball comedy directed and co-produced by Frank Capra, in collaboration with Harry Cohn, in which Ellen "Ellie" Andrews, a pampered socialite (Claudette Colbert) tries to get out from under her father's thumb and falls in love with a roguish reporter, Peter Warne (Clark Gable). The plot is based on the August 1933 short story "Night Bus" by Samuel Hopkins Adams, which provided the shooting title.

Scene: Who Needs a Thumb to Catch a Ride?

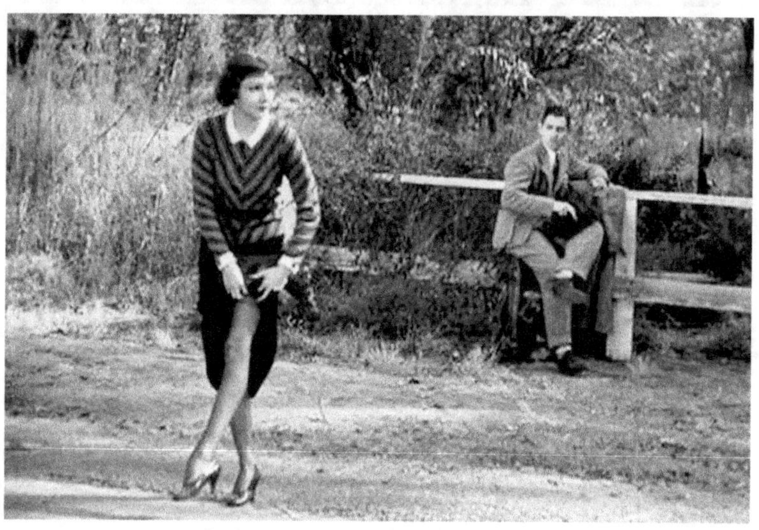

The famed hitchhiking scene in the film is a sheer riot. After Clark Gable brags that he's a hitchhiking expert, car after car zooms right by. In disgust at his lack of fulfillment and success, he ends up giving the passing cars a defiant gesture with his hand.

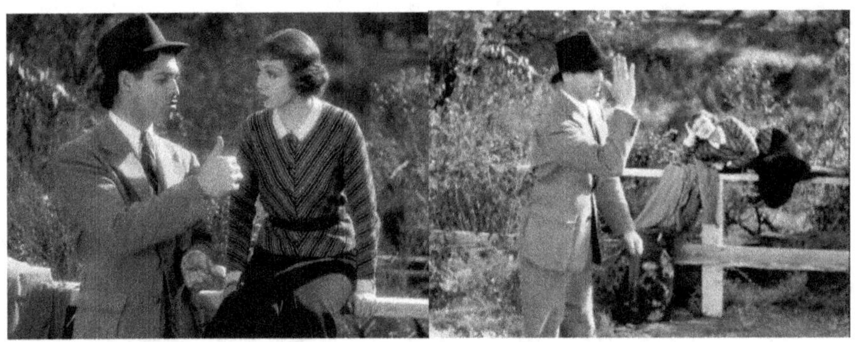

The following dialogue ensues:

Colbert: You mind if I try?
Gable (laughing): You? Don't make me laugh.
Colbert: You're such a smart aleck. Nobody knows any-
thing but you. I'll stop a car, and I won't use my thumb.
Gable: What are you going to do?
Colbert: A system all my own.

With that, Claudette Colbert hops off a fencepost and shows him how it's done, hiking up her skirt and causing the next driver to jam on his brakes. The moment is such a hoot because it's the first time Colbert turns the tables on Gable. And the skirt-hike hitchhike is only so funny because Gable had just lectured her with a detailed demonstration of proper thumb technique with three different "sure-fire" approaches.

She asks for a little credit for her alternative thumb-less meth-od: "Aren't you going to give me a little credit? Well, I proved once and for all that the limb is mightier than the thumb."

Defiant to the bitter end, Gable says: "Why didn't you take off all your clothes? You could have stopped forty cars."

Although Colbert had gladly disrobed for De Mille in *The Sign of the Cross* (1932), she refused to be shown taking off her clothes in the motel room sequence in *It Happened One Night*. No matter. Draping her unmentionables over the "walls of Jericho" made for a sexier scene anyway. More problematic was the hitchhiking scene. Colbert didn't want to pull up her skirt and flash her legs. So Capra hired a chorus girl, intending to have her legs stand-in for Colbert's in close-up.

Colbert saw the girl posing and said, "Get her out of here. I'll do it—that's not my leg!"

After shooting wrapped, Colbert told friends, "I've just finished the worst picture in the world!"

Of course, she was totally wrong. It turned out to be a major box office smash, easily Columbia Pictures' biggest hit to date. It garnished five Academy Awards at the ceremony in 1935, including best movie, best director (Frank Capra), best actor (Gable), and best actress (Colbert).

Famed film critic Roger Ebert summarized the significance of the scene beautifully when he said:

> "Peter's machismo and bravado are jabbed at so frequently in the course of the action, most spectacularly in the mock-phallic hitchhiking scene, when Peter's thumb is revealed as lacking and less powerful than some of Ellie's parts, that the whole film is blissfully devoid of the same masculine triumphalism that marred genuine classics like Woman of the Year and The Philadelphia Story."

Colbert's legs and Gable's chest were the sensations of the film. In the motel room scene, Gable demonstrates how a man undresses. When he took off his shirt, he wore no undershirt. Capra explained that the reason for this was that there was no way Gable could take off his undershirt gracefully, but once audiences saw Gable's naked torso, sales of men's undershirts plummeted.

The reviews for *It Happened One Night* were excellent, but no one really expected much from the film. After a slow opening, it received great word-of-mouth, and the film picked up steam at the box office.

James Harvey, in his 1998 book *Romantic Comedy in Hollywood: From Lubitsch to Sturges*, believes that the film succeeded because the couple transcended their stock characters. "There was some kind of new energy in their style: slangy, combative, humorous, unsentimental—and powerfully romantic. Audiences were bowled over by it."

Getting a car ride by using one's physical charms was again used in the 1991 film *Thelma and Louise*, directed by Ridley Scott. This time, a man dishes out the physical and personality vibes in order to obtain a car ride. Heading west, Thelma and Louise come across an attractive young drifter, JD (Brad Pitt), who Thelma quickly falls for, and Thelma convinces Louise to let him hitch a ride with them. Geena Davis played Thelma, and Susan Sarandon portrayed Louise in the film.

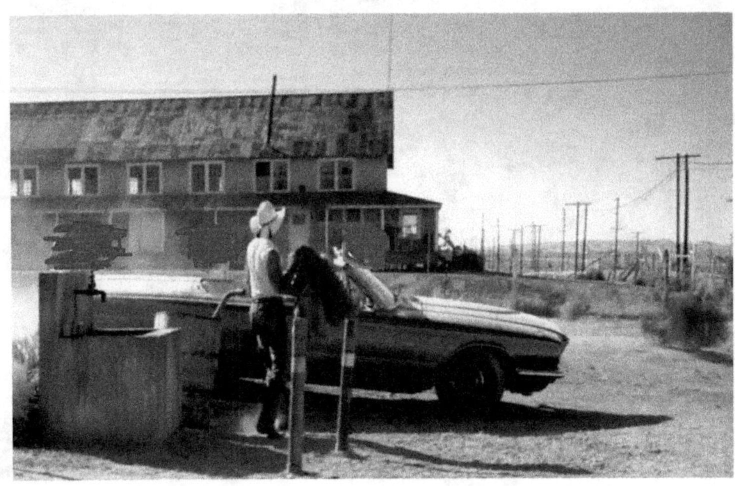

A Night at the Opera (1935)

A Night at the Opera is a comedy film starring the Marx Brothers and featuring Kitty Carlisle, Allan Jones, Margaret Dumont, Sig Ruman, and Walter Woolf King. It was the first of five films the Marx Brothers made for Metro-Goldwyn-Mayer after their departure from Paramount Pictures, and the first after Zeppo left the act. The film was adapted by George S. Kaufman and Morrie Ryskind from a story by James Kevin McGuinness, with additional dialogue by Al Boasberg. It was directed by Sam Wood and produced by Irving Thalberg. It tells the story of the antics of the Marx Brothers as they venture into the high-brow world of opera and change it forever.

Scene: The Stateroom

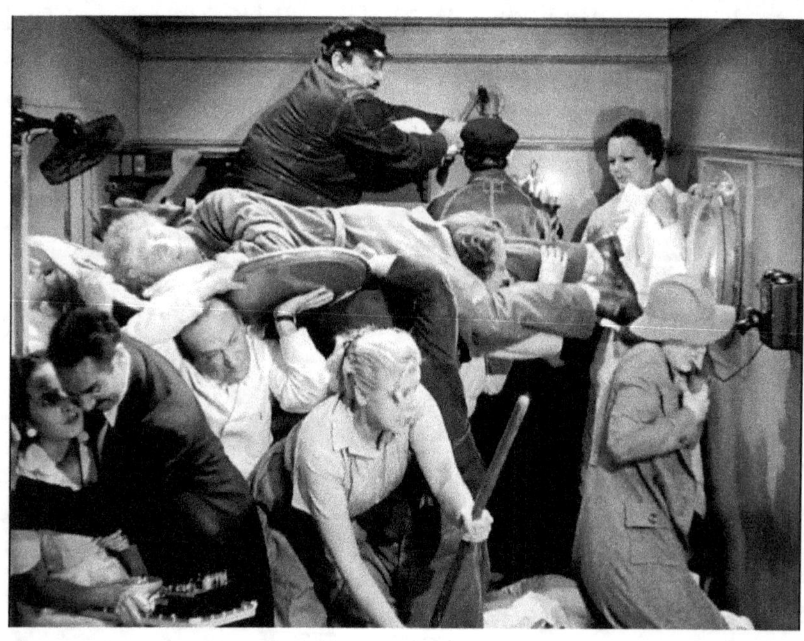

The famous "stateroom scene" was originally conceived as a way of getting a cheap laugh by having Groucho Marx, crowded out of his room, changing his pants in the corridor. This scene was written primarily by legendary gag man Al Boasberg. Boasberg's other film writing credits included *The General* (starring Buster Keaton), who was also heavily involved in designing this particular scene. Keaton, at the time, was an MGM studio comedy/gag writer. He contributed much of the content of this scene. He had performed a similar skit, a changing room scene, in one of his earlier films, *The Cameraman* (1928), his next-to-last silent comedy. Boasberg typed up the finished scene, then tore the pages into tiny pieces and tacked them to his ceiling. It took Irving Thalberg and the brothers hours to cut and paste the scene back together.

Driftwood plans a rendezvous with Mrs. Claypool in his stateroom. Then he finds out how small it is (a third-class cabin, about the size of a janitor's closet), and that he, his steamer trunk, and the bed barely fit in it. Driftwood discovers that Fiorello, Tomasso, and Ricardo have stowed away in his steamer trunk and discarded his clothes. So already, there are four people in the room, with three of them refusing to leave. Fiorello insists on eating ("We getta food or we don't go"). In order to get rid of them before Mr. Claypool arrives, Driftwood calls a steward ("I say, Stew") and orders dinner.

With that begins a persistent procession of eleven additional wanted and unwanted people from the ship's staff parading into Driftwood's tiny shoebox cabin no bigger than a closet. Already crowded with four individuals (Fiorello, Tomasso, Riccardo, and Driftwood himself), he takes a perverse pleasure in encouraging each new intruder to enter:

(Individuals #5–6): Two chambermaids to make up the room (they later prop up Tomasso). Driftwood encourages them to enter: "Come on in, girls, and leave all hope behind." [Groucho's greeting has a slight resemblance to the inscription at the gates of the inferno of Hell in Dante's *The Divine Comedy*: "ABANDON ALL HOPE, YE WHO ENTER HERE."]

(Individual #7): An engineer to turn off the heat.

(Individual #8): A manicurist to trim Driftwood's nails. ("I hadn't planned on a manicure, but I think on a journey like this, you ought to have every convenience you can get. You'd better make 'em short. It's getting kind of crowded in here.")

(Individual #9): The engineer's large assistant.

(Individual #10): An inquiring young woman wandering around for her Aunt Minnie and asking to use the phone. ("Well, you can come in and prowl around if you wanna. If she isn't in here, you can probably find somebody just as good.")

(Individual #11): A determined, gum-chewing, cleaning washwoman to mop up. ("Just the woman I'm looking for. Come right ahead. You'll have to start on the ceiling. It's the only place that isn't being occupied. Tell Aunt Minnie to send up a bigger room too, will ya?")

(Individuals #12–15): A large number of staff stewards bearing trays loaded with egg orders and dinner.

Each of the fifteen occupants that are entangled together must find space in a nook or cranny of the minuscule stateroom. The grande dame, Mrs. Claypool, shows up in her finest costume and opens the door, letting loose the above-mentioned people in an avalanching torrent of bodies into the corridor.

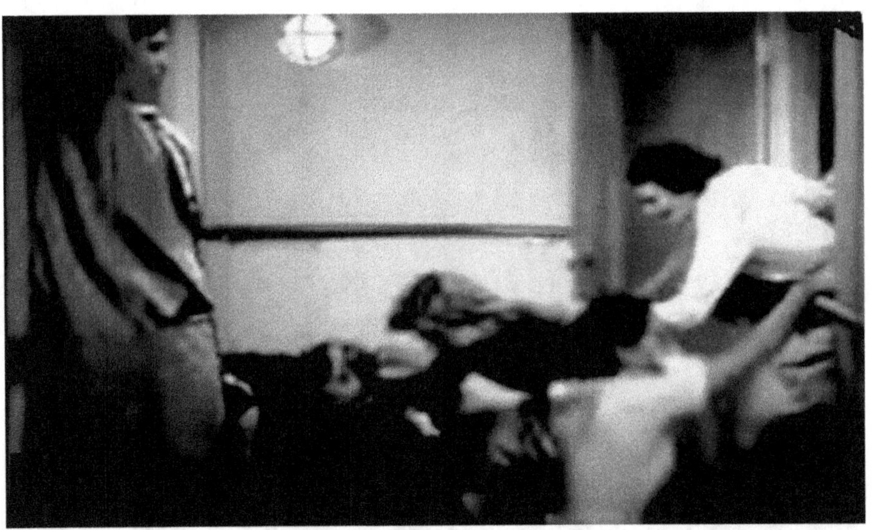

According to the documentary *The Marx Brother, The Making of a Night at the Opera* (2004), in order to maximize the comedic effect of a scene, you put the hero in the last place he wants to be. Groucho is in the place he wants to be, as Margaret Dumont is coming there, but in reality, with all the people in the room, it turns out to be the very last place he wants to be. This adds to the tension of the scene as Groucho wants all these people out ASAP as Dumont is on her way.

Another scene in a movie where a small stateroom's original occupant is invaded by unwanted guests was seen in the 1942 film *The Palm Beach Story*. In this scene, Claudette Colbert, portraying the charter Gerry, is being noisily serenaded by the probably slightly inebriated members of the Ale and Quail Club.

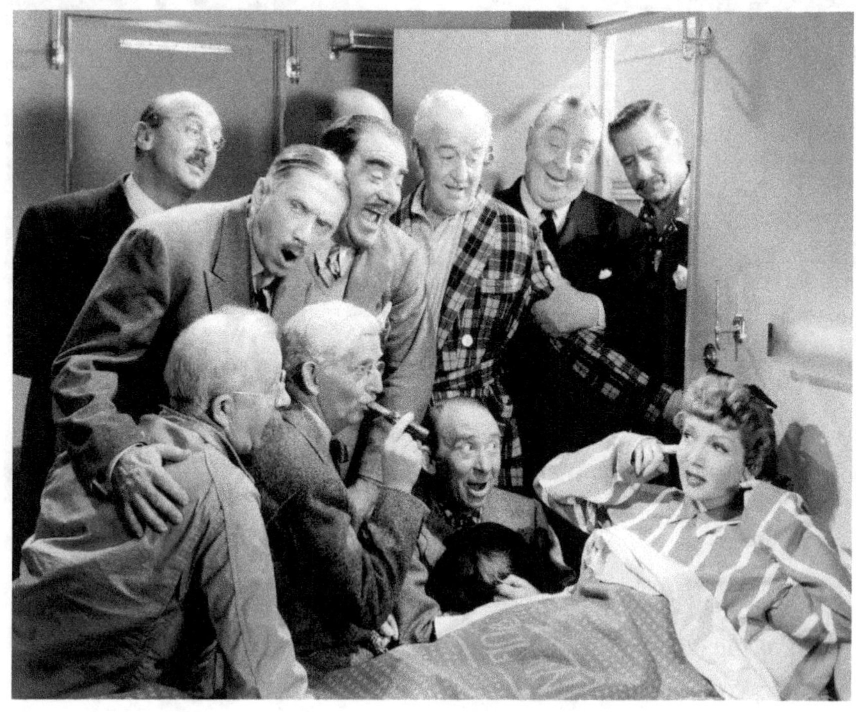

In both movies, Driftwood and Gerry embark on a journey with no money and no clothes, except what they are wearing on their back.

Top Hat (1935)

Top Hat is a screwball musical comedy film in which Fred Astaire plays an American dancer named Jerry Travers, who comes to London to star in a show produced by Horace Hardwick (Edward Everett Horton). He meets and attempts to impress Dale Tremont (Ginger Rogers) to win her affection. The film also features Eric Blore as Hardwick's valet Bates; Erik Rhodes as Alberto Beddini, a fashion designer and rival for Dale's affections; and Helen Broderick as Hardwick's long-suffering wife, Madge. The film was written by Allan Scott and Dwight Taylor. It was directed by Mark Sandrich. The songs were written by Irving Berlin. "Top Hat, White Tie, and Tails" and "Cheek to Cheek" have become American song classics.

Scene: Cheek to Cheek

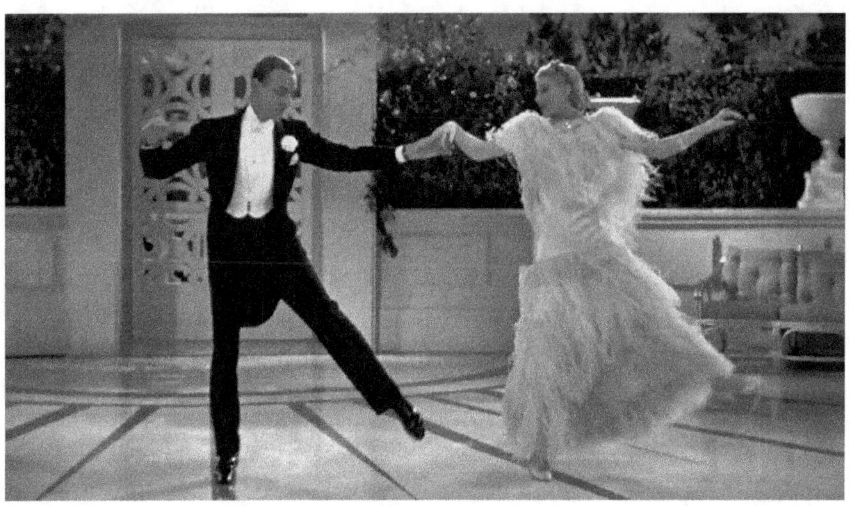

The famous "Cheek to Cheek" dance begins as a simple waltz, with Jerry Travers stopping several times to sing the famous lyrics ("Heaven, I'm in heaven / And my heart beats so loudly I can hardly speak / And I seem to find the happiness I seek / When we're out together dancing cheek to cheek"). After each stop, they dance for a while, until suddenly, at the music's crescendo, they swing upstairs, she spinning before laterally jumping, and Astaire moving into a soft tap. Both leap, moving backward, then forward, until in a final pas de deau, Ginger Rogers being gently lifted before Astaire lets her down, the two spin, returning to the quiet waltz.

Perhaps the most notable thing about this dance is Rogers' beautiful white feathered dress (at least it appears white on the screen; the lining was blue) that is so absolutely breathtaking a costume that we might forgive them, he in his tuxedo and she in the gown, if they merely stood there talking. Yet, their graceful dancing on top equally transports us into "Heaven."

The dancing partnership of Ginger Rogers and Fred Astaire, stretching over seven years for RKO Studios, has produced a priceless number of memorable dance duets. Most film aficionados consider it (their fourth film) to be their finest film together.

Together, the duo performs the romantic adagio Cheek to Cheek. He breaks into song in mid-sentence: "Heaven, I'm in heaven. And my heart beats so that I can hardly speak. And I seem to find the happiness I seek. When we're out together dancing, cheek to cheek."

First, they dance in the company of others on a crowded dance floor and then dance/drift across a bridge to a deserted, circular ballroom area. All alone in a dreamlike setting, they perform a romantic dance together.

Dale's ankle-length gown, (the most famous of all Rogers' dance dresses), light ice-blue satin covered with ostrich feathers, sheds as they whirl around. Beautifully, they stretch out an arm to each other (his left, her right), leading to her twirling spin into him. Briefly, they repeat their earlier tap-dancing routine from the bandstand, performing side by side. Several times, she bends deeply backward in his arms during their choreographed dance, surrendering his seductive, luring attraction. Mixed with standard ballroom dance positions, they also leap and turn boldly, separate, spin, and then return "cheek to cheek."

After a climactic ending with a full orchestral burst, the dance ends as they come to rest against a wall. They affectionately gaze at each other.

The famous "dress incident" is discussed in TCM factoids:

> Ginger Rogers gives a complete account, placing opposition to the costume well before the feathers started flying. In her autobiography, *Ginger: My Story* (1991, HarperCollins), she describes how she told costume designer Bernard Newman to make her a dress of pure blue, "like the blue you find in paintings of Monet … with myriads of ostrich feathers." When the completed dress was brought to the set, the actress wrote, director Mark Sandrich came to her dressing room with the suggestion that she wear the "much, much prettier" white dress she wore in The Gay Divorcee (1934). Rogers was certain that this "request" also reflected Fred Astaire's opinion. She immediately telephoned her mother, Lela Rogers, a tough, legendary stage mama, who stormed to the studio to her daughter's defense. Mother and daughter stood firm, and when Ginger threatened to walk off the picture if she couldn't use the gown, Sandrich allowed her to rehearse in it, despite the fact that she would have to pretend to be wowed by a love song sung by her

openly hostile co-star. Matters grew worse when, during the dance, feathers began to detach and fly all over the place, sticking to Astaire's skin and clothes. (Despite all-night work by the wardrobe department to reinforce each feather individually, you can still see errant feathers floating through still shots from the scene.) Rogers' book insisted only a few stray feathers came loose and that Sandrich and Astaire aloofly but eventually conceded the dress's beauty and appropriateness for the scene. Four days after the shoot, she said, Astaire sent her a gold feather for her charm bracelet and a note that read "Dear feathers, I love ya! Fred."

Astaire told the story a little differently in his autobiography, *Steps in Time* (1959, Cooper Square Press). According to him, he thought the look of the dress was "very nice" until the first time they rehearsed the dance with Ginger in it.

"Feathers started to fly as if a chicken had been attacked by a coyote... They were floating around like millions of moths." Astaire wrote that despite the hassle, the rushes revealed very little problems, everyone had a good laugh about it, and it became a running joke among the cast and crew. He and Hermes Pan even made up joke lyrics to the tune of "Cheek to Cheek":

> Feathers—I hate feathers
> And I hate them so that I can hardly speak
> And I never find the happiness I seek
> With those chicken feathers dancing
> Cheek to cheek.

Thereafter, Astaire nicknamed Rogers "Feathers"—also a title of one of the chapters in his autobiography—and parodied his experience in a song-and-dance routine with Judy Garland in *Easter Parade* (1948).

Astaire also chose and provided his own clothes. He is widely credited with influencing twentieth-century male fashion and, according to *Forbes* male fashion editor, G. Bruce Boyer, the "Isn't It a Lovely Day?" routine "shows Astaire dressed in the style he would make famous: soft-shouldered tweed sports jacket, button-down shirt, bold striped tie, easy-cut gray flannels, silk paisley pocket square, and suede shoes. It's an extraordinarily contemporary approach to nonchalant elegance, a look Ralph Lauren and a dozen other designers still rely on more than six decades later. Astaire introduced a new style of dress that broke step with the spats, celluloid collars, and homburgs worn by aristocratic European-molded father-figure heroes."

It has been nostalgically referred to, particularly the "Cheek to Cheek" segment, in many films, including *The Purple Rose of Cairo* (1985) and *The Green Mile* (1999).

This scene plays a prominent role in *The Green Mile*. First, at a Louisiana assisted-living facility, the elderly Paul Edgecomb (Dabbs Greer) becomes highly emotional, sobbing loudly, while watching the film *Top Hat*. His companion, Elaine, becomes concerned, and Paul tells her that the film reminded him of events in 1935, when he was a prison officer in charge of death row, also referred to as the "Green Mile," particularly his very personal association with one prisoner, John Coffey, played by actor Michael Clarke Duncan.

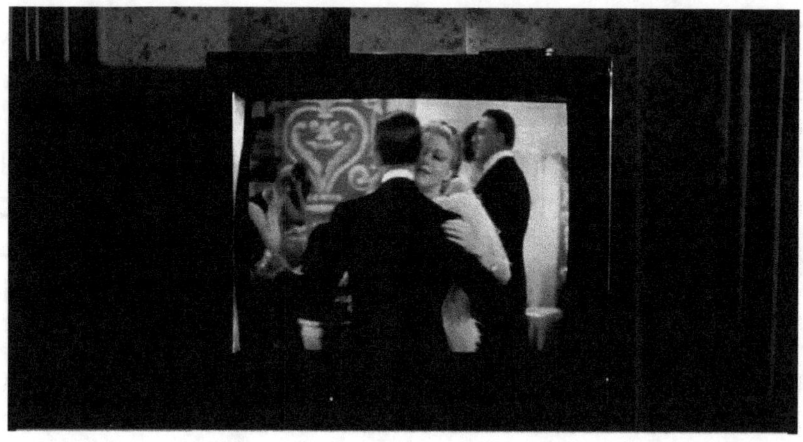

The "Cheek to Cheek" scene reappears in *The Green Mile*, when John Coffey mentions, as a final request before he is executed, that he has never seen a movie before, Coffey watches *Top Hat* with the guards as a last request. This particular incident explains why the elder Paul begins to cry in the earlier scene because it once again reminded him of Coffey, whom he considered one of God's own servants because of his acts of clairvoyance, humility, kindness, mercy, and "miracles."

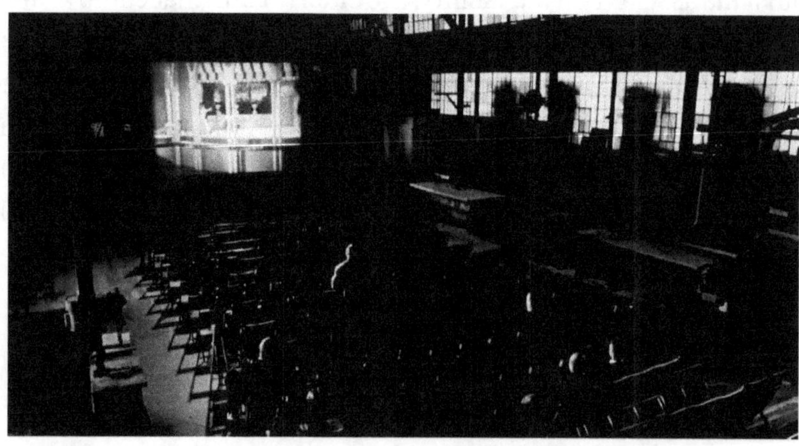

When Coffey sees this scene, he begins to cry and whispers, "Why, they's angels. Angels, just like up in heaven."

These are truly the perfect words to express the "Cheek to Cheek" scene. It magically transcends both space and time while slowly transporting the viewing audience into the blessed realm of heaven itself with enchanting and angelic music and song.

Modern Times (1936)

Modern Times is a comedy film written and directed by Charlie Chaplin in which his iconic Little Tramp character struggles to survive in the modern, industrialized world. The film is a comment on the desperate employment and financial conditions many people faced during the Great Depression—conditions created, in Chaplin's view, by the efficiencies of modern industrialization. The movie stars Chaplin and Paulette Goddard, who plays Ellen Peterson.

This social protest film is Chaplin's final stand against the synchronized sound film—and it is also his last full-length "silent film"—although it must be noted that it is a quasi-silent film. There is no traditional, synchronized voice dialogue in the film, but voices and sounds do emanate from machines (e.g., the feeding machine), television screens (i.e., the Big Brother screen—pre-dating George Orwell's book *1984*, written/published in 1949), and Chaplin's actual voice is heard singing an imaginary, nonsense song of gibberish. It is the last appearance of his Little Tramp character.

Set in the 1930s during the Great Depression era, the film's main concerns (and those of the oppressed Tramp) echo those of millions of people at the time—unemployment, poverty, and hunger. It has a number of wonderfully inventive and memorable routines and scenes that proclaim the frustrating struggle by proletarian men against the dehumanizing effects of the machine in the Industrial Age (at the time of Henry Ford's assembly line), and various social institutions.

Scene: Gone Crazy

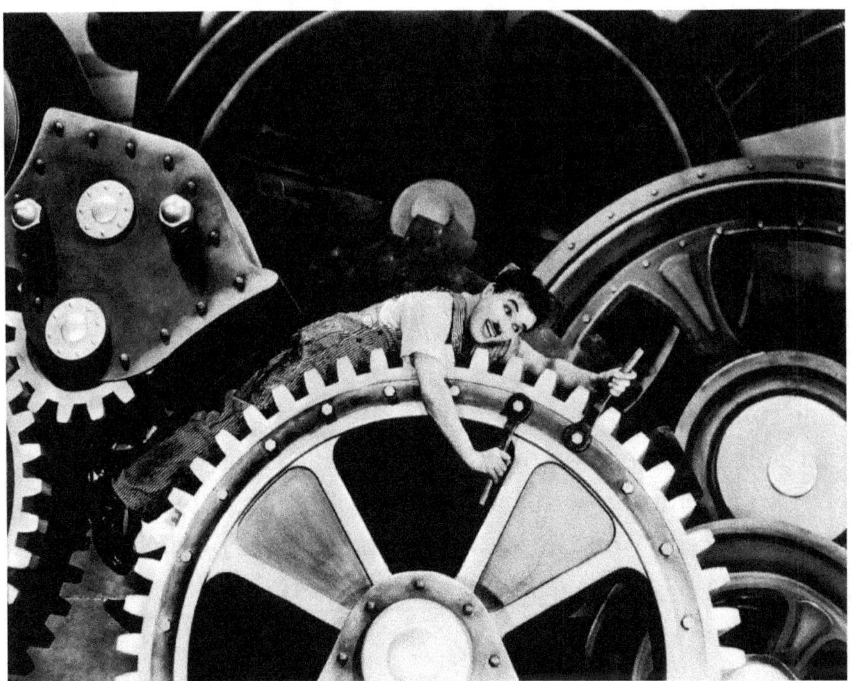

Setting: The Tramp has a disastrous, nightmarish lunch at a food-eating machine, a mechanical, automated, aerodynamically-styled, silent feeding machine that features a revolving table, an automaton soup plate, an automatic food pusher, a revolving low and high gear corncob feeder, and a hydro-compressed sterilized mouth wipe.

Back at his factory worker job, in the late afternoon, after rejoining his co-workers on the assembly line, his job is to tighten bolts on an endless series of machine parts—he is a small cog in the factory. The key to successful nut-tightening is to perform his movements and tasks with clocklike tempo and precision. From his workstation on the assembly line, he holds wrenches in both hands to tighten nuts on a long stream of steel plates carried on the conveyor belt production line. The boss, who monitors the work, in what looks like an isolation booth, has ordered production increases: "Section five—give 'em the limit," so the conveyor belt is sped up—a hilarious, frenzied scene as he makes a heroic effort to keep up.

Under the strain of the job, he finally goes berserk, slowly driven insane by the assembly line. He literally lies prone on the belt and is dragged, swallowed, and eaten up by the whizzing wheels, gears, and cogs of the monstrous machine. His body snakes its way through the gears until the production line's direction is reversed, and he finally emerges free—coughed out of the machine. He has gone completely crazy and insane.

The iconic depiction of Chaplin working frantically to keep up with an assembly line inspired later comedy routines, including Donald Duck in Walt Disney's *Der Fuehrer's Face* (1943), alternately assembling artillery shells and saluting portraits of Adolf Hitler.

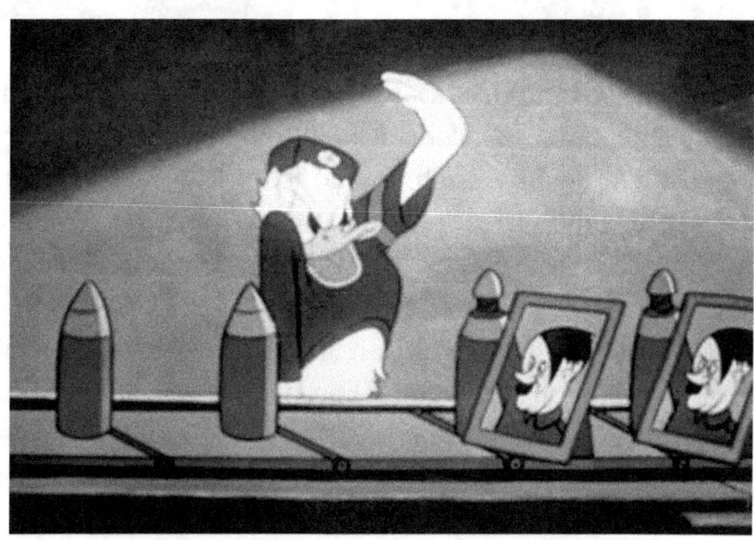

An episode of *I Love Lucy* entitled "Job Switching," Ricky and Fred try housework while the girls take jobs on a conveyer belt at a candy factory. Lucy and Ethel try in sheer desperation to keep up with an ever-increasing volume of chocolate candies, eventually stuffing them in their mouths, hats, and blouses. The episode originally aired on September 15, 1952.

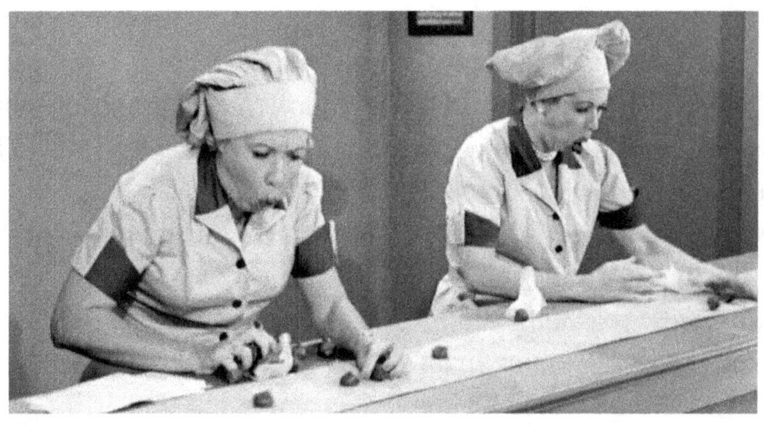

Scene: Hope Eternal

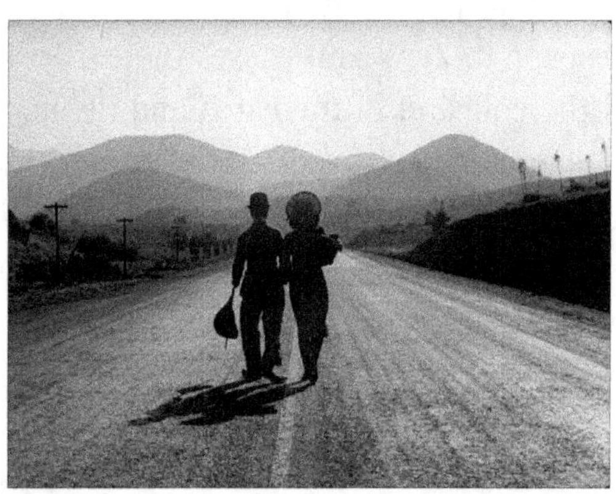

After a series of misadventures and tribulations together with the Tramp, Ellen is at the end of her ropes. Totally exasperated with the way her life has gone, she declares that there's no point to their struggling, but the Tramp assures her that they'll make it somehow. Like so many people caught in the throes of the Depression, they exist one day at a time, hoping that tomorrow will be a little better for them. As a new day dawns on the horizon, they walk down the road toward an uncertain but hopeful future. The scene was filmed on Sierra Highway and Penman Road in Santa Clarita, California.

This scene marks the end of the Little Tramp, and no one could possibly think of a more lovely and touching send-off to one of the most beloved characters in silent movie history.

In the classic 1951 film, *When Worlds Collide*, cataclysmic conflagrations caused by the approach of the planet Zyra, result in massive earthquakes, volcanic eruptions, and tsunamis that wreak havoc around the world, killing most of the earth's inhabitants. However, the news is even worse for the few survivors left on Earth. Zyra is the sole planet that orbits the star Bellus, and that star is on a direct collision course with Earth. Fortunately, forty-four people, most chosen by lottery, have one chance to escape the actual collision of the earth and Bellus in an atomic-powered rocket ship Space Ark. It was built in the last desperate months of the earth's existence, and the plan is to escape to Zyra as it passes the earth. The spacecraft barely escapes the collision of the earth and Bellus and leaves for Zyra just as the earth is destroyed. After a rough landing on Zyra, they discover that it is an Adonic new world where humanity can begin again, safe from fear and celestial collisions. Two of the earth's survivors step out of their spaceship to view "the first sunrise."

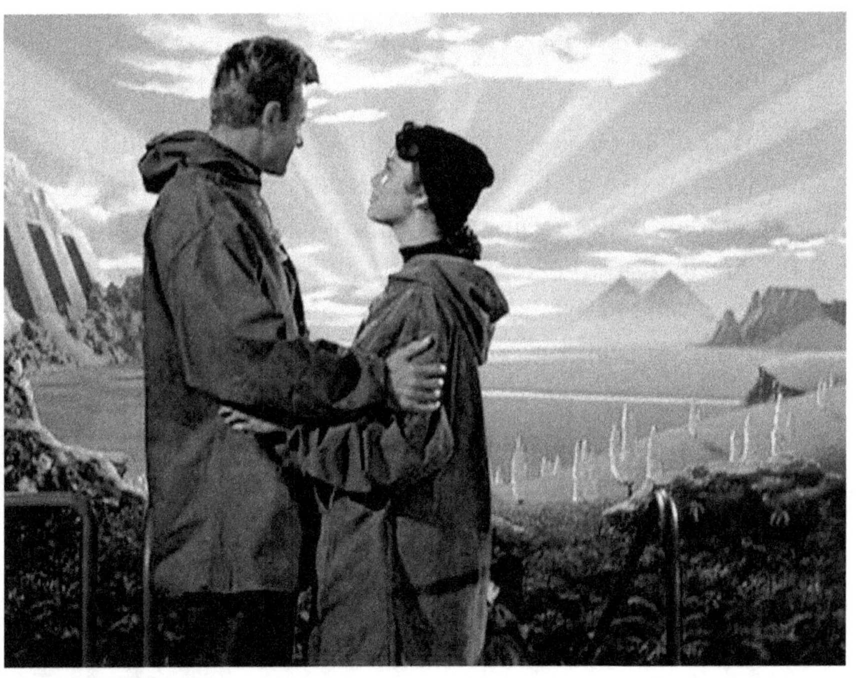

The Wizard of Oz (1939)

The Wizard of Oz is a musical fantasy film produced by Metro-Goldwyn-Mayer and widely regarded to be one of the greatest films in cinema history. Directed primarily by Victor Fleming (who left the production to take over the troubled *Gone With the Wind*), the film stars Judy Garland as Dorothy Gale.

In the film, a cyclone magically transports Dorothy to the Land of Oz, where she meets witches, munchkins, and assorted characters along the way until they finally meet the great and powerful Wizard himself who is the only one who can grant all of their wishes.

The movie was based on a novel called *The Wonderful Wizard of Oz* written by L. Frank Baum in the year 1900. The setting of the movie in rural Kansas and the name of its main character, Dorothy Gale, were not just random choices. Baum had been a newspaper editor in the "Dakota Territory" (now South Dakota) and recalled the story of twin tornadoes that destroyed the rural town of Irving, Kansas, in May 1879. The name of one of the victims of this tornado outbreak was found in a mud puddle—and her name was Dorothy Gale.

Scene: Over the Rainbow

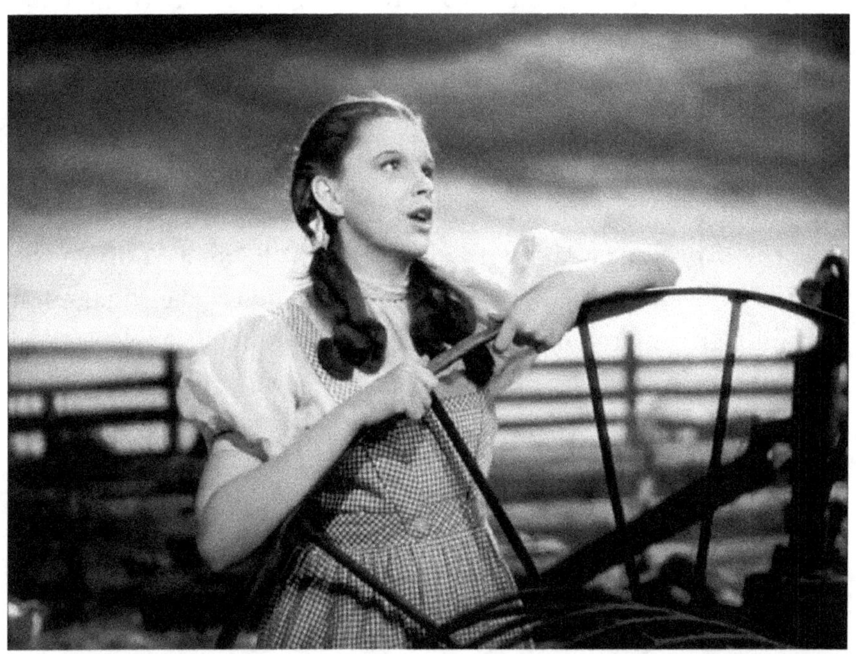

About five minutes into the film, Dorothy sings the song after failing to get Auntie Em (Clara Blandick), Uncle Henry (Charley Grapewin), and the farmhands to listen to her story of an unpleasant incident involving her dog, Toto, and the town spinster, Miss Gulch (Margaret Hamilton).

Auntie Em tells her, "Find yourself a place where you won't get into any trouble."

This prompts her to walk off by herself, musing to Toto, "Someplace where there isn't any trouble. Do you suppose there is such a place, Toto? There must be. It's not a place you can get to by a boat or a train. It's far, far away. Behind the moon, beyond the rain," at which point she begins singing her beloved, haunting, and plaintive but immortal song "Over the Rainbow." Dreaming, yearning, and wistfully longing for a trouble-free, fascinating, far-away world beyond her homeland, she strolls from a bale of hay (which she leans on) to an old wheel (which she pulls on) to a discarded buggy (which she and Toto sit on) as she sings.

The "Over the Rainbow" and Kansas scenes were directed by the uncredited King Vidor. The song was deleted from the film after a preview in San Luis Obispo because MGM Chief Executive Louis B. Mayer and producer Mervyn LeRoy thought it "slowed down the picture" and sounded "like something for Jeanette MacDonald, not for a little girl singing in a barnyard." But the song was returned to the film due to the persistence of associate producer Arthur Freed and Roger Edens, who was Judy Garland's vocal coach and mentor.

The song "Somewhere Over the Rainbow" has been featured in a number of subsequent motion pictures including the following:

James Stewart sings the song while carrying a drunken Katherine Hepburn in 1940 film *The Philadelphia Story*.

Myrna Loy hums the song after it plays in the background in the 1940 film *Third Finger Left Hand*.

An orchestral version appears several times in the 1941 movie *I Wake Up Screaming*.

The Abominable Dr. Phibes (1971) has an orchestral rendition of the song at the very end of the movie as the credits roll. Vincent Price sings the song to ironic effect at the very end of his 1972 cult classic fantasy-horror film, *Dr. Phibes Rises Again*.

For me, the other "star" of the movie, besides Judy Garland, is the twister (cyclone) that literally transports Dorothy to the Land of Oz and the beginning of her many adventures.

Scene: It's a Twister

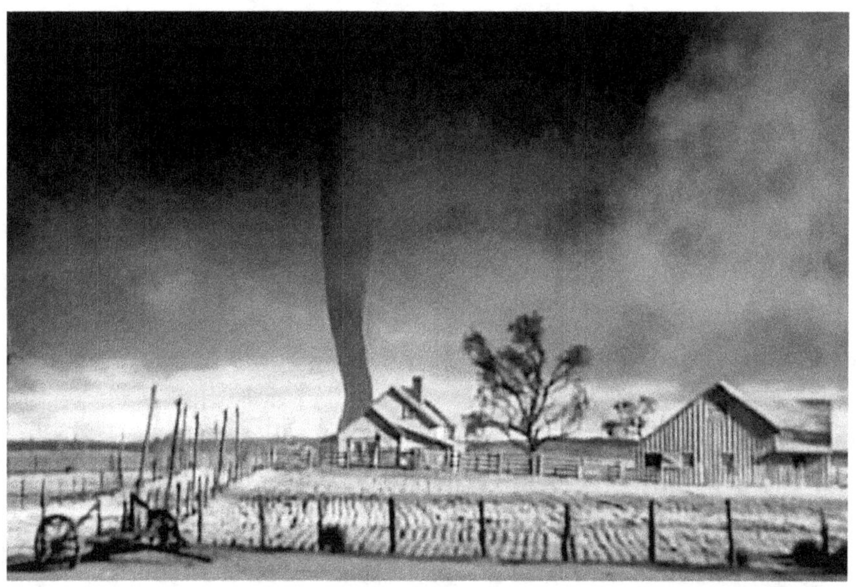

"It's a twister! It's a twister!"
—Zeke (The Wizard of Oz)

From the far north they heard a low wail of the wind, and they could see where the long grass bowed in waves before the coming storm. There now came a sharp whistling in the air from the south, and as they turned their eyes that way they saw ripples in the grass coming from that direction also. Suddenly, Uncle Henry stood up. "There's a cyclone coming, Em," he called to his wife. "I'll go look after the stock." Then he ran toward the sheds where the cows and horses were kept. Aunt Em dropped her work and came to the

door. One glance told her of the danger close at hand. "Quick, Dorothy!" she screamed. "Run for the cellar!"
—L. Frank Baum, *The Wonderful Wizard of Oz* (1900)

The date of August 25, 1939, was the official release date of *The Wizard of Oz*, which was the first movie to depict an authentic-looking tornado using improbable "1930s-style" special effects. Through the decades, this all-time classic has inspired movie-goers and "weather watchers" alike with the scene of a twister lifting Dorothy's home into the sky over the rural Kansas farmland.

As far as the tornado scene is concerned, it is still regarded as incredibly realistic, even in today's era of computer-generated special effects. It was created by Arnold Gillespie, the movie's special effects director. Gillespie began working at the studio during the filming of the silent version of *Ben-Hur*, and he was a veteran of natural disaster sequences, most notably in recreating the 1906 earthquake in San Francisco (1936). From 1936 to 1962, Gillespie served as the head of special effects at Metro-Goldwyn-Mayer on more than 180 feature films. His first attempt at a tornado was to use a thirty-five-foot tall rubber cone, but this turned out to be too rigid and simply wouldn't move. It didn't give Gillespie the undulating movements that he wanted to appear onscreen.

Then, Gillespie recalled from his experience as a pilot (he had his own airplane) that windsocks at airports had the classic funnel-shape of a tornado. He decided to make a tornado out of muslin (woven cloth), which would allow it to twist, bend, and move from side to side. He built a thirty-five-foot long tapered muslin sock and connected the top of it to a steel gantry suspended at the top of the stage. The gantry alone cost more than twelve-thousand dollars (in 1938 dollars) and was specifically built for the tornado by Bethlehem Steel. It was a mobile structure similar to those used in warehouses to lift heavy objects and could travel the entire length of the stage. The bottom of the sock disappeared into a slot on the stage floor where it connected to a car below the stage where the crew moved it back and forth along a track, giving the illusion of the tornado swaying to the left and right and back again.

To produce the dust and debris that makes a real tornado visible, they used compressed air hoses to spray powdery brown dust known as "Fullers Earth" from both the top and bottom of the funnel. The muslin sock was sufficiently porous that some of the dust sifted through, giving a blur or softness to the material and fuzziness to the edges so that it didn't look like a hard surface. Four or five feet in front of the cameras were two panels of glass on which gray balls of cotton (great for Mammatus clouds) had been pasted. The two panels moved in opposite directions, adding to the boiling sensation, and at the same time, they obscured the steel gantry and top portion of the tornado. Dense clouds of yellow-black smoke made from sulfur and carbon were injected onto the set from a catwalk above the gantry. The stagehands had no respirators and stayed up there breathing the stuff until they couldn't stand it. Many of them became ill, and some coughed up black-yellow mucous even days after the tornado was photographed.

Once the tornado had been filmed, there was still plenty of work to be done. Rear- projection was used to transfer the previously shot tornado image onto a translucent screen while actors such as Dorothy were placed in front of it. The farmhouse, fence, barn, and prairie all were done in miniature, and clouds were painted on glass. Wind machines provided the big blow while stagehands threw dried leaves and other debris in the air. When the tornado came close to the house at the end of the scene, more debris and dirt were added in the foreground to obscure the fake tornado while providing more realism. The tornado scene in *The Wizard of Oz* ended up costing more money than any other special effect in the movie. This film was made in 1938, so special effects were nothing like they are today. It's incredibly well done for its time.

Ironically, a tornado destroys the Hollywood sign in the 2004 film *The Day After Tomorrow*.

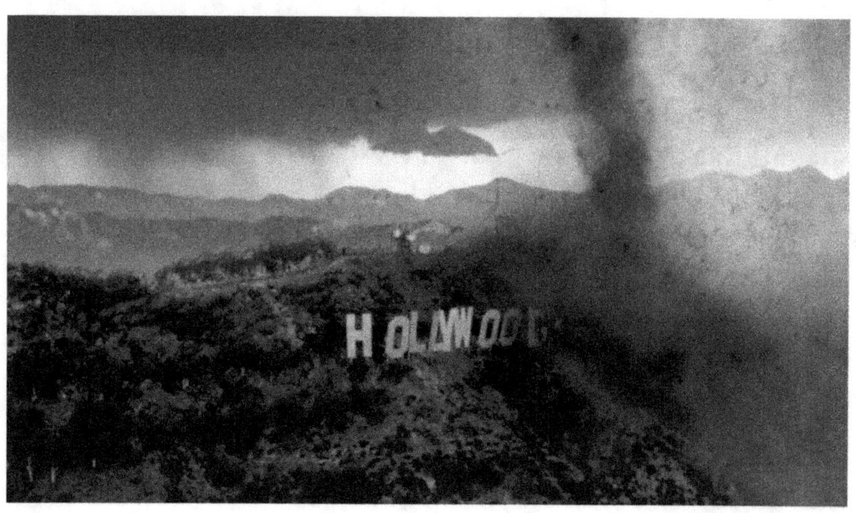

Gone With the Wind (1939)

Gone With the Wind is an epic historical romance film adapted from the 1936 novel by Margaret Mitchell. The film was produced by David O. Selznick of Selznick International Pictures and directed by Victor Fleming. Set in the American South against the backdrop of the American Civil War and the Reconstruction era, the film tells the story of Scarlett O'Hara, the strong-willed daughter of a Georgia plantation owner. It follows her romantic pursuit of Ashley Wilkes, who is married to his cousin, Melanie Hamilton, and her subsequent marriage to Rhett Butler. The leading roles are played by Vivien Leigh (Scarlett), Clark Gable (Rhett), Leslie Howard (Ashley), and Olivia de Havilland (Melanie).

Scene: "Frankly, my dear, I don't give a damn"

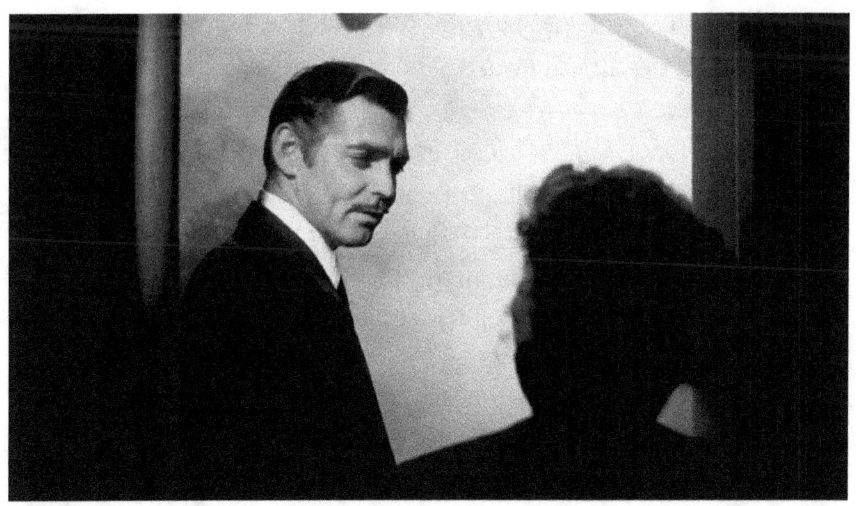

"Frankly, my dear, I don't give a damn" is the memorable line spoken by Rhett Butler (Gable), as his last words to Scarlett O'Hara (Leigh), in response to her tearful question: "Where shall I go? What shall I do?" Scarlett clings to the hope that she can win him back. This line is only slightly different in Margaret Mitchell's novel *Gone With the Wind*, published in 1936, from which the film is derived: "My dear, I don't give a damn."

Even today, the line is still one of the most famous utterances in motion picture history, a verbal confirmation that Rhett has finally given up on Scarlett and their tumultuous relationship over the years. After more than a decade of fruitlessly seeking her love, he no longer cares what happens to her, expressed in no uncertain terms.

Prior to the film's release, censors objected to the use of the word "damn" in the film, a word that had been prohibited by the 1930 Motion Picture Production Code, beginning in July 1934. However, before 1930, the word "damn" had been relatively common in films. In the silent era, John Gilbert even shouted "Goddamn you!" to the enemy during a battle in *The Big Parade* (1925). The Production Code was ratified on March 31, 1930, and was effective for motion pictures whose filming began afterward. Thus, talkies that used "damn" include *Glorifying the American Girl* (1929), *Flight* (1929), *Gold Diggers of Broadway* (1929), *Hell's Angels* (1930), *The Big Trail* (1930), *The Dawn Patrol* (1930), *The Green Goddess* (1930), and *Dracula* (1931).

Although legend persists that the Hays Office fined producer David O. Selznick five-thousand dollars for using the word "damn," in fact the MPPDA (Motion Pictures Producers and Distributors of America) board passed an amendment to the production code a month and a half before the film's release, on November 1, 1939, that allowed use of the words "hell" or "damn" when their use "shall be essential and required for portrayal, in proper historical context, of any scene or dialogue based upon historical fact or folklore … or a quotation from a literary work, provided that no such use shall be permitted which is intrinsically objectionable or offends good taste." With that amendment, the Production Code Administration had no further objection to Rhett's closing line. It is actually the second use of "damn" in the film. The term "damn Yankees" is heard in the parlor scene at Twelve Oaks.

Director Victor Fleming shot a different scene using the alternate line, "Frankly, my dear, I just don't care," in case the film censors objected to the word "damn." Of course, with the line being so famous, it stands without question as being left in the movie.

This system of governed filmmaking slowly started to collapse over the years and gave birth to the motion picture film rating system. Nowadays, film ratings and censorship are controlled by the film industry and not by a single controlling person or government. Now that we have the rating system, films can be classified by their rating. Today's ratings are, at least by idea, implemented by our peers. So as society changes, so do those who review and rate films. It can be argued that some swearing is overused and unnecessary, but some films contain swearing because some people swear in real-life, and it can make a film more dramatic or shocking. The use of the word "damn" in *Gone With the Wind* was certainly not the first time the word was used in movies, and it would hardly be the last time as even worse vulgarities have become commonplace in recent cinematic history as society accepts these words in common day usage and application.

The production shot below shows (from left to right) producer David O. Selznick, director Victor Fleming, Vivien Leigh as Scarlett O'Hara, and Clark Gable as Rhett Butler, as they relax on the set in preparation for the filming of the final scene of the most popular movie ever made and the utterance of probably the most famous line in motion picture history.

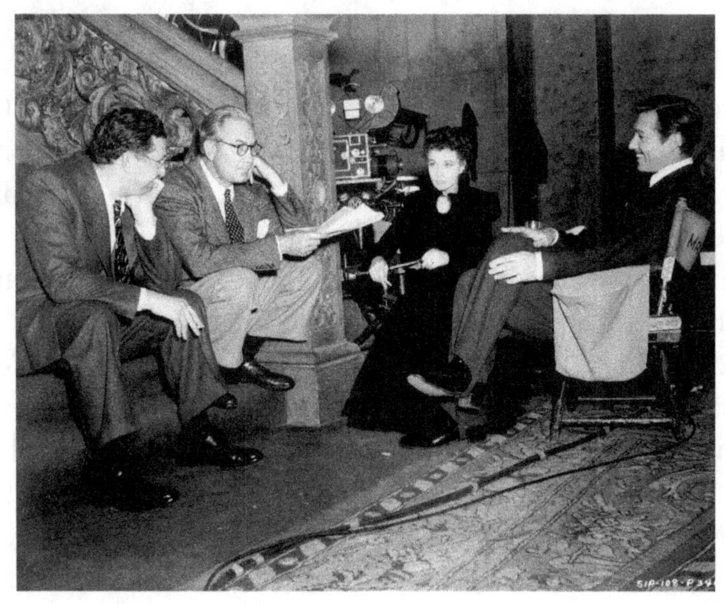

Scene: Open-Air Hospital

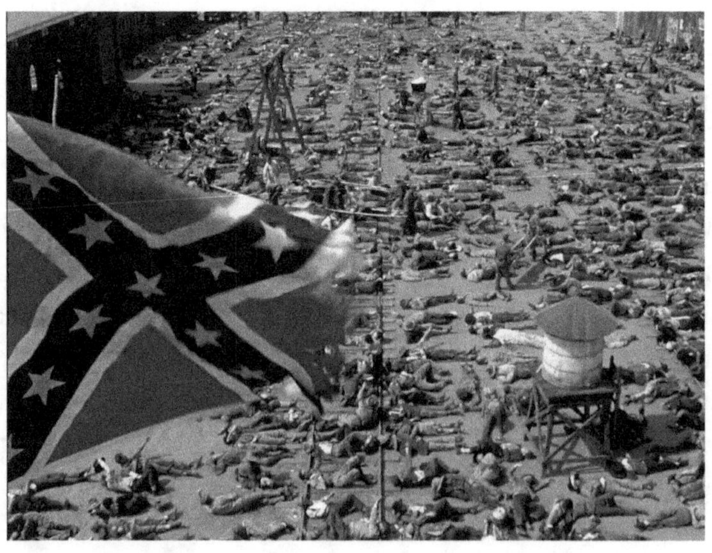

The scene above from *Gone With the Wind* is a depiction of the gathering of wounded Confederate soldiers as a result of the Atlanta Campaign, which lasted from May 7–July 17, 1864.

Earlier in the war, another gathering of Confederate wounded amassed after the valiant charge of 12,500 men under General Pickett and other troops under Generals Trimble and Pettigrew on July 3, 1863, at the Battle of Gettysburg. Literally, thousands of wounded Confederate soldiers lay on the valiant field of battle after the charge failed to breach the fortified and entrenched Union forces on Cemetery Ridge. Movies such as the 1993 *Gettysburg* depicted the aftermath of the charge on that fateful day of the Civil War. Again, wide-angle cameras were used in order to capture the sheer magnitude and horror of the scene, while extras, and in this case, Civil War reenactors, do their thing on the set.

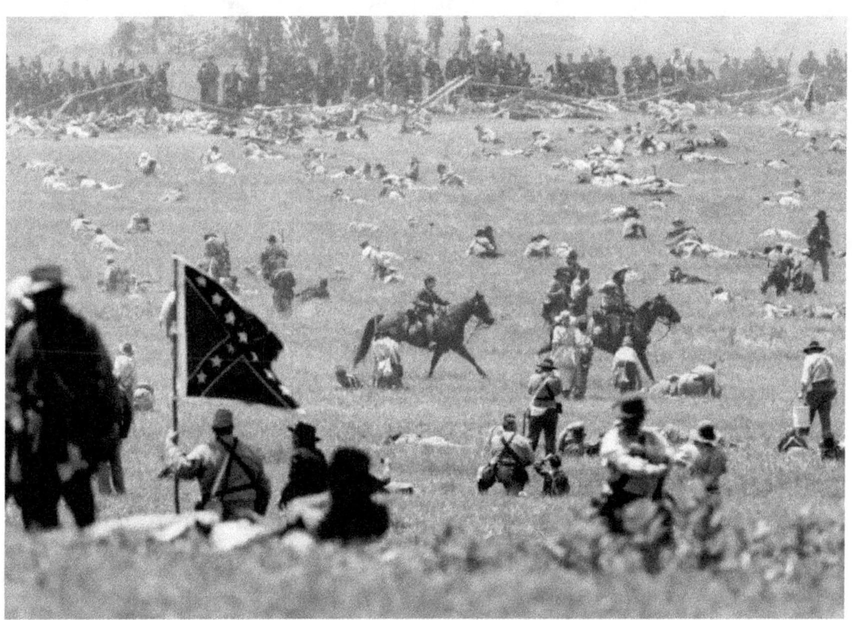

Movie extras gathered on the 40 Acres backlot for the filming of the famous train yard scene in *Gone With the Wind*. The Atlanta Railroad Depot set was built in the late 1930s specifically for the film *Gone With the Wind*. It became a fixture on the 40 Acres backlot for thirty-two years. The depot set was designed after the actual Atlanta Railroad Depot, which was destroyed by General Sherman in November 1864. The 40 Acres set was destroyed by fire in December 1971.

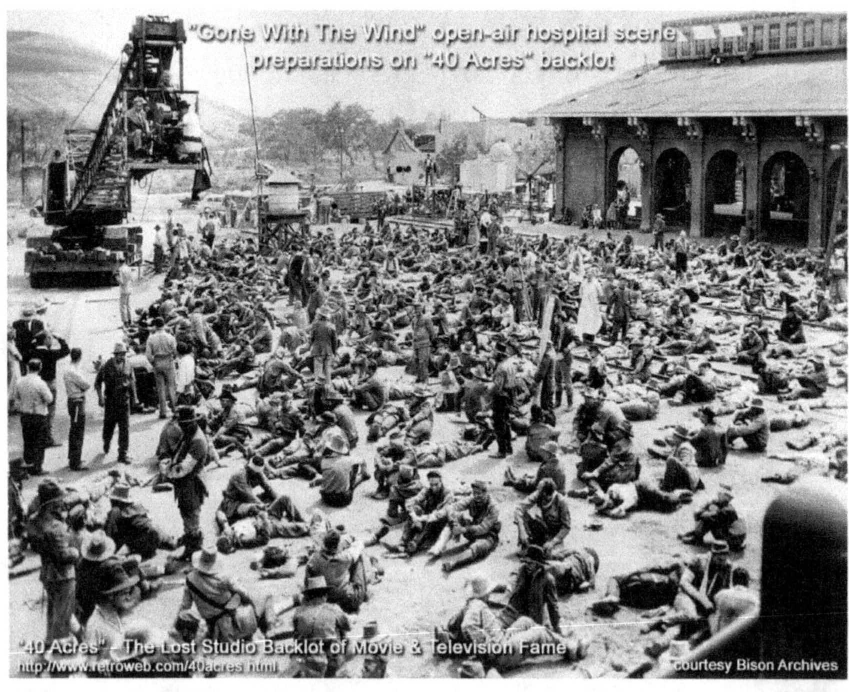

The location of the Railroad Station Set on the Pathe Studio Ranch leased by RKO Studios for *Gone With the Wind* is circled in black. The production crew had to be very careful in capturing the image of every extra and dummy in the scene without filming Culver City, which was located just behind the Pathe Studio Ranch.

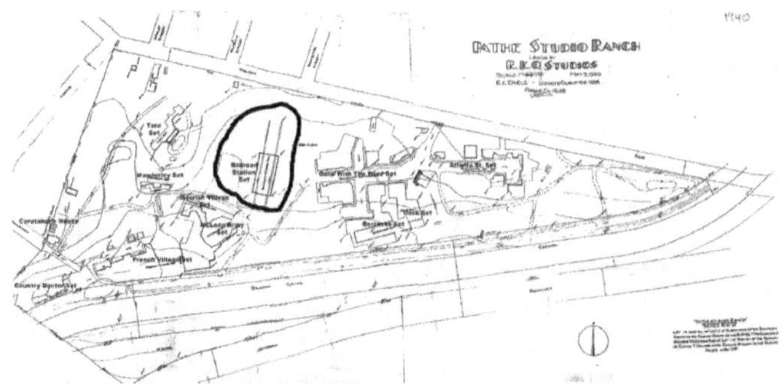

For the biggest scene in the movie, the filming of the open-air hospital was located in the yard adjacent to the reconstructed Railroad Depot originally located in Atlanta, Georgia. The scene required a full year of planning. In order to film this scene for the movie, Director Fleming had to find a crane that could raise the film crew high enough to encompass the enormous set. The biggest crane they could find was at the Long Beach Shipyard. The crane would lift the shooting crew eighty feet above the immense sea of extras and dummies. A runway made of two feet of concrete had to be constructed in order to support the sheer weight of the crane.

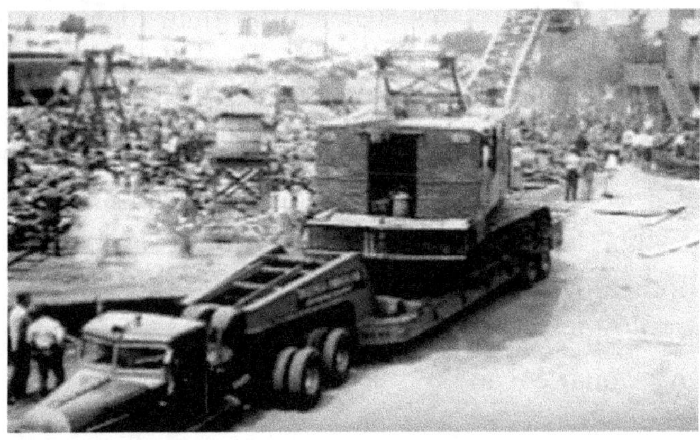

There is an interesting side story that goes along with this particular scene. Supposedly, Val Lewton, who served as producer David O. Selnick's story editor, claims, for fun, Lewton added an elaborate, costly elevator shot that would follow Scarlett as she makes her way through the hundreds of wounded and dying soldiers. To Lewton's surprise, Selznick loved it and called it to be filmed. We can assume that, at this point in time, the production crew secured the leasing of the crane and a call for more extras to fill the large film setting. At this point in time, a call to the Screen Actors Guild for more extras went out. The rest of the story continues: When Scarlett searches for Dr. Meade, making her way among 1,600 suffering and dying Confederate soldiers, in order to cut costs and still comply with a union rule that dictated the use of a certain percentage of extras in the cast, eight hundred dummies were scattered among the eight hundred extras. According to the documentary *The Making of a Legend: Gone With the Wind* (1988), in addition to saving money, the use of the dummies was required because there were not enough extras available the day of the filming due to the fact that four other films required a lot of extras as well.

This extra (Johnny Albright) was hired for the filming of this particular scene. He relates that a prop man placed a dummy next to him while he was lying on the ground, getting ready for the shooting to commence; then, an assistant director came by and told him to move a rod on the dummy that would move its arm. This action would make it appear that the dummy was actually alive when the filming commenced. When Margaret Mitchell's (author of the novel *Gone With the Wind*) husband saw the finished scene in the film, he said, "My, if we had that many soldiers, we would have won the war."

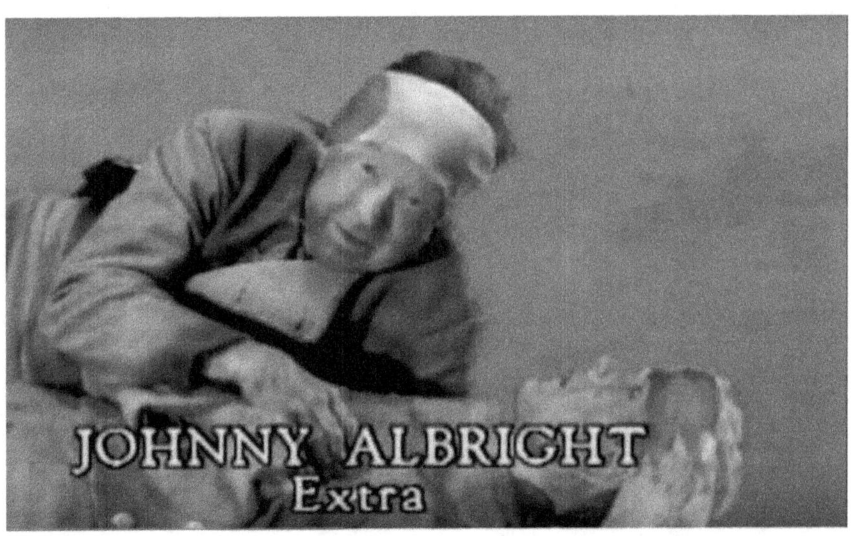

The crane is being set in order to make the "big shot."

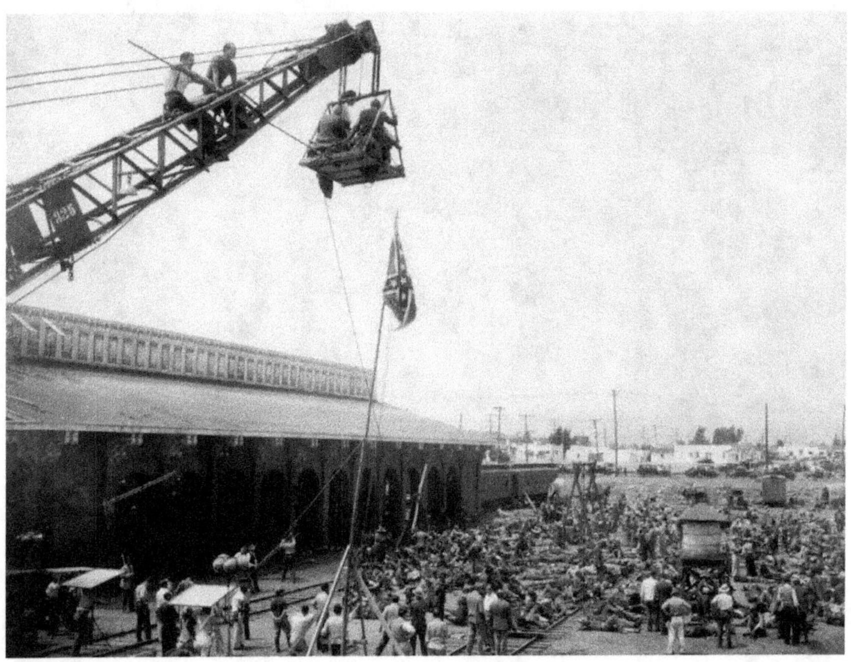

Mr. Smith Goes to Washington (1939)

Mr. Smith Goes to Washington is a political comedy-drama film directed by Frank Capra, starring Jean Arthur and James Stewart, and featuring Claude Rains and Edward Arnold. The film is about a newly appointed United States Senator who fights against a corrupt political system, and was written by Sidney Buchman, based on Lewis R. Foster's unpublished story "The Gentleman from Montana."

Scene: The Filibuster

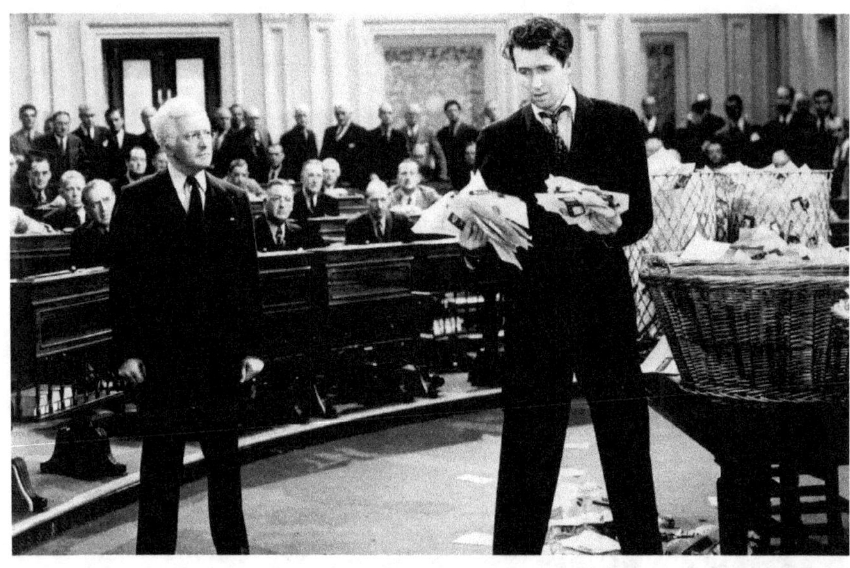

Radio commentator H. V. Kaltenborn (himself): "Half of official Washington is here to see democracy's finest show, the filibuster, the right to talk your head off, and the American privilege of free speech in its most dramatic form."

The classic filibuster scene at the conclusion of Frank Capra's film has to rank as one of the most-finely acted sequences ever recorded.

After almost twenty-four hours of filibustering, with an agonizingly, pathetically hoarse voice but also with an indomitable spirit, a weary, pleading Jefferson Smith (James Stewart) has a few more exhortations for the senators who have returned to the Senate chamber. In an extraordinary metaphor emphasizing the Capitol Dome high above him, Smith imaginatively suggests repositioning the Lady of the Dome back to an ethical center where she belongs:

> "And it's not too late. Because this country is bigger than the Taylors or you or me or anything else. Great principles don't get lost once they come to light. They're right here. You just have to see them again."

When baskets, wire barrels, and bundles of stacks of fifty-thousand "Taylor-made" phony telegrams from Senator Paine's (Claude Rains) state are brought in and deposited in the front of the Senate chamber, Paine holds up a fistful, telling Smith that they all demand that he yield the floor and give up his filibuster. In one of the most powerful scenes ever filmed, Jefferson staggers forward in disbelief to look at the telegrams, pawing through them and desperately looking for some evidence of support. In a symbolic crucifixion stance, he grabs two large fistfuls and holds them out. In a hoarse voice, he turns toward Senator Paine and delivers an impassioned speech, accusing Paine face-to-face of betraying his ideals.

Then, with heart-stirring courage, Smith finishes his heroic speech with the immortal eloquent words:

> "You think I'm licked. You all think I'm licked. Well, I'm not licked, and I'm gonna stay right here and fight for

> this lost cause even if this room gets filled with lies like
> these, and the Taylors and all their armies come march-
> ing into this place. Somebody'll listen to me. Some—"

Smith faints and collapses on the floor, dumping a basket of telegrams over onto himself. His supportive friend Saunders (Jean Arthur) screams from the gallery. With a strained look on his face, Senator Paine rushes from the Senate floor toward the vestibule/cloakroom as Smith is treated. Two or three shots ring out, and Paine is seen struggling with other senators. They prevent him from killing himself, as he screams in a public confession that he is unable to live with his guilt-ridden conscience any longer:

> "I'm not fit to be a senator. I'm not fit to live. Expel me!
> Expel me! Not him."

For the climactic filibuster scenes, Jefferson Smith had to sound hoarse after twenty-three straight hours of talking. Actor Stewart had trouble simulating the effect, so he consulted a throat doctor, asking how a gravelly voice could be induced rather than cured. As quoted again by Pickard, the actor said, "He dropped dichloride of mercury into my throat, not near my vocal chords but just in around there. It wasn't dangerous. And he said: 'How's that?' I said: 'rasp, rasp.' He said: 'You got it.'"

Stewart had the doctor apply the solution on the set; he was worried that Capra would disapprove and accuse Stewart of being a mechanical actor, but the director was delighted. Capra said, "The result was astonishing. No amount of acting could possibly simulate Jimmy's intense pathetic efforts to speak through real swollen chords."

A major effort went into a faithful reproduction of the Senate chamber on the Columbia lot. James D. Preston, a former superintendent of the Senate gallery, acted as technical director for the Senate set, as well as advising on political protocol. The Senate chamber had been faithfully recreated on the Columbia stages by art director Lionel Banks and a huge team of craftsmen, and the set was just that: a chamber. It was a tall, four-sided set filled with hundreds of people. Action required for the story would also be taking place simultaneously on three levels: the Senate floor, the rostrum where the Vice President sat, and the galleries holding the press, the pages, and the public. Capra wrote in *The Name Above the Title: An Autobiography*, "How to light, photograph, and record hundreds of scenes on three levels of a deep well, open only at the top, were the logistic nightmares that faced electricians, cameramen, and soundmen."

Capra would also rely heavily on reaction shots of the many observers in the scenes set in the Senate chamber. He wanted to retain a natural flow to these shots, and so, for these reasons, the usual one-camera set up could not be employed. "We might still be there," Capra said. The technical team "devised a multiple-camera, multiple-sound method of shooting which enabled us, in one big equipment move, to film as many as a half-dozen separate scenes before we made another big move."

Can Mr. Smith Get to Washington Anymore? is a 2006 documentary film directed by Frank Popper, which follows Missouri politician Jeff Smith's 2004 Democratic primary election campaign to the United States House of Representatives after the retirement of Dick Gephardt from his seat. The film follows Smith as he challenges Russ Carnahan, a member of the Carnahan political family and the frontrunner of a crowded Democratic primary, to capture the Democratic nomination for the seat. The movie's title references Frank Capra's *Mr. Smith Goes to Washington*, a film in which a naive but well-meaning idealistic man (named "Jefferson Smith") becomes a Senator and fights the cynical nature of Washington.

Many of the reviews for this movie mirror the same type of analysis attributed to Capra's groundbreaking film. *The Washington Post*'s Ann Horaday felt that it was a "funny, engrossing, and affectionate documentary." *The Boston Globe*'s Janice Page noted that the movie restored the viewer's faith in democracy, even if Jeff Smith failed to win the seat. Kevin Crust of the *Los Angeles Times* praised the movie: "[the film] captures ground-level political machinations in an utterly fascinating way."

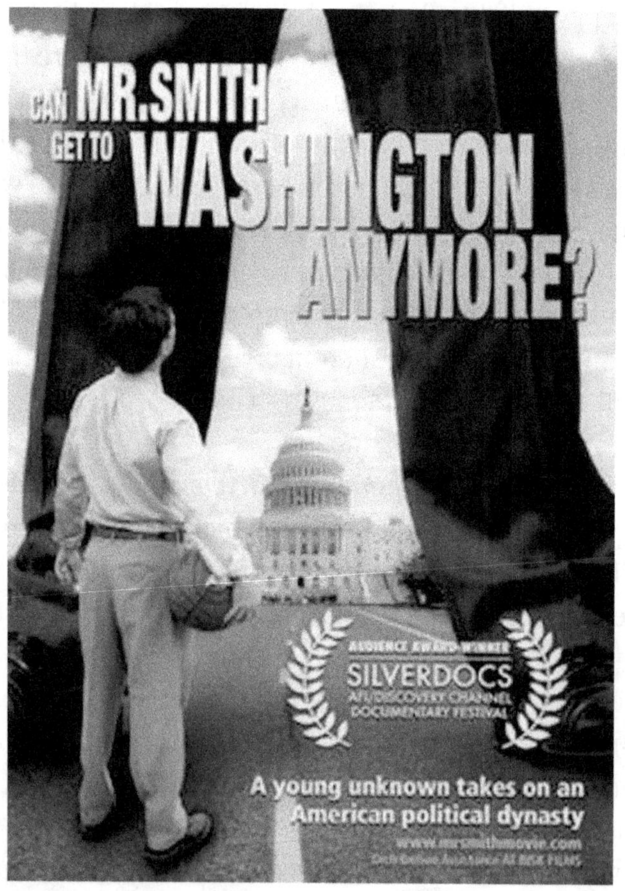

Stagecoach (1939)

Stagecoach is a Western film directed by John Ford and starring Claire Trevor and John Wayne in his breakthrough role. The screenplay by Dudley Nichols is an adaptation of "The Stage to Lordsburg," a 1937 short story by Ernest Haycox. The film follows a group of diverged and interesting strangers riding on a stagecoach through dangerous Apache territory.

Stagecoach was the first of many Westerns that Ford shot using Monument Valley, in the American Southwest on the Arizona-Utah border, as a location, many of which also starred John Wayne. Scenes from *Stagecoach* include a sequence introducing John Wayne's character, the Ringo Kid.

In director John Ford's first modern Western, John Wayne began his fertile acting partnership with the director (in his first major western role) with the inspired, legendary scene of his first appearance—in a role that made him famous and launched him as the most durable Western hero.

Scene: John Wayne and Monument Valley

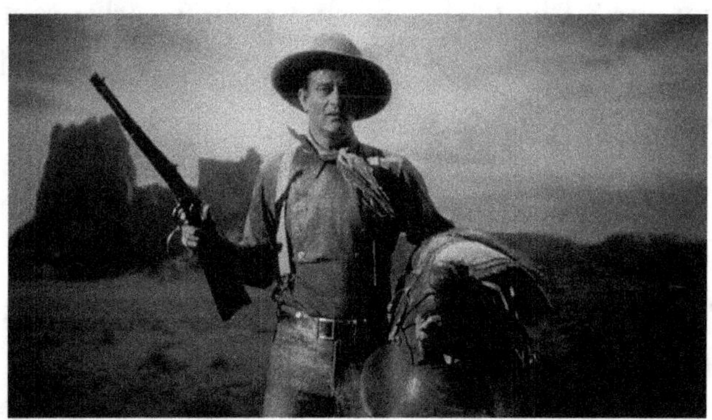

As Ringo Kid, an outlaw who is seeking revenge for the murder of his father and brother by the Plummers, he is first seen "holding up" the stagecoach (with an assortment of characters) on its way to Lordsburg. Along the way, after rounding a turn, a rifle shot is heard, and a tracking shot zooms in (losing focus for a moment) for a large clear close up of Ringo Kid standing tall from the perspective of the moving stagecoach. The camera rapidly tracks in on his face. Ringo is twirling and re-cocking his Winchester rifle in one hand, shouting out: "Hold it!" while holding his saddle in the other hand. He is standing in the middle of the desert by the trail, stranded without a horse. Ringo is wearing a paneled, placket-front shirt with a neckerchief, and jeans with its pants legs rolled up outside of the boots.

Stagecoach was John Wayne's eightieth film. The role made him a leading man in A-features, but he had to wait almost another decade until *Red River* (1948) to become a star in big-budget productions. By that time, he was in his early forties. His story is hardly the description of overnight success.

TCM factoids expressed it best:

> From the moment we are introduced to John Wayne as the Ringo Kid, with the camera tracking into an imposing close-up, we know we are in the presence of a major star. Although he had shown some early promise as an actor, Wayne's potential was being squandered in a series of forgettable B-Westerns for Republic Studios. Ford invited Wayne, who was already a good friend, on a weekend boat trip to read the screenplay.
>
> "I'm having a hell of a time deciding whom to cast as the Ringo Kid," he said. "You know a lot of young actors, Duke. See what you think."
>
> Wayne suggested Lloyd Nolan.

"Nolan?" Ford asked incredulously. "Jesus Christ, I just wish to hell I could find some young actor in this town who can ride a horse and act."

The next day, as the boat pulled into the harbor, Ford declared, "I have made up my mind. I want you to play the Ringo Kid."

It was likely that Ford had Wayne in mind for the role from the beginning. However, he had to work hard to convince Wanger to cast the star of mediocre B-Westerns in the part; and Republic Studios, to which Wayne was still under contract, proved to be a difficult negotiator.

Although it was not the first film to use Monument Valley as a location, Stagecoach did much to popularize it. The movie marked the beginning of a long friendship between John Ford and the Navajo Indians of Monument Valley. He employed scores of local Indians to play Apache warriors in Stagecoach and the various Indian tribes of many of his other Westerns. Part of the vast Navajo reservation near the Utah/Arizona border, the desolate landscape with its striking sandstone buttes and mesas, lends a mythic quality to the film, dwarfing the vulnerable stagecoach party in the presence of eternal and impersonal nature. It came to embody the very idea of the West for John Ford, who used Monument Valley in many of his later films. At the time the film was made, the region was still sparsely populated and not readily accessible, making work difficult for the film crew. Yet as prominent as it appears in the film, the location was, in fact, used surprisingly little. The Apache raid was shot on the Muroc dry lakebed near Victorville, California, and the river crossing took place on the Kern

River near Kernville, California, to name only a couple of other locations that were used. The interior scenes of the coach were all shot in a studio, and the town sequences were shot on Hollywood backlots. Moreover, to focus solely on the admittedly stunning outdoor landscapes is to lose sight of the film's stylistic richness as a whole: the beautifully lit nighttime scene in Lordsburg, with graceful tracking shots following Dallas and Ringo Kid on their stroll through the town; and the taut editing of the conversations inside the stagecoach, with their perfectly timed reaction shots. Orson Welles later claimed to have watched the film dozens of times before directing his own masterpiece, Citizen Kane (1941).

Monument Valley has made an appearance in a variety of Hollywood classics, including three in which actor John Wayne appeared in the movie, as well. After *Stagecoach*, they are *She Wore a Yellow Ribbon* (1949), *The Searchers* (1956), and *How the West Was Won* (1962). In the last film, Wayne and Monument Valley appeared in the same movie, but not in the same scenes.

Scene: The Artistry of Yakima Canutt

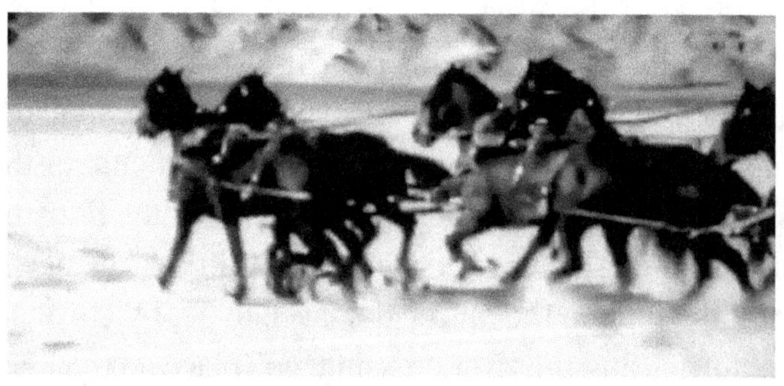

Legendary actor/stuntman Yakima Canutt also deserves to be noted for his contributions to the picture. One scene, which required the stagecoach full of passengers to be floated across a river, was deemed impossible by technicians to pull off, and John Ford considered removing it from the script altogether. Canutt, however, suggested using hollow logs tied to the coach; the air would give them increased buoyancy, offsetting the weight of the fully loaded coach. In addition, an underwater cable was used to help pull the stagecoach. Canutt's plan worked, and the scene was retained for the film. Ford rewarded Canutt's creativity by making him the stunt coordinator for the film. But it is Canutt's magnificent (and dangerous) stunts on this film that he is remembered today. In the most striking of these, he plays an Indian who rides alongside the coach at full speed—approximately forty miles per hour—and transfers from the horse he is riding to a horse on the team. The funny part of this story is that Canutt was a personal friend of Wayne, but Wayne winds up shooting him twice in the film's most famous stunt scene. After he is shot by Wayne, he falls between the two lead horses and hangs from the rig before letting go and allowing the horses and the stagecoach to pass over him. The stunt, which was broken up into two segments for the shoot, required precise timing and movements since any miscalculations or slips on Canutt's part could have been deadly.

According to the veteran stuntman, here's how it was accomplished: "You have to run the horses fast, so they'll run straight. If they run slow, they move around a lot. When you turn loose to go under the coach, you've got to bring your arms over your chest and stomach. You've got to hold your elbows close to your body, or that front axle will knock them off."

After the stunt was completed, Canutt ran to Ford to make sure they got the stunt on film. Ford replied, even if they hadn't, "I'll never shoot that again." Yakima Canutt performed the same stunt the next year in the movie *Virginia City.*

In *Thundering Hoofs* (1924), Fred Thomson performed the dangerous jump from a moving stagecoach to one of the horses pulling the coach. He fell and suffered a compound fracture of his right thigh when the weighted stagecoach ran over both of his legs. Yakima Canutt completed the stunt for director Al Rogell. Canutt was always fascinated with the mechanics of stunt work, and he was a true master of the art form.

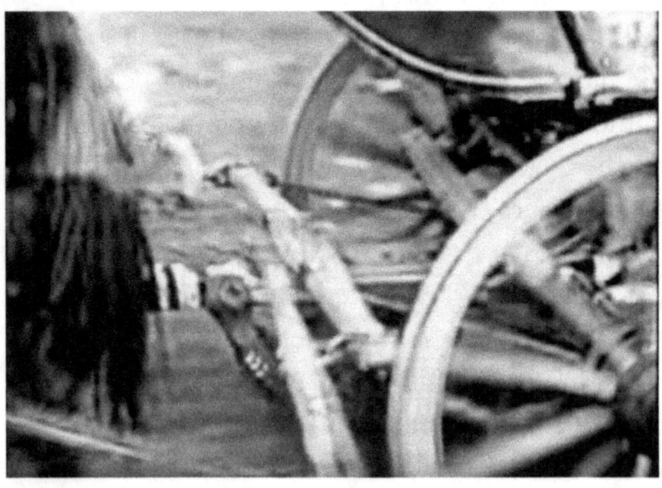

Steven Spielberg paid homage to this scene in *Raiders of the Lost Ark* (1981). Most of the truck chase was shot by second unit director Michael D. Moore, including Indiana Jones being dragged by the truck (performed by stuntman Terry Leonard), in tribute to a famous Yakima Canutt stunt. Spielberg then filmed all the shots with Ford himself in and around the truck cab.

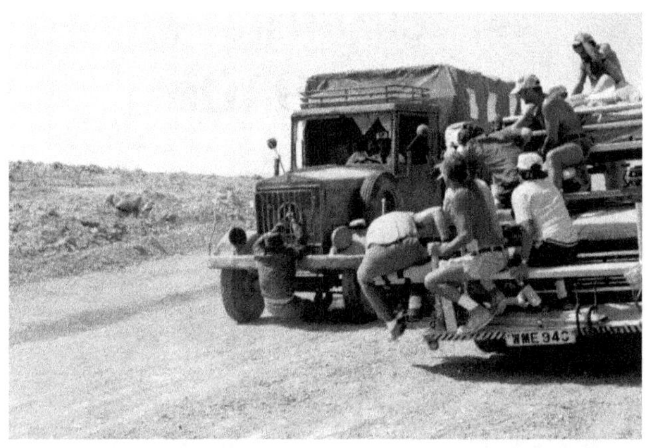

Harrison Ford narrated the behind-the-scenes 2018 documentary entitled *Filming the Truck Scene in Raiders of the Lost Ark* in which he stated that a trench was built under the path of the truck in order to give stuntman Terry Leonard enough clearance to do the stunt or "gag," as it is called in the industry. The scene took three days to film, and despite all the careful preparations and safety precautions surrounding the stunt, it was still a very dangerous feat for any stuntman to perform.

Here we see Terry actually performing the stunt for the film itself.

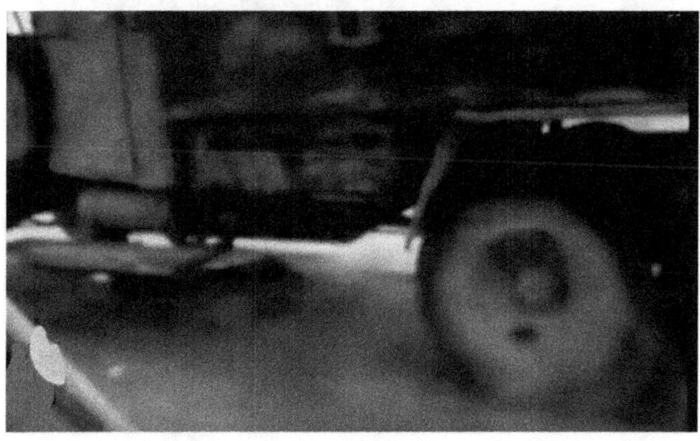

THE 1940s

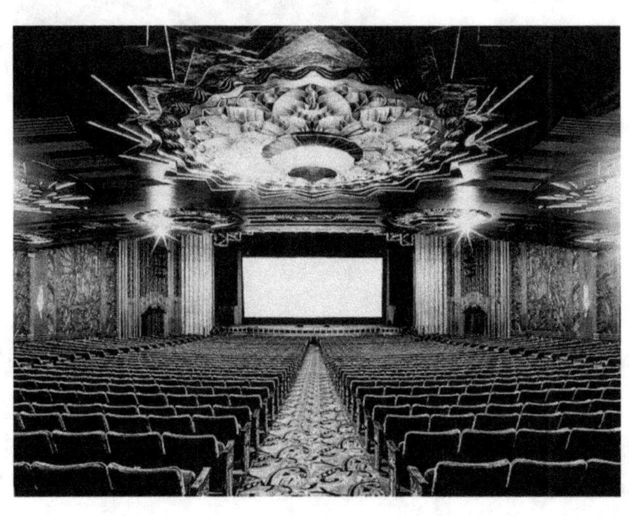

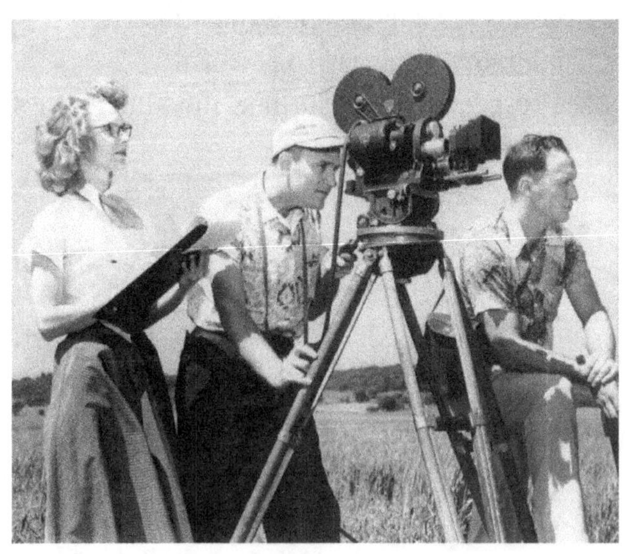

Dance, Girl, Dance (1940)

Dance, Girl, Dance is a gritty, gutsy, and trail-blazing movie drama directed by Dorothy Arzner and produced by Erich Pommer. It starred Maureen O'Hara as Judy O'Brien, Lucille Ball as Tiger Lily White, and Ralph Bellamy as Steve Adams.

Lucille Ball portrays a burlesque stripper while O'Hara plays an aspiring ballet dancer who is forced to share the stage with Ball. O'Hara performs a classical ballet/ballerina routine in order to make a living. Her performance is relentlessly heckled and berated by the lustful gentlemen in the audience. Bellamy plays a talent agent with whom O'Hara has been seeking an audition in the legitimate entertainment world. One night, Steve attends Judy's performance, and after she is once again severely heckled, as she always is when she is on stage, returns to the front of the stage and gives the audience a stern and forceful lecture about the evils of viewing and exploiting women as sex objects and how demeaning and totally offensive it is to woman in general. It is the highlight of the entire film. Her speech is met by applause led by Steve's secretary and then Steve. When Tiger Lily White comes on stage, she is soundly booed by the "enlightened" audience.

Scene: The Stage Lecture

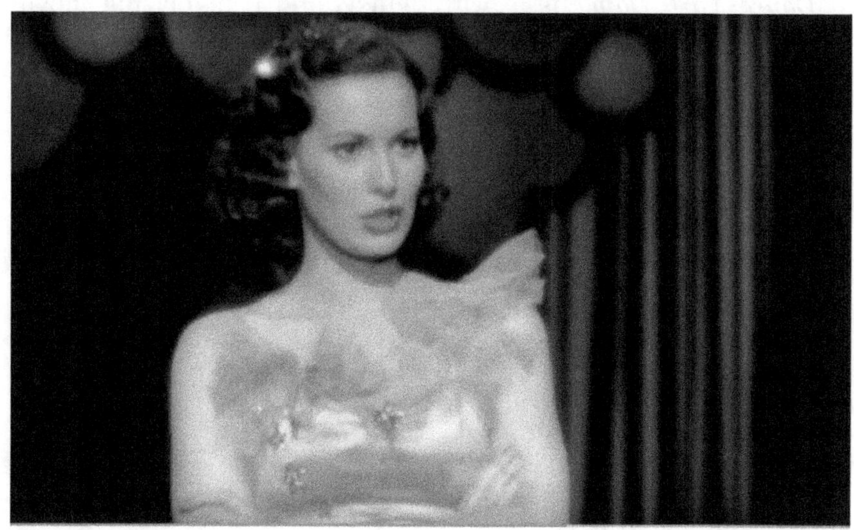

Judy O'Brien: "Go on, laugh, get your money's worth. No one's going to hurt you. I know you want me to tear my clothes off so you can look your fifty cents' worth. Fifty cents for the privilege of staring at a girl the way your wives won't let you. What do you suppose we think of you up here with your silly smirks your mothers would be ashamed of? . . . What's it for? So you can go home when the show's over, strut before your wives and sweethearts and play at being the stronger sex for a minute? I'm sure they see through you. I'm sure they see through you just like we do!"

Judy's most stunning set piece, a speech near the end berating the men who go to watch strippers on the burlesque stage, could be considered as a barbed attack on the movie audience. After all, part of the Hollywood myth was the objectification of women, and Arzner's film was one of the first to expose this exploitation.

Arzner spent her "retirement" from Hollywood directing fifty Pepsi-Cola commercials for good friend Joan Crawford (married at the time to Pepsi's chair of the board) and teaching filmmaking at UCLA in the 1960s before her death in 1979. In the 1970s, feminist film scholars applauded Arzner as a key pioneer in the small ranks of women directors working in classical Hollywood, with *Dance, Girl, Dance* often cited as a prime example of the Arzner touch.

History Channel
Oct 17, 2017
Written by Erin Blakemore
This Tinseltown Tyrant Used Sexual Exploitation to Build a Hollywood Empire
"King Cohn" lived up to his despicable reputation.
It seemed so easy: arrive in Hollywood with a suitcase and a pretty face. Get discovered by an agent or, better yet, a movie exec. Next step: stardom.
This seemingly simple formula was the dream of many aspiring Hollywood starlets—and the myth of Hollywood's Golden Age. For a significant number of movie stars, a career in pictures started instead with sexual exploitation on the "casting couch" of Harry Cohn, one of Hollywood's most powerful—and brutal—men.
As the head of Columbia Pictures from 1919 to 1958, Cohn expected sex in exchange for a chance at stardom. And as one of the most influential figures in Tinseltown, he usually got it.

He was one of the men responsible for instituting the system of Hollywood's "casting couch," which demanded women trade sexual favors with powerful executives for a chance at a movie role. Although the casting couch cliché predates the Columbia head's career in Hollywood, Cohn helped entrench the system in the movie industry during four decades in film.

Part of his success rested on his ruthlessness, and from the start Cohn used that aggression to exert control over female stars. Not only did he force them to change their names and their appearances, but he regularly forced them to trade sex for employment, then scrutinized and even spied on them.

This penchant for abusive behavior earned Cohn the nicknames "King Cohn" and "White Fang." He was known for having shelves of perfume and stockings in his office—trinkets he'd offer as "payment" for sexual favors. Cohn was not the only Hollywood harasser; other powerful studio executives like Darryl Zanuck at 20th Century Fox used their positions to bully women, too. But he was by far the most notorious, and his use and abuse of unequal power dynamics helped normalize the exploitation and harassment of women in Hollywood."

Fantasia (1940)

Fantasia is an animated film produced by Walt Disney and released by Walt Disney Productions. With story direction by Joe Grant and Dick Huemer and production supervision by Ben Sharpsteen, it is the third Disney animated feature film. The film consists of eight animated segments set to pieces of classical music conducted by Leopold Stokowski, seven of which are performed by the Philadelphia Orchestra. Music critic and composer Deems Taylor acts as the film's Master of Ceremonies, providing a live-action introduction to each animated segment.

Scene: The Sorcerer's Apprentice

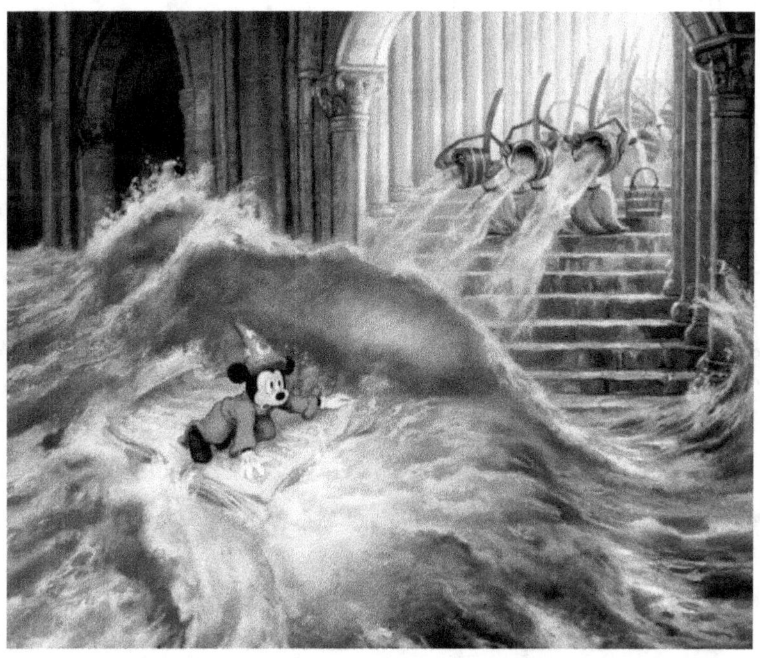

"And now we're going to hear a piece of music that tells a very definite story. As a matter of fact, in this case, the story came first and the composer wrote the music to go with it."
—*Deems Taylor*

The Sorcerer's Apprentice is the third and most famous segment in Disney's 1940 feature film, *Fantasia*, and the only returning segment in its sequel, *Fantasia 2000*. Based on the poem of the same name by Johann Wolfgang von Goethe and the musical piece by Paul Dukas, it stars Mickey Mouse as the titular apprentice. The origin of this film was when Disney began production of The Sorcerer's Apprentice as a stand-alone short. The resulting film proved to be so costly to film that Disney decided to act on Leopold Stokowski's advice and create a feature anthology of shorts in order to recoup the original's cost.

Unlike most of the tracks in the film, which were recorded by the Philadelphia Orchestra, this composition was the first to be recorded for the film by an ad-hoc one-hundred-piece handpicked orchestra of Los Angeles-based session musicians, which Stokowski conducted. The recording was done in January 1938 at the Pathe Studios in Culver City, California.

The scene starts with Sorcerer Yen Sid, who is working on his magic while his apprentice Mickey does the chores. After some magic, Yen Sid puts his hat down, yawns, and goes to his chambers.

When he goes out of sight, Mickey puts the hat on and tries the magic on a broom. He commands the broom to carry buckets of water to fill a cauldron. Since Mickey is satisfied, he sits down on the chair and falls asleep.

He dreams that he was a powerful sorcerer high on top of a pinnacle commanding the stars, planets, and water. Mickey wakes up to find that the room is filled with water, but since the cauldron is overflowing, the broom is not stopping. Mickey tries to stop the broom, but with no success, the broom walks right over him, bringing more and more water. Mickey even tries grabbing one of the buckets, but that too fails. Finally, when the water keeps rising, Mickey, in desperation, grabs a huge ax and chops the broom into pieces. Just when it is all over as Mickey is away, the little wooden split pieces, lying quietly on the floor, begin to come alive, stand upright, grow arms out of their sides, and turn into more brooms with buckets of water. They keep going to the vat and fill it up. Mickey tries to get the water out but finds that there are too many brooms. Mickey goes to a book and looks for a spell to stop the brooms. Mickey finds himself in a whirlpool. Just then, Yen Sid comes in and sees this, and with a wave of his hands, the water descends, and the army of brooms is decreased to one broom. Yen snarls at Mickey as he relinquishes Yen's magical hat back to him. As the downtrodden Mickey leaves, Yen gives him a firm but mischievous kick in the butt for good measure and as a lesson for him never to tamper with things he can't understand or control.

The "Silly Symphonies" shorts had demonstrated what the studio could do in terms of setting animation to music, and Disney was ready to present his animators with the challenge of working with a respected, complex orchestral composition. It was also time for Mickey himself to get what today we might call a "reboot."

By the late 1930s, Mickey—the hero of the Great Depression—had begun to be eclipsed by other characters who were, well, simply funnier. In particular, Donald Duck, who had first appeared in 1934, was leaving audiences in bellyaches with his high ambitions and short temper. How was the mundane Mickey supposed to compete?

For *The Sorcerer's Apprentice*, Mickey got a complete redesign to become both cuter and more expressive. Animator Riley Thompson redrafted the studio's signature character with a larger head and a pear-shaped body that made him more akin to a human child and less like a fishing bobber.

Through his role in the dramatic *Sorcerer's Apprentice*, Mickey also gained some depth of character. The little guy who violently assailed an anthropomorphic broom with an ax in a silhouetted scene influenced by German Expressionism was a far cry from the happy-go-lucky mouse of *Steamboat Willie* (1929)—his first on-screen appearance—a cartoon that, coincidentally, had made its public debut at the same New York theater (the Old Colony) where *Fantasia* would premiere.

Sorcerer's Apprentice was a masterwork of character animation, with a cinematic sweep. While Thompson and other animators worked on Mickey—bringing a UCLA athlete into model for Mickey's motions as the mouse ran and jumped through his flooding castle—Bill Tytla developed the Sorcerer himself. Tytla, who also created Stromboli in *Pinocchio* (1940) and the towering demon in *Fantasia*'s "Night on Bald Mountain" segment, modeled the Sorceror after actor Nigel De Brulier but also incorporated certain details inspired by Walt Disney himself—notably the eyebrow cocked by the Sorcerer (anagrammatically named Yen Sid).

Trivia

Originally at the part when Mickey uses an ax to chop the broom into pieces, thus ruling out the exposure of their shadows, they were going to show all images of Mickey chopping the broom. After chopping the broom to smithereens, the ax had appeared to have its blade broken. Mickey pouted in disgust, threw the ax away, and then sighed in exhaustion. This was considered to have too much grim drama, so, in the end, they only showed their shadows. Also, in comparison, the ax had a much rougher edge than in the final animation.

It was converted into a Little Golden Book by Don Ferguson and illustrated by Peter Emslie.

Mickey's role was originally intended for Dopey from *Snow White and the Seven Dwarfs* (1938), hence a similar wardrobe.

Here is a montage of the entire *Sorcerer's Apprentice* segment from *Fantasia*.

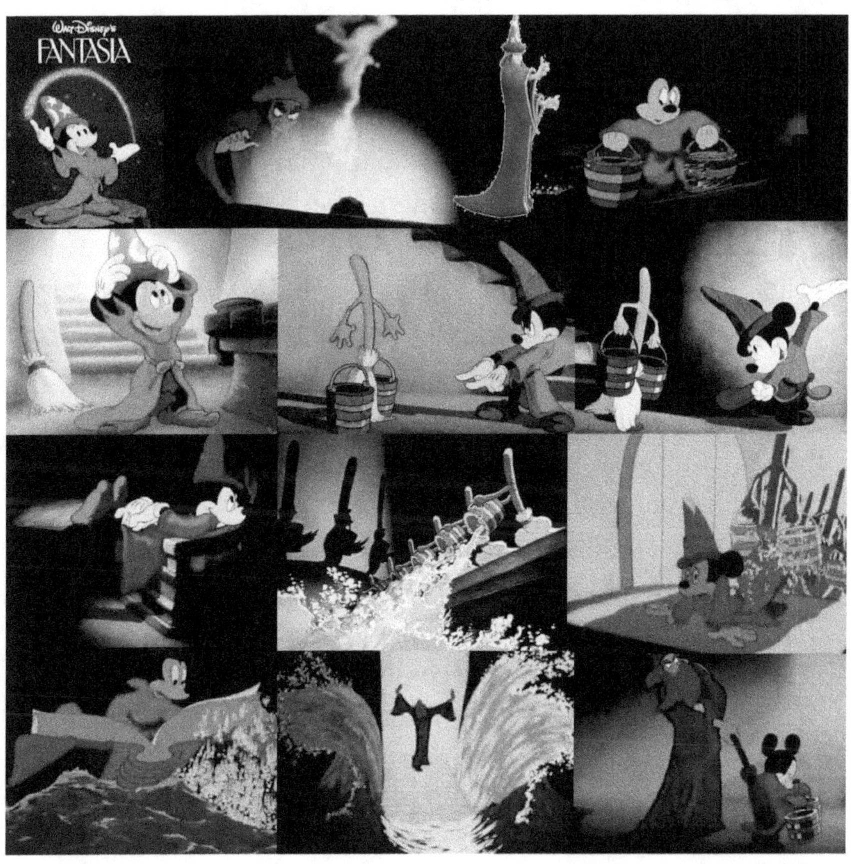

Following Goethe's poem and Dukas' symphonic piece and the film *Fantasia*, the term "Sorcerer's Apprentice" has had numerous iterations as the title of various media pieces. These include several fiction and nonfiction books, including novels by Elspeth Huxley and Hanns Heins Ewers. Nonfiction books with this title include a travel book, *Sorcerer's Apprentice*, by Tahir Shah. *The Sorcerer's Apprentice* is also the title of a Doctor Who novel by Christopher Bulis.

"The Sorcerer's Apprentice" is a 1962 episode of *Alfred Hitchcock Presents* featuring Brandon de Wilde as mentally-troubled youth Hugo, coveting the magic wand of a kindly magician.

"Top Secret Apprentice," is a segment of the *Tiny Toons Adventures* episode. Broadcast on February 1, 1991, it's a modern version of the story, with Buster Bunny messing around with Bugs Bunny's cartoon scenery machine and getting himself into a big heap of trouble. Like the *Fantasia* segment, there is no dialogue, saved for a line by Buster in the end.

There is a live-action film, *The Sorcerer's Apprentice* (2010), featuring a scene based on Goethe's poem (and the *Fantasia* version), produced by Jerry Bruckheimer and starring Nicolas Cage. In the scene, Dave (Jay Baruchel) tries to use magic to clean his lab, but loses control of his animated cleaning mops and forces him to cancel his date with Becky. He is saved because of Balthazar's (Nicholas Cage) intervention and, disillusioned, decides to give up on magic until Becky unknowingly changes his mind. Based on Yen Sid in *Fantasia* and Baruchel as David "Dave" Stutler, a highly intelligent college student who becomes Blake's reluctant apprentice

The scene from the movie can be seen in the left frame while the original scene from *Fantasia* can be seen to the right.

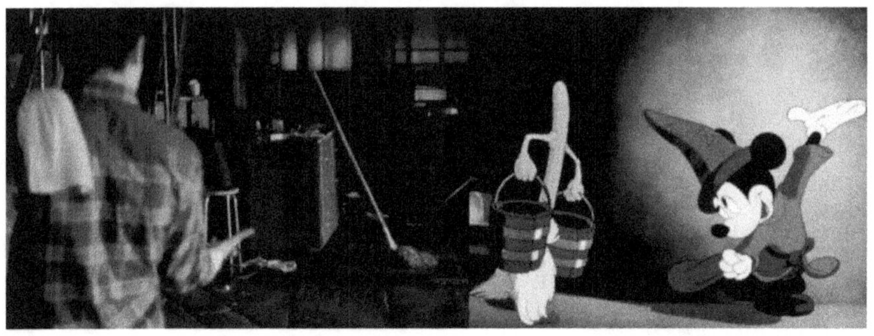

The cleaning spell scene from the 2010 film in this wide-angle shot.

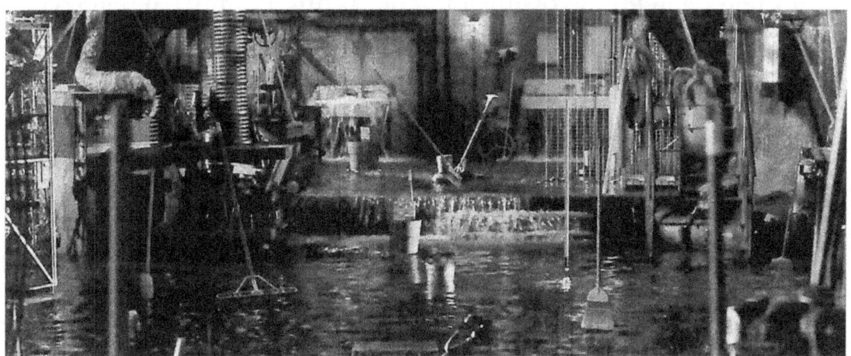

The Philadelphia Story (1940)

The Philadelphia Story is a romantic comedy film directed by George Cukor, starring Cary Grant, Katharine Hepburn, James Stewart, and featuring Ruth Hussey. The film was based on the 1939 Broadway play of the same name by Philip Barry. The film was produced by Joseph L. Mankiewicz. The music was composed by Franz Waxman, and the cinematography was done by Joseph Ruttenberg. The socialite character of the play of Tracy Lord (performed by Katharine Hepburn in the film) was inspired by Helen Hope Montgomery Scott (1904–1995), a beautiful socialite known for her hijinks, whose family had been Philly royalty for generations. (Vanity Fair called her "the unofficial queen of Philadelphia's WASP oligarchy.") Her husband, railroad heir Edgar Scott, had been friends with playwright Philip Barry since their days at Harvard, and the Scotts and Barrys often socialized. Barry used some of Helen's exploits during the 1920s and 1930s as inspiration for Tracy Lord's free-spirited ways.

Scene: The Face Shove

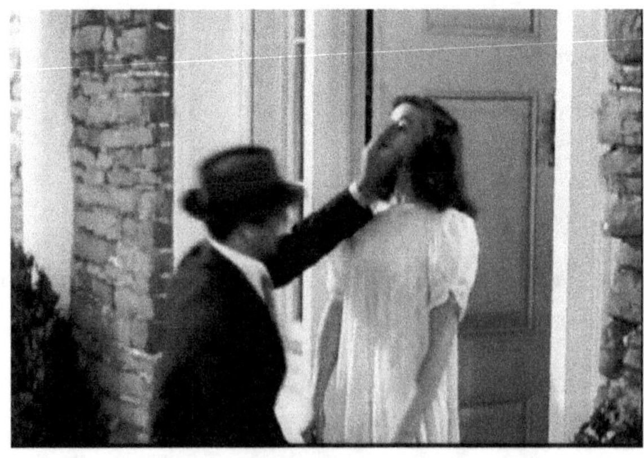

In the opening sequence to the movie, Tracy's attitude causes a marital rift with her childhood sweetheart, sportsman, and recovering alcoholic C. K. Dexter Haven (Cary Grant), leading to his eviction from their house and their eventual divorce. The famous comedic opening scene—or prologue—is a marvelous, expressive one that plays without dialogue at all. It immediately cues the audience into the personalities, interactions, and relationships of the main characters.

C. K. Dexter Haven (Cary Grant), with an angry expression on his face, slams the front door of a super-wealthy estate and carries his suitcases to a car parked in front. A moment later, his future ex-wife, a wealthy and spoiled but high-spirited socialite, Tracy Lord (Katharine Hepburn) with the pet name of "Red," dressed in her nightgown, follows him out the door—she holds his bag of golf clubs and a wooden pipe holder. She smashes the holder to the ground, and then with a cold, imperious look removes one of the clubs from the bag and throws the entire bag at him. Then, while he watches, she gives him a contemptuous and haughty smile and adds insult to injury. She deliberately breaks the club over her knee and tosses the two pieces at him, and then marches back toward the front door. He is infuriated and enraged—with an accompanying snare drumbeat, he follows her back to the house and cocks his fist to hit her, but then hesitates—he cannot quite bring himself to strike her. Instead, in a classic image, he palms her face and pushes her down to the floor (out of the frame) through the doorway. In superficial terms, the film is showing us just how bad relations got between Dexter and Tracy. We do not learn why they divorced until later in the film, but we do see that they both lost the ability to comport themselves peaceably. In addition, we see that their shows of frustration differ: Tracy takes her anger out on Dexter's possessions, while Dexter takes his anger out on Tracy.

This is the prelude to the "face shove." Tracy has deposited all of Dexter's belongings on the front porch and is about to attack his golf clubs.

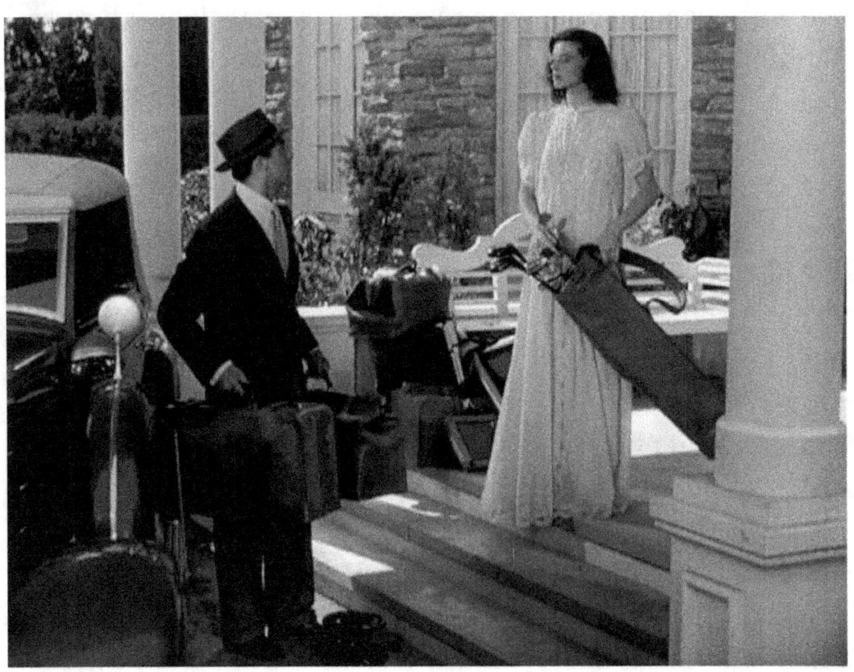

A cameraman on the set, Joseph Ruttenberg, recalling *The Philadelphia Story* in 1990, wrote: "Everyone had enormous fun on the movie. The days and nights were sweltering that summer of 1940, but nobody cared. Cary got along very well with Kate Hepburn." According to Ruttenberg, Hepburn enjoyed being pushed so much that she had Cary do it to her over and over again.

The Take of January 29, 2016, examined the question: What is the significance of the opening scene of *The Philadelphia Story*?

"If we consider the context of the film as well as its content, we can also note that Hepburn was labeled 'box office poison' in 1938, two years prior to the film's release. The label not only referred to the actress' recent string of flops but also to popular audience disapproval of Hepburn's perceived hardness of character, a cold pridefulness unbecoming to a properly feminine celebrity of the era. In this context, *The Philadelphia Story* portrays not only Tracy Lord's comeuppance but also Katharine Hepburn's as well. Beginning the film with a scene in which we see the haughty actress literally pushed down to the floor by rising star Cary Grant (whose flops—two of which co-starred Hepburn—did not harm his career) offered the perfect proof to an audience that an independent, headstrong woman could be humbled."

Seventy-five years later, Peter Bradshaw wrote, "*The Philadelphia Story* review—fun and wit rise like champagne bubbles." *The Guardian* (February 12, 2015) said, "However stagily preposterous, George Cukor's 1940 movie *The Philadelphia Story*, now rereleased, is also utterly beguiling, funny and romantic. ... The fun and wit rise like champagne bubbles, but there is a deceptive strength in the writing and performances." Bradshaw also notes that the film is the "most famous example of the intriguing and now-defunct prewar genre of comedy of remarriage."

The Fighting 69th (1940)

The Fighting 69th is a war film starring James Cagney, Pat O'Brien, and George Brent. The plot follows the actual exploits of New York City's infamous Irish 69th Infantry Regiment during World War I. The real Father Duffy was the regimental chaplain of "the fighting 69th," a group of Irish national guardsmen who were incorporated into the Rainbow Division in 1917 after distinguishing themselves in combat. The regiment was first penned that nickname by Confederate General Robert E. Lee during the Civil War. In addition, many of the events depicted (training at Camp Mills, the Mud March, dugout collapse at Rouge Bouquet, crossing the Ourcq River, etc.) actually happened in real life.

Scene: Opening Crawl

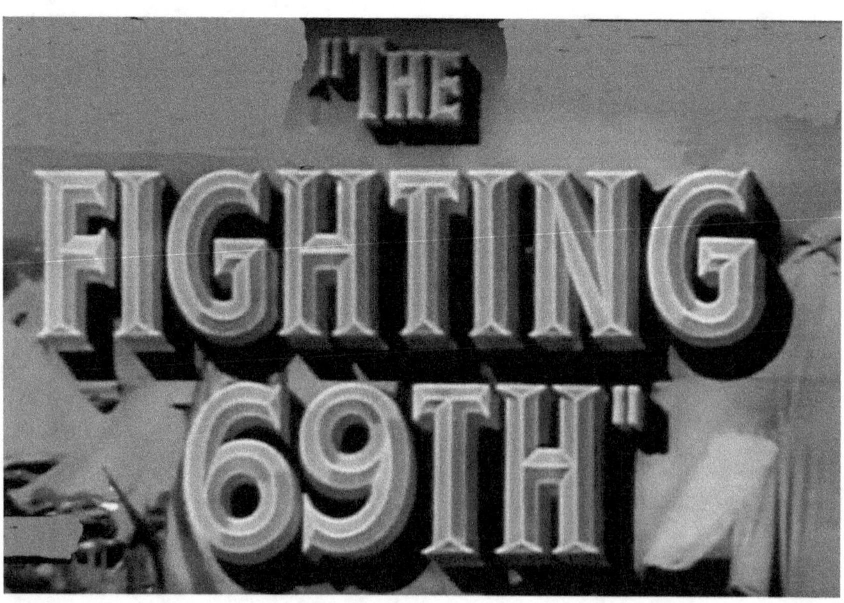

The movie opens with a very stirring rendition of the famous Irish jig "Garryowen." "Garryowen," also known as "Garyowen," "Garry Owen," and "Gary Owens," is an Irish tune for a quick-step dance. It was selected as a marching tune for Australian, British, Canadian, and American military formations, including General George Armstrong Custer's 7th Cavalry Regiment and Australia's 2 Cav Regiment. A crawl dedicates the film to the 69th Regiment and the Rainbow Division assembled for training at Camp Mills, New York, in 1917.

This is an actual photograph of the 69th Regiment at Camp Mills. It was taken on August 25, 1917. The narrative with the photograph reads as follows: "The 'Fighting 69th' which will form part of the new Rainbow Division, arriving last week at their temporary quarters Camp Mills, Garden City, L. I. for intensive training before being sent overseas."

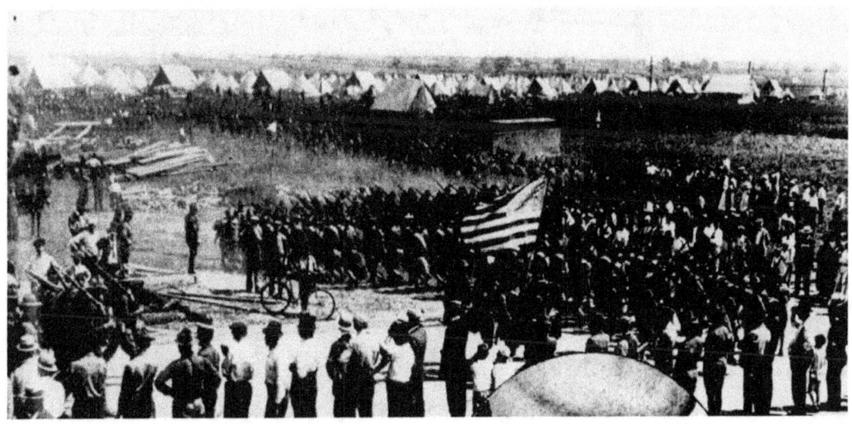

The movie crawl introduces the four real-life historical characters depicted in the film: the Colonel, William "Wild Bill" Donovan (George Brent); the Chaplin, Father Duffy (Pat O'Brien); the battalion commander, Lt. Oliver Ames (Dennis Morgan); a platoon commander; and the poet, Sergeant Joyce Kilmer (Jeffrey Lynn); along with the fictional character Jerry Plunkett (James Cagney).

Scene: Rouge Bouquet

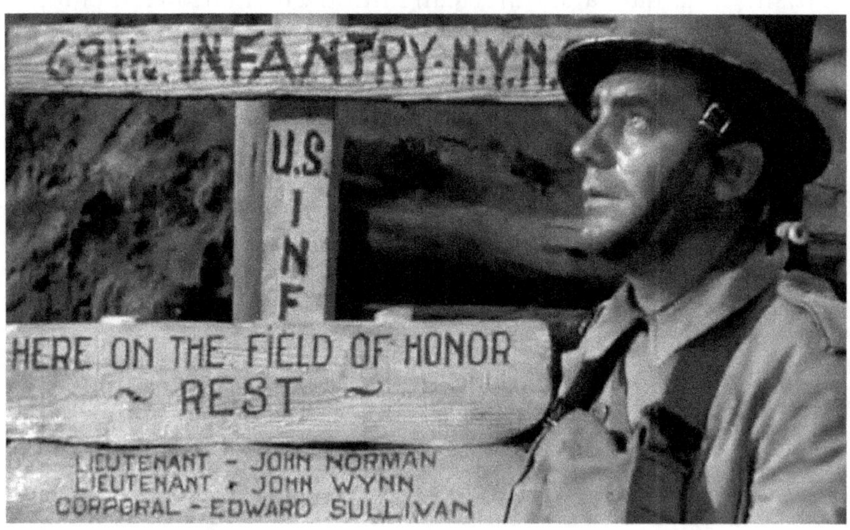

Despised by the other men, cocky and arrogant Jerry Plunkett causes a massacre at Rouge Bouquet when he disobeys orders and inadvertently incites the Germans to attack. This is a profoundly sad scene from *The Fighting 69th* depicting an actual event which (sadly) inspired the poem "Rouge Bouquet" by Sergeant/poet Joyce Kilmer, also a member of the 69th (known in WW1 as the 165th Regiment, 42nd "Rainbow" Division). Father Duffy pays homage to the fallen dead in the film. On March 7, 1918, a German artillery shell struck a dugout shelter and buried twenty-two members of E Company. Two men were rescued, five bodies were recovered during the rescue work, but fifteen remained entombed.

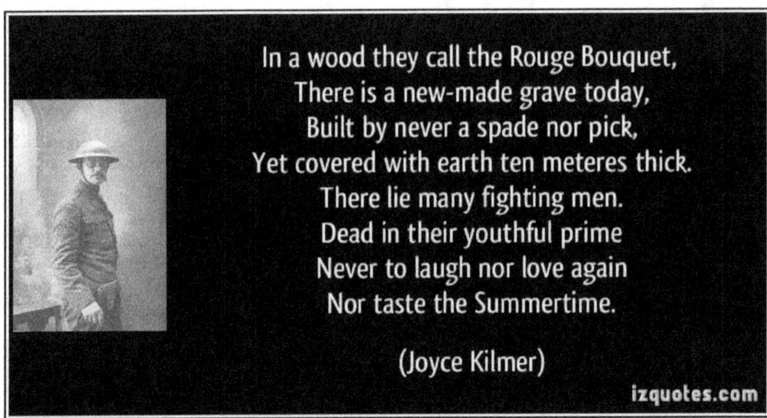

The 69th Infantry Regiment is an infantry regiment of the United States Army. It is from New York City, part of the New York Army National Guard. It is known as the "Fighting Sixty-Ninth."

Films depicting the service of the Fighting 69th Regiment:

1940: The World War I exploits of the regiment are the subject of the Warner Bros. film *The Fighting 69th*. An advisor to the film was former member Captain John T. Prout, who later was a major general in the Irish Army. The film was shown at drills to all persons joining the regiment through the 1970s.

1941: The comedy *Buck Privates* has the character Julia mention that her father was a captain in the "Fighting 69th."

1948: In the movie *Fort Apache*, Sergeant Major Michael O'Rourke (Ward Bond) had been a major in the 69th.

1993: The regiment is shown receiving general absolution from Reverend William Corby before going into battle at Gettysburg in the film *Gettysburg*.

2003: The regiment's attack on Marye's Heights during the Battle of Fredericksburg is depicted in the film *Gods and Generals*. They can be seen wearing the regiment's traditional green boxwood sprigs in their kepis during the attack.

2006: Fictional veterans of the Fighting 69th are portrayed in season three of HBO's *Deadwood* series, as agents of George Hearst.

2007: The military units in the film remake *I Am Legend* are members of the Fighting 69th.

2008: The film *Cloverfield* depicts the 69th Infantry Regiment and other elements of the regular and reserve military doing battle with a giant monster in the streets of New York City.

The Grapes of Wrath (1940)

The Grapes of Wrath is a drama film directed by John Ford. It was based on John Steinbeck's 1939 Pulitzer Prize-winning novel of the same name. It relates the heart-wrenching story of one fictional family (Joads), like so many real ones, who were caught up in one of the largest forced mitigations in American history. During the 1930s, due to severe drought and decades of farming without crop rotation or other means of erosion prevention, severe dust storms blew away the topsoil of vast areas of the central plains of the US and Canada, which became known as the Dust Bowl. Coupled with the economic disaster of the Great Depression, this ecological-agricultural crisis forced hundreds of thousands of people, many of them tenant farmers, off their lands, migrating from place to place in search of farm work to survive. Many of these people, lured by promises of abundant opportunities, headed to California. Although they were from a number of states and regions, the term "Okie"—coined for a native of Oklahoma, one of the hardest-hit areas—was attached to the waves of families desperately heading West, their few remaining possessions piled high on old, barely operating vehicles. Those who made it to California found little work, poor living conditions, a great deal of hatred, resentment, and prejudice, and even physical violence directed against them.

The film features Henry Fonda as Tom Joad and Jane Darwell as Ma Joad in the starring roles.

Scene: I'll Be There

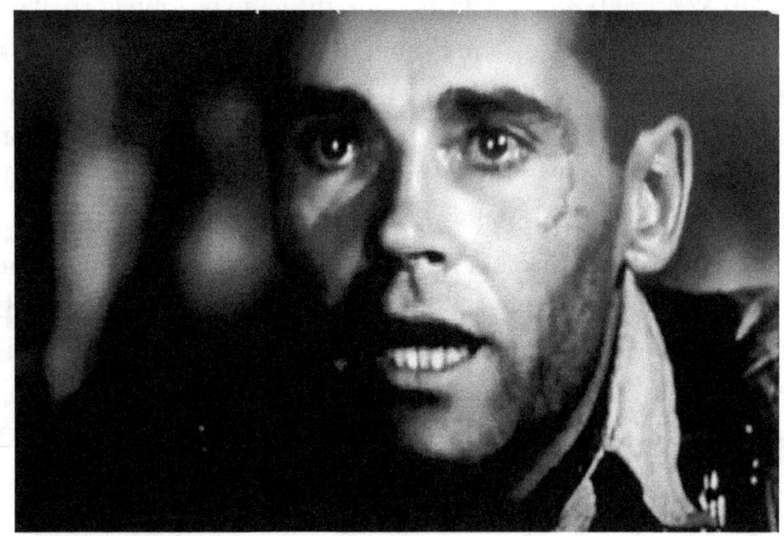

Tom Joad: [Speaking to Ma Joad] Well, maybe it's like Casey says. A fellow ain't got a soul of his own, just little piece of a big soul, the one big soul that belongs to everybody, then...

Ma Joad: Then what, Tom?

Tom Joad: Then it don't matter. I'll be all around in the dark—I'll be everywhere. Wherever you can look—wherever there's a fight, so hungry people can eat, I'll be there. Wherever there's a cop beatin' up a guy, I'll be there. I'll be in the way guys yell when they're mad. I'll be in the way kids laugh when they're hungry, and they know supper's ready, and when the people are eatin' the stuff they raise and livin' in the houses they build—I'll be there, too.

"The Grapes of Wrath still looks like an earnest and touching attempt by the film industry to honor years of national hardship and sacrifice, and Fonda's Tom Joad is timeless and true and a key warning of how a society may make outlaws out of its best material."
—David Thomson, *Have You Seen...?* 1975

Scene: We're the People

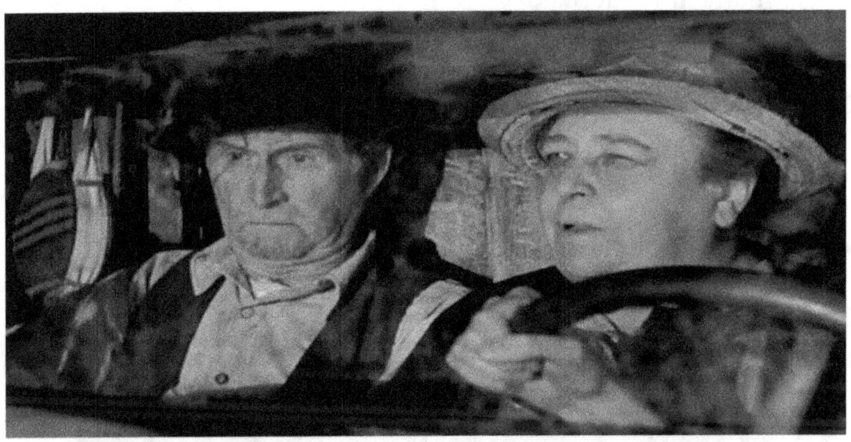

When Darryl F. Zanuck suggested to John Ford that, to create an upbeat ending, he used Ma Joad's "we're the people" monologue for a closing scene, Ford told Zanuck to direct it himself—which he did. Ma Joad, despite the loss of her home, the breakup of her family, and the physical hardships, prejudice, and ridicule that she and her family have had to endure, still retains her undying belief in the common people and their undying resilience. "We keep a-coming. We're the people that live. They can't wipe us out; they can't lick us. We'll go on forever, Pa, cos we're the people."

In this scene, Darwell beautifully captured what poet Carl

Sandburg penned in his 1936 work *The People, Yes*. The Depression years provoked in Sandburg a profound desire to console "the people of the earth, the family of man," and to lift the hopes of the people. Believing that economic inequity lay at the root of all social injustice, from labor conflict to racial and civil strife, he responded to the economic and social upheavals of the 1930s with *The People, Yes:*

> The people is the grand canyon of humanity and many
> many miles across.
> The people rest on land and weather, on time, and the
> changing winds.
> The people have come far and can look back and say,
> "We will go farther yet."

In recognition of her gritty, resilient, and tenacious role of Ma Joad, Jane Darwell won Best Actress at the thirteenth Academy Awards ceremony.

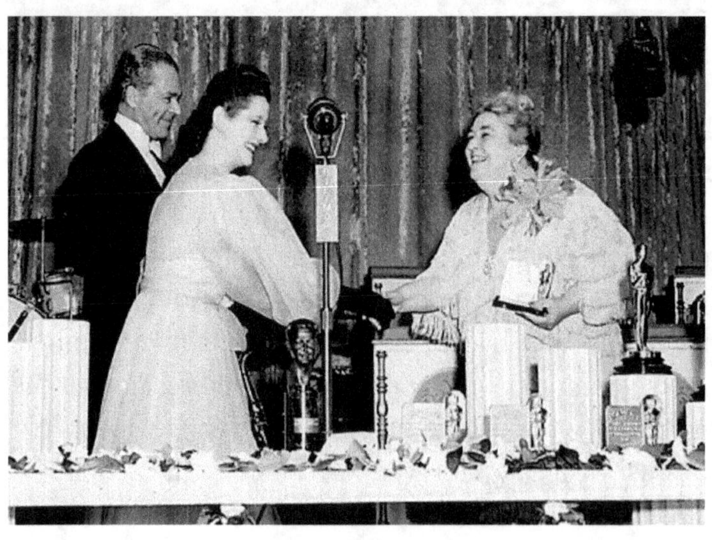

The Great Dictator (1940)

The Great Dictator is a powerful political satire comedy-drama film written, directed, produced, scored by, and starring British comedian Charlie Chaplin, following the tradition of many of his other films. Having been the only Hollywood filmmaker to continue to make silent films well into the period of sound films, this was Chaplin's first "all-talking, all-sound" feature film.

Chaplin's film advanced a stirring, controversial condemnation of Adolf Hitler, Benito Mussolini, fascism, antisemitism, and the Nazis. At the time of its first release, the United States was still formally at peace with Nazi Germany. Chaplin wanted to address the escalating violence and repression of Jews by the Nazis throughout the late 1930s, the magnitude of which was conveyed to him personally by his European Jewish friends and fellow artists. The Third Reich's repressive nature and militarist tendencies were well-known at the time. Later, Chaplin states that had he known the full extent of the Nazi atrocities, he "could not have made fun of their homicidal insanity."

Scene: The Globe

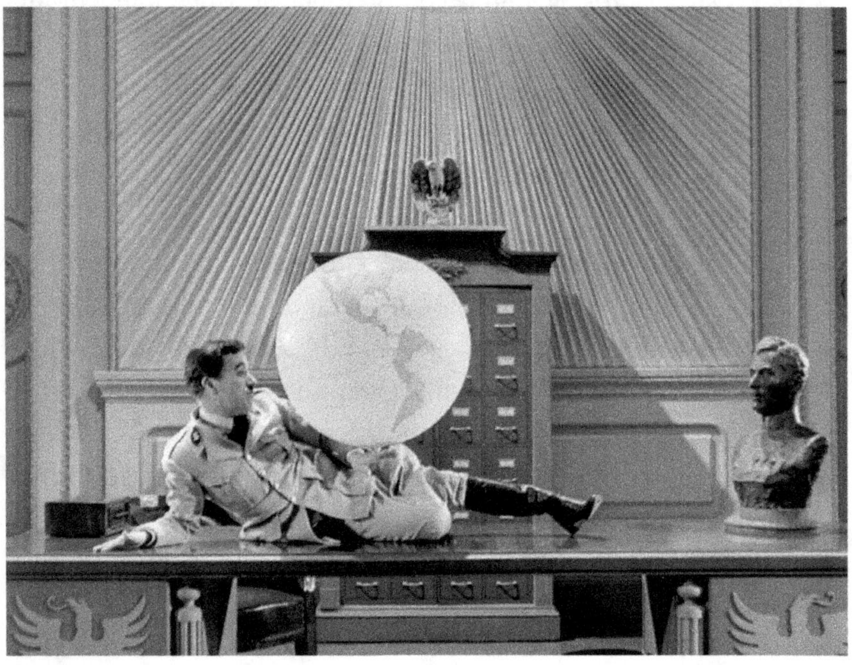

The film contains sequences of great humor and poetry. The scene with Hitler and the globe is one of the most memorable on film. Music from composer Richard Wagner's "Prelude" to his opera *Lohengrin* was used during this scene. After longingly gazing at the globe wanting to possess, dominate, control, and care for all that he sees, he declares himself "Emperor of the World." He then begins a delicate ballet/dance playfully bouncing the globe into the air with his hands, head, feet, and butt. As he holds out the conquered world, it suddenly explodes in front of his face—he holds up the tattered rubber rag—all that is left of his world. Distressed, he whirls away, puts his head on his desk, and with his back to the camera, he bursts into tears.

Adenoid Hynkel's (Charlie Chaplin) dance with the globe was originally written as a scene in which he cuts up a map of the world to rearrange the countries the way he wants. When this evolved into the globe dance, Chaplin spent six days over a two-month period filming the sequence, plus three days of retakes.

In 1928, in a home movie, Chaplin reviewed his interest in playing a god-like figure admiring the globe, even donning it with a German helmet.

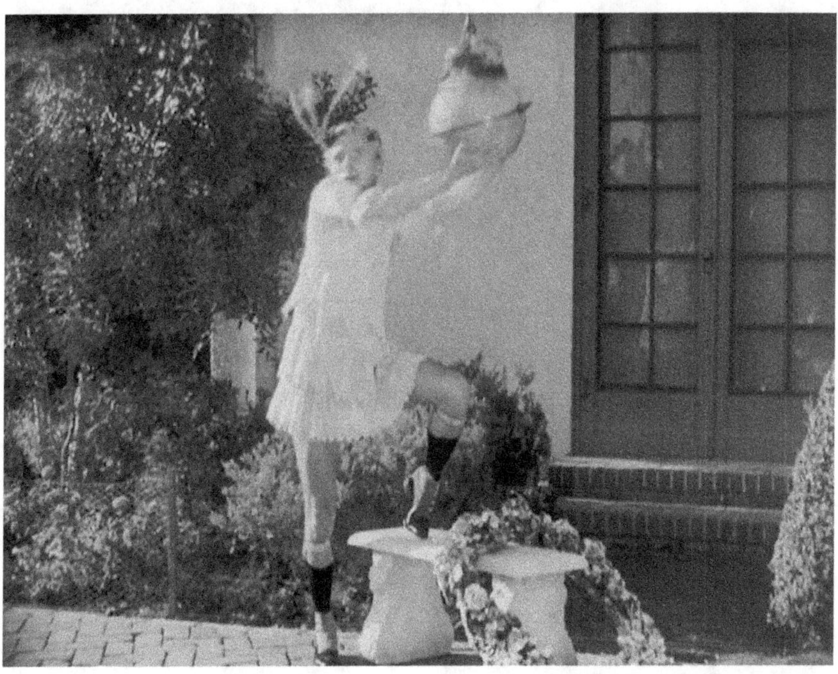

This globe is said to be inspired by a large globe at the German New Reich Chancellery during the Nazi regime (1933–1945).

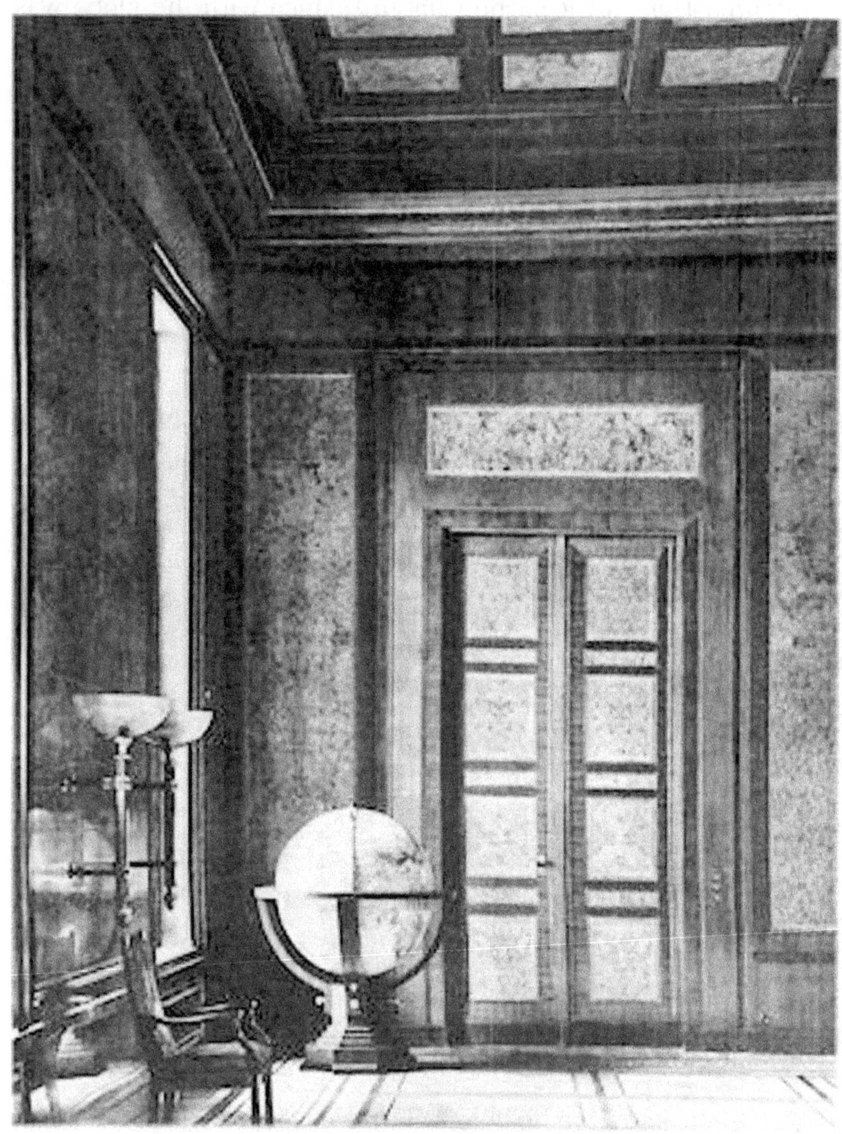

Jeff Saporito wrote a brilliant essay in *The Take* (October 15, 2015) entitled "After 75 years, what is the cinematic legacy of *The Great Dictator?*"

Political satire is important. Its power is obvious, and, decade after decade, satirical films manage to shake the foundation beneath the people and subjects they jest... Charlie Chaplin's first true talking picture which took jabs at history's most prolific terror by outwardly mocking him. It's quite possibly the most daring and poignant political satire in cinema, and the one to which all its successors owe a debt. It's perfectly executed slapstick set against the greatest atrocity in world history...

Hollywood was hesitant to produce anti-Hitler propaganda. United States involvement in the war in 1940 was still a tumultuous concept. The Hays Code in place even deemed anti-Nazi films to be in violation of American's neutrality stance and advised against their creation. But Chaplin didn't care. He had an important point to make, and found a way to make it. His films had always been about people—about regular, every day, sensible folks getting the opportunities they deserved and fighting against injustice. The absurdity of Hitler's concept of a 'master race' and the generally pompous nature of diplomats shouting, posturing, and needing to be heard was conceptually insane to him...

Vue Weekly notes:

Chaplin remained prescient and circumspect enough to make a comedy lashing out at a tragedy's progenitor, taking the failed artist-turned-genocidal-tyrant seriously enough to mock him on-screen. (Chaplin realized that stonily self-serious right-wingers tend to hate, most of all, people laughing at them.) From the 21st century's first celebrity and cinema's first great comic visionary, this was a feat of artistic ambition and bravery, in the face of a brutal fascist nightmare, that hasn't been matched since in commercial movie-making...

The backing music as Chaplin speaks is Wagner's Lohengrin, the same tune heard earlier in the film when Hynkel dances with the balloon version of Earth, choreographing his takeover of the world (Wagner was Hitler's favorite composer). There's a potent parallel between Hynkel's dreams of universal empire and Chaplin's universal humanity. Hynkel's balloon eventually pops, after all, and Chaplin's legacy lives on.

Waterloo Bridge (1940)

Waterloo Bridge is a remake of both the 1931 American drama film and the 1930 play of the same name. The film was made by Metro-Goldwyn-Mayer, directed by Mervyn LeRoy and produced by Sidney Franklin and Mervyn LeRoy. The movie about star-crossed lovers is filmed with the backdrop of World War I with intermixes of scenes of World War II. It is Leigh's first movie after *Gone With the Wind* (1939). Vivien Leigh wanted Laurence Olivier to play the role of Roy Cronin in this film and was unhappy that Robert Taylor, one of MGM's top stars at the time, had been cast instead, although she had enjoyed working with him, in a supporting role on *A Yank at Oxford* (1938).

Scene: Aude Lang Syne

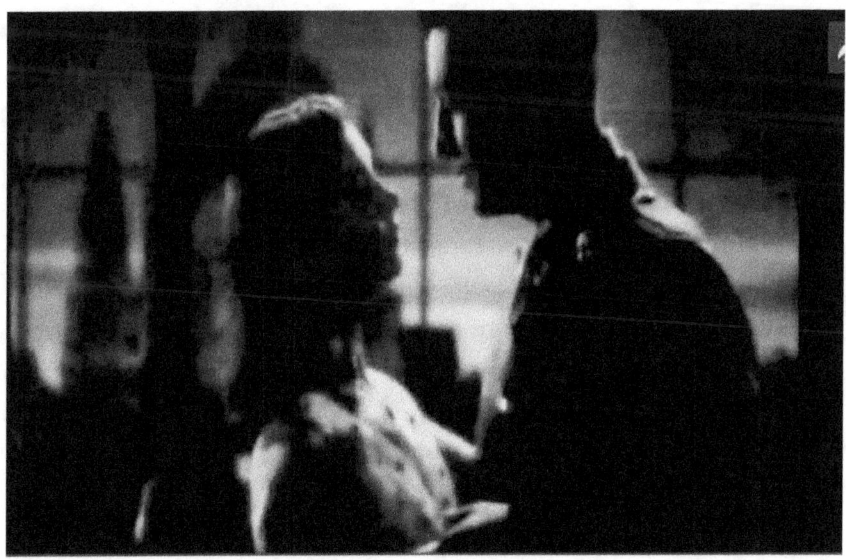

Director Mervyn Leroy, who had begun his career in silent films, knew when to let the images tell the story without dialogue, and this cinematic nuance is quite evident in the memorable scene in the nightclub. It is also my favorite scene in the entire movie. It's the last dance of the evening, and Myra (Vivian Leigh) and Roy (Robert Taylor) are dancing to "Auld Lang Syne." One by one, the musicians finish playing their parts and snuff out the candles, until, finally, the music ends, and in darkness and silence, the lovers kiss. As Leroy explained, "A look, a gesture, a touch can convey much more meaning than spoken sentences."

"Auld Lang Syne" is a Scots-language poem written by Robert Burns. It is well known in many countries, especially in the English-speaking world, its traditional use being to bid farewell to the old year at the stroke of midnight on New Year's Eve. By extension, it is also sung at funerals, graduations, and as a farewell or ending to other occasions.

The poem's Scots title may be translated into standard English as "old long since" or, more idiomatically, "long long ago," "days gone by," or "old times."

Since *Waterloo Bridge*, the song "Auld Lang Syne" has appeared in no less than twenty-one movies in various forms. These are as follows: *The Gold Rush* (1942), *Meet Me in St. Louis* (1944), *It's a Wonderful Life* (1946), *Scandal* (1950), *The Steel Helmet* (1951), *Operation Petticoat* (1959), *The Apartment* (1960), *Ocean's Eleven* (1960), *The Poseidon Adventure* (1972), *More American Graffiti* (1979), *The Quiet Earth* (1985), *Out of Africa* (1985), *The Last Emperor* (1987), *Young Guns* (1988), *Ghostbusters* (1989), *When Harry Met Sally* (1989), *Forrest Gump* (1994), *Elf* (2003), *A Brand New Life* (2009), *The Time Traveler's Wife* (2009), and *New Year's Eve* (2011).

Perhaps the most romantic of these, in tune with *Waterloo Bridge*, is the 1989 film *When Harry Met Sally*. I still remember that wonderful New Year's Eve scene when Harry (Billy Crystal) asks

Sally (Meg Ryan) about the meaning of Auld Lang Syne. She answers, "Auld Lang Syne is about old friends who have parted and meet again." Perfect answer!

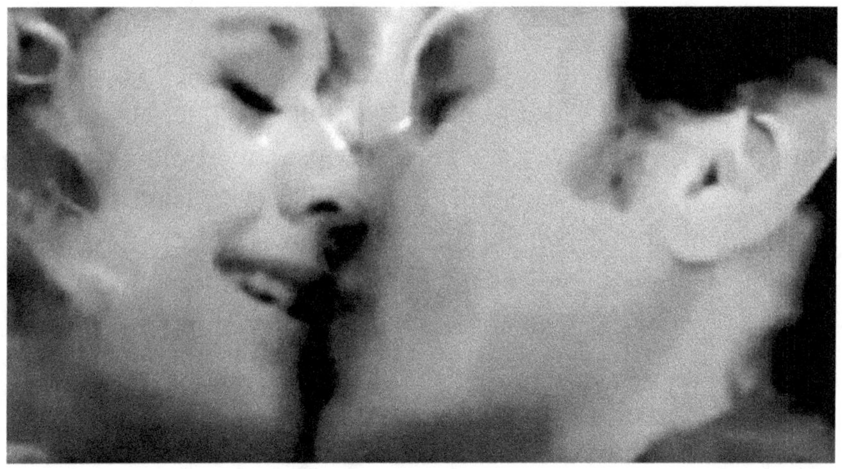

Citizen Kane (1941)

Citizen Kane is an epic drama film by Orson Welles, its producer, co-screenwriter, director, and star. The picture was Welles's first feature film. Nominated for Academy Awards in nine categories, it won an Academy Award for Best Writing (Original Screenplay) by Herman J. Mankiewicz and Welles. Considered by many critics, filmmakers, and fans to be the greatest film ever made, the quasi-biographical film examines the life and legacy of Charles Foster Kane, played by Welles, a character based in part upon the American newspaper magnates William Randolph Hearst and Joseph Pulitzer, Chicago tycoons Samuel Insull and Harold McCormick, and aspects of the screenwriters' own lives.

Scene: Opening Sequence

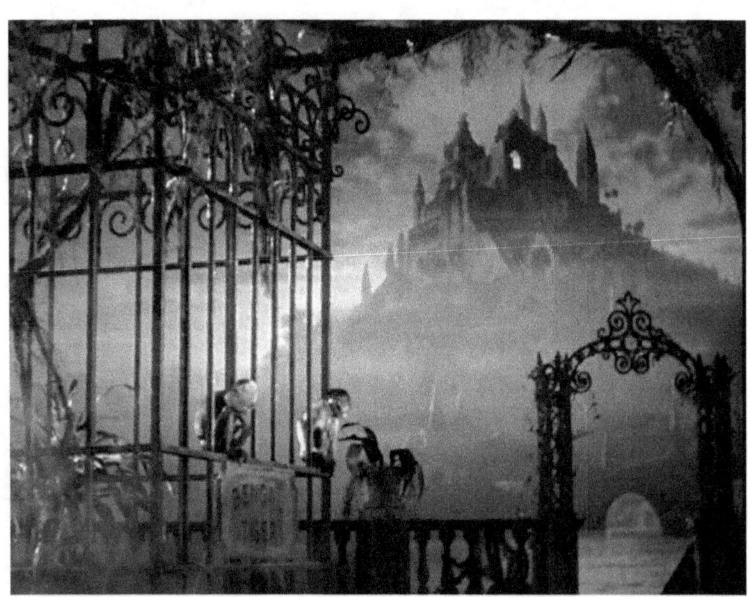

From its very opening sequence, the film displays its bravura visual intelligence. The foreboding introduction to Kane's Xanadu fortress shows a single light from an upper room within.

Through a series of brilliant Wellesian close-ups, the single light in the window remains the focus of the scene in exactly the same place within the frame—simple, artful, fluid, and elegant. The window is the living quarters of the tycoon John Foster Kane. The last sequence of these scenes shows a light in the final close-up of the window. However, almost immediately, this light is extinguished. This marks the last night that Kane will see alive, for the coming dawn will bring an end of a cruel and turbulent life in which the innocence of his youth was stolen, never to be regained during his life. Only as he dies, does he, for an instant, recall the one shining moment of his youth embodied in his dying word: "rosebud."

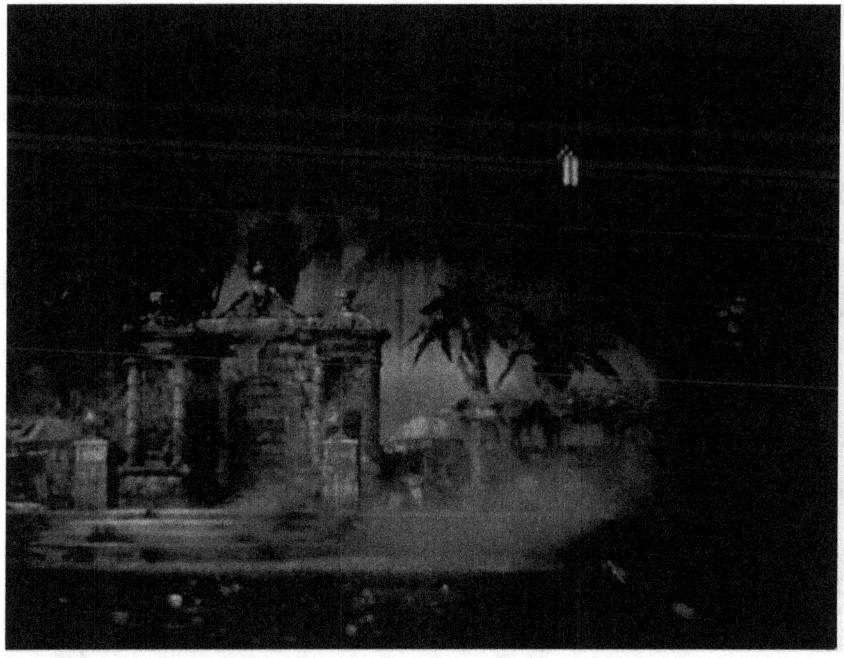

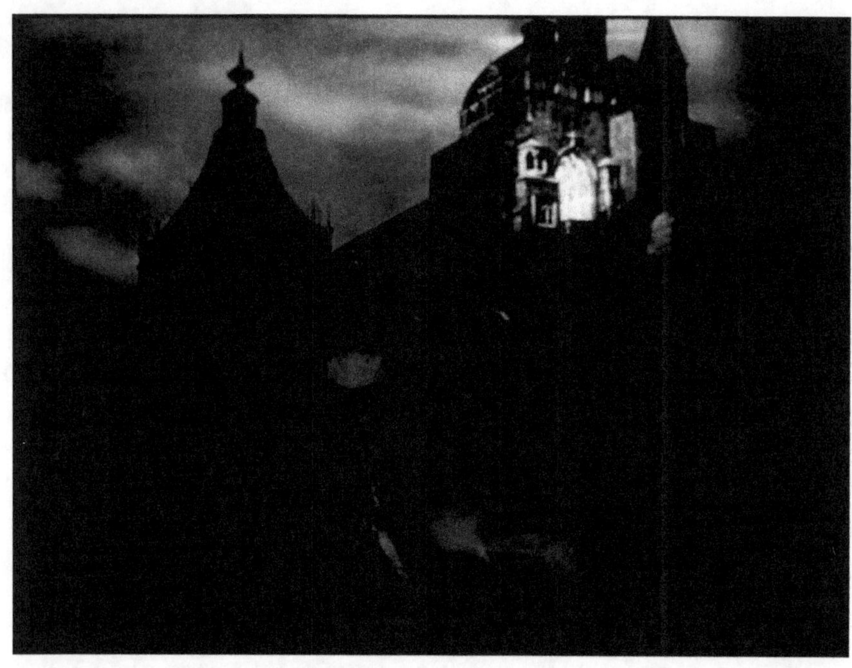

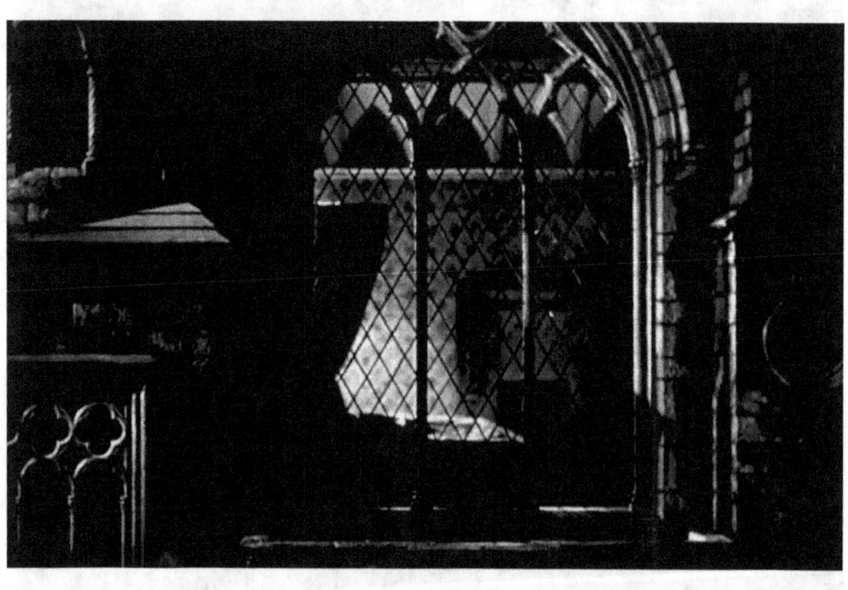

Scene: The Death of Charles Foster Kane

In this almost simultaneous scene, Charles Foster Kane utters the word "rosebud" as the snow globe he is clutching in his hand falls from his hand, as he dies, and crashes onto the titled floor below smashing it into oblivion symbolizing the destiny of Kane's own life.

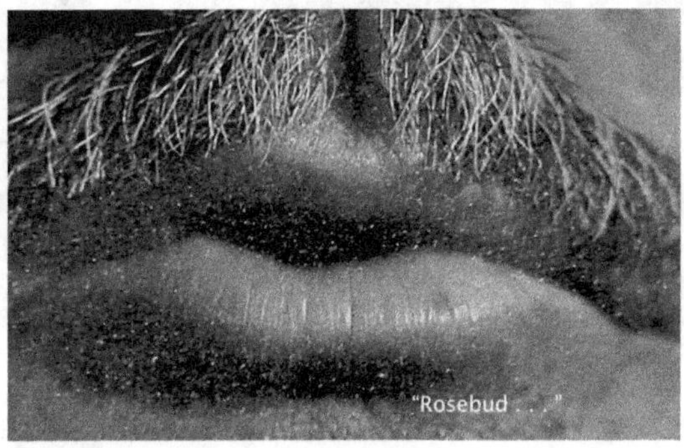

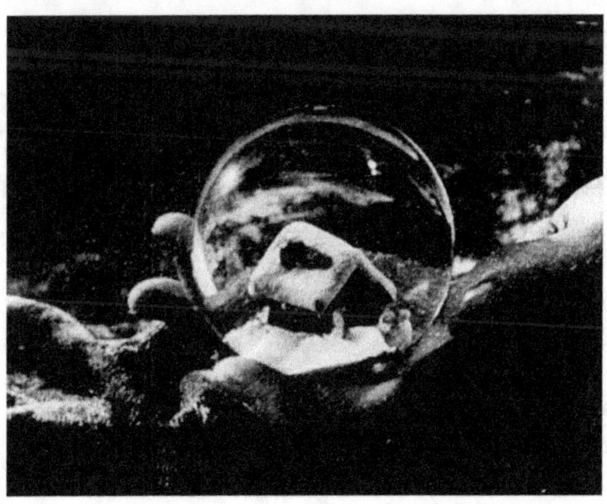

Scene: The Room Trashing

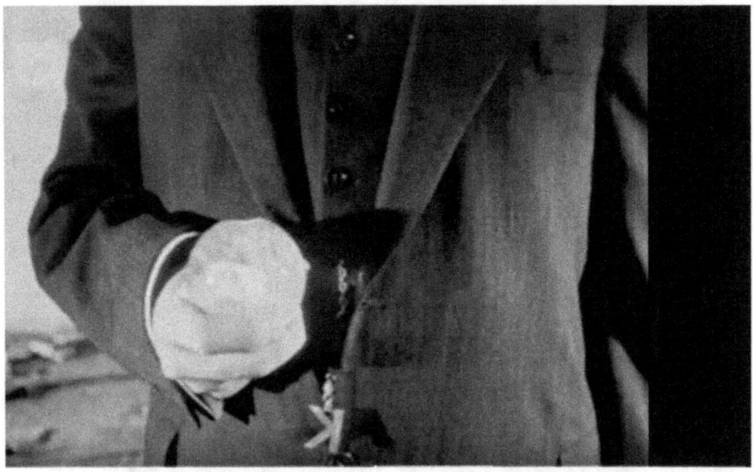

This scene is where we witness Kane destroying Susan's (Susan Alexander Kane, portrayed by Dorothy Comingore) bedroom after she finally leaves him. It is near the end of the film and is seen as one of the film's most iconic scenes.

The scene starts silently, with Kane's anger slowly building up. A low angle is used by Welles to make us feel inferior to and threatened by Kane. He starts by throwing suitcases at the door, symbolizing the anger he feels toward Susan and how he wants to get rid of her. The way he moves about is with stiffness and violence, showing the audience that, in old age, Kane does not come with grace, but defeat. Another series of extreme low-angle shots are used to again connote the power of Kane and that he feels unstoppable. At one point, there is a long shot of Kane while he moves to the other side of the room to continue his reign of utter destruction. This long shot could have been used to represent how the audience might be feeling; they may want to distance themselves from this man due to what he is doing on screen.

As Kane comes back toward the camera, the low angle is used to pan across so that we are at an eye-level view with the snow globe. The camera rests on it before Kane notices it, reinforcing the significance and allowing the audience to link it to his childhood. It is the one time in his life when he was truly happy, and life was truly worth living.

After this, we see the lull after the storm, as he tentatively walks away from the camera, snow globe in hand. Kane holds the snow globe, the camera pans up to his face, and he utters, "Rosebud." This is the first time that the audience has some information on the true meaning and significance of rosebud, very near the end of the film, despite it being what the entire film revolves around. The snow globe has triggered a childhood memory, and also made him realize he is acting like a spoiled child. The contrast of this slow camera shot to the violent eruption we have just witnessed shows a different side of Kane.

Scene: The Basement at Xanadu

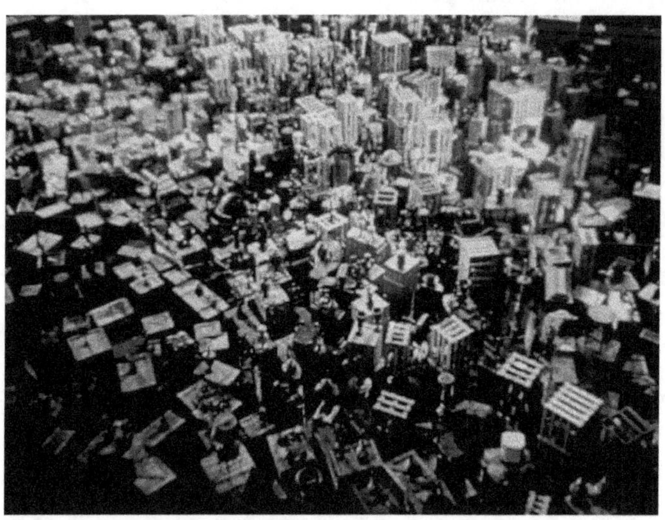

One of its greatest sequences is at the end of the film, when the secret of the word "rosebud," the last word uttered by Charles Foster Kane before he died, is finally revealed.

The camera pulls away from the basement floor to show the incredible accumulation of Kane's acquisitions over a lifetime. Then, the camera slowly glides over years and years of his pitiless pieces of material goods and collected art objects, looking like a broken jigsaw puzzle, a deserted skyscraper city, or a metropolis when photographed from high above. There, in the piles of possessions, are:

Iron bedframes

An open, wooden toy box (with a few dolls and a picture of Kane around the time of his first marriage)

Statues both crated and uncrated

A pile of old newspapers wrapped in twine

A photograph of Kane as a boy with his mother

A snow sled (which is picked up by a workman)

Kane's life appears as a disjointed collection of failed energy to productively use resources.

Director Steven Spielberg paid homage to this basement scene in his closing scene of *Raiders of the Lost Ark* (1981) when the Ark of the Covenant is "buried" in a secret US Government facility amongst literally thousands of packing crates.

Scene: Rosebud

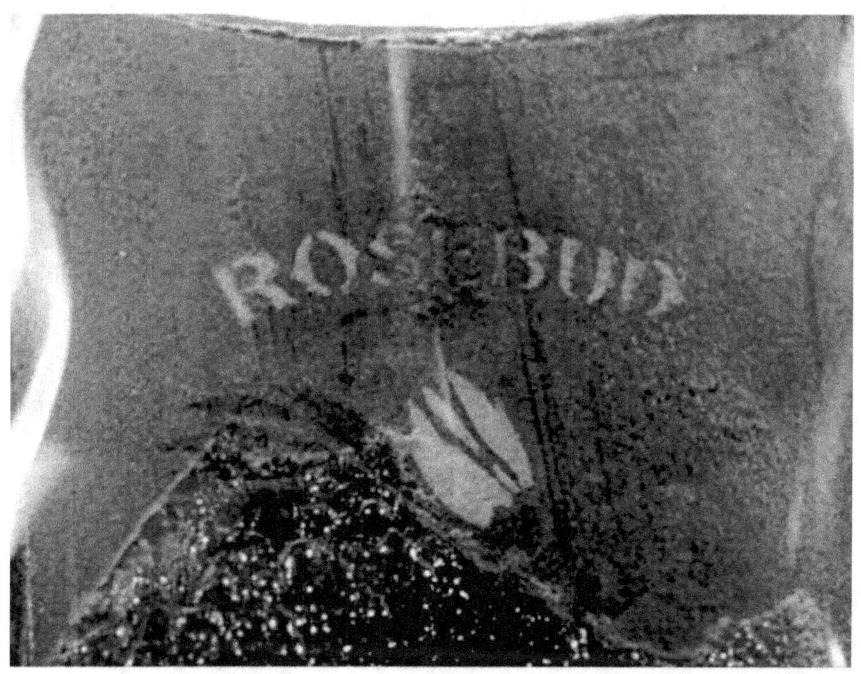

In the basement beneath Xanadu, workers clear away the vast array of junk and articles. A workman is sorting and crating his possessions near an incinerator, a blazing furnace where items are thrown that are considered junk. The worker with the sled in his hands is told by Raymond, the butler, to "throw that junk" into the flames of the incinerator to be consumed, along with an accumulation of other possessions. The sled, the one that young Charles played with when he was with his father and mother early in the film, is an enduring and beautiful symbol of Kane's life.

The name "rosebud" (and its decorative flower) is briefly seen on the sled in a close-up before flames lick the wood, the heat warps and blisters the paint of the wooden surface, and it is consumed by the flames. The "rosebud" sled is a memento from Kane's childhood with his mother, a childhood that was interrupted by the opportunities wealth and fortune bestowed upon him. He rammed banker Walter Park Thatcher (George Coulouris) with the sled when he was forcibly taken away to New York to be raised in more affluent surroundings. The sled symbolized the innocence, beauty, and love that he lost, the love that eluded him—a dying man's memory of a childhood possession that held special meaning.

The Columbia University School of the Arts' Film Language Glossary defines deep focus as "a style or technique of cinematography and staging with great depth of field, using relatively wide-angle lenses and small lens apertures to render in sharp focus near and distant planes simultaneously. A deep-focus shot includes foreground, middle-ground, and extreme-background objects, all in focus."

While other directors and other films employed it earlier in cinematic history, back to the silent era, deep focus is most commonly associated with Orson Welles and his cinematographer Gregg Toland's use of the technique in *Citizen Kane*. The film's use of deep focus and high-contrast lighting established a distinctive, idiosyncratic visual style that Welles would employ throughout his career, with later films employing it to increasingly expressionistic, baroque effect. All the scenes shown in this segment of my book incorporate the deep focus technique.

Directors may use deep focus in only some scenes or even just some shots. Other auteurs choose to use it consistently throughout the movie, either as a stylistic choice or because they believe it represents reality better. Filmmakers such as Steven Spielberg, Akira Kurosaa, Stanley Kubrick, Kenji Mizoguchi, James Wong Howe, Jean Renoir, Terry Gilliam, and so many others used deep focus as part of their signature style.

In 1962, Orson Welles directed the film *The Trial* with Anthony Perkins (in the foreground). Notice how the entire scene is in focus from in front of the camera to way back in the room.

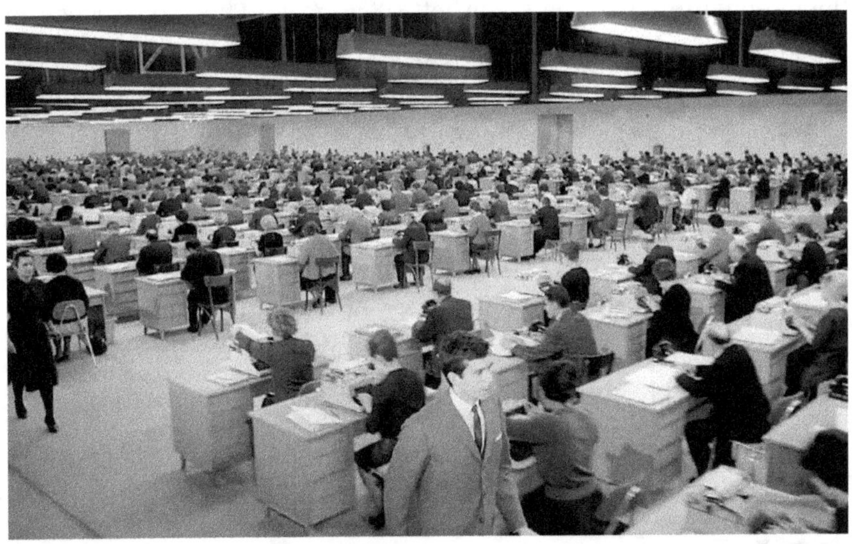

Deep focus is a difficult cinematic technique—it requires intense attention to the details of mise-en-scene and complicates the process of focusing the audience's attention on the most pertinent information in a scene. Notably, the trend in contemporary cinema has been away from deep focus and toward shallow focus. However, when done right, as in the works of Jean Renoir and Orson Welles, deep focus creates a sense of observing a complete world and explores the way time, movement, and space interact in a way that only cinema can.

Gentleman Jim (1942)

Gentleman Jim is a drama starring Errol Flynn as heavyweight boxing champion James J. Corbett (1866–1933). The film traces the life and times of this famous boxer of the past. As bare-knuckled boxing enters the modern era, the brash extrovert Jim Corbett uses new rules and dazzlingly innovative footwork to rise to the top of the boxing world. The supporting cast includes Alexis Smith, Jack Carson, Alan Hale, William Frawley, and Ward Bond as boxer John L. Sullivan. The movie was based upon Corbett's autobiography, *The Roar of the Crowd*, and directed by Raoul Walsh. The role was one of Flynn's favorites. The story was serialized by the *Saturday Evening Post* in six weekly installments during October/November 1894. The following year, G.P. Putnam's Sons published it in book form, marketing it as *The True Tale of the Rise and Fall of a Champion*.

Scene: John L. Sullivan Surrenders the Championship Boxing Belt to Gentleman Jim

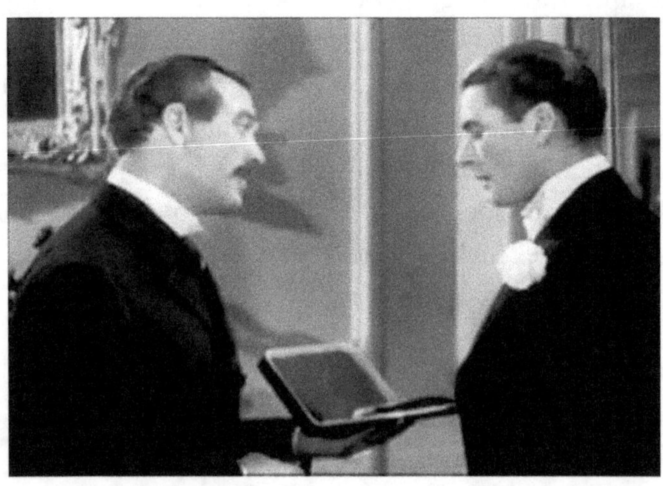

When Corbett becomes a professional prizefighter, he acquires a manager, Billy Delaney (William Frawley), and introduces a new, more sophisticated style of boxing, emphasizing footwork over the unscientific brawling epitomized by world champion John L. Sullivan. After winning several matches, Corbett finally gets the opportunity to take on the great man. Corbett's method of boxing baffles Sullivan, and Corbett wins the Heavyweight Championship title. For the record, Corbett scored a knockout of Sullivan at 1:30 of the 21st round on September 7, 1892 at the Olympic Club in New Orleans, Louisiana. His victory party is unexpectedly interrupted by the defeated Sullivan, who has come to personally present the championship belt to Corbett. They speak graciously of each other, and Jim expresses his deep appreciation of Sullivan's skills and his place in history.

No such scene ever happened, though—in real life, the two men were bitter enemies to the end of their days, with Corbett always showing a particular contempt for Sullivan.

Ward Bond and Errol Flynn appeared in three other films together: *Dodge City* (1939), *Virginia City* (1940), and *Santa Fe Trail* in 1940. *Filmink* magazine called the film:

> "Terrific fun and Flynn is splendid—he rarely acted with such infectious enjoyment and is obviously having the time of his life in the title role, a part which obviously was close to his real-life personality: big-headed, cocky, a bit of a prat, the sort of person who has himself paged all the time at a gym just for the thrill of hearing his name spoken out loud, but with a likable sheen" (Stephen Vagg, "The Films of Errol Flynn." *Filmink,* November 17, 2019).

The famously hard-partying Flynn had been wracked with assorted health problems in 1942, and it all culminated with his collapse during the filming of one of *Gentleman Jim*'s fight sequences. Flynn developed a reputation for womanizing, hard drinking, chain-smoking, and, for a time in the 1940s, narcotics abuse. While the studio had publicly chalked it up to fatigue, the doctors diagnosed a mild heart attack. Alexis Smith recounted in the 1979 biography *The Two Lives of Errol Flynn* by Michael Freedland, how she took the star aside and told him, "It's so silly, working all day and then playing all night and dissipating yourself. Don't you want to live a long life?"

Errol was his usually apparently unconcerned self: "I'm only interested in this half," he told her. "I don't care for the future."

Health issues would plague Flynn for the rest of his film career; he would die at the age of fifty on October 14, 1959, due to a combination of coronary and liver diseases.

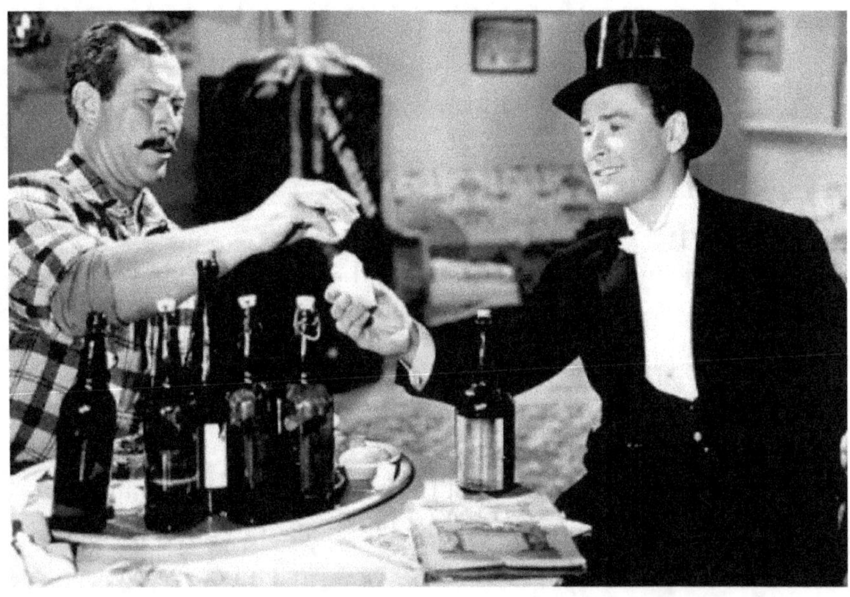

Ward Bond is terrific as John L., especially when he bounds into a bar and makes his famous announcement: "I can lick any man in the house!" He is utterly convincing as a man invariably described as "larger than life." Bond captures Sullivan's gusto and Vesuvian temperament, though in a scene when he and Corbett nearly come to blows, he probably overdoes it. My favorite moment is the shot of Sullivan walking down a city street with a crowd of kids following him—a scene memorably etched by Charles Dana Gibson.

Bond's triumph is even more telling when put up against the only other film portrayal of Sullivan of which I'm aware: Frank Tuttle's *The Great John L.* (1945), in which the novice actor Gregg McClure plays Sullivan.

As for Flynn, he was allegedly quite the brawler at his Sydney grammar school. "I was bigger than most," the actor wrote in his autobiography. "I was an athlete, quite good at tennis, swimming, boxing, and ready to fight if picked on."

In 1927, Flynn entered the world of amateur boxing, ducking it out with heavyweights and earning praise for his "elusiveness" and straight left. According to biographer Thomas McNulty, Flynn was infamous for his "deceptive dance." As he circled around his rival, Flynn would quickly look down at his feet. His opponent would instinctively follow his glance, and that's when the actor would send his foe tumbling to the mat.

In 1937, Flynn played the role of Gerald Beresford Wicks in the movie *The Perfect Specimen.* In one scene, he wins a boxing match in place of another character in the movie.

When Flynn finally went to work for Warner Bros., he was placed under the tutelage of Mushy Callahan. A former Junior Welterweight Champion, Callahan taught boxing to some of the biggest stars in the business, including Frank Sinatra, Paul Newman, and Elvis Presley When Flynn was cast as the legendary Jim Corbett in Gentleman Jim (1942), Mushy was the man who helped Errol improve his game.

Callahan was actually quite impressed with Flynn's talents and claimed, "Next to [James] Cagney, Errol Flynn is the best fighter on the Warner lot...He can take punishment and isn't afraid to wade in." In fact, according to The Sydney Morning Herald, Flynn was such a natural boxer that the Warner Bros. publicity team cooked up a crazy story claiming he'd competed for Great Britain in the 1928 Olympics and had "whaled the stuffing out of assorted lads of various nationalities."

In 1966, the actor James Davidson played Corbett in the episode "The Fight San Francisco Never Forgot" of the syndicated western television series Death Valley Days, hosted by Ronald Reagan.

Casablanca (1942)

Casablanca is a romantic drama film directed by Michael Curtiz based on Murray Burnett and Joan Alison's unproduced stage play *Everybody Comes to Rick's*. The film stars Humphrey Bogart (Rick Blaine), Ingrid Bergman (Ilsa Lund), and Paul Henreid (Victor Laszlo); it also features Claude Rains (Captain Louis Renault), Conrad Veidt (Major Strasser), Sydney Greenstreet (Signor Ferrari), Peter Lorre (Signor Ugarte), and Dooley Wilson (Sam). Set during World War II, it focuses on an American expatriate who must choose between his love for a woman and helping her and her husband, a Czech resistance leader, escape from the Vichy-controlled city of Casablanca to continue his fight against the Germans.

Major Strasser leads a group of officers in singing "Die Wacht am Rhein" ("The Watch on the Rhine") in Rick's club. This sets the stage for one of the classic scenes from the movie.

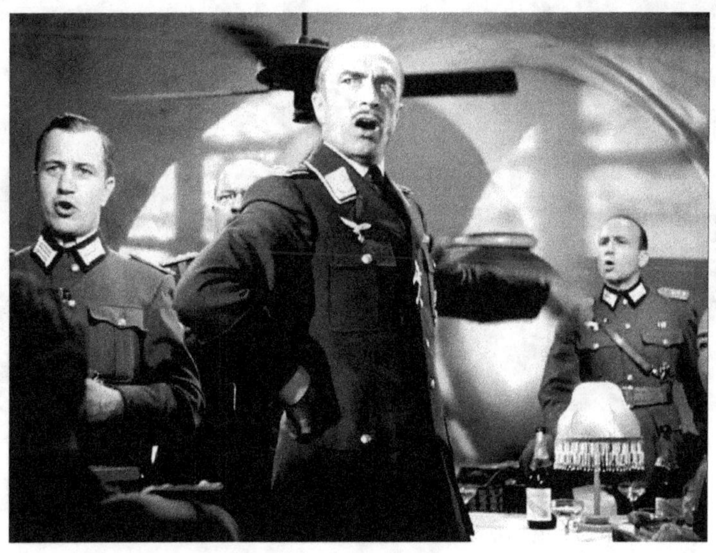

Angered and outraged by this, Laszlo orders the house band to play "La Marseillaise." When the band looks to Rick for guidance, he nods his head, displaying his solidarity against the Germans. With this, Laszlo starts singing, alone at first, then patriotic fervor grips the crowd, and everyone joins in, drowning out the Germans. Strasser, in retaliation, demands that Renault close the club, which he does on the pretext of suddenly discovering there is gambling on the premises. This scene speaks volumes. The arrogance and ruthlessness of tyranny are often expressed in bombastic posturing and behavior. However, in the end, all such attempts fail under the sweet lyrical song of patriotism, love, and devotion to peace.

Scene: The Marseillaise

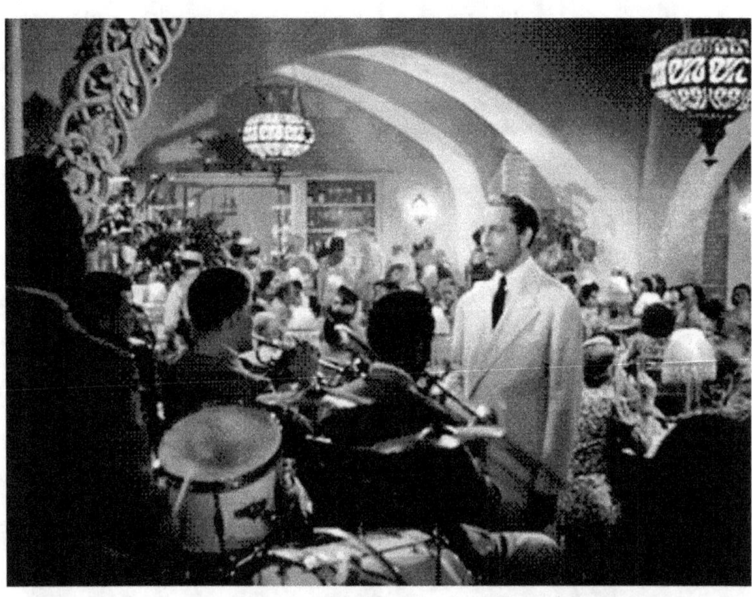

TCM offers some great background tidbits concerning this scene:

Conrad Veidt and Paul Henreid, far from being murderous adversaries, were actually the best of friends. Veidt had intervened on Henreid's behalf to prevent the Austrian refugee from being interned in Britain near the beginning of World War II. Veidt appeared in another milestone of world cinema as the somnambulist Cesare in the silent German film, *The Cabinet of Dr. Caligari* (1919). He was also an exotic presence as the mysterious prince in *The Indian Tomb* (1921).

After escaping Nazi Germany, Veidt settled into a Hollywood career, doing his best to portray the Nazis in the worst possible light. Sadly, Veidt, whose performance as the villainous Major Strasser was completely different from his own character, died in April 1944, one month after *Casablanca* swept the Academy Awards.

Scene: Parting at the Airport

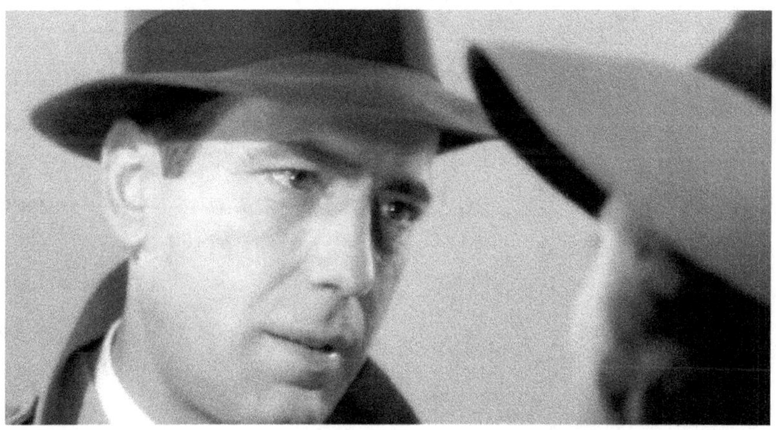

As a result of working with an incomplete screenplay, many of the lines we remember from the film were made up on the spot by the remarkably-talented actors.

The romantic drama ends in the dense airport mist and fog, after

American cafe proprietor Rick says goodbye to the only woman he has ever loved, the luminous Ilsa with her Resistance-leader husband, Victor. For Rick, no sacrifice is too great—he touches her cheek with one finger after delivering one of the film's most famous speeches:

> "Ilsa, I'm no good at being noble, but it doesn't take much to see that the problems of three little people don't amount to a hill of beans in this crazy world. Someday you'll understand that. Not now. Here's looking at you, kid."

In the end, this scene reminds the audience that the needs of the many are so much more important than the personal needs of the few. Tyranny must be conquered all over the world, and Ilsa's husband and his noble quest must take precedence over anything else, now and forever.

TCM notes that the sentence, "Here's looking at you, kid," was originally written as "Here's good luck to you."

Though not written for the film, the song "As Time Goes By" became a popular standard thanks to *Casablanca*. A few bars are sampled during the current Warner Bros. Studios logo.

Scene: New Friendship

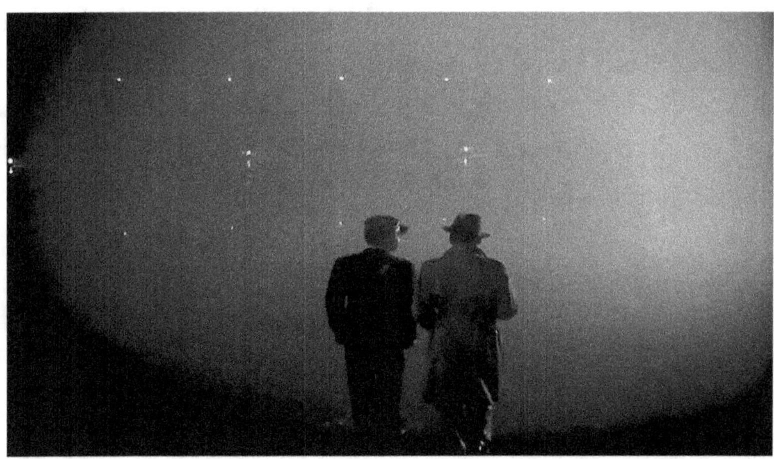

After Rick kills Major Strasser, who is trying to apprehend them at the airport, the crafty Captain Renault, being sympathetic toward Rick, ultimately lets him off the hook by commanding his men: "Round up the usual suspects."

Then, in the fog, they watch the plane leave the ground for neutral Lisbon. Renault offers Rick a way out of Casablanca—the cafe owner is willing to accept the transit letter, but not in exchange for canceling their wager. Rick walks off with Captain Renault across the wet runway, as they discuss what they might do together with the ten thousand francs [three hundred dollars], the payment due on their earlier bet over whether or not Laszlo would ever get out of Casablanca.

The closing in the fog brings another great classic line as Rick tells Renault that they have forged a new alliance as they head off for an uncertain future together: "Louis, I think this is the beginning of a beautiful friendship." Nothing in life is more precious than an enduring friendship that transcends both space and time.

Their new partnership is underscored with the sounds of "La Marseillaise," which, as noted earlier, was sung in the cafe (and led by Laszlo) as a statement of solidarity against the Germans.

This closing scene was actually initially filmed without any dialogue actually being exchanged between Rick and the captain as they walk off into the fog. The cast had left the set, and the dialogue would be later recorded by Bogart and Raines and dubbed into the final film.

TCM offers some wonderful trivia regarding the particulars of this scene.

Since their backs were to the camera, the studio had more time to come up with a suitable closing line to their scene. Before producer Hal Wallis himself came up with the perfect line ("Louis, I think this is the beginning of a beautiful friendship"), there were a few other possible lines considered:

"Louis, I begin to see a reason for your sudden attack of patriotism. While you defend your country, you also protect your investment."

"If you ever die a hero's death, heaven protect the angels!"

"Louis, I might have known you'd mix your patriotism with a little larceny."

Another possible ending that was considered was to shoot a coda with Rick and Louis on a battleship taking the war to Hitler's front doorstep. Thankfully, the idea was scrapped when preview audiences responded enthusiastically to the airport-in-the-fog ending. Besides, a new ending would have required more time and money than their schedule allowed.

In conclusion, the *New York Times* called *Casablanca:*

> "a picture which makes the spine tingle and the heart take
> a leap...they have so combined sentiment, humor, and

pathos with taut melodrama and bristling intrigue that
the result is a highly entertaining and even inspiring film."

The *Horse's Head* analyzed the continued relevance and interest
in the movie *Casablanca* in an essay entitled "The Legacy of *Casa-blanca*," on June 29, 2018:

> "This is another one of those movies that started off as
> a hit and became a classic over time. Its regular airings
> on television, as well as the annual screenings of the
> film at Harvard (and other colleges) throughout the
> '70s helped boost the film's standing as a classic, to the
> point where Francois Truffaut cited these showings
> when refusing to direct a potential remake."

Warner Bros. originally planned on making a sequel shortly after
the film's release. *Brazzaville* would have followed Rick and Louis as
they traveled to the Congo to join the Free French. It never happened.

Unproduced for decades, the play *Everybody Comes to Rick's*
made its West End premiere in 1991, a run that lasted three weeks.

There have been two attempts to turn *Casablanca* into a TV series,
one in the fifties that acted as a prequel, and one in the eighties that was
set a year after the events of the movie. The first was entitled *Passage to
Danger*, and the other was sponsored by NBC and called *Casablanca*. It
starred David Soul as Rick and Scatman Crothers as Sam.

Play It Again, Sam is a 1972 comedy film written by and starring
Woody Allen, based on his 1969 Broadway play of the same name.
The film was directed by Herbert Ross.

The film is about a recently divorced film critic, Allan Felix, who
is urged to begin dating again by his best friend and his best friend's
wife. Allan identifies with the movie *Casablanca* and the character

Rick Blaine as played by Humphrey Bogart. The film is liberally sprinkled with clips from the movie and ghost-like appearances of Bogart (Jerry Lacy) giving advice on how to treat women.

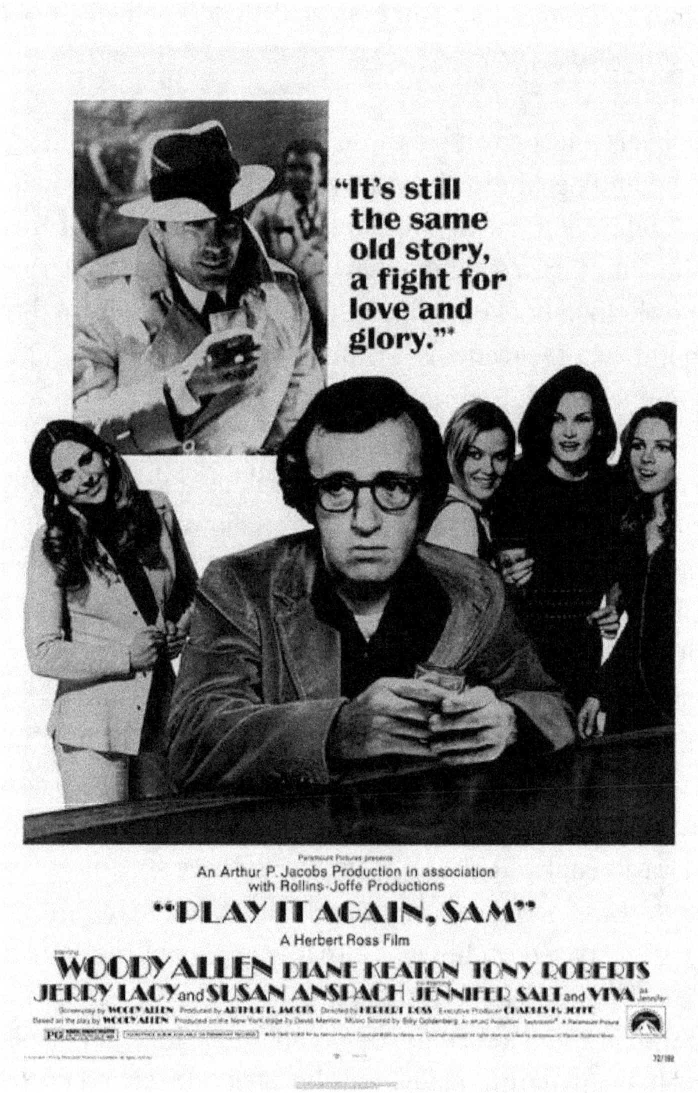

Yankee Doodle Dandy (1942)

Yankee Doodle Dandy is a biographical musical film about George M. Cohan, known as "The Man Who Owned Broadway." It stars James Cagney, Joan Leslie, Walter Huston, and Richard Whorf, and features Irene Manning, George Tobias, Rosemary DeCamp, Jeanne Cagney, and Vera Lewis. The film was written by Robert Buckner and Edmund Joseph and directed by Michael Curtiz. The Hungarian director, who often mangled the English language, called this film "the pinochle of my career."

The movie is an enduring tribute to the adage that patriotism, love of one's country and flag-waving, are never old-fashioned.

Scene: Little Johnny Jones

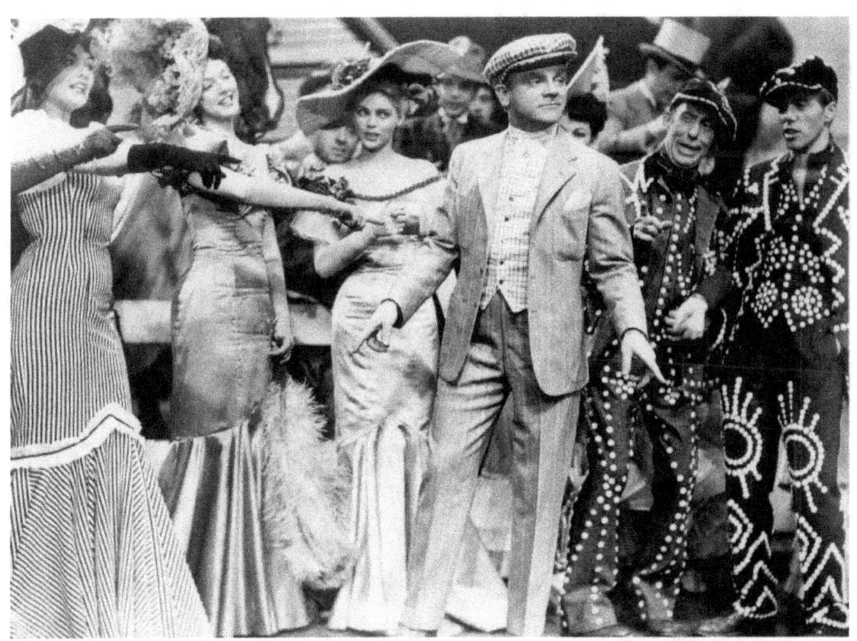

This tribute to the patriotic song-and-dance man George M. Cohan rates as the favorite film of its star, James Cagney.

In his role as adviser to the film, George M. Cohan, who admired Fred Astaire's work, let it be known that he preferred Astaire, who also bore a passing resemblance to him, to star in his life story. Warner Bros. first offered him the role, but Astaire turned it down because Cohan's eccentric, stiff-legged dancing was far removed from Astaire's own, more fluid style.

Care was taken to make the sets, costumes, and dance steps match the original stage presentations. Twice, Cagney sprained an ankle while mastering Cohan's stiff-legged dance style. This effort was aided significantly by a former associate of Cohan's, Jack Boyle, who knew the original productions well. Boyle also appeared in the film in some of the dancing groups.

Cagney, like Cohan, was an Irish-American who had been a song-and-dance man early in his career. His unique and seemingly odd presentation style, of half-singing and half-reciting the songs, reflected the style that Cohan himself used. His natural dance style and physique were also a good match for Cohan. Newspapers at the time reported that Cagney intended to consciously imitate Cohan's song-and-dance style but to play the normal part of the acting in his own style. Although director Curtiz was known as a taskmaster, he also gave his actors some latitude. Cagney and other players came up with a number of "bits of business," as Cagney called them, meaning improvised lines or action in theater parlance.

The spirited, spunky, and domineering acting performance of James Cagney as song-and-dance man George M. Cohan in this biopic is unbelievably arousing.

Especially in the title number, George, as horse jockey Johnny Jones—the Yankee Doodle Boy himself, stands on a pedestal next to a racehorse and is soon surrounded by long-gowned, glittering dancers/singers. He sings the film's classic, all-time favorite title song, "Yankee Doodle Dandy":

> I'm a Yankee Doodle Dandy,
> A Yankee Doodle, do or die;
> A real live nephew of my Uncle Sam,
> Born on the Fourth of July.
> I've got a Yankee Doodle sweetheart,
> She's my Yankee Doodle joy.
> Yankee Doodle came to London,
> Just to ride the ponies;
> I am that Yankee Doodle boy.

As the chorus is sung, the limber song and dance hoofer George struts back and forth across the stage with a stiff-legged gait, bent forward with a straight upper torso. His high, straight-toed kicks, jerky convolutions (like an unwieldy marionette), and a bit of bouncing, twirling, tap-dancing, and other assorted, arrogant movements make the dynamic, vigorous dance number come alive. The side walls of the immense stage become part of his dance floor as he walks up them to make his turns. Cagney's style mimicked the rollickingly and unorthodox dance moves of George M. Cohen him-self as when Cohen appeared on Broadway in *Little Johnny Jones.*

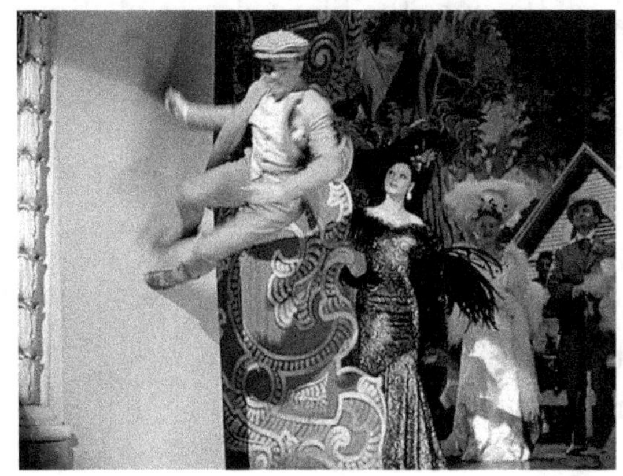

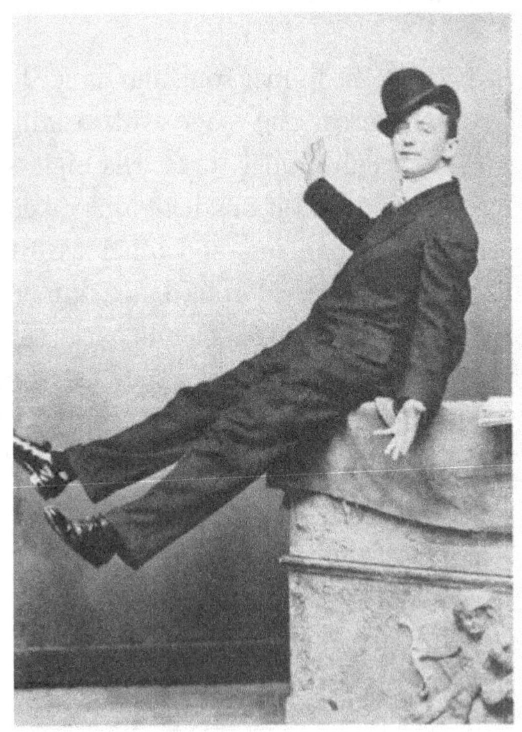

Scene: Impromptu Tap Dance

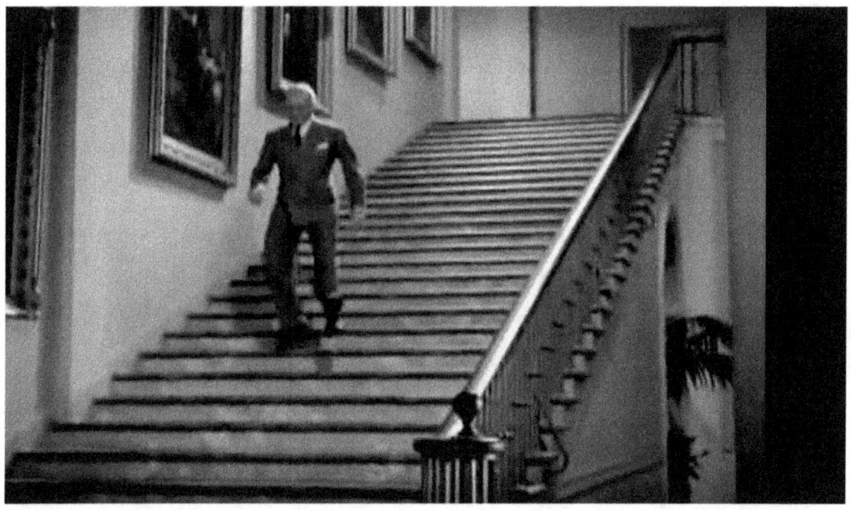

After Cohan retires from show business, with the death of his show business family, he does return periodically to the stage several times, culminating in the role of U.S. President Franklin Delano Roosevelt in the Broadway play *I'd Rather Be Right*. The play opened on Broadway, at the Alvin Theatre on November 2, 1937 and closed on May 1938 and was performed at the Music Box Theatre from May 1938 until it closed on July 9, 1938. It was produced by Sam H. Harris with music by Richard Rodgers and lyrics by Lorenz Hart based on the book written by George S. Kaufman and Moss Hart. It was a musical in two acts set in Central Park, New York on July 4. At the White House, FDR praises the enormous contribution of Irish-Americans, and other ethnic groups, to this country. As the last member of the Cohan Troupe, George thanks the president for all of his family one by one. He then receives the Congressional Gold Medal from the president. As he leaves the White House, he descends a set of stairs while performing a tap dance (which Cagney personally thought up before the scene was filmed and undertook without rehearsal).

One of Curtiz's keys to success was the decision to allow Cagney free rein in his scenes, permitting the actor to improvise as the cameras were rolling. A prime example, and reportedly Cagney's favorite moment in the film, is when he suddenly breaks into a tap dance as he comes down the stairs in a scene at the White House where Cohan has just met with President Franklin Roosevelt.

"I didn't think of it till five minutes before I went on," Cagney later recalled. "And I didn't check with the director or anything; I just did it."

The ordinarily hard-boiled Curtiz was so moved by the scene in which Cohan bids farewell to his dying father (Walter Huston) that he reportedly ruined a take with his loud sobs. According to Cagney biographer Michael Freedland, tears streamed down Curtiz's face as he stumbled away to find a handkerchief and exclaimed to Cagney, "Gott, Jeemy, that was marvelous!"

James Cagney played Cohan in the 1955 film *The Seven Little Foys* along with Bob Hope as Eddie Foy.

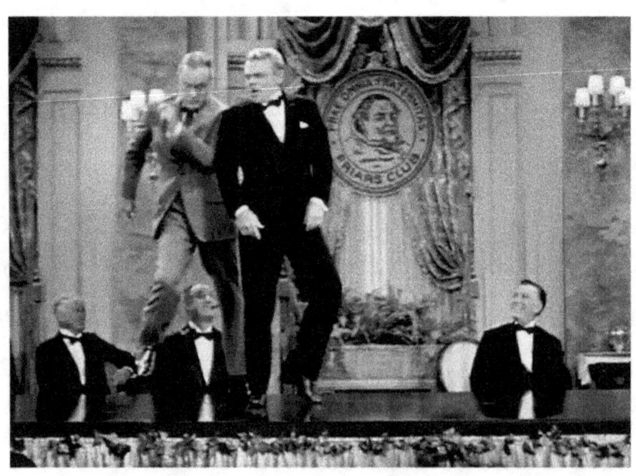

Mickey Rooney played Cohan in *Mr. Broadway*, a television special broadcast on May 11, 1957. The same month, Rooney released a 78-RPM record, *The A-Side,* featuring Rooney singing Cohan's best-known songs.

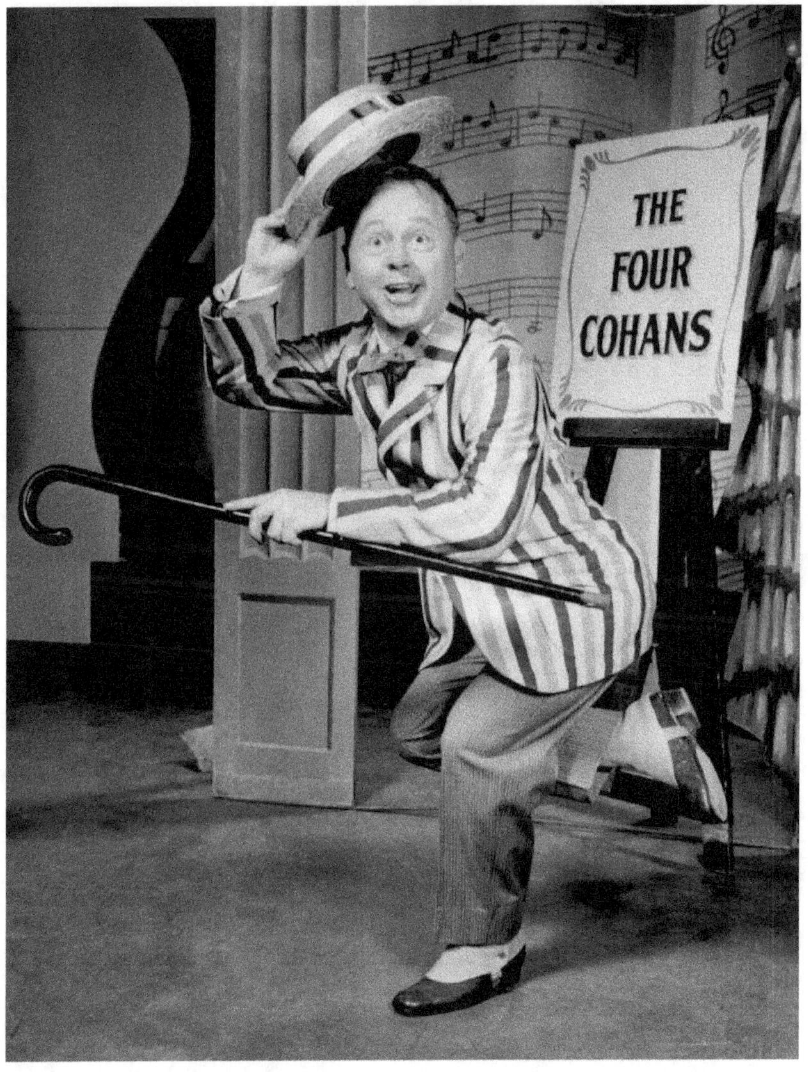

Joel Gray starred on Broadway as Cohan in the musical *George M* (1968), which was adapted into a television special in 1970.

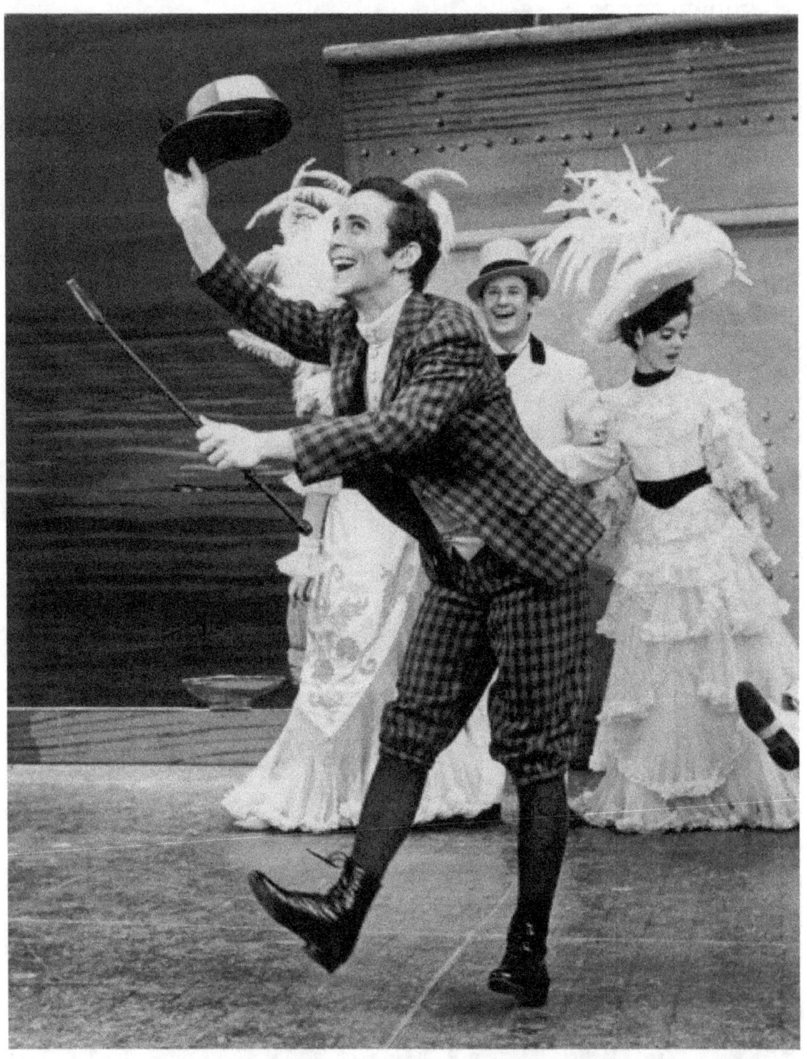

To Have and Have Not (1944)

To Have and Have Not is a romance-war-adventure film direct-ed by Howard Hawks, loosely based on Ernest Hemingway's 1937 novel of the same name. It stars Humphrey Bogart (Harry "Steve" Morgan) and nineteen-year-old Lauren "Slim" Browning. The screenplay was written by Jules Furthman and William Faulkner. The plot centers on the romance between a freelancing fisherman in Martinique and a beautiful American drifter, which is compli-cated by the growing French resistance in Vichy France.

As a prelude to one of the screen's most famous seductions, Slim sits on Steve's lap. Before kissing the seated man for the first time, she acts the aggressor role as they engage in flirtatious sexu-al repartee. Her verdict of his kissing talent requires a second kiss. Then, after kissing him again, he appears baffled. She suggests to her passive partner as she stands: "It's even better when you help."

Scene: How to Whistle

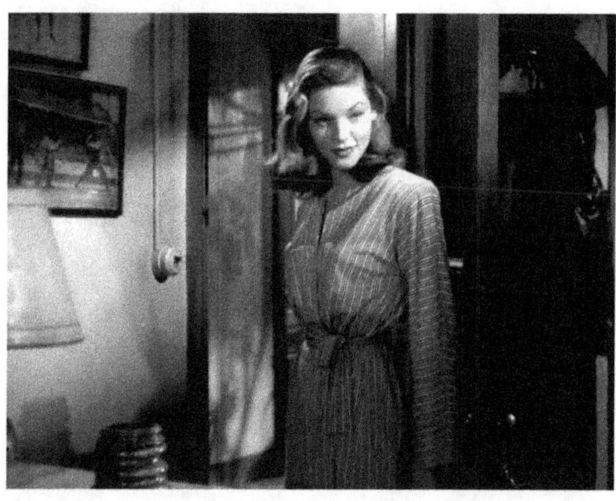

When this remark doesn't have the immediate and desired response she had expected, Bacall propositions him midway from leaving his room with other famous lines, delivered with a calculated coolness:

> "You know, you don't have to act with me, Steve. You don't have to say anything and you don't have to do anything. Not a thing. Oh, maybe just whistle. (She opens his door and pauses.) You know how to whistle, don't you, Steve? You just put your lips together—and blow."

He continues to remain seated in his chair, smoking a cigarette. After she has left, he makes the sound of a cat-call whistle—and then chuckles to himself. At the time of casting, Bacall was an eighteen-year-old model. She appeared on the cover of *Harper's Bazaar* and was noticed by Hawks' wife, Nancy "Slim" Keith, who showed the cover photo to her husband.

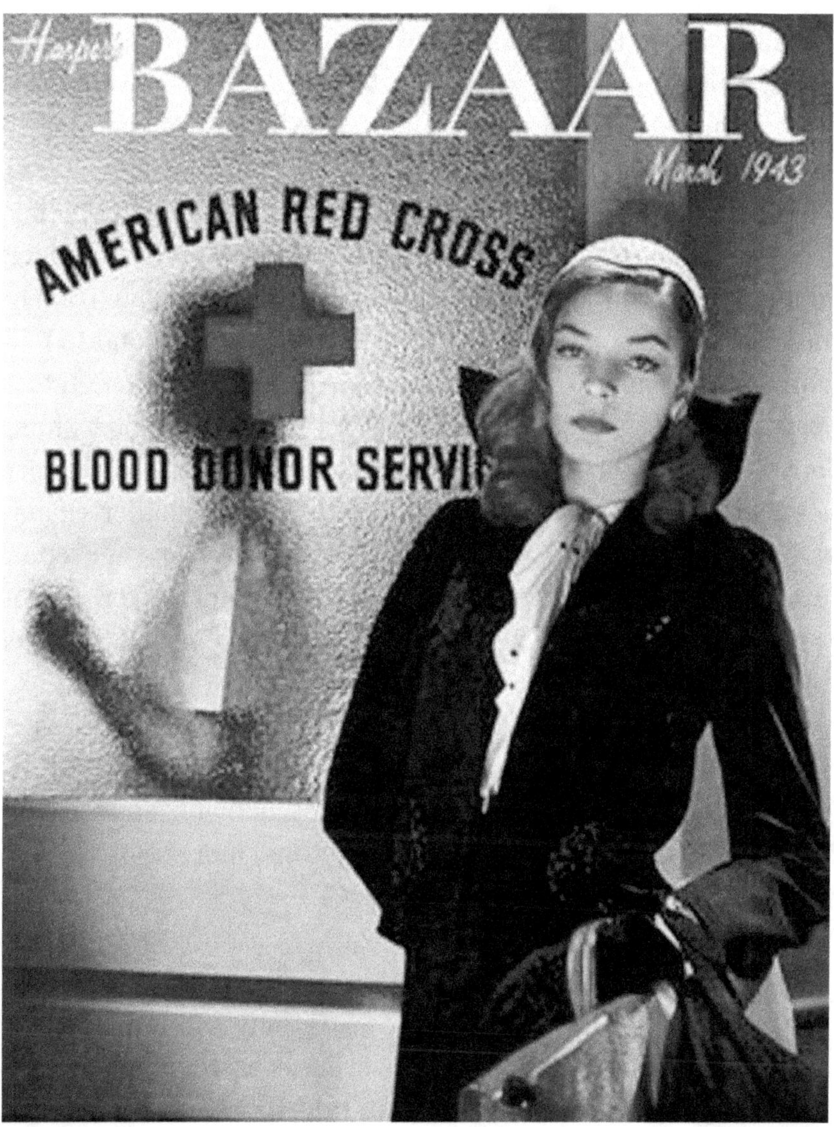

Hawks sought Bacall out in April 1943 and signed her for the role. It would be her first movie appearance. In the film, Harry calls her by the nickname "Slim," and she calls him "Steve," the nicknames used between Keith and Hawks. Hawks shot her screen test in January 1944. Her screen test was the seduction and "whistle" scene. The famous "you know how to whistle" line was not written by Ernest Hemingway, Furthman, or William Faulkner, but by Howard Hawks. Hawks wrote the scene as a screen test for Bacall, with no real intention that it would necessarily end up in the film. The test was shot with Warner Bros.' contract player John Ridgely acting opposite Bacall. Jack L. Warner likes the line so much that he told Hawks that he needed to integrate it into the film, and so William Faulkner later adapted it into the film. After the screen test, Hawks signed his first personal contract with an up-and-coming actress with Bacall. After Bacall turned nineteen, Hawks changed her name to Lauren, and she used a variation of her mother's maiden name "Bacal" (Bacall was born Betty Perske). During her screen test, Bacall was so nervous that, to minimize her quivering, she pressed her chin against her chest, faced the camera, and tilted her eyes upward. This effect, which came to be known as "the Look," became another Bacall trademark, along with her deep sultry voice.

Bacall writes in her autobiography, *Lauren Bacall by Myself* (1978) that it was in the third week of shooting that friendly banter between her and Bogart turned to something more. At the end of shooting one day,

> "he leaned over, put his hand under my chin, and kissed me. It was impulsive—he was a bit shy—no lunging wolf tactics. He took a worn package of matches out of his pocket and asked me to put my phone number on the back. I did."

Bogart was forty-four years old and in an unhappy third marriage. The relationship with Bacall was obvious on the set, and while it sparked the onscreen chemistry for his movie, Hawks was furious. He warned Bacall away and threatened that the relation-ship could damage her career—that she could end up at Monogram Pictures. (By some accounts, Hawks was jealous and had designs on Bacall himself.) Hawks warned that Bogart would drop Betty after filming was completed, but nothing could be further from the truth. Bogart was divorced and married Bacall in 1945. They made three more films together and remained married until Bogart's death from cancer in January 1957.

Most contemporary reviews of the movie were reviews fixated on the sultry Lauren Bacall and her steamy scenes with Bogart. The usually cool and judicious film critic James Agee was inspired to write: "Lauren Bacall has cinema personality to burn ... a javelin like vitality, a born dancer's eloquence in movement, a fierce female shrewdness, and a special sweet-sourness."

During the Golden Age of cartoons, it was common for animators to caricature movie stars or to parody certain movie genres, but it was uncommon for cartoons to feature full-blown parodies of specific movies. In 1946, Warner Bros. released Bacall to Arms. In it, a group of cartoon animals find their seats in a movie theater, including a raucous wolf, and watch *To Have and Have Not* starring Bogey GoCart and Laurie BeCool. The wolf has particular troubles keeping his cool while watching the sultry BeCool character. There is not a director credited, because it is an awkward amalgam of two cartoons. Much of the movie theater audience material was lifted from a 1937 Friz Freleng cartoon called "She Was an Acrobat's Daughter." The other material was new and was directed by the great Bob Clampett. The film functions as a tribute to Bacall and her sexual attractiveness. It was probably produced to promote the release of an upcoming feature film, *The Big Sleep* (1946). The film conflates two scenes from *To Have and Have Not*, the scene where the protagonists are introduced to each other and the whistle scene. The animators were clearly inspired by Lauren Bacall's performance in *To Have and Have Not*—when the cartoon Bacall walks across the screen, she leaves fiery footprints. Certain specific lines and situations from the film are parodied.

When Bogey and Bacall kiss, Bogey asks afterward, "What did you do that for?"

A young duck in the audience enthusiastically squeals to his father, "I know why, Daddy! I know why!"

The Bacall character delivers the famous line, "You know how to whistle, don't you?" and proceeds to give a wildly exaggerated New York-style taxi whistle, fingers in mouth. The animator for this shot was probably Clampett mainstay Rod Scribner.

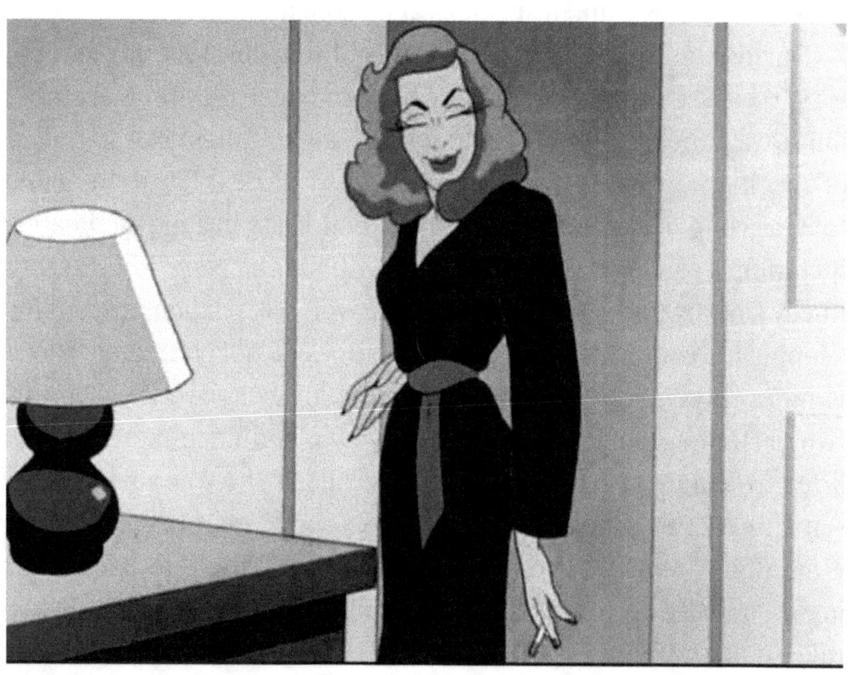

The Best Years of Our Lives (1946)

The Best Years of Our Lives is a truly powerful drama film directed by William Wyler and starring Myrna Loy, Fredric March, Dana Andrews, Teresa Wright, Virginia Mayo, and Harold Russell. The film is about three United States servicemen readjusting to civilian life after coming home from World War II. Samuel Goldwyn was inspired to produce a film about veterans after reading an August 7, 1944, article in *Time* about the difficulties experienced by men returning to civilian life. Director Wyler had flown combat missions over Europe in filming *Memphis Belle* (1944) and worked hard to get accurate depictions of the combat veterans he had encountered. Wyler changed the original casting that had featured a veteran with post-traumatic stress disorder, and sought out Harold Russell, a non-actor, to take on the exacting role of Homer Parrish. The film was the very first time Hollywood openly addressed the enormous problems returning World War II wounded and disabled soldiers faced in adjusting to physical challenges, mental anguish, their own fear of pity, addressing real human relationships, and the attitude of others. Their tenacity and forbearance to these challenges and hardships captured the spirit and inspiration of a country recovering from a war that affected the lives of every American. The film's legacy is that it brought to Americans' consciousness the importance of caring for the physical and psychological well-being of all of our servicemen and women after their sacrifice to our country.

Scene: Homer Parrish

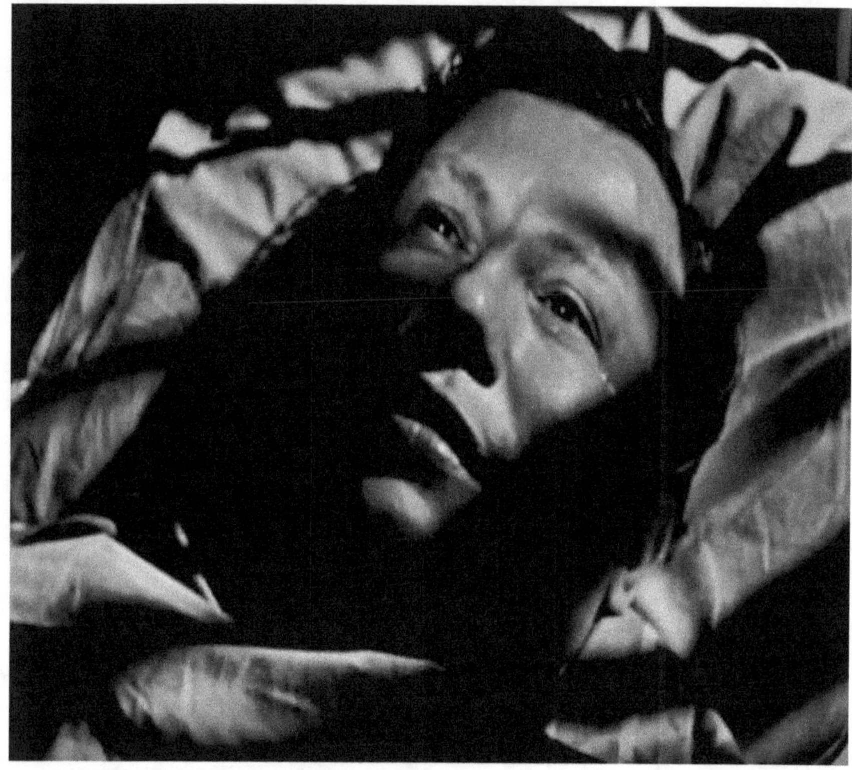

Setting: Upon his return from the war, Homer is reluctant to renew his love for his old girlfriend, Wilma Cameron (Cathy O'Donnell), because of his disability. He is very aware of people staring and him and very self-conscious about his condition and feels that she can't truly love him anymore because of this. He intentionally shuns her and avoids talking about his condition and feelings openly with her. Finally, in desperation, Wilma comes to see Homer in his home, saying that her parents want her to go away because it is obvious that Homer no longer loves her. He argues that she does not know what it would be like living with him, but because she wants to try, he decides to let her see the worst. In his room, Homer gets out of his robe, is able to drop the harness that holds his prosthetics, and put on his pajama top without help, but after that, he is completely vulnerable and helpless, for he has no arms. Rather than being repulsed, Wilma lovingly places his harness on top of his other clothes, says that she will never leave him, and tenderly kisses him and tucks him into bed. After she leaves the room, Homer lays in bed, and tears appear in his eyes, for he realizes that he has now been given two very special gifts from above in his life. The first was the fact that he survived the war, and now he has been blessed with the gift of love from someone who wants to marry him and spent the rest of her life with him, facing the joys and tribulations of life together as one.

Harold Russell was born in North Sydney, Nova Scotia, Canada, and moved to Massachusetts with his family in 1921, after his father's death in 1920.

At the time of the December 7, 1941, attack on Pearl Harbor, he was living in Cambridge, Massachusetts, working at a food market. In his 1949 autobiography, *Victory in My Hands*, he wrote that he rushed to enlist in the United States Army, "not out of patriotism, but because I thought of myself a failure."

On June 6, 1944, while he was an Army instructor, teaching demolition work with the U.S. 13th Airborne Division at Camp Mackall, North Carolina, a defective fuse detonated TNT explosives he was handling. As a result, he lost both hands and was given two hooks to serve as hands. After his recovery, and while attending Boston University as a full-time student, Russell was featured in *Diary of a Sergeant* (1945), an Army film about rehabilitating war veterans.

When film director William Wyler saw the film on Russell, he cast him in *The Best Years of Our Lives*, playing the major role of Homer

Parrish, which marked his feature film debut. Russell's ease using the metal prosthetics that replaced his hands, and his naturalness in front of the camera, convinced Wyler and Goldwyn that Russell could play the role. According to TCM, director William Wyler was furious when he learned that Samuel Goldwyn had sent Harold Russell for acting lessons; he preferred Russell's untrained, natural acting.

For his realistic, sympatric, and powerful portrayal as Homer Parrish in the film, Harold Russell won the Academy Award for Best Supporting Actor in 1947. Earlier in the ceremony, he was awarded an honorary Oscar for "bringing hope and courage to his fellow veterans." The special award had been created because the Board of Governors very much wanted to salute Russell, a non-professional actor, but assumed he had little chance for a competitive win. It was the only time in Oscar history that the Academy has awarded two Oscars for the same performance.

Upon completion of the film, Wyler told Russell to return to school since there "weren't many roles for actors without hands." Russell returned to Boston University and graduated with a business degree in 1949.

Russell authored two autobiographies, *Victory in My Hands* (1949) and *The Best Years of My Life* (1981).

Kiss of Death (1947)

Kiss of Death is a film noir directed by Henry Hathaway and written by Ben Hecht and Charles Lederer from a story by Eleazar Lipsky. The story revolves around an ex-con, played by Victor Mature, and his former partner-in-crime, Tommy Udo (Richard Widmark in his first film). *Kiss of Death* is a movie that's well-remembered, but mostly for the wrong reasons.

Like *From Here to Eternity* (1953), it's a film that's come to be summed up in the popular gestalt for a single scene, even though that scene isn't particularly representative of the movie around it. For *Eternity,* it was the beachside kiss. For *Kiss of Death*, it's a giggling, soulless, maniacal, diabolic, two-bid hood pushing a poor woman in a wheelchair down a flight of stairs to her demise.

Scene: The Wheelchair Push

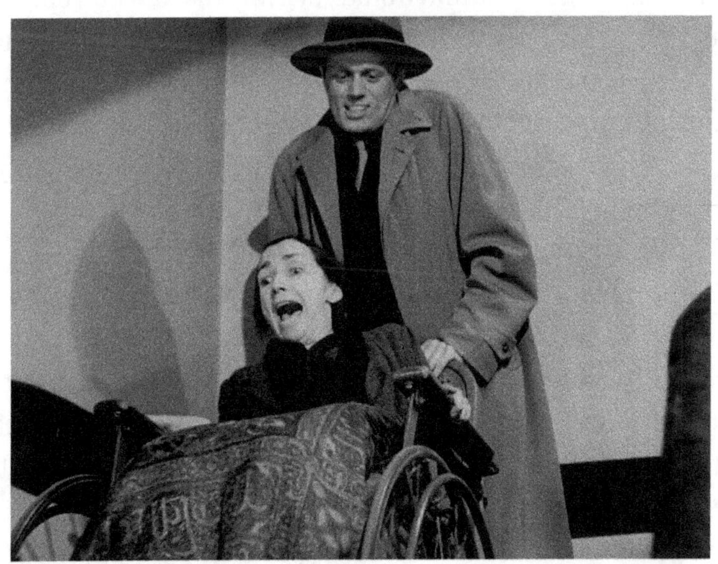

Probably like many movie lovers, I have seen the wheelchair scene, but not the whole movie. Within the context of the story, it's a rather brief, almost a throwaway scene. It exists not because the woman is important—we're introduced to her moments before she dies—or that her death plays a pivotal role in the story. It's simply intended as a shocking moment to depict how despicable the villain, Tommy Udo, really is.

To audiences in 1947, it surely must have been quite a surprise to see a disabled woman ("crippled," they would have said in those days) killed by a giggling lunatic for no good reason at all. But it's a shame that people more readily recall that act of depravity than the character behind it or the actor who created him.

Tommy Udo should be right up there with Keyser Soze and Hannibal Lecter on the list of greatest cinematic villains. He's a jittery, shivery figure who makes you feel like bugs are crawling all over you whenever he's onscreen.

It was the first film role for Richard Widmark, who'd mostly been known for his stage work, and would earn him his first and only Oscar nomination. It also set the tone for his career, in which he largely played men who easily turn to violence during his younger years and corrupt cops or misguided soldiers as he got older. Even his heroic roles, like *Warlock* (1959), are shot through with moral ambiguity.

After Tommy Udo, straight heroics were out for Widmark.

Widmark's look and mannerisms in the film are highly stylized and memorable. He always wears dark shirts with a light-colored tie, the mark of an operator. He moves in a languid style, almost as if the world around him bores him. When he's talking to someone, he tends to stare them straight in the eyes, virtually without blinking, a rictus smile seeming to split his skull horizontally. His teeth somehow seem malevolent.

He speaks in a nasally Noo Yawk pattern, warping his vowels

and swallowing his consonants to the point where it can be hard to understand what he's saying. At one point, on a train, he announces that it's his birthday, but it comes out something like, "Ehz meeh boithdoy!"

If Widmark's Tommy Udo seems evocative of another character, that's because he is. Widmark was reputedly fascinated with the Joker in the Batman comics of that era and patterned his look, smile, and laughter after the famed psychopath who would later be portrayed by Jack Nicholson, Heath Ledger, and others.

The only difference is there's no joking to Udo despite his nearly non-stop laughter. That giggle seems to escape out of him like noxious gas out of a cesspool, unable to be contained. According to biographer Kim Holston, Widmark would be approached by strangers for years afterward, asking him to reproduce the famous laughter or even record it for them.

Udo laughs at those around him, whom he divides into two categories: "squirts," the everyday folks who deserve only to be browbeaten and murdered, and a "big man" who carries himself above the rest.

Interestingly, Widmark was not considered by the studio to be any big shakes when they were marketing the movie; his name does not even appear on the poster. Coleen Gray, who was also making her film debut playing Nick's nanny-turned-new-wife, got the glamorous "and introducing ..." treatment.

Richard Widmark followed *Kiss of Death* with other villainous performances in *The Street with No Name*, *Road House*, and the western *Yellow Sky* (all 1948), the latter film with Gregory Peck and Anne Baxter. Another standout villainous role was in the racial melodrama *No Way Out* (1950), with Sidney Poitier. But the best film which displays Widmark's ability to portray a sadistic and heartless SOB, like Udo, is *The Bedford Incident.* It is a 1965 British–American

Cold War film starring Richard Widmark and Sidney Poitier and co-produced by Widmark.

Widmark plays Captain Eric Finlander, the captain of the American destroyer *USS Bedford* (DLG-113) detects a Soviet submarine in the GIUK gap near the coast of Greenland. It is an area in the northern Atlantic Ocean that forms a naval chokepoint. Its name is an acronym for Greenland, Iceland, and the United Kingdom, the gap being the open ocean between these three landmasses. Finlander exploits the fact that the Russian sub has to surface periodically to replenish air and recharge batteries because it is not nuclear-powered; knowing full well, it will make the Soviets more desperate. Finlander mercilessly and sadistically pursues his prey, forcing the sub underwater for extended periods of time in order to escape detection. Sidney Poitier, as Ben Munceford, plays a civilian photojournalist who constantly questions Finlander's motives for his seemingly unprovoked actions, which only infuriate the captain even further. The entire crew of the destroyer is on high alert without any relief or pause endangering their health and well-being and greatly reducing their overall ability to respond to an actual emergency. Wally Cox, as Seaman Merlin Queffle, is driven to the brink of a total nervous breakdown by the captain's continuous harassment of him as the radar technician tries to track the Russian vessel on his radar. He finally goes berserk under the continuous strain. Martin Balsam, as Lt. Cmdr. Chester Potter, MD, USN, comes to his aid and wants Queffle declared unfit for unity. The captain refuses and only gives Potter a short time to get him back on duty. Eric Portman, as Commodore Wolfgang Schrepke Deutsche Merine, warns Finlander that he is playing a deadly game which can only have one terrible consequence for all concerned. When the Russian submarine surfaces in order to recharge its batteries and replenish its air, Finlander deliberately ignores the

Commodore's warning and runs over the exposed snorkel of the submarine, which, in all intent, is an act of war. James MacArthur, as Ensign Ralston, is also taxed beyond human endurance and, in the end, mistakenly interprets the captain's orders and actually fires an anti-surface rocket at the Russian vessel. It is too late to disarm it, and the submarine is destroyed. But before they are destroyed, the submarine releases torpedoes that hit the *Bedford*, destroying it and all on board.

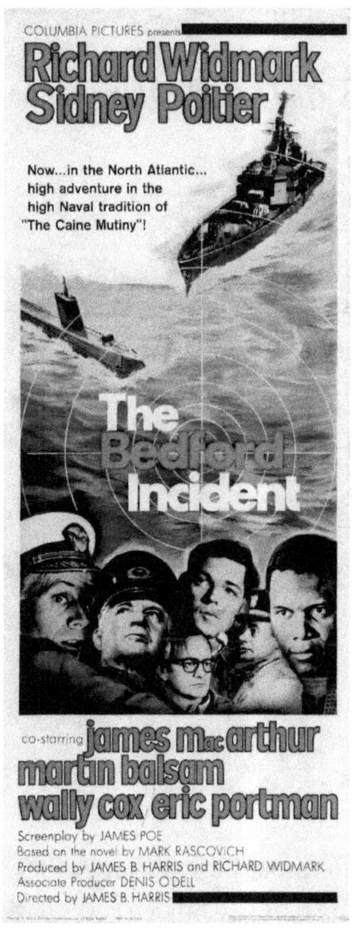

White Heat (1949)

White Heat is a film noir film directed by Raoul Walsh and starring James Cagney, Virginia Mayo, Edmond O'Brien, Margaret Wycherly, and Steve Cochran. Written by Ivan Goff and Ben Roberts, *White Heat* is based on a story by Virginia Kellogg and is considered to be one of the best gangster movies of all time. It traces the life and times of the notorious and often deranged gangster, Cody Jarrett, up to his final "flaming" demise.

Scene: News of the Death of Cody's Mother

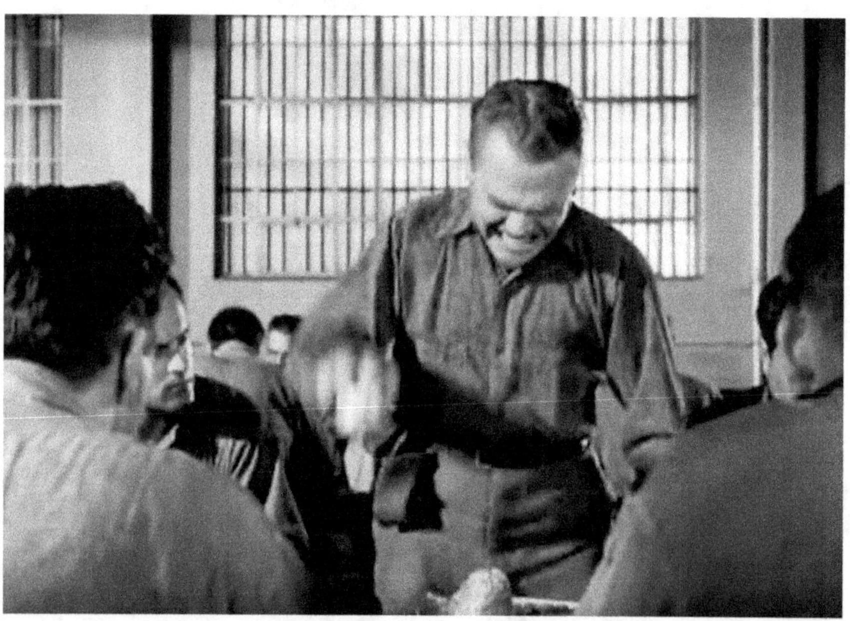

Probably the scene most people remember from the film *White Heat* is the very ending where Cody Jarrett deliberately shoots bullet holes in the tanks of a petroleum refinery and is almost immediately killed in an immense explosion just after yelling, "Made it, Ma! Top o' the world!" However, for me, the most famous scene in *White Heat* is undoubtedly the one in which Cody Jarrett, in prison, gets the news of his mother's death. His reaction resembles that of a volcano slowly building up pressure from within and then finally exploding. The news is passed down from inmate to inmate at the prison mess hall tables until it finally reaches Jarrett, who explodes into psychotic grief, staggering around the room, landing punches on everyone who gets in his way while letting out a kind of strangled, primal cry. According to TCM, Cagney was once asked by a reporter if he had to "psych" himself up for the scene. Cagney responded, "You don't psych yourself up for these things, you do them," reiterating his very non-method philosophy that working on inward emotional motivation is a waste of time leading to a performance solely for the actor himself. According to Cagney, an actor shouldn't psych himself up to be the character; he should simply understand the character and play it for the audience. His only preparation for the scene, he later said, was remembering a visit as a youngster to see a friend's uncle who was in a psychiatric hospital.

"My God, what an education," he said. "The shrieks, the screams of those people under restraint. I remembered those cries, saw that they fitted, and I called on my memory to do as required."

When Cody gets the news of his mother's death, Cagney plays his first reaction merely looking down, building into the emotional explosion. Years later, he explained to *Los Angeles Times* film critic Charles Champlin,

> "That first agony is private. If I'd looked up right away and started bellowing, it would have been stock company, 1912."

Director Raoul Walsh said of his star: "Jimmy, I can honestly say, was the best actor I ever directed."

According to TCM, studio mogul Jack Warner wanted the prison mess hall scene replaced for budgetary reasons, stating the "cost of a single scene with six hundred extras and only one line of dialogue would be exorbitant." For this reason, Warner wanted the scene shot in a chapel, but relented when "the writers pointed out that, apart from the fact that Jarrett would [never be willingly caught in a] chapel," the whole point of the scene was to "have a lot of noise, with rattling knives and forks and chatter, that suddenly goes completely silent when Jarrett first screams." The scream was improvised by Cagney, and the shock on everyone's face was real, for neither Cagney nor Walsh informed any of the extras of what was going to happen. Warner agreed to the scene on the condition that it be shot in three hours, so "that the extras were through by lunchtime."

White Heat was not James Cagney's last gangster role, but it is generally considered his most extreme and enjoyable performance as a trigger-happy criminal; he would again play mobsters in *Kiss Tomorrow Goodbye* (1950) opposite Barbara Payton and *Love Me or Leave Me* (1955), which earned him an Oscar nomination for Best Actor as the gangster boyfriend of real-life singer Ruth Etting (portrayed by Doris Day in the film).

The script for *White Heat* was based on a story written for the screen by Virginia Kellogg. She followed this film with another stark and brutal prison drama, with the added twist of setting it in a women's institution: *Caged* (1950).

According to Turner Classic Movies:

> *White Heat* remains one of the crowning achievements
> of Cagney's career. It's hard to imagine another actor
> of the time convincingly pulling off this all-stops-out

portrayal of Cody Jarrett. And this is no mere farewell or throwback to another era. It has the volatile dynamism of the best gangster flicks of the 30s and 40s, but it mixes in important tendencies taking shape in postwar cinema. The train robbery heralds the attention to the logistical details of a crime that would play such a vital element in films like John Huston's *The Asphalt Jungle* (1950) and Stanley Kubrick's *The Killing* (1956). It displays elements of the documentary style made popular by the film noir *Naked City* (1948), directed by Jules Dassin, and similar movies. The term *film noir* is French for 'black film' (literal) or 'dark film.' It shares something of the film noir style in its often shadowy cinematography and focus on its lead character's twisted psychology.

CHAPTER 4

THE 1950s

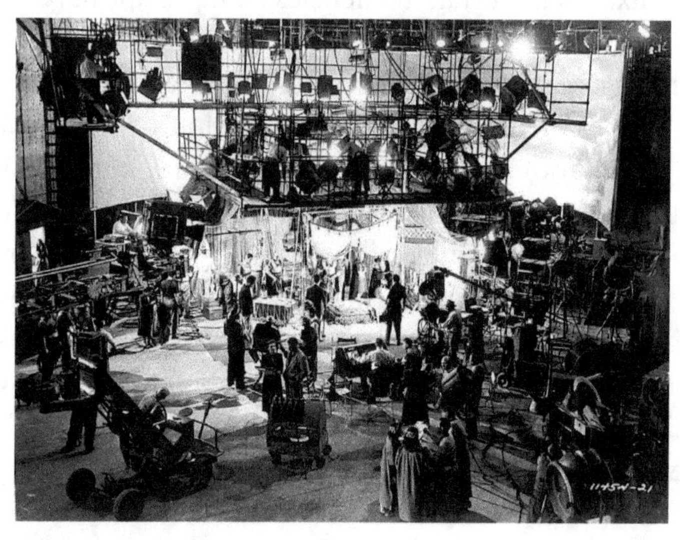

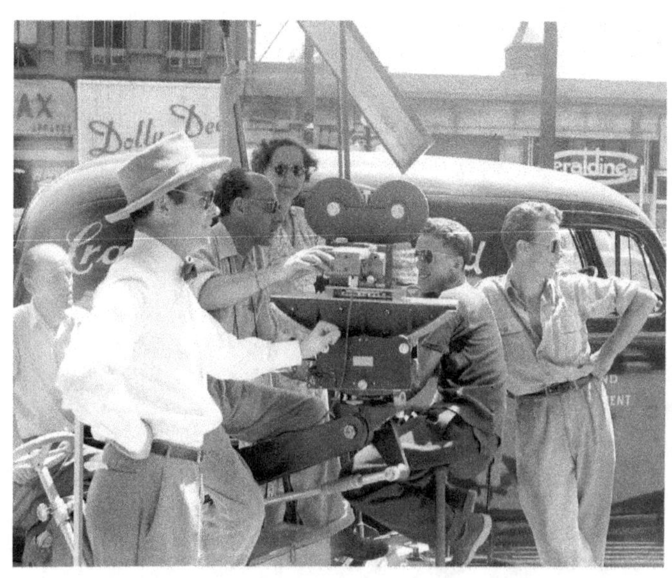

Sunset Boulevard (1950)

Sunset Boulevard is a film noir directed and co-written by Billy Wilder and produced and co-written by Charles Brackett. It was named after the thoroughfare with the same name that runs through Los Angeles and Beverly Hills, California. The film is Wilder's dark, classic comedy/drama and is perhaps the most acclaimed, "behind the scenes" film about Hollywood and its legacies.

The film stars William Holden as Joe Gillis, an unsuccessful screenwriter who narrates the story from his perspective, and Gloria Swanson as Norma Desmond, a faded and deluded silent-film star who draws him into her fantasy world, where she dreams of making a triumphant return to the screen. Joe is caught between a rock and a hard place loving the fact that is can live high on the hog in her rundown but still luxurious mansion as her ghostwriter, while trying to live his own life outside, co-writing a movie script with a lady friend (Betty Schaefer played by Nancy Olsen), who unfortunately has fallen in love with him. In the end, Joe forgoes Betty and tries to leave Norma in a vain attempt to rediscover his roots by returning back to his hometown of Dayton, Ohio, but Norma can't stand to lose him and kills him before going completely insane, escaping inside her own disillusioned reality. Norma is "tricked" into leaving her room by Max (Erich von Stroheim as Max von Mayerling) by cleverly using the reporters and studio and news camera people, already gathered there to cover her surrender to the authorities, as a ploy to pretend that they have all assembled there to film her big scene for the movie *Salome*. Max even portrays himself as Cecil B. DeMille himself. The ploy works, and she descends the stairs and stops to address her millions of fans and the news media. She announces her triumphant return to the silver screen and pledges never to leave her adoring movie fans again.

As a prelude to the film's memorable conclusion, Norma is lured from her mansion in Beverly Hills to go quietly downstairs to a waiting police car, to whisk her away to wherever through a group of assembled reporters and cameramen—only by being made to think she is returning to the screen and shooting a scene for famous movie director Cecil B. DeMille. DeMille had actually helped make Swanson a star, directing her in such early hits as *Male and Female* and *Don't Change Your Husband* (both 1919). Like the DeMille in the movie, the real-life director used to address Swanson on the set as "young fellow." Her bald-headed butler Max von Mayerling (Erich von Stroheim) prepares the newsreel cameramen and also asks if the lights are ready. Then, looking up toward the balcony where Norma will enter the scene, he shouts: "Quiet everybody! Lights!"

Max must explain the scene to a confused Norma: "This is the staircase of the palace."

Norma readies herself: "Oh yes, yes. Down below, they're waiting for the princess. I'm ready." Sweeping her gown around with one hand, she begins to descend the staircase for her final close-up.

Max shouts more directions: "Cameras! Action!"

The dead screenwriter narrates in voice-over, introducing her exit down the marble staircase in her decaying Hollywood mansion to the whir of cameras:

> "So they were turning, after all—those cameras. Life, which can be strangely merciful, had taken pity on Norma Desmond. The dream she had clung to so desperately had enfolded her."

Scene: Lost in an Illusion

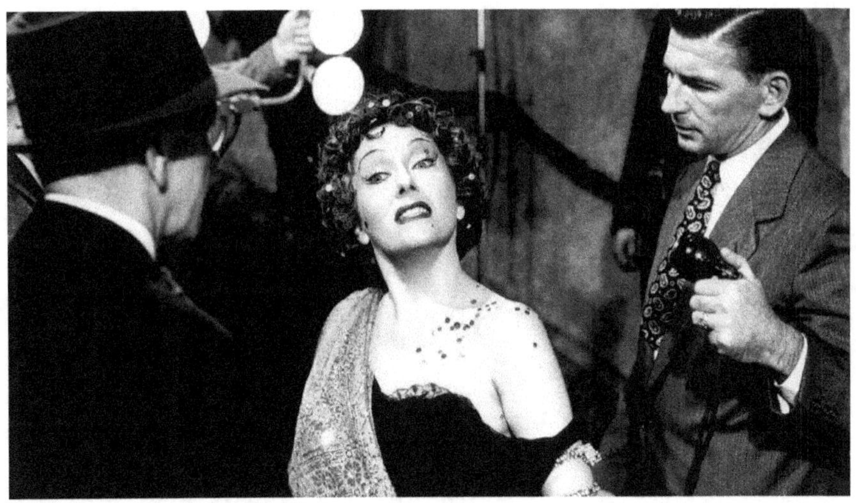

The film queen descends the marble staircase believing she is playing Salome in the most important scene of her career. At the bottom of the stairs, she has become so overjoyed that she has to have a word for the crew:

I can't go on with the scene. I'm too happy! Mr. DeMille, do you mind if I say a few words? Thank you. I just want to tell you all how happy I am to be back in the studio, making a picture again! You don't know how much I've missed all of you. And I promise you, I'll never desert you again because after Salome we'll make another picture and another picture! You see, this is my life. It always will be! There's nothing else—just us—and the cameras—and those wonderful people out there in the dark. All right, Mr. DeMille, I'm ready for my close-up.

Then, Norma walks past the newsreel cameras and directly toward the off-screen cameras filming the scene. As one camera closes in on her face, her image goes into a blurry soft-focus, as Norma slips transcendently backward in time to her glory days, a time of illusion.

What a tour de force of performance for Gloria Swanson. She was what they say, "born to play the role of Norma Desmond." In fact, her own life mirrored the role she played in *Sunset Boulevard* to a T. Swanson was the silent screen's most successful and highest-paid star, earning twenty-thousand dollars a week in the mid-1920s. Noted for her extravagance, Miss Swanson earned eight million dollars from 1918 to 1929 and spent nearly all of it without blinking an eye.

Swanson starred in dozens of silent films, often under the direction of Cecil B. DeMille, who appears in *Sunset Boulevard*, as a movie director. Great casting! In 1928, she was nominated for the first Academy Award ever given for Best Actress. Seen below, in the first photograph, is DeMille with Swanson (in the silk gown) during the silent era days and, in the second photograph, DeMille as he appeared (right) with her in *Sunset Boulevard*, along with director Billy Wilder seen in the light tan shirt.

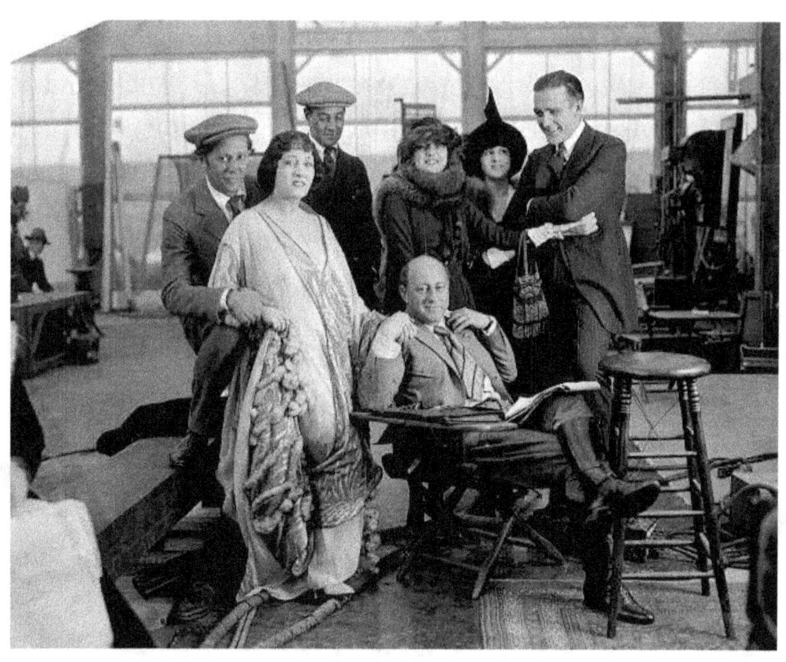

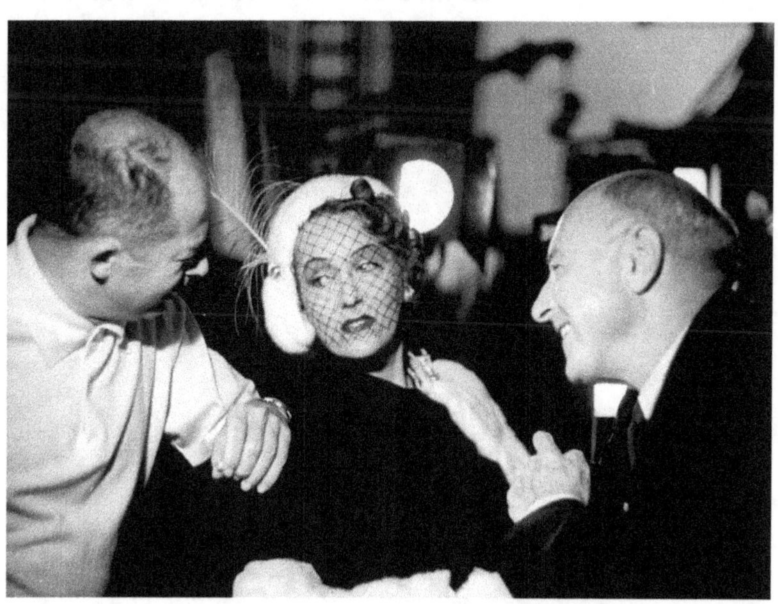

Swanson was also one of the first women to produce her own films, making *The Love of Sunya* (1927) and *Sadie Thompson* (1928). In 1929, Swanson transitioned into talkies with her performance in *The Trespasser*. Personal problems and changing tastes saw her popularity wane during the 1930s, and she subsequently ventured into theater and television.

In 1950, after a virtual sixteen-year absence from the screen, Swanson would achieve widespread critical acclaim and recognition for her role as Norma Desmond, a reclusive silent film star, in the critically acclaimed 1950 film, *Sunset Boulevard*.

Often hailed as the definitive insider portrait of Hollywood, *Sunset Boulevard* was one of the first serious treatments of life in Hollywood, coming at a time when most movies about movies were irony-free comedies and musicals. The picture exposes the film capital at its worst as a world of fleeting fame where almost everybody is on the hustle for success, money, and sex. As such, it was a key influence on such films as *The Bad and the Beautiful, The Star* (both 1952), and *The Barefoot Contessa* (1954).

A Streetcar Named Desire (1951)

A Streetcar Named Desire is an epic film drama, adapted from Tennessee Williams' Pulitzer-Prize-winning 1847 play of the same name. It was directed by Elia Kazan. The film challenged the Production Code's censors with its bold adult drama and sexual subjects (rape, domestic violence, homosexuality, and female promiscuity or nymphomania). It is the story of the pathetic mental and emotional demise of a determined yet fragile, repressed, and delicate Southern lady Blanche DuBois (Vivien Leigh), born to a once-wealthy family of Mississippi planters. Her downfall in the squalid, two-room French Quarter apartment of her married sister Stella Kowalski (Kim Hunter) and animalistic husband Stanley (Marlon Brando) is at the hands of savage, brutal forces in modern society.

Marlon Brando, in his second screen appearance (Brando's first screen role was a bitter paraplegic veteran in *The Men* (1950), and recreating his Broadway role, delivers an overpowering, memorable performance. During a drunken, losing poker hand, Stanley becomes uncontrollably berserk, charges after his wife, and assaults her with a few blows, causing a fight to break out to control his "lunacy." His poker buddies hold him under a cold shower to sober him up. Dripping wet with water, Stanley realizes he has struck and abused Stella, and feeling repentant, he searches for her.

Stella and Blanche have sought protective refuge in an upstairs apartment. Animalistic and virile in a wet, torn T-shirt, he repeatedly bellows for Stella from the street in front of their building, begging for her return: "Hey Stellahhhhh!"

Scene: "Hey Stellahhhhh!"

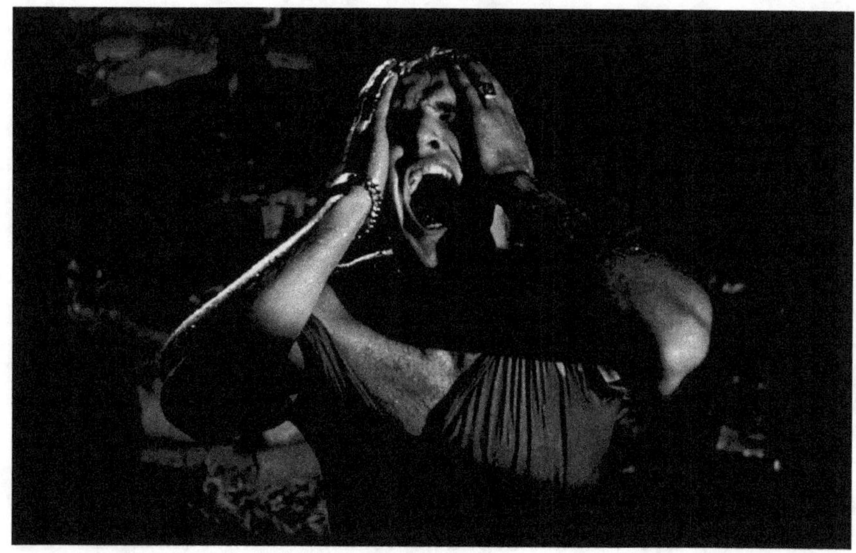

This scene is one of the most regularly-chosen clips played in film excerpts from cinematic history. With the low moan of a clarinet, Stella finally responds to her contradictory impulses—her anger melts into forgiveness, her fear into desire. She leaves the shelter of the upstairs apartment and stands, staring down at him from the upper landing. Then, she surrenders herself to him—she slowly descends the spiraling stairs to him and comes down to his level. He drops to his knees, crying. She sympathizes with him as he presses his face to her pregnant belly, and they embrace and kiss. Stanley begs: "Don't ever leave me, baby," and then literally sweeps her off her feet—he carries her into their dark apartment for a night of passion.

Brando's reputation as a difficult actor has been confirmed by several directors, but Elia Kazan isn't among them. He was one of the few who commanded the actor's complete respect. In his 1994 autobiography, *Brando: Songs My Mother Taught Me*, Marlon wrote,

> "I have worked with many movie directors—some good, some fair, some terrible. Kazan was the best actors' director by far of any I've worked for Gadg, who got his nickname because of an affection for gadgets, was the only one who ever really stimulated me, got into a part with me and virtually acted it with me."

This is a photograph of Brando talking to director Kazan on the set of *A Streetcar Named Desire*.

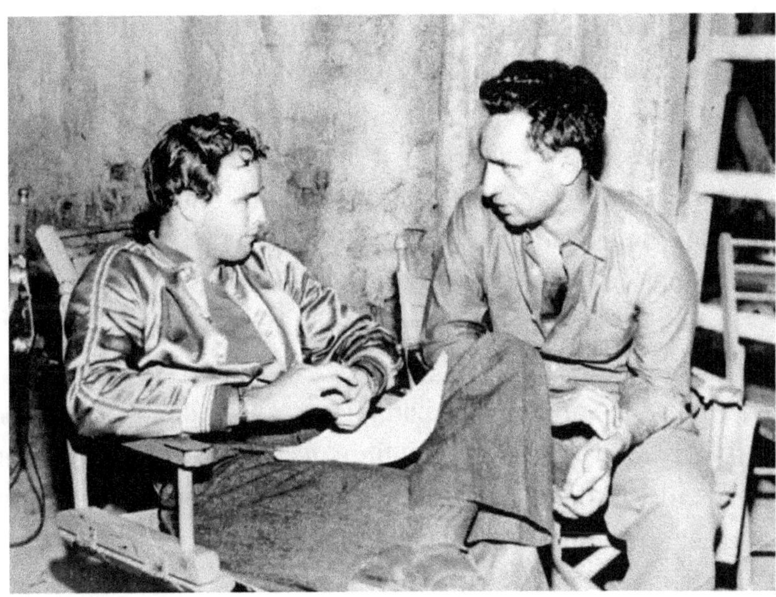

The role is regarded as one of Brando's greatest. The reception of Brando's performance was so positive that Brando quickly became a male sex symbol in Hollywood. The role earned him his first Academy Award nomination in the Best Actor category.

A Turner Classic Movies article discussed how the movie would change the traditional studio system:

> A Streetcar Named Desire also deserves another footnote in Hollywood history because of its revolutionary mode of production. While Hollywood filmmaking was still firmly entrenched in the studio system which used only studio-contracted actors and craftsmen, A Streetcar Named Desire turned out to be a harbinger of things to come. Independent agent-producer Charles Feldman purchased the property and brought it to Jack L. Warner, the head of Warner Bros. Studios. Independent director Elia Kazan was brought on board to direct, and playwright Tennessee Williams adapted his own work to the screen. Furthermore, none of the cast members were Warner contract players, and only a few crewmembers came from outside of Warner Bros. This film put one more crack in the studio system's ironclad hold on filmmaking in America, leading to even more power for independent producers and smaller filmmaking companies.

There have been a few film adaptions of the original 1951 film, notably by Woody Allen. His 1973 film *Sleeper* includes a late scene in which Miles (Woody) and Luna (Diane Keaton) briefly take on the roles of Stanley (Luna) and Blanche (Miles).

It was noted by many critics that the 2013 Academy Award–winning Woody Allen film *Blue Jasmine* had much in common with *Streetcar* and is most likely a loose adaptation. It shares a very similar plot and characters, although it has been suitably updated for modern film audiences.

There have been two different television movies based on the

Tennessee Williams play. In 1984, Treat Williams and Ann-Margret starred as Stanley and Blanche, while Beverly D'Angelo and Randy Quaid filled out the cast as Stella and Mitch, respectively. Then in 1995, Alec Baldwin and Jessica Lange starred in another TV-movie adaptation of Williams' play as Stanley and Blanche. Diane Lane and John Goodman co-starred as Stella and Mitch.

In an October 1992 episode of *The Simpsons* that spoofs *A Streetcar Named Desire*, Marge decides to try out for the Springfield Community Center's musical production of *Oh! Streetcar!* Marge plays Blanche, while next-door neighbor Ned Flanders is Stanley and Reverend Lovejoy's wife Helen, is Stella. Homer is not in the cast, but he does get into the homage act: when the tab breaks off his pudding can, he stands outside in the yard and screams, "Marge!" just as Marlon Brando shouted, "Stella!"

Tweety and Sylvester the Cat starred in a Warner Bros. animated short called *A Street Cat Named Sylvester* in September 1953, but all connections with *A Streetcar Named Desire* ended with the title.

The first Broadway revival of the play was in 1973. It was produced by the Lincoln Center at the Vivian Beaumont Theater and starred Rosemary Harris as Blanche, James Farentino as Stanley, and Patricia Conolly as Stella. A highly publicized revival in 1992 starred Alec Baldwin as Stanley and Jessica Lange as Blanche. It was staged at the Ethel Barrymore Theatre on Broadway, the same theatre that the original production was staged in 1947 with Jessica Tandy and Brando in the lead roles. The 2005 Broadway revival was directed by Edward Hall and produced by The Roundabout Theater Company. It starred John C. Reilly as Stanley, Amy Ryan as Stella, and Natasha Richardson as Blanche. In March 2019, the American Theatre Company of Brussels, Belgium, played it on its fiftieth anniversary at Le Jacques Franck Theatre.

High Noon (1952)

High Noon is possibly the all-time best Western film ever made—a successful box-office production by Stanley Kramer and director Fred Zinnemann. The Western genre was employed to tell an uncharacteristic social problem tale about civic responsibility, without much of the typical frontier violence, panoramic land-scapes, or tribes of marauding Indians.

This iconic moment occurs when Sheriff Kane (Gary Cooper) recognizes that the townspeople will not aid him in his struggle against a band of murderous outlaws. The time span of the film (about 105 minutes) approximates the actual screen length of the film—eighty-five minutes—accentuated by frequent images of the clock as time rapidly dissipates before the final showdown.

The story of a man who was too proud to run, even though it most likely will result in his death!

The dramatic, tightly-compressed, austere black-and-white film with high-contrast images was shot in a spare thirty-one days, and the physically pained, ravaged look etched on fifty-one-year-old Gary Cooper's gaunt face was due to actual illness (a recurring hip problem, bleeding stomach ulcers, and lower back pain) and emotional stress due to his recent breakup with actress Patricia Neal after a three-year, well-publicized affair while sep-arated from his wife.

Scene: Alone to Face His Destiny

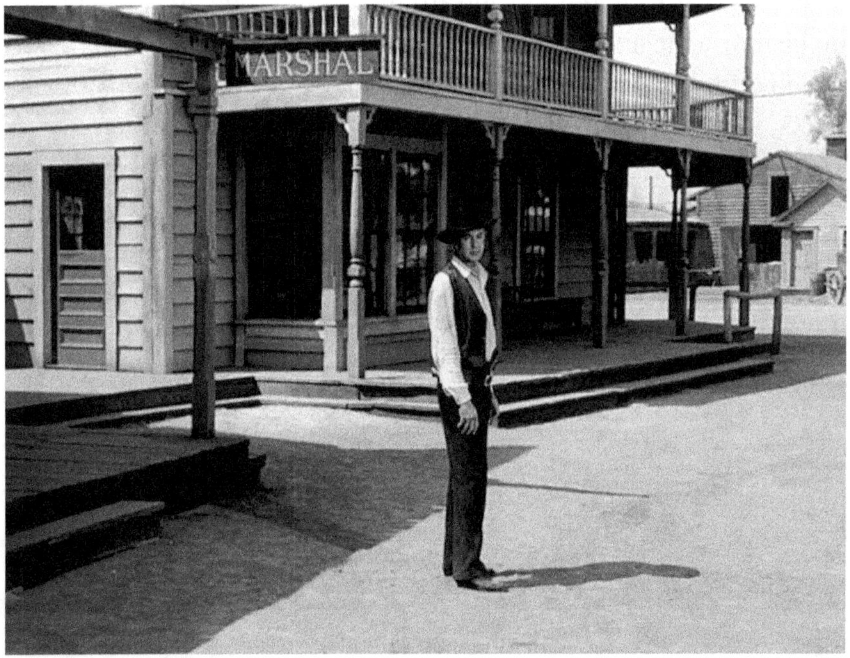

In the exciting finale and gripping shootout sequence on Hadleyville's main street, Kane is betrayed and all alone, surveying and walking up the deserted streets of the ghost town toward the four tough killers. No one is there to support him and come to his aid: not the judge, not his immature deputy Harvey, not the retired sheriff, nor any of the cross-section of townspeople or his friends. Not even his wife, whom he just married minutes ago!

In the film's most famous, memorable shot—a dramatic reverse high-crane shot in broad daylight—the camera pulls up and away from the lone, abandoned, and frightened figure of the Marshal, leaving him dwarfed by the buildings on either side of the town's dusty street. It is a perfect example where character size within the visual space proves symbolic. He is alone both physically and metaphorically. He is a solitary man implacably forced to confront destiny and face the real issue at hand. He turns and walks toward the train station. At this moment in the film, a melancholy refrain of "The Ballad of High Noon" is heard punctuating the stark loneliness and helplessness of the scene.

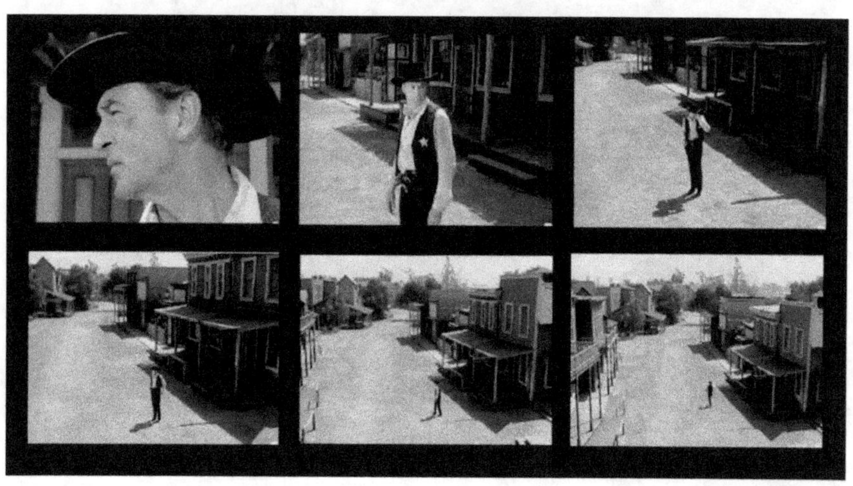

"The climax follows in a fairly spectacular shot (impossible to obtain with a zoom lens) starting close on the Marshal and moving into the longest possible boom-shot of the entire town, the empty street, and the tiny forlorn shape of the man turning and starting to walk toward his destiny," as quoted by Fred Zinnemann in his 1992 book *Fred Zinnemann, An Autobiography*. He achieved this by using a long crane that he borrowed from fellow director George Stevens. If you look closely, you can see, in the upper frame, the nearby Warner Bros. studio lot.

The famous street scene was used in the opening credit for the long-running and beloved television series *Gunsmoke* (1955–1975) for at least part of its run.

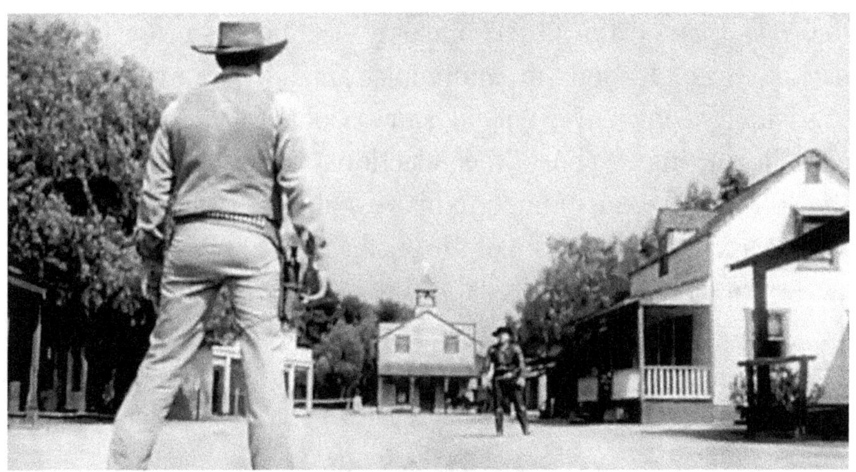

High Noon is referenced several times on the highly acclaimed HBO drama series *The Sopranos*. Tony Soprano cites Gary Cooper's character as the archetype of what a man should be, mentally tough and stoic. He frequently laments, "Whatever happened to Gary Cooper?" and refers to Will Kane as the "strong, silent type." The iconic ending to the film is shown on a television during an extended dream sequence in the fifth-season episode "The Test Dream."

A television sequel, *High Noon Part II, The Return of Will Kane,* was produced in 1980 and aired on CBS in November of that year. Lee Majors and Katherine Cannon played the Cooper and Kelly roles. Elmore Leonard wrote the original screenplay.

Outland is a 1981 British science-fiction thriller film written and directed by Peter Hyams and starring Sean Connery, Peter Boyle, and Frances Sternhagen, and was inspired by *High Noon*.

In 2000, Stanley Kramer's widow, Karen Sharpe Kramer, produced a remake of *High Noon* as a TV-movie for the cable channel TBS, with Tom Skerritt playing the lead role.

In 1989, twenty-two-year-old Polish graphic designer Tomasz Sarnecki transformed Marian Stachurski's 1959 Polish variant of the *High Noon* poster into a Solidarity election poster for the first partially free elections in communist Poland. The poster, which was widely seen all over Poland, shows Cooper armed with a folded ballot saying "Wybory" (i.e., elections) in his right hand while the Solidarity logo is pinned to his vest above the sheriff's badge. The message at the bottom of the poster reads: "W samo południe: 4 czerwca 1989," which translates to "*High Noon*: 4 June 1989."

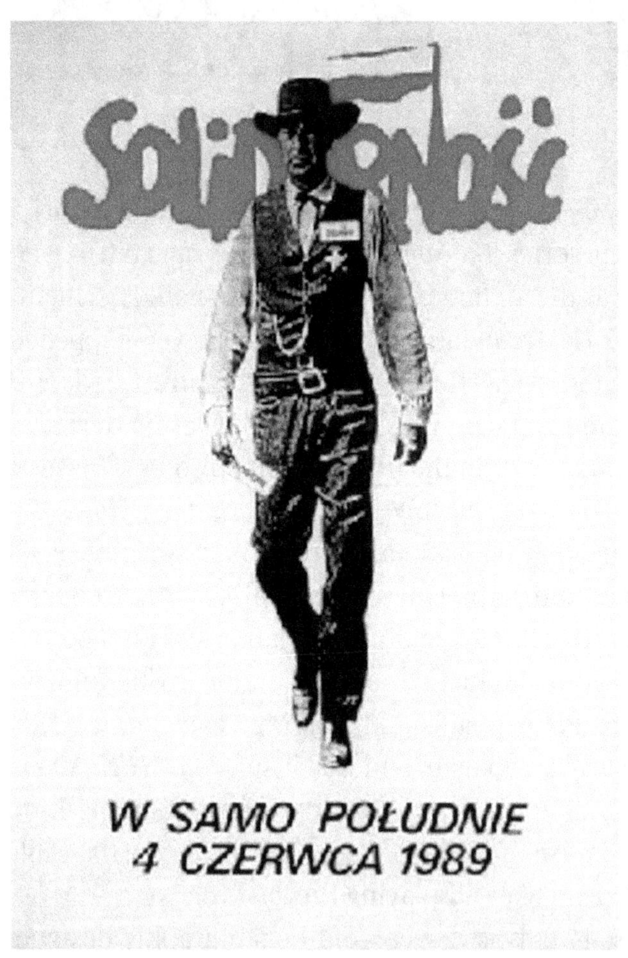

Singin' in the Rain (1952)

Singin' in the Rain is truly one of the most-loved and celebrated film musicals of all time from MGM. The joyous film, co-directed by Stanley Donen and acrobatic dancer-star-choreographer Gene Kelly, is a charming, upbeat, graceful, and thoroughly enjoyable experience with great songs, lots of flashbacks, and wonderful dances. This was another extraordinary example of the organic "integrated musical" in which the story's characters naturally express their emotions in the midst of their lives. Song and dance replace the dialogue, usually during moments of high spirits or passionate romance. And over half of the film, a "let's put on a play" type of film, is composed of musical numbers.

The film offers a lighthearted depiction of Hollywood in the late 1920s, with the three stars portraying performers caught up in the transition from silent films to "talkies."

The joyous title song sequence from this musical has become movie legend as the most famous dance number in American film—and it is Gene Kelly's finest solo performance ever. In a classic, heart-lifting, enchanting dance scene during a cloudburst, Don Lockwood (Gene Kelly) does a glorious performance of the title song "Singin' in the Rain," a spontaneous expression of his euphoric mood and happiness over his new-found love for Kathy Selden (Debbie Reynolds).

Scene: The Dance Sequence

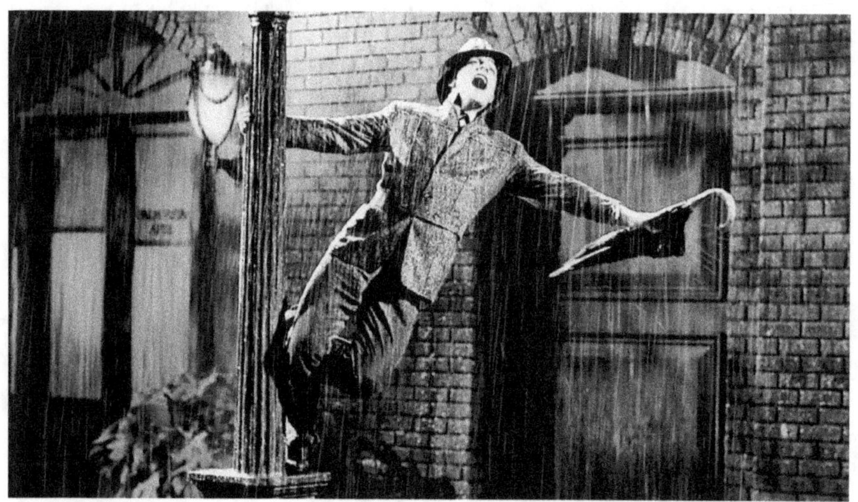

He strolls down the empty two blocks in the rain, passing shop windows (including a pharmacy/drugstore with a "Smoke Mahout" window display, the Richard Carlane Music Studio, the LaValle Millinery Shop, the First Editions Bookstore, and Mount Hollywood Art School). At first, he keeps his umbrella open above him to keep dry, but after a few short steps, he shrugs and closes it (and either lays it on his shoulder, swings it, keeps it to his side, or imaginatively incorporates it into the number).

He skips on the sidewalk, climbs on and swings around a lamppost, and saunters and sloshes along. Then, he jumps and tap-dances through the puddles—becoming more and more child-like. He lets a drainpipe of rainwater drain on his upturned face, kicks up water, splashes, cavorts, and stamps around with sheer delight. After twirling on the cobblestoned street, he balances on the street curb like a tightrope walker. When a mystified and vaguely hostile policeman finally walks over to find out what he is doing jumping up and down in deep puddles and looks at him suspiciously, he reacts guiltily toward the authority figure. (When the camera cuts from one view to another, Kelly's two hands on the umbrella change to only his right hand on the umbrella.) He slows down, turns, and answers simply: "I'm dancin' and singin' in the rain." He closes his umbrella, grins boldly, walks off, hands his umbrella off to a needy passerby, and waves back toward the policeman from afar.

While the film is chock-full of musical highlights, Gene Kelly's "Singin' in the Rain" number is the genuine showstopper. Regarding his immortal solo, Kelly later commented, quite graciously and modestly, on what made the scene work so well:

> "The concept was so simple I shied away from explaining it to the brass at the studio in case I couldn't make it sound worth doing. The real work for this one was done by the technicians who had to pipe two city blocks on the backlot with overhead sprays, and the poor cameraman who had to shoot through all that water. All I had to do was dance."

The technicians' efforts are all the more remarkable since there was a severe water shortage in Culver City, California, the day the sequence was shot.

In the sequence in which Gene Kelly dances and sings the title song while spinning an umbrella, splashing through puddles and getting soaked with rain, Kelly was sick with a 103°F (39°C) fever. (The water used in the scene caused Kelly's wool suit to shrink during filming.) A common myth is that Kelly managed to perform the entire song in one take, thanks to cameras placed at predetermined locations. However, this was not the case; filming the sequence took two to three days. Another myth is that the rain was mixed with milk in order for the drops to show up better on camera, but the desired visual effect was produced, albeit with difficulty, through backlighting.

The song "Singin' in the Rain" has been featured in many films, but it was Stanley Kubrick who made ironic use of the song in his bleak vision of a dystopian future, *A Clockwork Orange* (1971). Kubrick mulled for days over a way to shoot the scene where Alex (Malcolm McDowell) brutalizes a woman.

Out of the blue, he turned to McDowell and asked, "Can you sing?"

McDowell replied, "I only know one song," and he started to do "Singin' in the Rain."

Kubrick then left the room and called Warner Bros. in Hollywood to ask if he could obtain the rights to "Singin' in the Rain." He came back to the set an hour later and wryly told Adrienne Corri (cast as the rape/murder victim), "You're playing the Debbie Reynolds part, Corri."

Coincidentally, Stanley Donen was in London at the time and not far from the location site for *A Clockwork Orange*. When Kubrick asked Donen for his opinion of this new use of the song, Donen surprisingly raised no objections.

Shane (1953)

Shane is a timeless, classic western tale—a very familiar and highly regarded seminal western and the most successful western of the 1950s. The film's rich color cinematography captures the beautiful environment of the legendary frontier (filmed on location in Jackson Hole, Wyoming) with its gray-blue Grand Tetons as a backdrop.

Veteran director/producer George Stevens self-consciously fashioned this simple western into a wide-screen, Technicolored, panoramic masterpiece to create a symbolic myth: the age-old story of the duel between good and evil, the advent of civilization (with families, law and order, and homesteaders) and progress into the wilderness (a world of roaming cattlemen, lawless gunslingers, and loners on horseback), a land-dispute conflict between a homesteader and cattle baron, and the coming of age of a young boy. In this particular allegory, Alan Ladd plays the gunfighter trying to forget his past by moving in with the Starrett's (Joe played by Van Heflin, Marian played by Jean Arthur, and Joey played by Brandon de Wilde). Unfortunately, his past catches up with him quickly when the Starretts are threatened, which forces him to become what he really is and reluctantly relinquish his attempt to settle down.

Scene: "Shane Come Back"

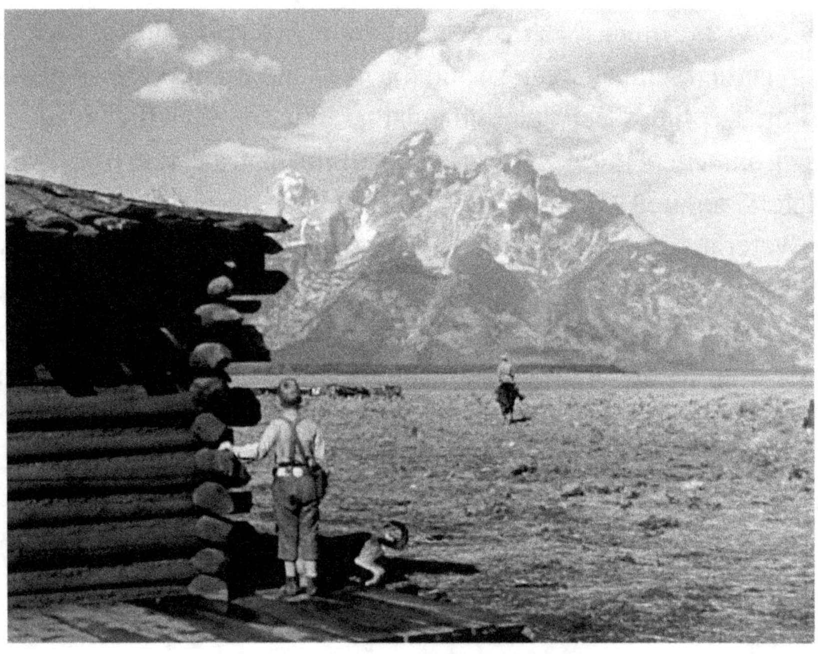

The echoing finale, as Shane rides off into the bluish distance of the empty Wyoming landscape after a poignant goodbye and farewell, is an unforgettable sequence.

Young Joey is the only one to bid Shane, his mythical idolized hero, farewell. As gunfighter Shane starts to leave, he indicates to Joey that he will never return. Tears well up in Joey's eyes, and Shane whispers quietly: "Bye, little Joe." The fringe-jacketed, lonely hero then rides off into the twilight meadow toward the distant hills framed against the sky and mountains, growing smaller and smaller in the distance. Young, anguished, and heartbroken, Joey sadly calls out to his hero/idol in one of filmdom's most famous and haunting endings, as tears streak down his face:

"Pa's got things for you to do, and Mother wants you. I know she does. Shane. Shane. Come back. Bye, Shane."

Badly (and possibly lethally) injured in the gun battle, Shane disappears into the twilight meadow toward the distant hills framed against the sky and mountains, growing smaller and smaller in the distance. Young, anguished, and heartbroken, Joey sadly calls out to his hero/idol in one of filmdom's most famous, melancholic and haunting endings, as tears streak down his face. (He is left abandoned and stranded there, summarizing the needs that the members of his family—including himself—have had for Shane.)

"Pa's got things for you to do, and Mother wants you." (The words "wants you" echo twice.) "I know she does. Shane. Shane!" (echoes) "Come back!" (echoes)

The mountains echo Joey's plaintive call as Shane (slightly slumped over in his saddle, wounded and dying—and almost dead?) rides up the crest to a second small-town cemetery (not Cemetery Hill). He rides through the tombstones as he ascends toward the snow-capped Tetons (metaphorically ascending into heaven?). In a mirror-image of the film's opening, he follows the same path that he had taken in his descent into the valley.

Joey's final call, mostly spoken as a thought to himself, is softly heard (so faint that Shane doesn't even hear it)—implying that symbolically, Shane's life (or way of life) is over: "Bye, Shane."

In the film's final few seconds, however, Shane and his horse mythically descend until both move completely out of camera range, possibly implying that Shane's mortal body returns to the earth.

But wait—*Shane*'s ending has become famous for the "did he live or die?" nature of its ending, but the point isn't really anything to do with whether or not Shane survives (most seem to think he dies, despite the fact that he only appears to have suffered a relatively minor wound).

The ending actually wraps the film up as an allegory for the gun-slinging way of life in general—Shane is a dying breed, and the ambiguity of the movie's ending serves to nail this point home: Shane is moving on not because he's injured and doesn't want to die in front of Joey, but because the film leaves that question unanswered, although viewers can be found to support either side of the argument. Those who conclude that Shane dies argue that the last scene in which he rides through a cemetery is an indication that he is dying or is already dead. They point out that he is slumping slightly with his arm to his side and that, in the novel, the gunshot was to his abdomen. They reason that he goes off to die as one last favor to the Starretts. Shane admires and likes Joe but is in love with Marian. He leaves so that they do not know for sure that he has died; he knows that the guilt Joe and Marian would feel at his death would poison their marriage. Those who conclude that Shane is not dying counter that the cemetery is simply on the way back to the mountains and that he is leaning forward because he is going uphill, as horseback riders tend to do. Although he was shot, they argue, it appears to be a superficial wound to his upper arm. The wound isn't bleeding profusely; Shane isn't acting like the wound is serious; he could mount and ride his horse; he is holding up the reins.

Others circumvent the argument entirely by pointing out that it matters little whether or not Shane dies from his wound. The movie itself is an allegory saying that the gunfighter, like the free-range cattle rancher, is a dying breed. The West is being settled, civilized, and developed. It's giving way to a new era where the rugged individual was being replaced by families, where peace would prevail, and gunfighters no longer had a place. There's really no place left for him anymore in the changing world.

This is the ultimate trope of Westerns and many assorted action movies. It is the eternal western conflict between the rootless drifter and the community. The heroic drifter who rides into town (or in this case, valley) who supposedly possesses mythical gunmanship. The drifter who tries re-integrating himself into a community, yearning for its emotional/communal safety and wholesomeness, yet is unable to do so because of his own self-identity, because of his very nature.

It is said that *Shane* is the most iconic western. Here is proof of that. *Shane* tells this age-old, archetypal story without any subversions, inversions, or other trope-changers. It presented the story at its purest and achieved it closest to perfection. It is the age-old-same-old, just done better than any other film. For what truly distinguishes Shane from other movie characters of this genre, is the earnestness of which he desires the community. Shane is the character that wants, more than any other character, to be integrated into a community, and hence it is all the more tragic when he fails.

The 1980 Japanese film *A Distant Cry* from Spring (遙かなる山の呼び声) features a similar plot.

The 1985 film *Pale Rider* is partly inspired by *Shane*, with Clint Eastwood playing a mysterious stranger who comes to the aid of gold prospectors terrorized by a mining tycoon.

The film *Soldier*, released in 1998, takes the basic *Shane* plot and sets it in the motif of a *Blade Runner* (1982) universe. Kurt Russell plays a battle-hardened replicate who is dumped on a garbage planet. He is taken in by a colony of humans similarly marooned and eventually defends them when they come under attack.

In the 1998 film *The Negotiator*, the two leading characters have a discussion about Western genre films, *Shane* in particular. Arguing about the ending, one character says Shane died, and the other says, "He's slumped 'cause he's shot, and shot don't mean dead."

The 2017 film *Logan* drew substantial thematic influence from *Shane* and formally acknowledged it with a series of specific dialogue references and scene clips. As the film ends, Shane's farewell words to Joey are recited, verbatim, at the title character's grave.

On the Waterfront (1954)

On the Waterfront is a gritty and controversial film directed by Elia Kazan—a part drama and part gangster film. The authentic-looking, powerful film is concerned with the problems of trade unionism, corruption, and racketeering. And it is set on New York's oppressive waterfront docks, where dock workers struggled for work, dignity, and to make ends meet under the control of hard-knuckled, mob-run labor unions that would force them to submit to daily "shape-ups" by cruel hiring bosses.

The film's morality tale of corruption ends with its ultimate defeat and the saving of the community by a morally-redeemed martyr (a common man with a conscience). With a naturalistic acting style, Marlon Brando portrayed an inarticulate, struggling, brutish hero and small-time, washed-up ex-boxer who took a regrettable fall in the ring. Now just an errand boy and "owned" by the union boss, he is unaware of his own personal power. But eventually, because of torment over his actions and his realization of new choices in life, he disavows the advice of his older brother Rod Steiger and joins forces with a tough-minded, courageous, and crusading priest, Father Barry (Karl Malden) and a loving, angelic blonde woman (Eddie Doyle played by Eva Marie Saint), a sister of one of the victims, to seek reform and challenge the mob.

Scene: Confrontation in the Taxicab

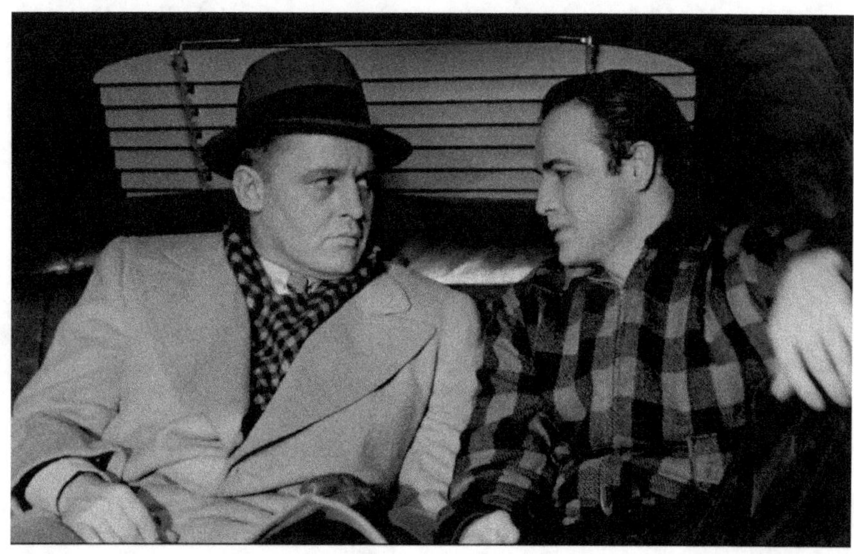

The most famous, truthful scene of Elia Kazan's film is the one in the back of a New York taxicab between two brothers: Charley Malloy (Rod Steiger), a smartly-dressed lawyer for the criminal union boss; and Terry Malloy (Marlon Brando), his younger brother, an ex-prize-fighter and waterfront bum.

Charley advises Terry to keep his mouth shut and not testify about what he knows about the corrupt union bosses. He becomes exasperated with his stubborn brother's unwillingness to comply immediately. Charley suggests that if they get to their destination, 437 River Street, and Terry hasn't made up his mind, there may be serious consequences. Terry is stunned by his brother's words. Suddenly, Charley pulls a gun, threatening him to accept an easy dock job in exchange for keeping quiet. Surprised, Terry pushes the gun away, gently guiding it down: "Charley, Charley, oh Charley. Wow."

Embittered, Terry faces up to the fact that he has made nothing of his life, blaming his brother instead of his ex-boxing manager. Terry is reminded of how he was given "a one-way ticket to Palookaville" in his boxing days when he knew he had a winner inside himself but was told to lose. At one point in his life, he could have risen about his low-life condition through his skill as a prizefighter. He poignantly looks back to the night of the fight when he lost all his sense of personal worth and integrity. He realizes that his brother betrayed him and sold him out. He continues his sad, pitiable lament, and blames his brother for compromising and sacrificing his boxing career and his life, preventing him from becoming a contender for the title:

> "You was my brother, Charley. You should've looked out for me a little bit. You should've taken care of me—just a little bit—so I wouldn't have to take them dives for the short-end money... You don't understand! I could've had class. I could've been a contender. I could've been somebody, instead of a bum, which is what I am. Let's face it... It was you, Charley."

Director Elia Kazan originally intended to shoot the famous taxicab scene between Rod Steiger and Marlon Brando in an actual cab. But producer Sam Spiegel opted instead to use a shabby old taxicab shell. When the crucial rear-projection equipment was not available to shoot the scene, cameraman Boris Kaufman had to put a small Venetian blind across the window and small, flickering lights on the side of the cab to create the illusion of movement.

The famous taxicab scene between Rod Steiger and Marlon Brando is now considered one of the great sequences in American cinema, performed by two master Method actors who partially improvised their dialogue with little to no direction from Elia Kazan.

"The finest thing ever done by an American film actor" was how director Elia Kazan had characterized the performance of Marlon Brando in *On the Waterfront*.

It is one of the most justly famous scenes in the history of the American cinema, and surely one of the simplest: two brothers, talking in the back seat of a cab. Once, they were joined by the hope of climbing out of their slum childhood through the patronage of "important people." Now they are divided by the emerging moral sense of one of the brothers, and the rising fear of the other that the important people may turn on them both and rend them.

It is, of course, Elia Kazan's *On The Waterfront*, a film whose themes of brotherly loyalty and political betrayal have become so integral to the American film that another brilliant film, the 1980 *Raging Bull*, is so unashamedly inspired by it that the protagonist of the latter film recites the indelible lines of the taxicab scene.

Rear Window (1954)

Rear Window is a wonderfully exciting and suspenseful Technicolor mystery thriller film directed by Alfred Hitchcock and written by John Michael Hayes, based on Cornell Woolrich's 1942 short story entitled "It Had to Be Murder." The film is considered by many filmgoers, critics, and scholars to be one of Hitchcock's best.

Recuperating from a broken leg, adventuresome professional photographer L. B. "Jeff" Jefferies (James Stewart) is confined to a wheelchair in his Greenwich Village apartment. His rear window looks out onto a courtyard and several other apartments. During a powerful heatwave, he watches his neighbors who keep their windows open to stay cool.

He observes a flamboyant dancer he nicknames "Miss Torso;" a single woman he calls "Miss Lonelyhearts;" a talented, single, composer-pianist; several married couples, one of them newlyweds; a female sculptor; and Lars Thorwald (Raymond Burr), a traveling jewelry salesman with a bedridden wife. It is this particular tenant whose suspicious nocturnal activities will receive most of Jeff's attention along with his socialite girlfriend, Lisa Fremont (Grace Kelly) and insurance company's nurse, Stella (played by Thelma Ritter).

Scene: The Hunter Becomes the Hunted

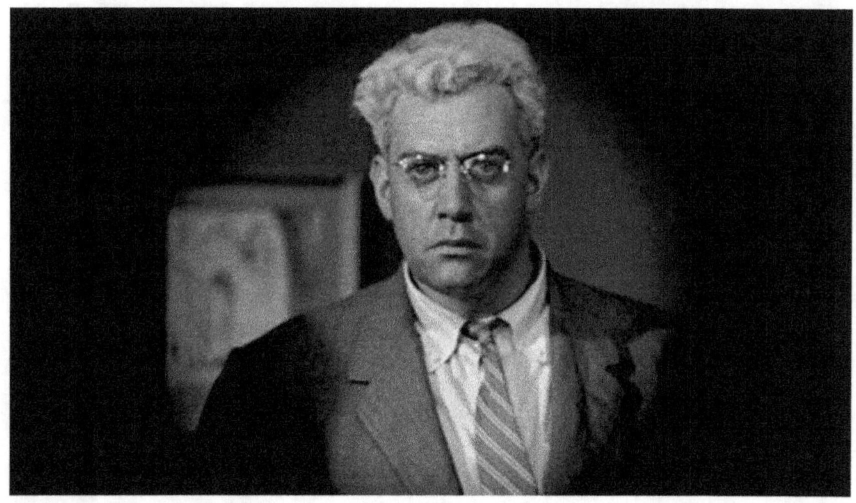

Let me set the scene: Ida is in Thorwald's apartment and has found the wedding ring belonging to Burr's wife, whom he has killed, butchered, and disposed, in separate packages, all over the city. Kelly is wearing her ring on one of her fingers to show Jeff looking at her through his camera equipped with a telephoto lens. Burr sees her signaling to someone as she repeatedly points to the wedding ring on her hand. Burr's eyes slowly move from her hands upward in the direction of Stewart, looking directly into his camera. Stewart's head snaps back from holding his camera and yells to Thelma Ritter to shut off the lights, but it is too late. Stewart has been caught snooping and is now in mortal danger.

The angle of the shot is eye level, as seen through Stewart's camera lens. The shot is a close-up, although Stewart and Burr are actually far away from each other in their respective apartments across a large courtyard. The close-out is because Stewart's camera has a telephoto lens attached to it. The lighting in Burr's apartment is low-key and subdued, and Burr stands squarely in the center of the shot, so all the audience's focus and attention are solely on him and him alone. Burr stands erect, alert, and totally serious as he glares out, across the courtyard, expressionless. He is now wearing his glasses so he can see Stewart clearly. Although the shot appears to be at eye level, we know for a fact that Stewart's apartment is actually higher than Burr's. Hitchcock does this deliberately as the hunter has suddenly become the hunted. He is emphasizing that they are now on the same level playing field, the game is afoot, and that their deadly confrontation is inevitable.

When Thorwald slowly looks up and gazes directly into Stewart's camera—and into the eyes of the viewer—the sense of the watcher becoming the watched is like a punch in the gut. That the gaze belongs to a man with a discomfiting silver mane atop his head—a hairdo that would not look out of place on a schoolmarm, stalking the rows of a classroom, slapping her palm with a ruler—only makes the moment that much more disturbing. But here is another perspective on the Burr character. Thorwald is a thoroughly beaten man from the moment we set eyes on him: beaten down by life, by his job, by his marriage. Despite his size, we get the impression that he has little strength remaining. Even his crumpled hat and wrinkled suit seem to say, "What's the use? This is all I've got left." Perhaps, he does deserve maybe an ounce of sympathy.

More on Raymond Burr's "look." Hitchcock had a long-standing grudge with his former producer, David O. Selznick. The director believed Selznick had meddled too much with his movies, so much so that Hitchcock effectively disowned his first film with the producer, *Rebecca* (1940). His ties to Selznick ended with the 1947 movie *The Paradine Case*, though, so Hitch decided to enact a sly bit of revenge onscreen. It involved Raymond Burr, the actor playing

Rear Window villain Lars Thorwald. Hitchcock gave Burr glasses just like Selznick's and curly gray hair to match. He also instructed Burr to adopt many of the producer's mannerisms, such as the way he cradled a telephone in his neck. When all was said and done, Burr's murderous character looked a lot like Selznick, no doubt to the producer's supreme annoyance.

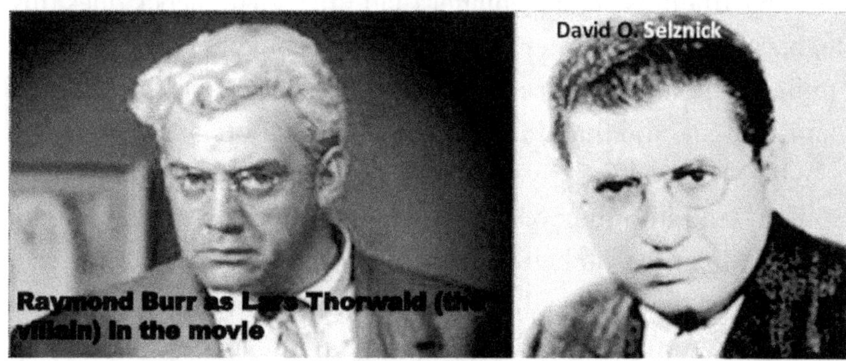

Sixty-four years after its release, *Rear Window* is referenced in public art commissioned for the Treefort Music Fest in Boise, Idaho.

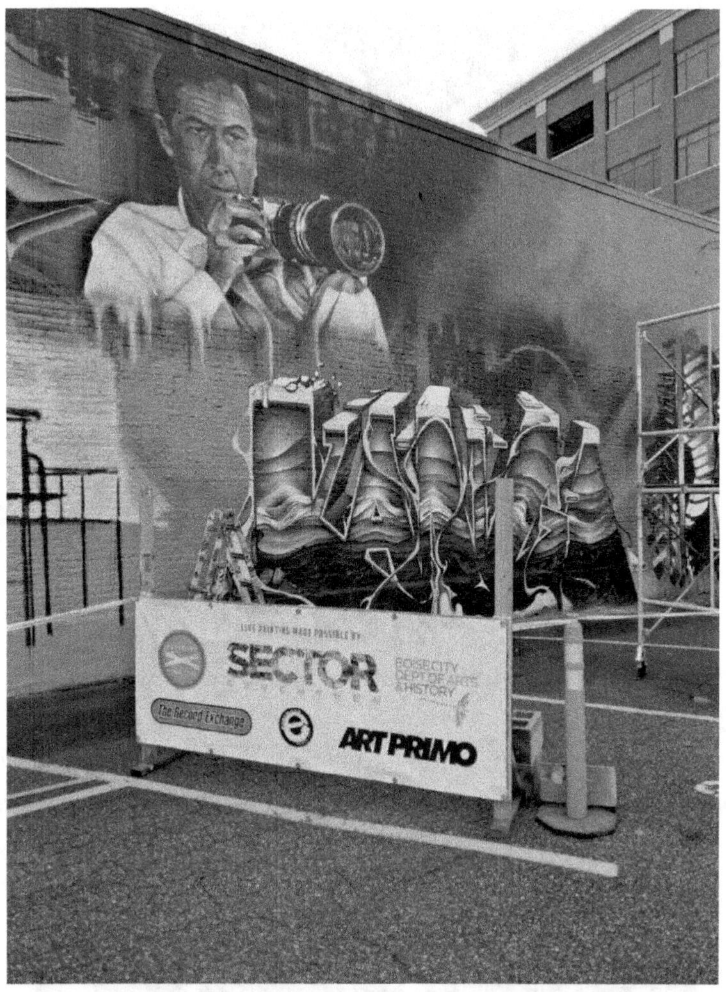

Rear Window was remade as a television movie (1998) of the same name, with an updated storyline in which the lead character is paralyzed and lives in a high-tech home filled with assistive technology. Actor Christopher Reeve, himself paralyzed as a result of a 1995 horse-riding accident, was cast in the lead role. It aired November 22, 1998, on the ABC television network. The poster for this movie and the scene where Reeves is "spotted" is now shown.

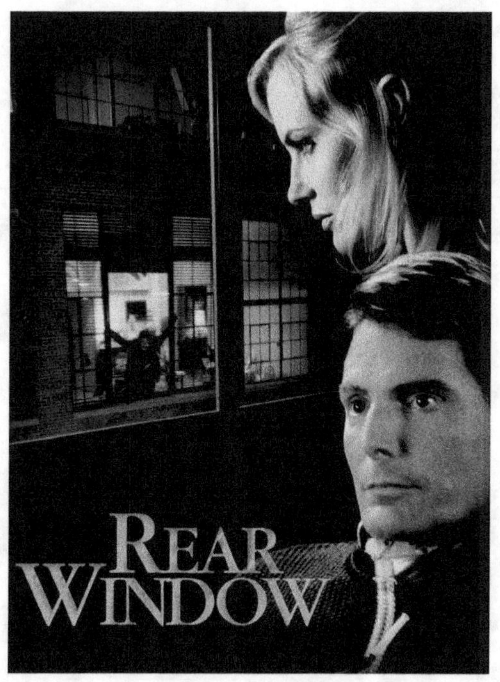

Disturbia (2007) is a modern-day retelling, with the protagonist (Shia LaBeouf)) under house arrest instead of laid up with a broken leg and who believes that his neighbor is a serial killer rather than having committed a single murder.

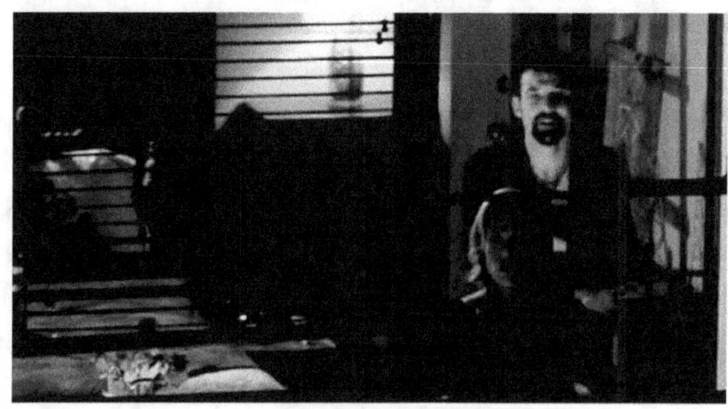

The Ten Commandments (1956)

The legendary film legend Cecil D. DeMille produced and directed two movies entitled *The Ten Commandments*. The second version
was made in 1956 and is an epic religious drama film produced,
directed, and narrated by Cecil B. DeMille, shot in VistaVision (color
by Technicolor), and released by Paramount Pictures. The film is
based on *Prince of Egypt* by Dorothy Clarke Wilson, *Pillar of Fire* by JH
Ingraham, *On Eagle's Wings* by AE Southon, and the book of Exodus.
As the earlier version of this movie conveyed, *The Ten Commandments* dramatizes the biblical story of the life of Moses, an adopted
Egyptian prince who becomes the deliverer of his real brethren, the
enslaved Hebrews, and therefore leads the Exodus to Mount Sinai,
where he receives, from God, the Ten Commandments.

Scene: The Parting of the Red Sea

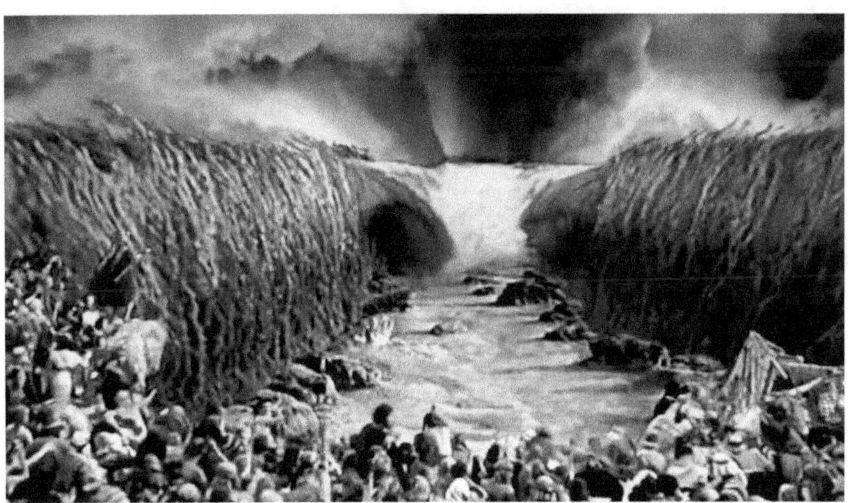

DeMille was reluctant to discuss technical details of how the film was made, especially the optical tricks used in the parting of the Red Sea. Although separated by many years, the special effects wizardry used to create the parting of the Red Sea marveled audience when both movies were released, so this scene will be discussed together. The special photographic effects in 1956 edition of *The Ten Commandments* were created by John P. Fulton, ASC (who received an Oscar for his effects in the film), head of the special effects department at Paramount Pictures, assisted by Paul Lerpae, ASC in Optical Photography (blue screen "traveling matte" composites) and Farciot Edouart, ASC, in Process Photography (rear projection effects). Because the 1956 version had the immense advantage of superior technological tools and expertise, we have to give the nod to that version as far as rankings.

To set the scene, the Hebrews are trapped at the edge of the Red Sea and are threatened by the approaching Egyptians on chariots and bend on their total destruction when Moses declares: "The Lord of Hosts will do battle for us. Behold his mighty hand!"

According to Turner Classic Movies (TCM):

> "The huge Red Sea set included two giant water tanks, according to an April 1955 New York Times report, which covered not only a 300 by 300-foot square area of the Paramount backlot but also part of the RKO backlot. According to a contemporary *Time* review, the special effects team 'built a 200,000 cubic-foot swimming pool, [and] installed hydraulic equipment that could deluge the area with 360,000 gallons of water in two minutes flat.'"

According to modern sources, John Fulton simply projected the film of the water pouring out of the tanks in reverse to stimulate the parting of the sea, with footage of the actors then superimposed over the shots of the water. Rear projection, an in-camera effect, placed cloud effects in the background for this scene. According to TCM, part of the live-action footage for the Red Sea sequence was shot on location in Egypt, and part of it in studio soundstages in front of blue screen backings. A contemporary Paramount Studio Report stated the water "in the first scenes of the encampment is actually the Red Sea," while miniatures and the water in the tanks were used for the rest of the sequence. Matte paintings of the bottom of the sea and of the sky were combined with the rest of the footage. The report concluded that "the opening and closing scenes of the sea are a combination of as many as twelve original negatives printed together with stationery split screen mattes, rotoscope hand-made mattes, and blue screen mattes."

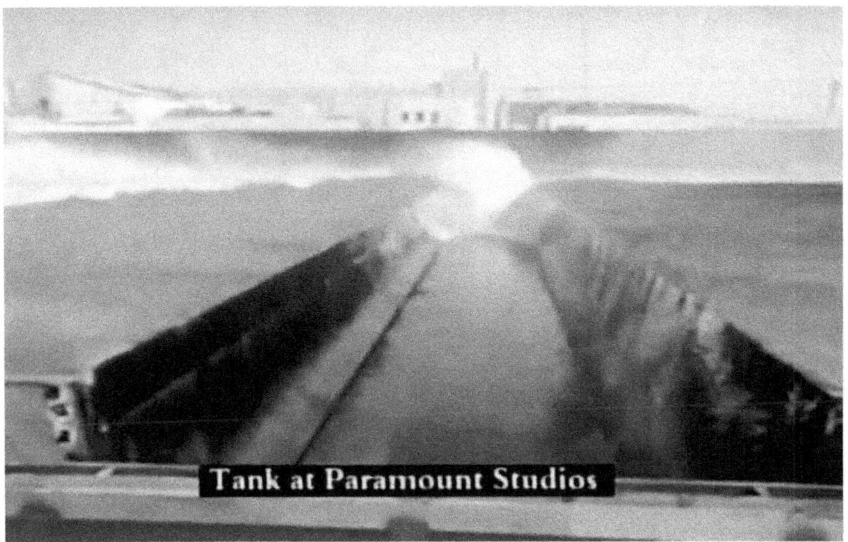

In order to kill the Egyptians, tons of water was captured running forward through the tank.

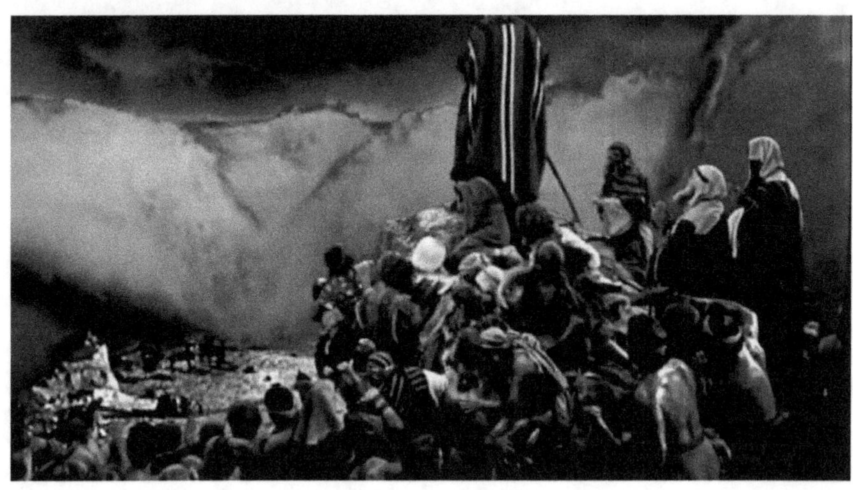

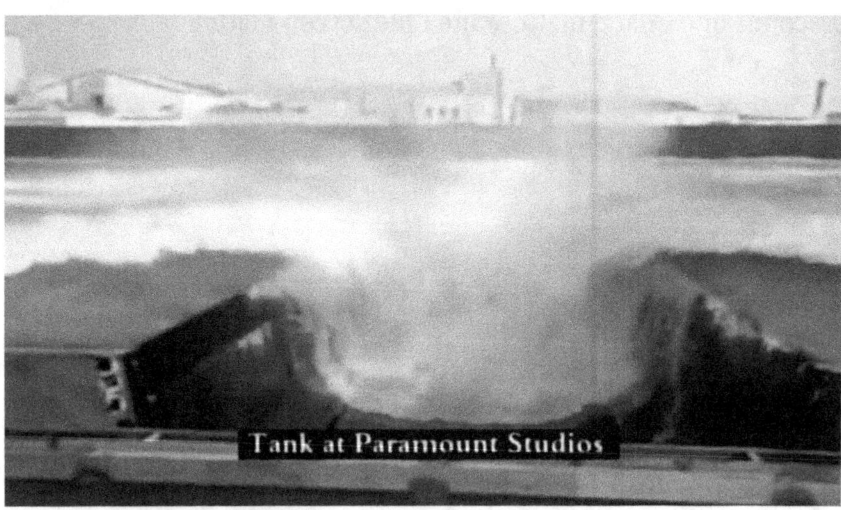

In order to film the scene where the water is held back so the Hebrews can escape, the sides of the tanks at Paramount Studios were filmed sideways and separately and then combined together to give the illusion of two walls of water being held in suspension.

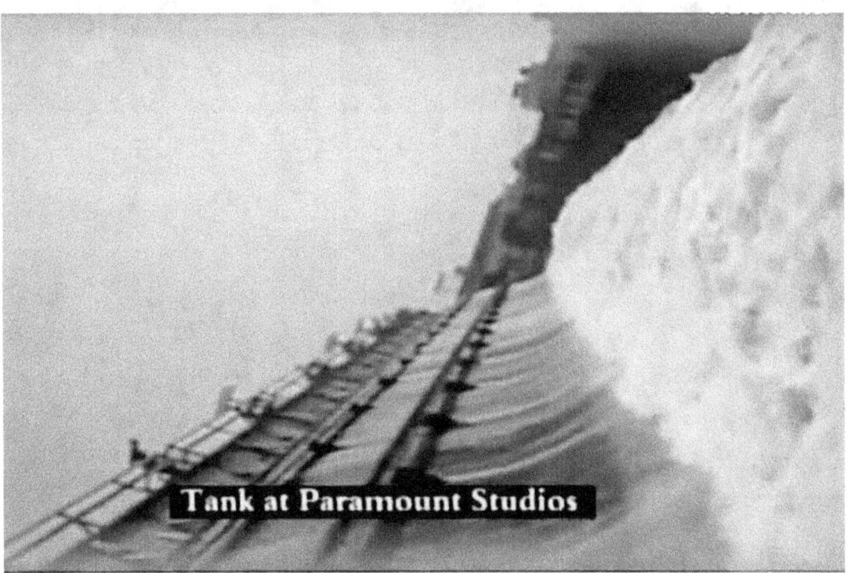

Tank at Paramount Studios

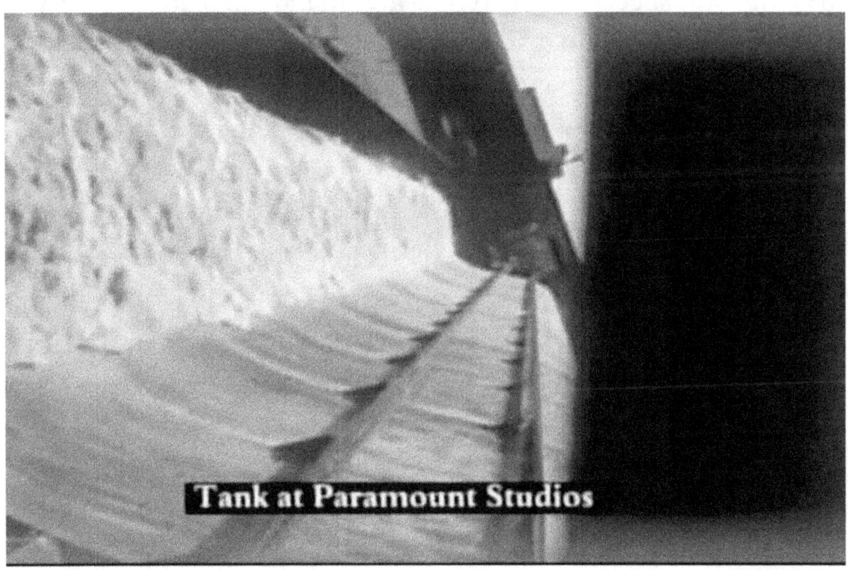

Tank at Paramount Studios

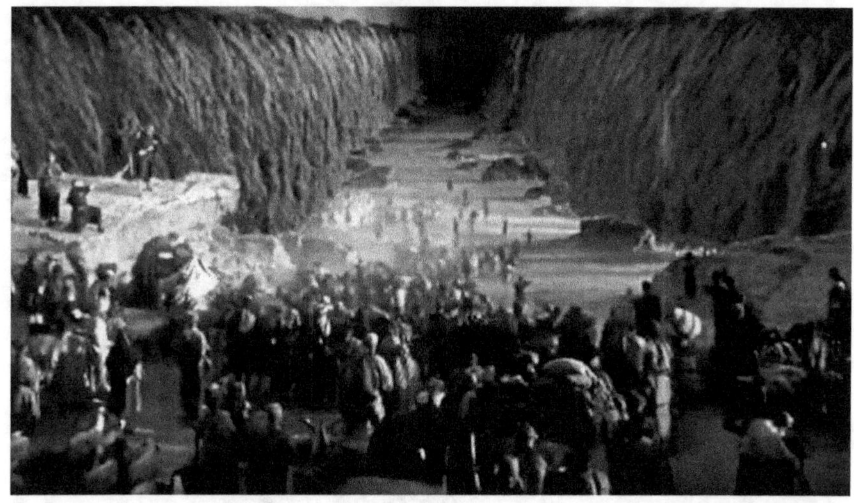

We have already discussed the fact that the parting of the Red Sea sequence in the 1956 version of *The Ten Commandments* is considered to be the best special effects renderings in motion picture history.

Therefore, I wanted to instead discuss the legacy of the "human" star of the film, and so many others, Mr. Charlton Heston.

Heston was born John Charles Carter on October 4, 1923, to Lilla Baines (1899–1994) and Russell Whitford Carter (1897–1966), a saw-mill operator.

As a versatile and highly talented Hollywood star, he appeared in almost one hundred films over the course of sixty years, ranging from westerns, biblical heroes, science fiction thrillers, and drama.

Richard Corliss wrote in *Time* magazine:

"From start to finish, Heston was a grand, ornery anach-ronism, the sinewy symbol of a time when Hollywood took itself seriously when heroes came from history books, not comic books. Epics like *Ben-Hur* or *El Cid* simply couldn't be made today, in part because popular culture has changed as much as political fashion. But mainly because there's no one remotely like Charlton Heston to infuse the form with his stature, fire, and guts."

In his obituary for the actor, film critic Roger Ebert noted,

"Heston made at least three movies that almost everybody eventually sees: *Ben-Hur*, *The Ten Commandments,* and *Planet of the Apes.*"

Heston's cinematic legacy was the subject of *Cinematic Atlas: The Triumphs of Charlton Heston*, an eleven-film retrospective by the Film Society of the Lincoln Center that was shown at the Walter Reade Theatre from August 29 to September 4, 2008.

On April 17, 2010, Heston was inducted into the National Cowboy and Western Heritage Museum's Hall of Great Western Performers.

In his childhood hometown of St. Helen, Michigan, a charter school, Charlton Heston Academy, opened on September 4, 2012. It is housed in the former St. Helen Elementary School. Enrollment on the first day was 220 students in grades kindergarten through eighth.

Charlton Heston was commemorated on a United States postage stamp issued on April 11, 2014.

Charlton Heston was inducted as a Laureate of the Lincoln Academy of Illinois and awarded the Order of Lincoln (the State's highest honor) by the Governor of Illinois in 1977 in the area of Performing Arts.

From 1965 until 1971, Heston served as president of the Screen Actors Guild. The Guild had been created in 1933 for the benefit of actors, who had different interests from the producers and directors who controlled the Academy of Motion Pictures Arts and Sciences.

The Searchers (1956)

The Searchers is considered by many to be a true American masterpiece of filmmaking, and the best, most influential, and perhaps most-admired film of director John Ford. The film's complex, deeply nuanced themes included racism, individuality, the American character, and the opposition between civilization (exemplified by homes, caves, and other domestic interiors) and the untamed frontier wilderness.

The Searchers tells the emotionally complex story of a perilous, hate-ridden quest and Homeric-style odyssey of self-discovery after a Comanche massacre, while also exploring the themes of racial prejudice and sexism. Its meandering tale examines the inner psychological turmoil of a fiercely independent, crusading man obsessed with revenge and hatred, who searches for his two nieces (Pippa Scott and Natalie Wood) among the "savages" over a five-year period.

With dazzling on-location, gorgeous VistaVision cinematography (including the stunning red sandstone rock formations of Monument Valley) by Winton C. Hoch in Ford's most beloved locale, the film handsomely captures the beauty and isolating danger of the frontier.

Both the beginning and end of John Ford's classic western symmetrically involve a framed door. The film begins with a frontier cabin door opening onto the horizon of the Monument Valley wilderness, the passageway between two worlds. The interior area in the cabin represents civilized values and the settled family. The bright, glaring, sunny outdoor area represents the savage and threatening land of the frontier loner. The black silhouette of a frontier woman Martha Edwards (Dorothy Jordan), moves from the darkness through the door to the brightly sunlit wilderness outside. Moving excitedly to the porch, she notices a man approaching—in the center of the frame—who slowly rides in from the desert in a mythic entrance. The man is framed between two distant buttes. After several years of mysterious absence following the Civil War, loner Ethan Edwards (John Wayne), her brother-in-law, suddenly appears with no explanation, returning on horseback to his brother Aaron Edwards' (Walter Coy) family, living on a solitary Texas frontier farm.

Scene: The Doorway

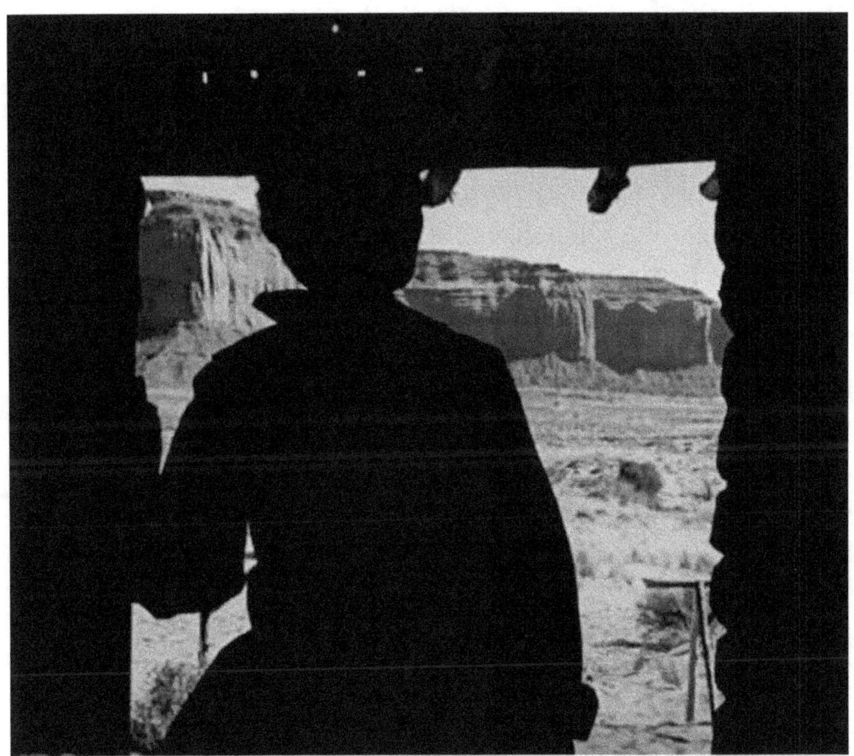

In the film's finale, after Ethan's obsessive, long, vengeful campaign to retrieve his kidnapped niece Debbie Edwards (Natalie Wood) from Comanche Indians, he remains a tragic figure—a loner and outsider.

He stands for a few moments, lingering outside as the camera pulls back into the darkened inside of the home, the doorway framing the scene. Ethan steps up onto the porch, then hesitates and steps to one side as others behind him enter, reunited once and for all—unlike Ethan, who is fated to wander and cannot live in a civilized, family-based community. He grasps his right elbow with his left hand (a fond remembrance of the stance of silent western star Harry Carey, Sr.), and then decides to remain behind, looking after them.

He turns away, his silhouette framed in the open doorway, walking into the swirling dust. The eternal loner, he wanders alone (like the fate of the dead Indian whose eyes he shot out) back into the alien, desert wilderness, similar to how he entered the picture so many years before, but now reversed. The door to civilization and the family hearthside swings shut on him, making the screen black. This ending symbolizes our hero returning to the wilderness from which he first came at the very beginning of the movie.

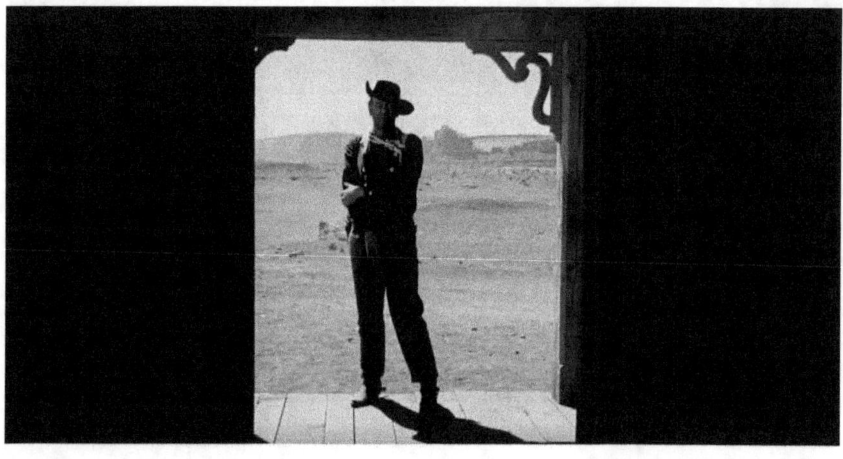

For most viewers, however, it is John Wayne's performance in *The Searchers* that is a revelation. "I've always thought [Wayne is] underrated as an actor," James Stewart once said. "I think *The Searchers* is one of the most marvelous performances of all time."

The Searchers has influenced many films. David Lean, for instance, watched the film repeatedly while preparing for Lawrence of Arabia in to help him get a sense of how to shoot a landscape. The entrance of Ethan Edwards in *The Searchers*, across a vast prairie, is echoed in the across-the-desert entrance of Sheriff Ali in the classic 1962 film *Lawrence of Arabia.*

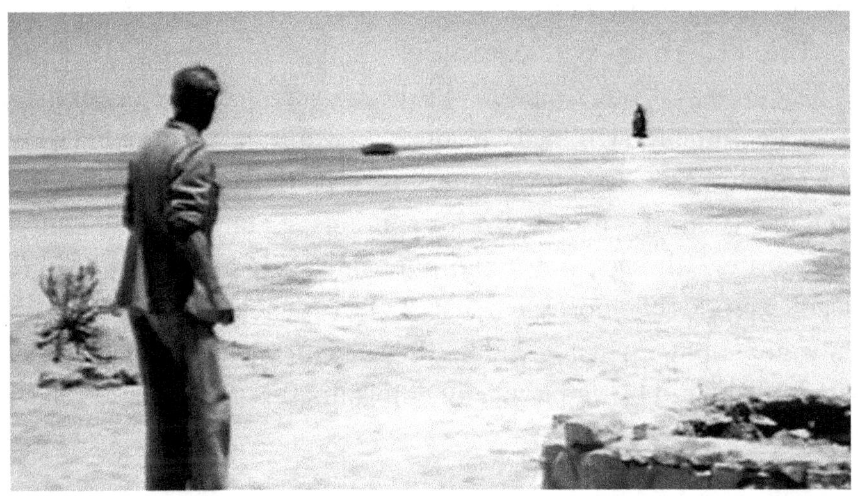

Scott McGee, writing for Turner Classic Movies, notes,

"Steven Spielberg, Wim Wenders, John Milius, Martin Scorsese, Paul Shrader, Jean-Luc Godard, ad George Lucas have all been influenced and paid some form of homage to *The Searchers* in their work."

The Defiant Ones (1958)

The Defiant Ones is a swift and exciting, dramatic action-crime film, known for its symbolic and memorable image of two escaped convicts (Joker and Cullen), one white and one black. The two were tied together by twenty-nine-inch long shackles and faced a hostile posse of townspeople and authorities, a lynching mob, barking bloodhounds, and a swamp. As they struggled together, they slowly began to accept each other.

The single-most symbolic image of the encouraging state of the development of race relations in the US was in Stanley Kramer's social commentary film. Two convicts—white John Jackson (Tony Curtis) and black Noah Cullen (Sidney Poitier), are shackled together. When they escape from a southern chain gang, they must cooperate with each other and put aside their racial animosities as they evade the oppressive search of the police. Held together by a twenty-nine-inch steel chain, they are manacled to each other, and only bound by their will and determination to escape.

Scene: The Train

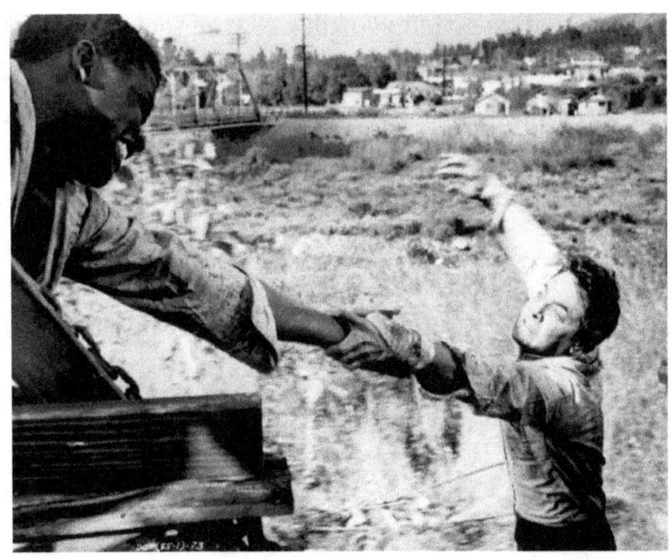

In the film's final sequence, the two men hear an approaching freight train. They frantically pursue it, and Cullen is able to get onto one of the moving cars. He reaches back with one free hand and pleads for his white companion to "run" faster. However, Jackson has been wounded in the shoulder and doesn't have the strength. They lock hands with each other (a memorable image of black and white hands and arms locked together), but he cannot pull Jackson up onto the moving train. So he sacrifices his own freedom and falls back off the train onto the ground.

In their final few moments of freedom, they share a cigarette, and Cullen sings the blues classic "Long Gone" as the sounds of bloodhounds on their trail closing in on them are heard in the distance.

Despite the mutual admiration and camaraderie among the cast and crew, *The Defiant Ones* wasn't necessarily a breeze to shoot. It was physically exhausting for Curtis and Poitier, who had to run through fields, swamps, and woods and fight each other bare-fisted, all while being chained together. There was also the famous climactic run for the train. Most grueling of all were the scenes where the two chained men are swept down the rapids of a river and their desperate attempt to climb out of a deep clay pit during a rainstorm. Curtis said there were no doubles for the clay pit scene, which he deemed the hardest sequence in the film. He also said he had a stunt double for some of the water scenes while Poitier had a dummy as a stand-in for at least one shot—look for it. It's pretty obvious. However, most of the grueling stunt work was done by the two stars themselves.

In this production photograph, director Stanley Kramer (extreme right) goes over the train arduous sequence with Poitier and Curtis.

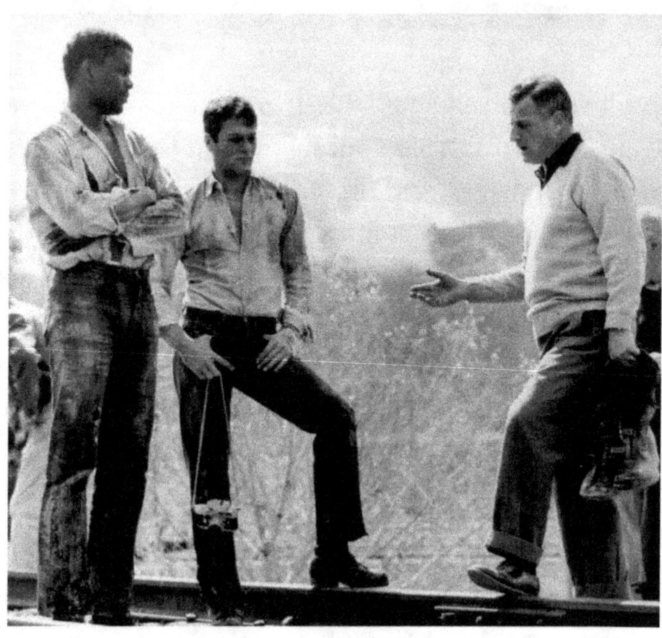

When the film was completed, Curtis paid tribute to his co-star in a unique way. Poitier said:

> "Tony performed the most generous act I ever received from an actor in my life. My contract called for me to be listed among the supporting actors. Tony had top billing alone, but he went to Stanley Kramer and said, 'I want you to put Sidney's name up there with mine.' And that's exactly what happened. That's how I got top billing for the first time in my life. I think that speaks a lot of him."

The basis of *The Defiant Ones* was revisited several times in popular media:

Warner Bros. parodied the film in Friz Freleng's 1961 cartoon *D'Fightin' Ones*, in which Sylvester the Cat escapes from captivity in a dogcatcher truck while chained to a bulldog.

In 1972, with gender reversal, as *Black Mama White Mama,* starring Pam Grier and Margaret Markov.

Another 1972 B-movie added a science-fiction Blaxploitation twist as *The Thing with Two Heads*, in which a racist white man (played by Ray Milland) has his head grafted onto the body of a living black man (played by former NFL player Rosey Grier).

In 1984, in the season-one episode "Some Like It Hot" of the American sitcom *Night Court*, the movie plot was briefly alluded to by a maintenance man as Dan and Liz (white and black characters, respectively) are handcuffed together, as he says, "Tony Curtis, Sidney Poitier. What was the name of that movie?"

The 1985 sci-fi film *Enemy Mine* is a West German-American science fiction film directed by Wolfgang Petersen and written by Edward Khmara, based on Barry B. Longyear's novella of the same name. The film stars Dennis Quaid and Louis Gossett, Jr. as a human and alien soldier, respectively, who become stranded together on an inhospitable planet and must overcome their mutual distrust in order to cooperate and survive.

For television in 1986, as *The Defiant Ones* starred Robert Urich and Carl Weathers.

Homage is paid to the film in the 1992 *Quantum Leap* science fiction television series episode "Unchained." Protagonist Sam Beckett lands in the body of a white Mississippi road gang worker chained to a wrongly convicted black man, and the two must escape together or be murdered by the corrupt warden. In the BBC2 television sitcom *Red Dwarf* episode (first broadcast on February 27, 1992) "The Inquisitor," Arnold Rimmer says, in reference to Dave Lister and Kryten showing up on the ship chained together, "Look, they come here with some cock-and-bull story, they're chained together like Sidney Poitier and Tony Curtis—I say open the door to oblivion and kick 'em through!"

Fled is a 1996 American buddy action comedy film directed by Kevin Hooks. It stars Laurence Fishburne and Stephen Baldwin as two prisoners chained together who flee during an escape attempt gone bad.

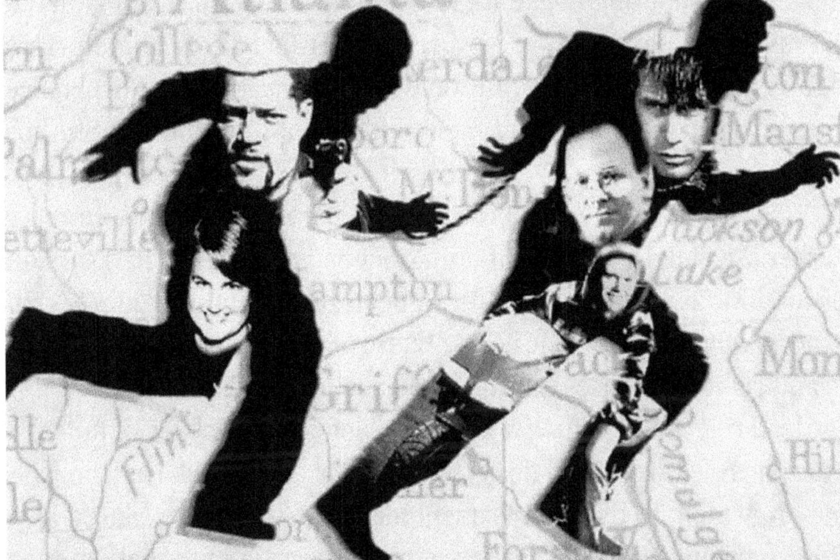
LauRence FishburNe
StePhen BalDwIn
Karen FiScher
MichaeL wySeSSion
ThE MaNtLe StriKes BaCk
FLED-
For the Love of
Earthquake Detection
WASHU-BROWN PICTURES PRESENTS A J. PASSCAL & B. IRIS PRODUCTION DIRECTED BY PATRICK SHORE STARRING LAWRENCE FISHBURNE, STEPHEN BALDWIN, KAREN FISCHER, AND MICHAEL WYSESSION
AND INTRODUCING STEPHANE RONDENAY, GHASSAN AL-EQABI, JESSE FISHER AND BRIAN WHITE DESIGN AND CONCEPT SARAH ZEE PHOTOGRAPHY DAVID LACHACHAPELLE SOUND STRECKEISEN MUSIC U2, TOM PETTY CATERING WAFFLE HOUSE

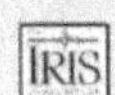
IRIS
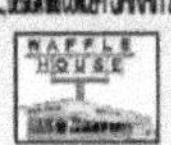
WAFFLE
HOUSE
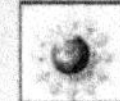
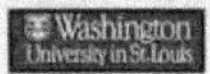
Washington
University in St.Louis

Ben-Hur (1959)

Director William Wyler's film was a retelling of the spectacular (1925) silent film of the same name. Both films were adapted from the novel (first published in 1880) by former Civil War General Lew Wallace's *Ben-Hur: A Tale of the Christ*. In fact, Wyler had been an "extras" director on the set of DeMille's original film of the silent era. This film featured a cast of 125,000 and cost about $4 million to make after shooting began on location in Italy in 1923, and starred silent screen idols Ramon Novarro and Francis X. Bushman. This figure is equivalent to $33 million today—it was the most expensive silent film ever made. *Ben-Hur* was filmed at the Cinceitta Studios in Italy.

This remake of the novel was inspired by the fact that three years earlier, Cecil B. DeMille and Paramount had remade the 1925 version of his film as a successful fifties epoch biblical tale titled *The Ten Commandments* (1956). The heroic figure of Charlton Heston (an iconic and righteous Moses figure) would again be commissioned to play the lead role in this film of a Jewish nobleman (the Prince of Judea)—after the role was turned down by Burt Lancaster, Rock Hudson, and Paul Newman. In the plot, Prince Judah Ben-Hur was enslaved by a Roman tribunal friend, but then returned years later to seek revenge in the film's centerpiece, a chariot race. Ultimately, he would find redemption and forgiveness in the inspiring and enlightening finale.

On May 24, 1958, the first spectacular scene for *Ben-Hur* was shot: the entrance of the chariots into the arena, with 1,500 extras on hand in order to fill the stadium.

Scene: The Chariot Race

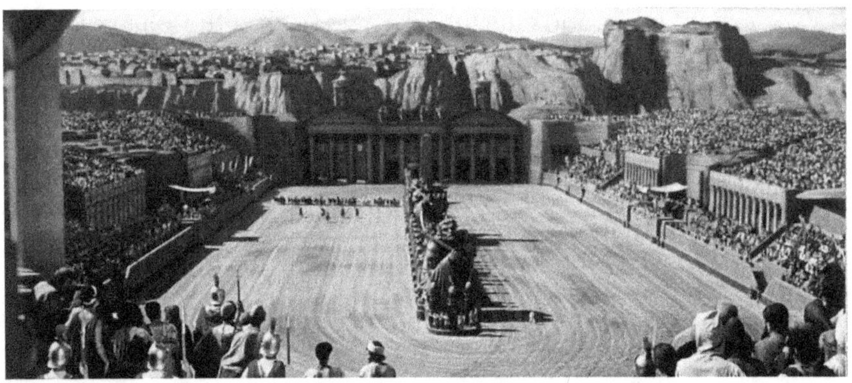

For the movie's centerpiece sequence, the chariot race, the producers built what was then the biggest movie set ever constructed. The arena, an accurate duplicate of an actual Roman stadium outside Jerusalem, was five stories tall and big enough to enclose a track two-thousand feet long and sixty-five feet wide. There were actually two such tracks, one built outside of camera range for the horses and riders to train and rehearse. For the track surface, some forty-thousand tons of white sand was imported from Mexico. The arena cost $1 million to build and spanned eighteen acres on the Cinecittà lot.

The spectacular, memorable eleven-minute chariot race in this epic was filmed on a gigantic racing set—the largest single film set in cinematic history. The setting for the exciting action scene is majestically impressive with a central divider strip composed of three statues thirty feet high, and grandstands on all sides, rising five stories high and filled with thousands of extras. Before the race, the charioteers parade around the ring in a display of pageantry—the focus is on the two chariots of Ben-Hur (Charlton

Heston) and arch-enemy Messala (Stephen Boyd) with white and black horses respectively. A crown of victory will be given to the victor—the chariot that first completes nine rounds.

The eager horses and chariots are held back at the starting point until the signal to begin the race is given. The battle between the competitors is highlighted by a series of close-ups of the action, as the chariots race around the great stone idols in the center of the arena. One by one, Messala eliminates the other drivers in the ferocious race, shattering their chariots.

The climactic ending to the race occurs when the chariots of the two dueling rivals run neck-and-neck and slash at each other. Messala tries to destroy Ben-Hur's chariot by moving close with its rotating blades, but as the wheels lock and he loses one of his wheels, Messala's chariot is splintered into pieces. He is dragged by his own team, then trampled, and run over by other teams of horses. Defeated, he lies in the dirt, his body a broken, bloody pulp.

The chariot arena was built by more than one thousand workers beginning in January 1958, according to some reports. It was two-thousand feet long by sixty-five feet wide and covered eighteen acres, the largest single set in motion picture history at that time. Reputedly, forty-thousand tons of white sand was imported from Mexico for the track.

Wyler left oversight of the chariot race sequence to second unit director Andrew Marton and legendary stuntman Yakima Canutt. He coordinated all the chariot race stunt work and trained the drivers. (An assistant director on the sequence was future spaghetti-western maestro Sergio Leone.) Joe Canutt, the stunt coordinator's son, was Heston's double.

Heston was among the first to begin training, arriving on location a few months ahead of scheduled shooting. He was also there to do costume fittings. Heston mastered the driving of the four-horse team more quickly than anyone else in the chariot scene, probably because of his experience with the smaller two-horse chariots he drove in *The Ten Commandments* (1956). Nevertheless, he was concerned about his ability to pull off the race with all the other teams on the track. Canutt assured him, "You just stay in the chariot; I guarantee you'll win the damn race."

Stephen Boyd had a much more difficult time driving the chariots. His hands and wrists blistered, and rest time had to be scheduled.

Although only about thirty-six horses would ever be seen on screen during the race, eighty-two animals (to cover for accidents and rest periods) were brought in from Yugoslavia.

The chariot scene alone cost about $4 million, or about a fourth of the entire budget, and took ten weeks to shoot.

According to Andrew Marton, who directed the chariot race, the track was constructed of steamrolled ground rock debris covered with ten inches of ground lava and finished with eight inches of crushed yellow rock to make the surface hard enough to hold the weight of the chariots and horses while still having enough give not to make the horses lame (which Marton said was achieved by a top of sand). After one day of shooting, the upper layer of rock was removed because it had slowed the pace of the race considerably. The lava layer, which Marton and Canutt had initially opposed, proved to be the most workable element.

Marton had three 65mm cameras at his disposal for shooting the race. The larger format film proved to be an issue. The standard close-up lens for 35mm photography was 100mm; it became, in the wide-screen process, a 200mm lens, which could not be focused closer than fifty feet. So he had to use a 140mm lens, requiring him and his crew to move closer to the dangerous action of the race.

After a few days of shooting, Marton discovered the most effective way to shoot in the arena would be to have the cameras right in the midst of the race, necessitating a camera car that moved with the chariots. He also noted that the best shots on the curves were done using a specially built camera chariot with rubber tires.

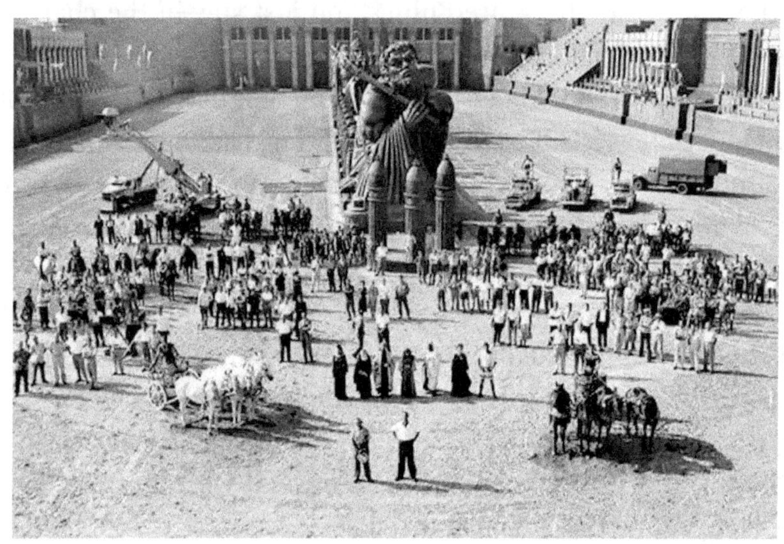

The heat of Rome proved to be a serious drawback for the action scenes in *Ben-Hur*. Horses could only make about eight runs a day at most. Because of this, most of the shots in the race were done on the first take.

Ben-Hur is a 2016 American epic historical drama film directed by Timur Bekmambetov and written by Keith Clarke and John Ridley. It is the fifth film adaption of the original 1880 novel *Ben-Hur: A Tale of the Christ* by Lew Wallace following the 1907 silent short film, the 1925 silent film, the 1959 film, and the 2003 animated film of the same name. It is the third version of *Ben-Hur* released by Metro-Goldwyn-Mayer.

In *Film* of April 4, 2016, written by Jack Giroux, Timur tells us about the planning and work that went into shooting the sequence:

"If anyone is worried that the end of *Ben-Hur* is going to be packed with CGI, worry no more, because that may not be the case. Bekmambetov wanted to rely more on practical effects for the film, which he considers more of a drama than a 'huge tentpole attraction.' The director didn't set out to make a more stylized version of the past, as he did with *Abraham Lincoln: Vampire Hunter*, he wanted to make a film that's more grounded and tangible."

To create a believable Roman chariot race, Bekmambetov and his crew used mostly practical elements:

We shoot everything in Italy. We built a 1,000-foot-long surface, with a track, stands, and gates. We had 90 horses trained for several months to be able to race. We built very unique chariots based on original references, which is very different from previous movies, because usually chariots are like these huge battle axes [Laughs]. In reality, it was a very low, almost Formula 1-type of design. It was very difficult to race, because nothing protects you. You're just staying on a bench with two wheels, flying with a 40 or 50 mph speed, with a lot of horses around you. It was very, very dangerous work. What's very contemporary is there were teams—blue or red—and they were very popular in the Roman Empire. They were so rich. They were paid well, if they survived. One of the champions, he'd be worth 40 billion dollars [Laughs]. It's a whole culture. The famous chariot race sequence, which runs about 10 minutes, almost exactly the same as in the prior films, was originally planned to be filmed in the Circus

Maximus arena in Rome; however, producers were denied access by Italy's national cultural authorities due to fears that the stunts would damage the fragile historic site, which was under restoration at that time. We shot it in Rome, in Cinecittá studio, and also found a great medieval town, Latera. What's interesting is—it's all real. We shot the chariot race for 45 days. It was 45 days with a crowd, horses, and great stunt drivers. Phil Neilson is a very good person, the second unit director, and he was my hero. He helped me make it right. You can't really change things on the fly. Horses need to be prepared. Actors spend months to prepare, to learn how to drive chariot races. There were stunt guys, but only for the really dangerous things. Overall, it was the actors in the chariots.

To capture the thunderous feel of the race, the film crew attached microphones to the horses to record the sound of pounding hooves, and GoPro cameras were buried in the sand. The cameras were also planted on chariots and people, one of which was placed on a soccer ball in the middle of the track while the horses ran over it. A total of twenty chariots were used. Around four hundred extras were used as spectators (which were then increased to around one hundred thousand with special effects). Unlike the chariots in the 1959 version, made by Italian craftsmen and weighed nine hundred pounds, this time, the team wanted to use the equivalent of a Ferrari—small and fast.

Some Like It Hot (1959)

Some Like It Hot is a hilarious romantic comedy film directed and produced by Billy Wilder, starring Marilyn Monroe as Sugar "Kane" Kowalczyk, a ukulele player and singer; Tony Curtis as Joe/"Josephine"/"Shell Oil Junior," a saxophone player; and Jack Lemon as Jerry (Gerald)/"Daphne," a double bass player. Joe E. Brown portrays Osgood Fielding III. The film is about two musicians who are forced by circumstances to dress in drag in order to escape from mafia gangsters whom they witnessed commit a crime inspired by the Saint Valentine's Day Massacre. The all-time outrageous, satirical comedy farce favorite, *Some Like It Hot*, is one of the most hilarious, raucous films ever made. The exceptional film was the all-time highest-grossing comedy up to its time, one of the most successful films of 1959, and director Billy Wilder's funniest comedy in his career and is often considered to be the funniest film in motion picture history. The ribald film is a clever combination of many elements: a spoof of 1920–30s gangster films with period costumes and speakeasies, and romance in a quasi-screwball comedy with one central joke—entangled and deceptive identities, reversed sex roles, and cross-dressing. In fact, one of the film's major themes is disguise and masquerade—e.g., the drag costumes of the two male musicians, Joe's disguise as a Cary Grant-like impotent millionaire, and Jerry's happiness with a real wealthy, yacht-owning retiree.

Scene: The Romantic Getaway

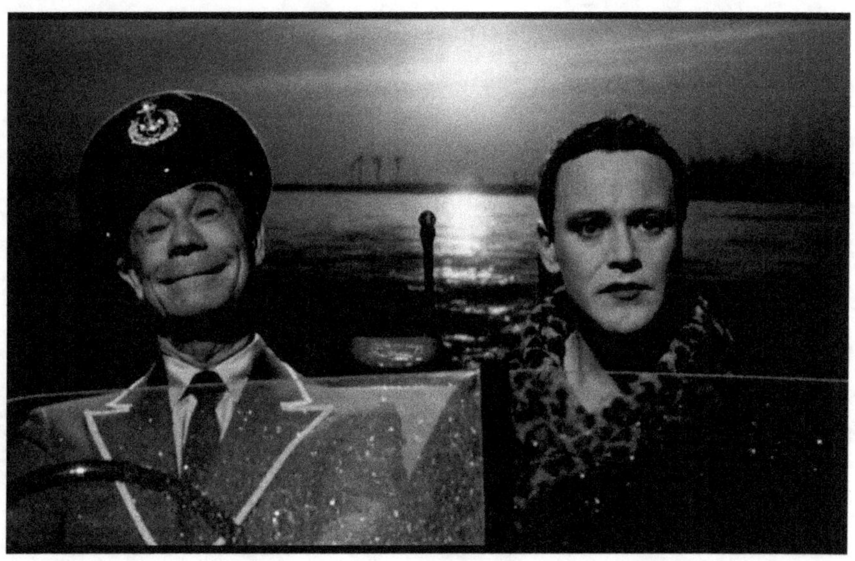

In the film's classic closing scene in a pre-arranged getaway boat, Jerry attempts to end his relationship with Osgood, breaking the news gently to him by discouraging his affection, but he isn't successful:

> Osgood: I called Mama. She was so happy she cried. She wants you to have her wedding gown. It's white lace.
> Jerry-Daphne: Yeah, Osgood. I can't get married in your mother's dress. Ha ha. That—she and I, we are not built the same way.
> Osgood (unflappable): We can have it altered.
> Jerry-Daphne: Aw, no you don't! Osgood, I'm gonna level with you. We can't get married at all.
> Osgood: Why not?

Jerry: Well, in the first place, I'm not a natural blonde.

Osgood: Doesn't matter.

Jerry-Daphne: I smoke. I smoke all the time.

Osgood: I don't care.

Jerry-Daphne: Well, I have a terrible past. For three years now, I've been living with a saxophone player.

Osgood: I forgive you.

Jerry-Daphne: I can never have children.

Osgood (unperturbed): We can adopt some.

Jerry-Daphne (whipping off his wig, utterly exasperated): You don't understand, Osgood. (Changing to manly voice.) I'm a man.

Osgood (unruffled and still in love): Well, nobody's perfect.

Although the two always had a strict rule about who wrote which line, Wilder always credited Diamond with the film's justly famous closing line. The original ending, suggested by Monroe, was to have been a fade-out with Sugar and Spats (George Raft) doing the tango together. But Monroe's unpredictability made Wilder seek a solution that wouldn't require shooting *one more scene* with her. The night before the ending had to be shot, Diamond came up with the idea of having Jerry (Lemmon) as Daphne on a motorboat speeding away from Miami with his rich older suitor, played by veteran comic Joe E. Brown. Daphne tries a number of ways to explain to Osgood why "she" can't marry him, but the undaunted millionaire overlooks them all.

Finally, Jerry tears off his wig and says in exasperation, "Aah, I'm a man."

Osgood amiably replies, "Well, nobody's perfect!"

"This line is entirely from the brain of IAL Diamond," Wilder said. "I had nothing to do with it. Not even the exclamation point!"

The studio hired female impersonator Barbette to coach Lemmon and Curtis on gender illusion for the film. Lemmon totally threw himself into it his role in the movie spending hours with makeup technician Harry Ray to get the right look, taking tango lessons (from co-star George Raft), frustrating the professional female impersonator brought in to teach him and Curtis how to act like women (Lemmon felt that too much regal perfection would be wrong for the character and dangerously unfunny).

Once they got their drag look down, Lemmon and Curtis decided to test it by going to the ladies' room at the studio commissary. According to Lemmon, "not one of the girls going in or out ever batted an eyeball! They thought we were extras doing a period film on the lot."

When Tony Curtis and Jack Lemmon appeared together in 1999 for a *Vanity Fair* photo spread about Hollywood, they did it partially in drag since their roles as Daphne and Josephine in *Some Like It Hot* are forever linked in the memories of film lovers everywhere.

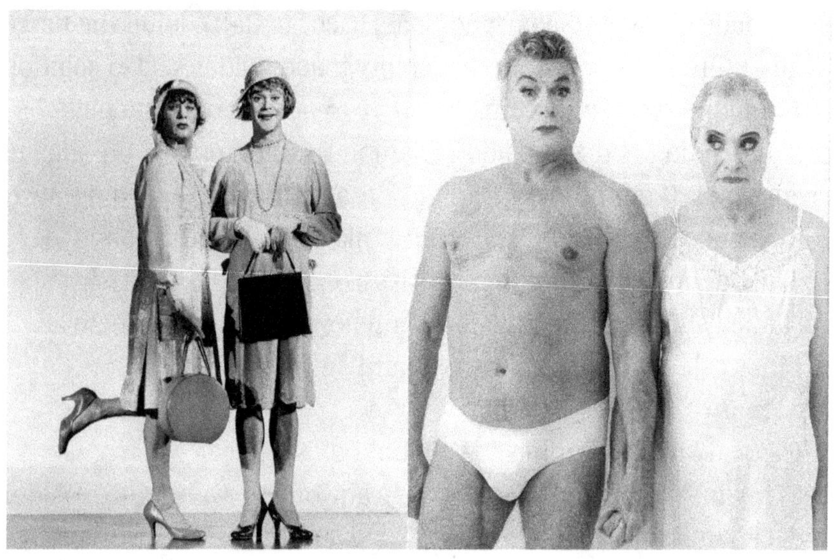

Tootsie (1982): The character Michael Dorsey (portrayed by Dustin Hoffman) stars as Dorothy Michaels in the show-within-show soap opera *Southwest General.*

Mrs. Doubtfire (1993): The character Daniel Hillard (Robin Williams) dresses as nanny Mrs. Doubtfire so he can be with his kids and is later hired to host a children's show.

Like Jack Lemon in *Some Like It Hot*, both of these movie characters were able to convince "loved ones" and many others that they were women up until the very end of the movie when "The s__t hit the fire," at least for a little while, for both of them.

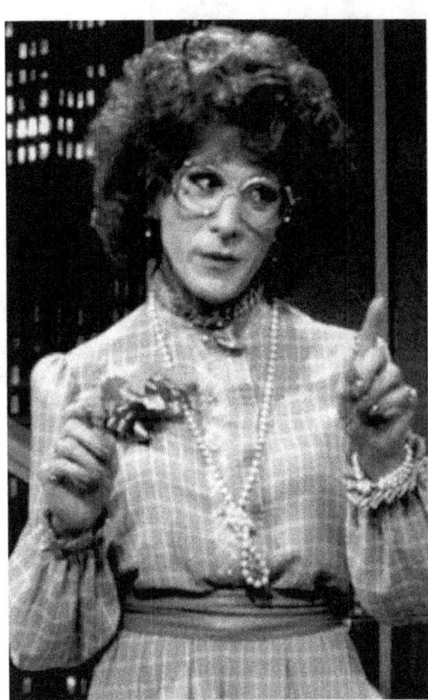
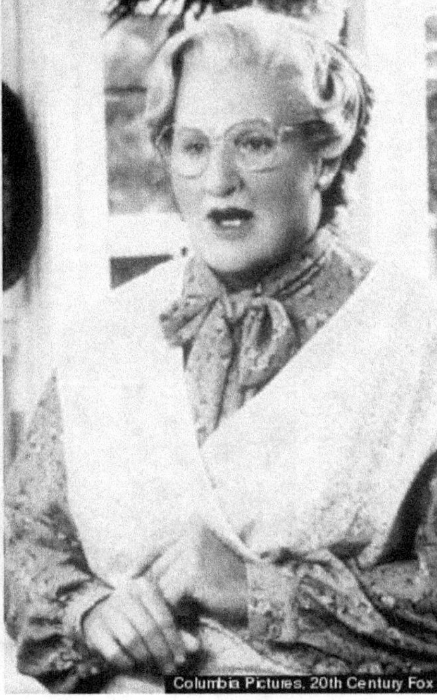

THE 1960s

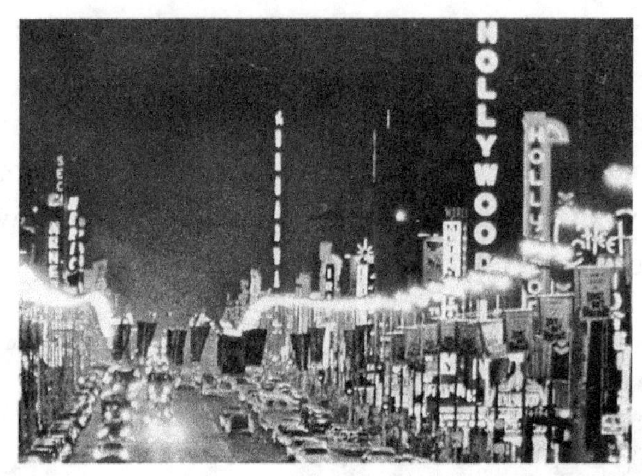

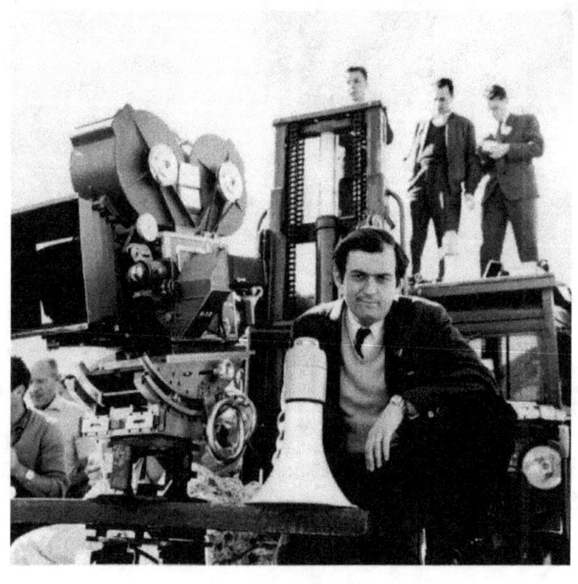

Psycho (1960)

Psycho is a psychological horror film directed and produced by Alfred Hitchcock and written by Joseph Stefano. Its principal stars are Anthony Perkins and Janet Leigh. The film centers on an encounter between a secretary, Marion Crane (Leigh), who ends up at a secluded motel after stealing money from her employer, and the motel's owner-manager, Norman Bates (Perkins), and its aftermath. The thrilling and suspenseful music for the film was composed by Bernard Herrmann. It was based on the 1959 novel of the same name by Robert Bloch.

Scene: The Shower

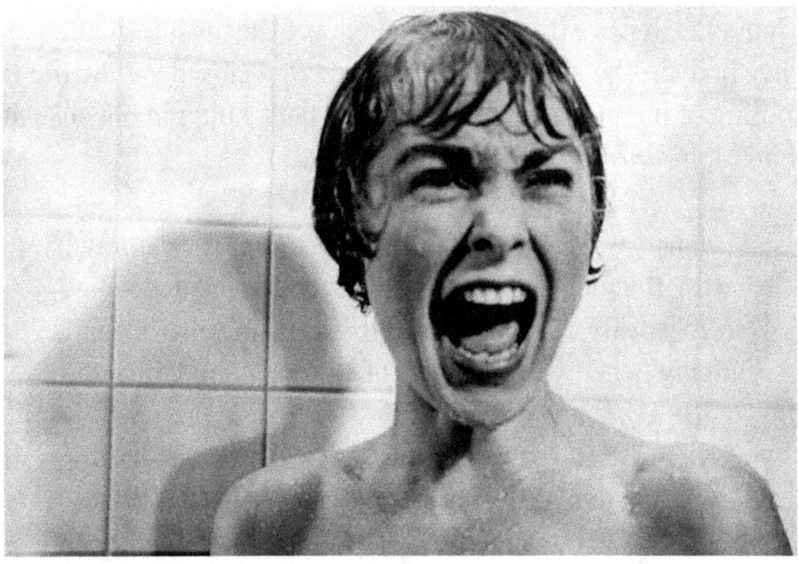

The famous forty-five-second shower scene in *Psycho* required seventy-eight camera set-ups and took seven days to film. The set was built so that any of the walls could be removed, allowing the camera to get in close from every angle. Although other scenes were shot with more than one camera, this one used only one cameraman.

Graphics designer Saul Bass created forty-eight storyboards for the shower scene and claimed that he actually directed the scene. However, Hitchcock contends that he himself directed the sequence. Whoever actually "directed" the scene obviously used Bass's storyboards extensively.

The shower scene was originally written to see only the knife-wielding hand of the murderer. Hitchcock suggested to Saul Bass, who was storyboarding the sequence, a number of angles that would capture screenwriter Joseph Stefano's description of "an impression of a knife slashing, as if tearing at the very screen, ripping the film."

Janet Leigh wore thin moleskin to cover the most intimate parts of her body in the shower. Hitchcock kept a closed set during the shooting of the murder. Even so, Leigh later noted in her 1984 autobiography *There Really Was a Hollywood:*

> "Security was a constant source of trouble. Even though
> I wore the moleskin, I was still pretty much 'on display,'
> so to speak. I didn't want strangers lurking around,
> hoping to get a peek in case of any accidental mishap."

Marli Renfro was paid $400 as Leigh's body double for some shots (according to some reports, she was only used for the scene of Marion's body being wrapped in the shower curtain). Although Leigh said for many years that there was never anyone actually naked in the shower, she admitted late in her life that Renfro did some shots nude. She also mentioned in her autobiography that she was nude in some scenes as the flesh-colored moleskin was washed away from her breasts. "What to do? ... To spoil the so-far successful shot and be modest? Or get it over with and be immodest? I opted for immodesty."

Reportedly, a fast-motion reverse shot was used to give the impression that the knife actually enters Marion's abdomen.

To achieve the effect of the water coming out of the showerhead and streaming down past the camera on all sides, Hitchcock had a huge shower head made to order and shot with his camera very close to it.

During shooting, Hitchcock was forced to uncharacteristically do retakes for some scenes. The final shot in the shower scene, which starts with an extreme close-up on Marion's eye and pulls up and out, proved difficult for Leigh, since the water splashing in her face made her want to blink, and the cameraman had trouble as well since he had to manually focus while moving the camera.

This particular scene is the reason Hitchcock wanted to make *Psycho* in the first place. He purposefully cast Janet Leigh, an established celebrity, because he knew that it would be that much more shocking when he killed off her character midway through the film. The shower scene is also why Hitchcock wouldn't allow viewers to enter the movie theater after the film had started to roll, because they might come in expecting to see Janet Leigh and miss out on the shocking revelation of her death.

"I was directing the viewers," Hitchcock told Francois Truffaut. "You might say I was playing them like an organ."

In addition, the shower scene reveals that everything that comes before it—Marion stealing the money and running away—has been a red herring. The audience no longer knows whom to follow; there is a vacuum. After Marion's slaughter, even the camera seems to be uncertain about what to do next, meandering from her glassy-eyed corpse on the ground, through her room, to the newspaper containing the money, still lying on the nightstand, and finally, to the window where we hear Norman's screams.

The irony of the shower scene is that Marion has just decided to give back the money when "Mrs. Bates" kills her. Norman's inability to achieve salvation from his private island has driven Marion to reconsider her actions, as she still has the opportunity to get out of her trap. She has effectively snapped out of her madness and has decided to (pun intended) come clean, which is what the shower represents. The bathroom is blindingly white, echoing Marion's white bra and slip from her tryst with Sam and reminding the audience of her duality; this character still has the potential to come back from the dark side. The shower, then, begins like a baptism, removing the corruption from her mind and returning her to a state of purity. Indeed, she is left naked on the white floor as her blood circles the drain; this image reminds the viewer that in death, Marion's guilt or innocence no longer matters.

Hitchcock thought that filming in black and white would be more economical than filming in color and would also soften the shocking, gory nature of the images (he used chocolate syrup for the blood floating down the drain), but despite that, newspapers in 1960 reported moviegoers were fainting, vomiting, and staggering out of theaters screaming after viewing the sequence, which occurs just thirty minutes into the film. Even in 2008, film fans in an international poll voted the frenzied shower scene "the most nail-biting movie moment" in the history of cinema. Many moviegoers, even today, claim that the movie was actually filmed in color because of the gore and realism of this particular scene.

Anthony Perkins was, in fact, not on the set during the filming of the shower scene. Instead, he was in New York rehearsing a play he would open after *Psycho* was completed. The fact that Perkins had to be in New York that week was quite intentional.

"Hitchcock was very worried that the dual role and nature of Norman Bates would be exposed if I were to appear in that scene. I think it was the recognizability of my silhouette, which is rather slim and broad in the shoulder. That worried him."

Perkins added that the director, in effect, broke his own long-standing rule with that decision.

"He was outspokenly eager to not play any tricks on the audience in his films, to do anything that couldn't be thought of as fair play, but in that instance, he, in fact, did. The guy he chose, from the 'extra' pool, was very unlike the silhouette of Norman Bates, as played by me. So in a way, Hitchcock didn't exactly play by the book when he cast someone else in that scene."

Hermann achieved the shrieking sound of the shower scene by having a group of violinists saw the same note over and over. He called the motif "a return to pure ice water."

Hitchcock originally wanted the shower scene to play with no music. In post-production, while the director was out of town, Herrmann composed the famous theme and showed it to Hitchcock with the music upon his return. Hitchcock had to admit his original notion was an "improper suggestion."

In this production shot, Hitchcock is instructing Leigh on how he wants to shower scene to go.

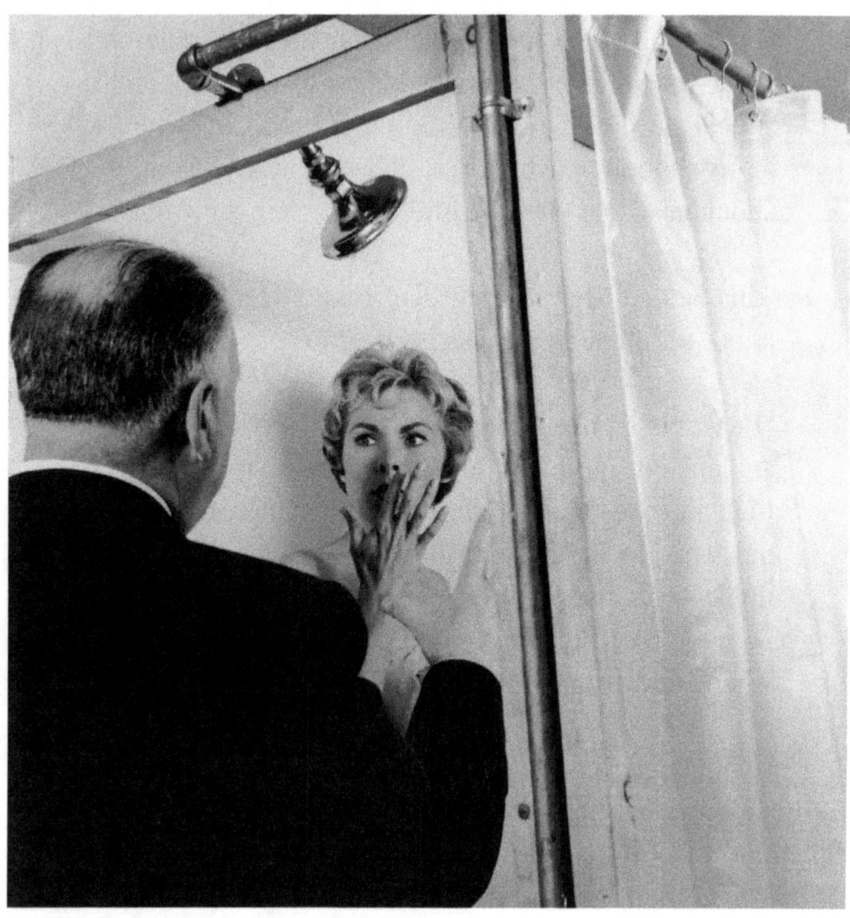

Unfortunately, in the course of human events, someone insists that a prequel, sequel, or even a remake of the original film masterpiece is absolutely required. Such is the case with *Psycho*. The following is this list of films that followed the original.

Psycho, an American horror-thriller film franchise based on the Robert Bloch novel

Psycho II (1983), a sequel to the original film, following the plot of the previous novel

Psycho III (1986), a follow-up to the second film

Psycho IV: The Beginning, a 1990 sequel to the 1986 film, made for cable television

Psycho (1998 film), a remake of the original film by Gus Van Sant starring Vince Vaughn

Psycho (2008 film), an Indian film (in the Kannada language) directed by Devadatta

Psycho (2013 film), a Telugu film directed by Kishore Bhargava

Psycho (2018 film), a Tamil film by Mysskin

As far as the original 1960 film and the 1998 remake, there are some similarities and differences, notably in the famous shower scene (Janet Leigh in the original top image and Anne Hecht in the remake, bottom image).

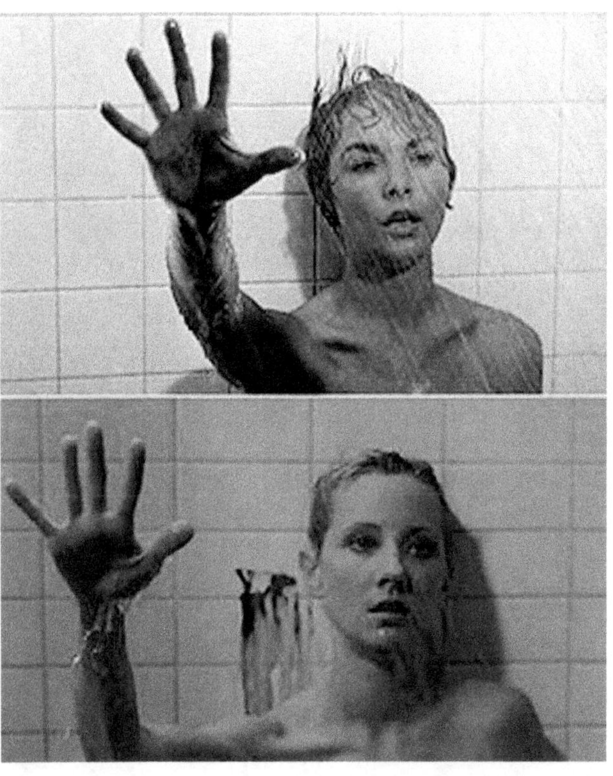

The cinematography and the cinematic techniques were consistent between the two films in many of the most memorable scenes, including the shower scene, scenes of the mother, scenes of the swamp, and the scene of Arbogast on the staircase, but other scenes changed significantly, particularly the climax, and the Dr. Simon monologue at the end, which was much shorter in the remake. Van Sant's comments from the commentary track attribute many of the updates to the need to make the film more accessible to a new audience.

The famous shower scene was filmed in the same way; the stabbing sound effects were produced by stabbing a melon. Fake blood was used instead of chocolate syrup.

Dr. Strangelove (1964)

Dr. Strangelove or: How I Learned to Stop Worrying and Love the Bomb, more commonly known simply as *Dr. Strangelove*, is a political satire comedy film that satirizes the Cold War fears of a nuclear conflict between the Soviet Union and the United States. The film was directed, produced, and co-written by Stanley Kubrick, stars Peter Sellers (various roles); George C. Scott as General Buck Turgidson, the USAF Chief of Staff; Sterling Hayden as Brigadier General Jack D. Ripper, a paranoid Strategic Air Command commander; and Slim Pickens as Major Kong.

The story concerns an unhinged US Air Force commander who orders a first-strike nuclear attack on the Soviet Union. It follows the President of the United States, his advisors, the Joints Chiefs of Staff, and a Royal Air Force (RAF) officer as they try to recall the bombers to prevent a nuclear apocalypse. It separately follows the crew of one B-52 bomber as they try to deliver their payload.

Scene: Major Kong Rides the Bomb

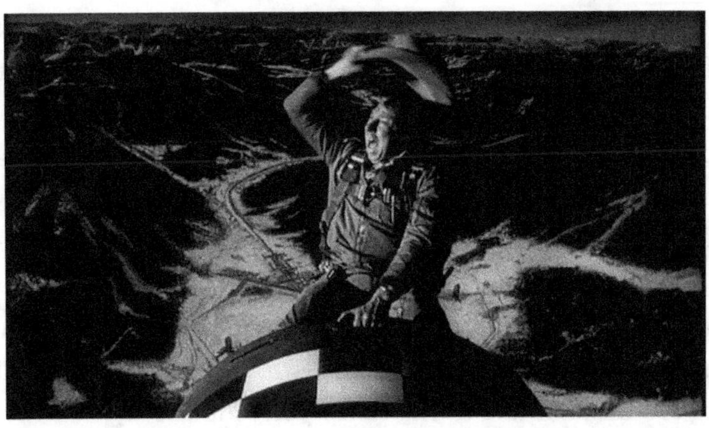

Slim Pickens played B-52 pilot Major TJ "King" Kong in *Dr. Strangelove*. According to the 2013 documentary film *Inside the Making of Dr. Strangelove*, Stanley Kubrick cast Pickens after Peter Sellers, who was initially slated to play the role of Major Kong, as well as three other roles in the film, broke his leg when he accidentally fell fifteen feet from the suspended stage cockpit during a heated argument with director Stanley Kubrick. The injury would not allow Sellers to sit in the cramped cockpit. Besides that, Sellers had a dreaded fear of heights. Pickens was chosen because his accent and comic sense were perfect for the role of Kong, a cartoonish, patriotic, and gung-ho B-52 commander. As a fellow actor, in his screen debut, James Earl Jones stated, "Pickens just played himself on and off the set."

Kubrick remembered Pickens when he met him on the set of the 1961 western movie *One-Eyed Jacks* with Marlon Brando. Pickens was not given the script for the entire film, but only those portions in which he played a part. Pickens had three memorable scenes in the film. However, he would be best known for riding a dropped H-bomb to certain death, whooping and waving his cowboy hat (in the manner of a rodeo performer bronc-riding or bull-riding) toward the Russian missile complex. The film was laden with numerous sexual overtones, and this particular scene was no exception. Pickens' memorable scene was characterized as him "riding a phallic symbol, the bomb, into a nuclear orgasm."

Pickens credited *Dr. Strangelove* as a turning point in his career. Previously, he was "Hey you" on sets, and afterward, he was addressed as "Mr. Pickens." He once said, "After *Dr. Strangelove*, the roles, the dressing rooms, and the checks all started gettin' bigger." Pickens said he was amazed at the difference a single movie could make. However, Pickens also said that working with Stanley Kubrick proved too difficult due to Kubrick's perfectionist style of directing with multiple takes for nearly every shot, especially with the climactic H-bomb riding scene, which was done in just over one hundred takes.

In the late 1970s, Pickens was offered the part of Dick Hallorann in Kubrick's adaptation of Stephen Kings' 1980 novel *The Shining*, but Pickens stipulated that he would appear in the film only if Kubrick was required to shoot Pickens' scenes in fewer than one hundred takes. According to the documentary *Inside the Making*, Kubrick, at the eleventh hour, decided to have Major Kong ride the H-bomb down to its target, a Russian missile base. Kong was "trapped" on the bomb when he managed to rewire the damaged bomb bay doors so they would be opened and the bomb could be released. Unfortunately, there were no bomb bay doors in the constructed sixty-foot-long bomb bay. The film's special effects specialist Wally Veevers conceived a novel idea. Since the scene would be in black and white, he simply took stills of the bomb bay and cut out an opening for the doors. The bomb was suspended from a crane at the Shepperton Studios, and the scene was shot from the top of the crane itself. As the bomb drops, the crane was mechanically backed-up, allowing them to optically reduce the size of the bomb as it fell from the confines of the bomb bay toward its target with Pickens, sitting on the bomb itself, framed against a blue background. In the end, it was a truly wonderful special effect.

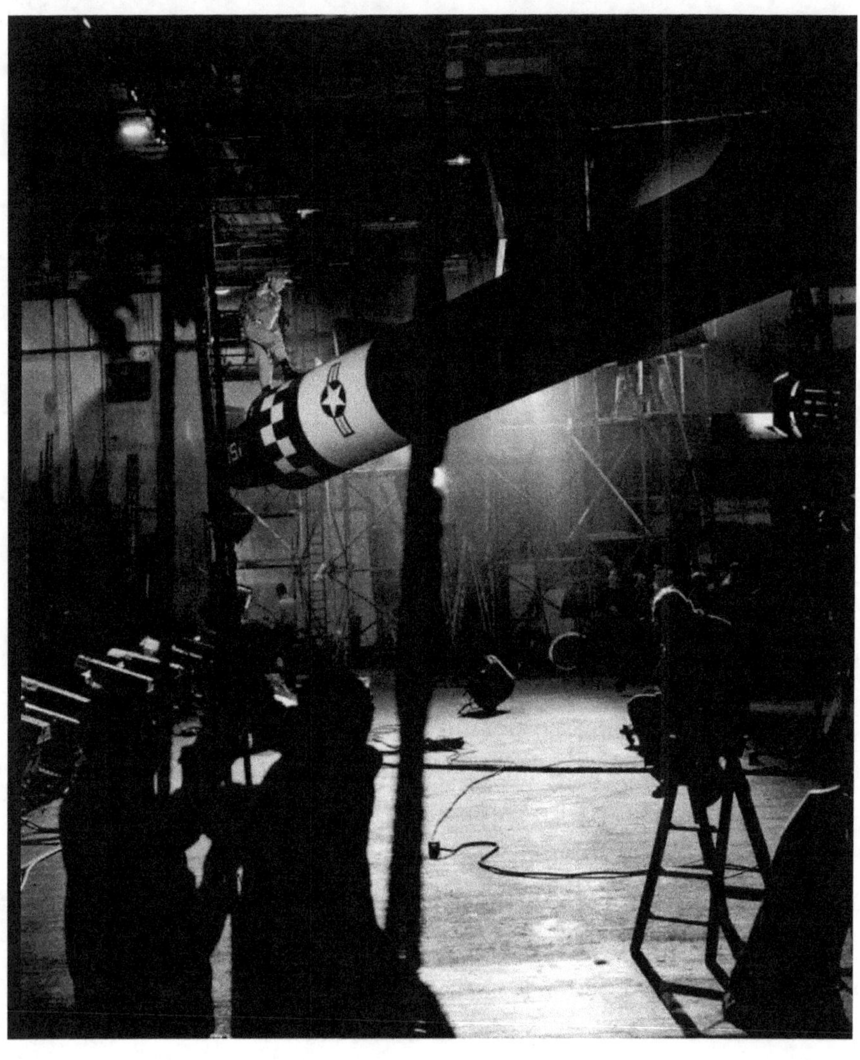

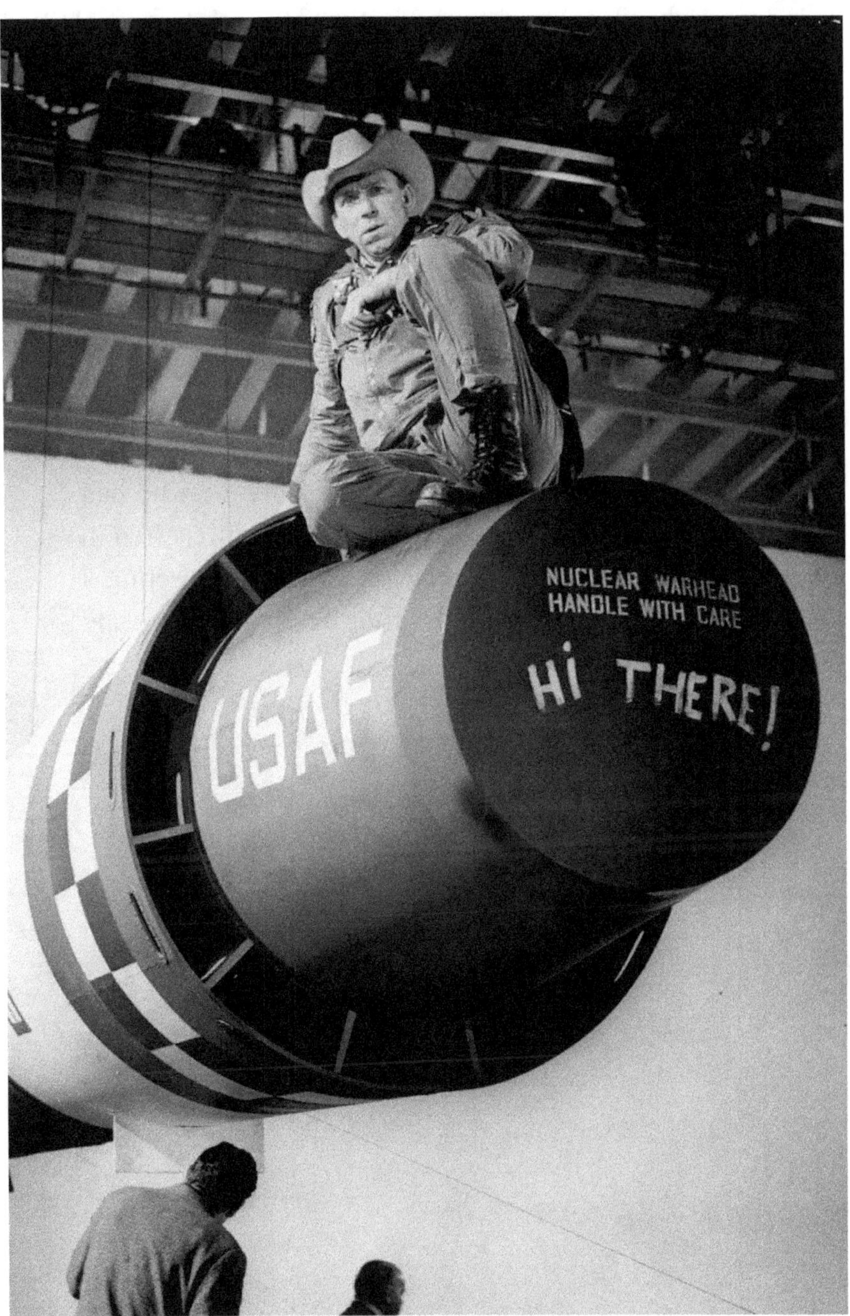
NUCLEAR WARHEAD
HANDLE WITH CARE
Hi THERE!
USAF

In 1995, Kubrick enlisted Terry Southern to script a sequel titled *Son of Strangelove*. Kubrick had Terry Gilliam in mind to direct. The script was never completed, but index cards laying out the story's basic structure were found among Southern's papers after he died in October 1995. It was set largely in underground bunkers, where Dr. Strangelove had taken refuge with a group of women. This situation is due in part to Slim's hand-delivering a bomb on a Russian missile base, thus activating their "Doomsday Machine," eventually killing everything above ground.

In 2013, Gilliam commented,

> "I was told after Kubrick died—by someone who had been dealing with him—that he had been interested in trying to do another Strangelove with me directing. I never knew about that until after he died, but I would have loved to."

Scene: Dr. Strangelove in His Wheelchair

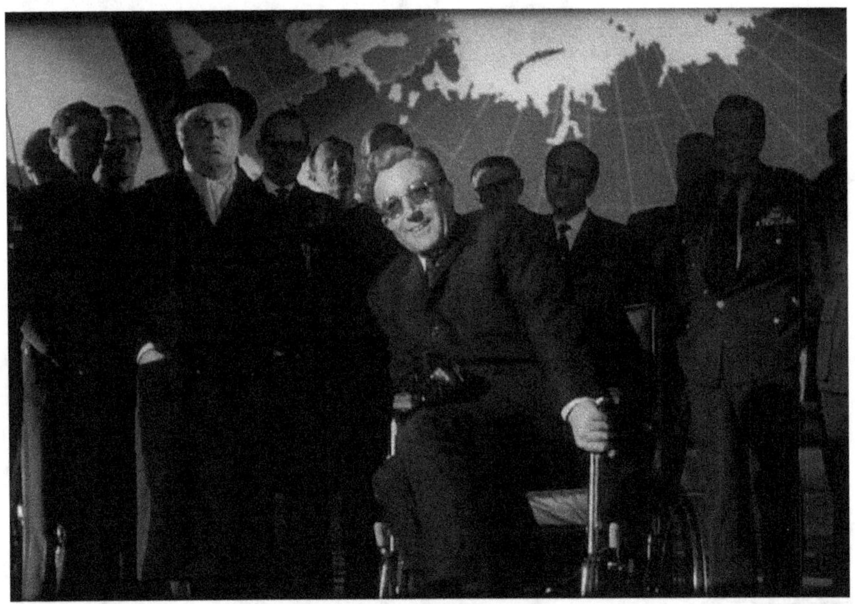

Sellers was a master of accents. In fact, initially, he was cast in four major roles, all of which underwent considerable changes before filming ended. He was originally going to play US President Merkin Muffley, B-52 pilot Major "King" Kong, Colonel Lionel Mandrake, and the mysterious Dr. Strangelove. The role of Kong, as we already know now, eventually went to Slim Pickins.

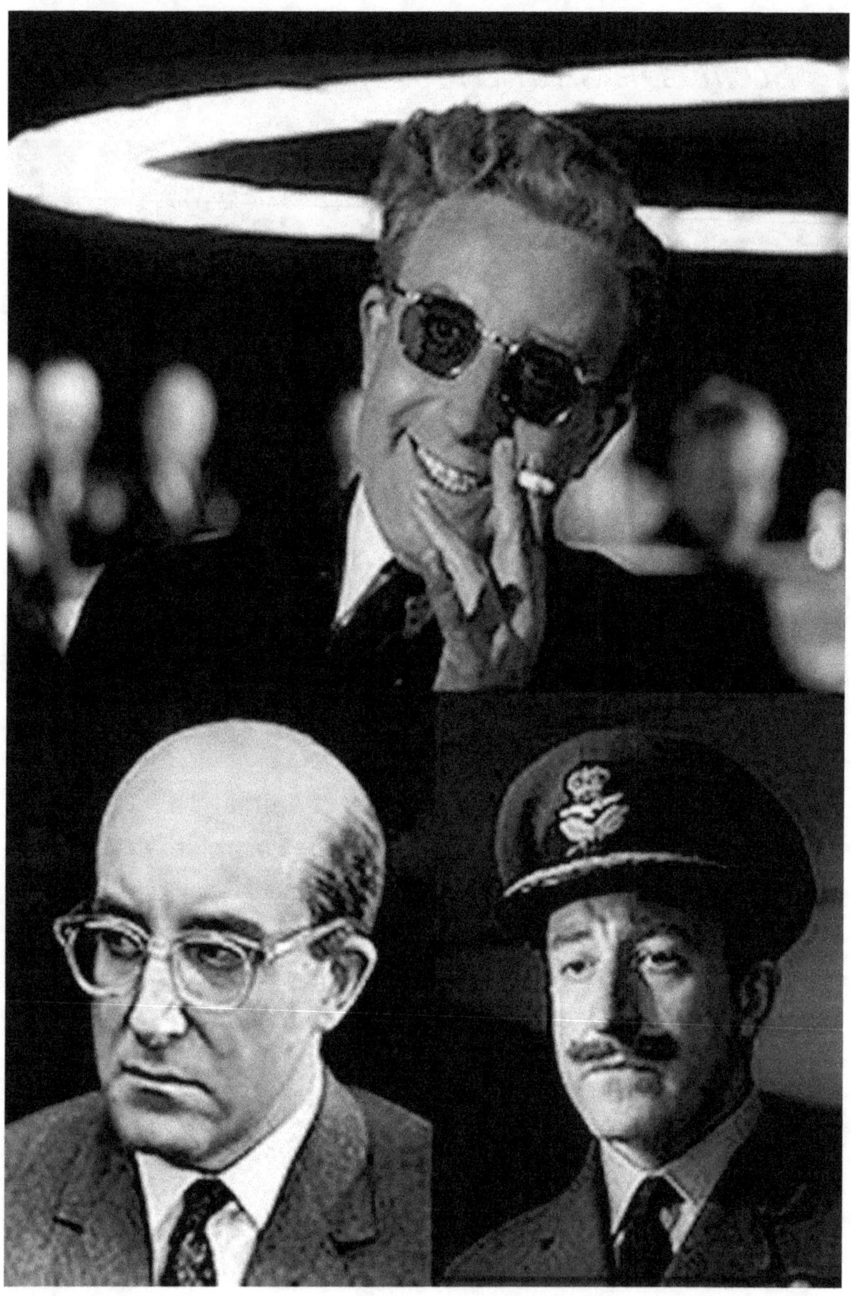

This was Sellers at his best, inventing bits of comic action that added immeasurably to the role, such as the bit of Dr. Strangelove's uncontrollable, homicidal hand, which tries to choke him and involuntarily presents the Nazi salute while he talks to the president about a post-apocalyptic world.

Dr. Strangelove is an ex-Nazi. He serves as President Muffley's scientific adviser in the War Room. We learn in the course of the film that Strangelove's original German surname was Merkwürdigliebe ("strange love" in German) and that he changed it when he became a US citizen after the war. But old habits are hard to break; twice in the film, Strangelove accidentally addresses the president as Mein Führer. The character is an amalgamation of RAND Corporation strategist Herman Kahn, mathematician and Manhattan Project principal John von Neumann, maybe most notably, rocket scientist Wernher von Braun (a central figure in Nazi Germany's rocket development program recruited to the US after the war), and Edward Teller, the "father of the hydrogen bomb." There is a common misconception that the character was based on Henry Kissinger, but Kubrick and Sellers denied this; Sellers said, "Strangelove was never modeled after Kissinger—that's a popular misconception. It was always Wernher von Braun." Furthermore, Henry Kissinger points out in his memoirs that at the time of the writing of *Dr. Strangelove*, he was an unknown academic.

The wheelchair-using Strangelove furthers a Kubrick trope of the menacing, seated antagonist, first depicted in *Lolita* (1962) through the character Dr. Zaempf. Strangelove's accent was influenced by that of Austrian-American photographer Weegee, who worked for Kubrick as a special photographic effects consultant. Strangelove's appearance echoes the mad scientist archetype, as seen in the character Rotwang in Fritz Lang's film *Metropolis* (1927). Sellers's Strangelove takes from the character Rotwang, the single black-gloved hand (which, in Rotwang's case is mechanical, because of a lab accident), the wild hair, and, most importantly, his ability to avoid being controlled by political power. According to Alexander Walker, Sellers improvised Dr. Strangelove's lapse into the Nazi salute, borrowing one of Kubrick's black leather gloves for the uncontrollable hand that makes the gesture.

Dr. Strangelove apparently suffers from alien hand syndrome. Kubrick wore the gloves on the set to avoid being burned when handling hot lights, and Sellers, recognizing the potential connection to Lang's work, found them to be menacing, so he borrowed them for his scenes in the movie. The mechanical hand would later become the motif of Darth Vader's cybernetic right hand in the *Star Wars* movies, suggesting a soul divided against itself—a legacy passed from father to son when he chops off Luke's hand, and back from son to father when Luke does the same thing in *Return of the Jedi* (1983).

In the Heat of the Night (1967)

In the Heat of the Night is a mystery drama film directed by Norman Jewison. It is based on John Ball's 1985 novel of the same name. The film tells the story of Virgil Tibbs (Sidney Poitier), a black police detective from Philadelphia, who involuntarily becomes involved in a murder investigation in the small town of Sparta, Mississippi. It stars Poitier and Rod Steiger (Sheriff William "Bill" Gillespie). Both Gillespie and Tibbs are so anxious to solve the murder case that they both either arrest and openly accuse a number of innocent people before the real culprit is discovered. The film was produced by Walter Mirisch. The screenplay was written by Stirling Silliphant.

The slapping scene occurs in the film when Tibbs, who is determined to establish the guilt of the murder of Eric Endicott (Larry Gates), an influential but insolent and bigoted conservative who opposed Colbert's progressive plans for a modern factory, that he makes a false accusation, whereupon Gates, using his left hand, suddenly and without warning, slaps Poitier across the face.

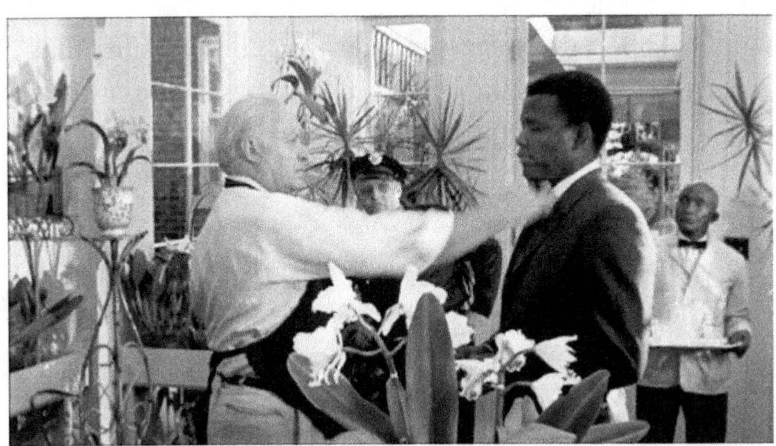

Without hesitation, Poitier retaliates using his right hand and strikes Gates with an even more forceful slap across the face that shocked both white and black audiences of the day. Director Norman Jewison said, "A black man had never slapped a white man back in an American film. We broke that taboo."

Scene: The Slap in the Greenhouse

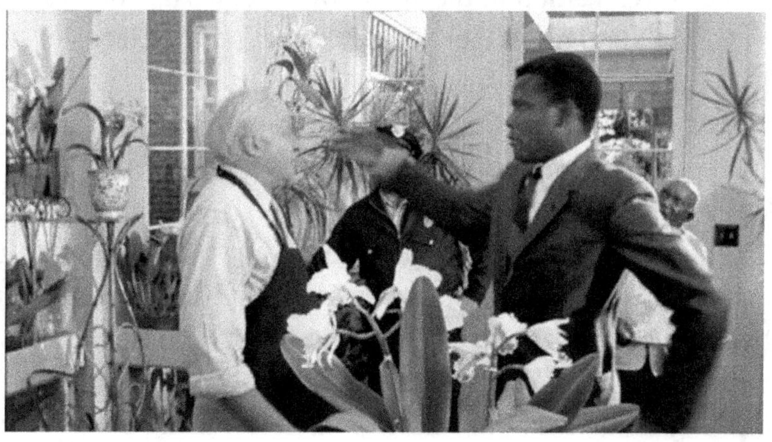

The shocked Gates asks Gillespie, "What are you gonna do about it?" Gillespie replies, "I don't know."

Gates is shocked to hear this and says, "I'll remember that." He then looks Poitier straight in the eye and says, "There was a time when I could have had you shot."

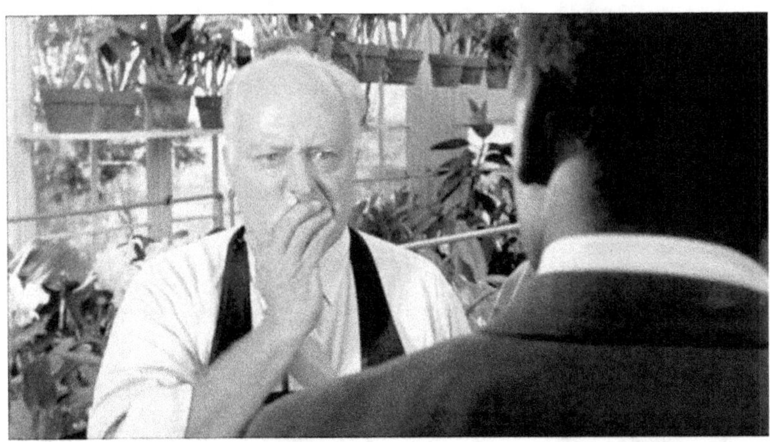

The greenhouse scene ends with Gates crying to himself, either from the embarrassment of losing control of his own passion, or his perceived indignity of being slapped by a black man without there being an immediate retaliation for this gross insult or both.

The famous scene of Tibbs slapping Endicott is not present in the John Ball novel. According to Poitier, the scene was almost not in the movie. In the textbook *Civil Rights and Race Relations in the USA 1850–2009* (Access to History), Poitier states:

> "I said, 'I'll tell you what, I'll make this movie for you if you give me your absolute guarantee when he slaps me I slap him right back and you guarantee that it will play in every version of this movie.' I try not to do things that are against nature."

However, Poitier's version of the story is contradicted by Mark Harris in his 2009 book *Pictures at a Revolution.* Harris states that copies of the original draft of the screenplay that he obtained clearly contain the scene as filmed, which is backed up by Jewison and Silliphant.

In the *Directors Guild American* (DGA) issue of Spring 2011, director Norman Jewison, in an article entitled "The Slap Heard Around the World," written by Robert Abela, said:

> When we rehearsed the slap, we always stopped and said, "bang, bang, bang," or "slap, slap." Because it hurts to get slapped that hard, I took Larry Gates aside, the chap who played Endicott, and had to teach him, since he wasn't a trained film actor, he was a theatrical actor. I said, "Try not to hit the ear. Hit him on the fatty part of the cheek, underneath the ear. Then you can take a pretty hard slap. Go ahead, slap me."
> He says, "I can't do that."
> I said, "Go ahead." So he slapped me. I said, "That's not a slap. Slap me harder!" When he got to the point when he was stunning me a little, I said, "You got it!"
> I could see Larry was afraid of slapping Sidney. But Sidney, I didn't have to direct. He was a film actor. I said, "I want you to hit him hard enough so that he feels it. In other words, you can't hold back." I remember working on this technically, trying to get both actors to the point where they're not afraid of hurting each other. That was the main thing. I think we did it in two takes, and I think we used the first. Because there's something about being caught off guard that was essential to the moment. Nobody expected him to slap Sidney.

Race relations were boiling over in the country when Norman Jewison shot *In the Heat of the Night* in 1967. The director explains how he captured that tension in the film's most famous scene.

Canadian-born Norman Jewison was eighteen years old when he came face-to-face with Southern racism on a bus in Memphis just after his service in World War II. The experience stayed with him. Two decades later, in the heyday of the civil rights era, he was able to answer back.

The legacy of "the slap" can be summarized as follows: After too many years of repression and cruelty, African-Americans had become empowered to react to situations just like their white counterparts. No longer did they need to walk off a sidewalk when a white person approached, use separate toilet facilities, sit at the back of the bus, get paid less than others for doing the same exact job, having to eat in separate areas of a restaurant, marry only with their own race, not being able to drink out of the same water fountain, not being able to vote, or turn the other cheek, and the list goes on and on.

2001: A Space Odyssey (1968)

2001: A Space Odyssey is a truly epic science-fiction film produced and directed by Stanley Kubrick. The screenplay was written by Kubrick and Arthur C. Clarke and was inspired by Clarke's short story "The Sentinel" and other short stories by Clarke. The film follows a voyage to the planet Jupiter, with the super-smart computer HAL, after the discovery of a featureless alien monolith, which affects traditional theories of human evolution, is unearthed on the moon. The film deals with themes of existentialism, human evolution, technology, artificial intelligence, and the possibility of extraterrestrial life.

The film is noted for its scientifically accurate depiction of space flight, pioneering special effects, and ambiguous imagery. Sound and dialogue are used sparingly and often in place of traditional cinematic and narrative techniques.

Scene: Humanity's Final Evolution

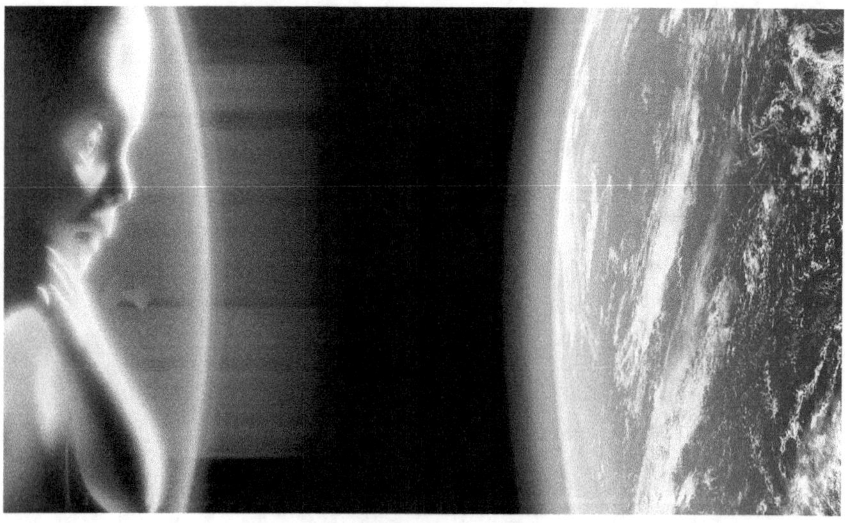

"There before him, a glittering toy no Star-Child could resist,
floated the planet Earth with all its peoples."
—Arthur C. Clarke, 2001: A Space Odyssey

Dr. David "Dave" Bowman, the mission commander of the *Discovery One* and the sole survivor of the Jupiter mission, is reborn at the end of the movie and emerges within an embryo with his own serene and wise-eyed features. This scene is enriched, in the movie, with the thrilling strains of *Also Sprach Zarathustra* by Johann Strauss. Bowman becomes reborn as a cosmic, innocent, orbiting "Star Child" that travels through the universe without technological assistance. The last enigmatic, open-ended image of the film is of the large, bright-eyed (with pin-pointed, glowing stars for pupils), luminous embryo in a translucent uterine amnion or bluish globe—an enhanced, reborn superhuman floating through space. Next to the globe of Earth on one half of the screen is the Star Child's globe of about the same size. The cyclical evolution from ape to man to spaceman to angel—Star Child—superman is now complete. Evolution has also been outwardly directed toward another level of existence—from isolated cave dwellings to the entire earth to the moon to the solar system to the universe. Humankind's unfathomed potential for the future is hopeful and optimistic.

What is the next stage in man's cosmic evolution beyond this powerful, immense, immortal, space-journeying creature? The last lines of Arthur C. Clark's science-fiction short story "The Sentinel" echo this sentiment:

> Then he waited, marshaling his thoughts and brooding over his still untested powers. For though he was master of the world, he was not quite sure what to do next. But he would think of something.

In director Stanley Kubrick's own words,

> "He is reborn, an enhanced being, a star child, an angel, a superman, if you like, and returns to earth prepared for the next leap forward of man's evolutionary destiny."

Liz Moore was a painter and sculptress who created the Star Child for the movie 2001. Her work became one of the most powerful and recognizable symbols of the movie.

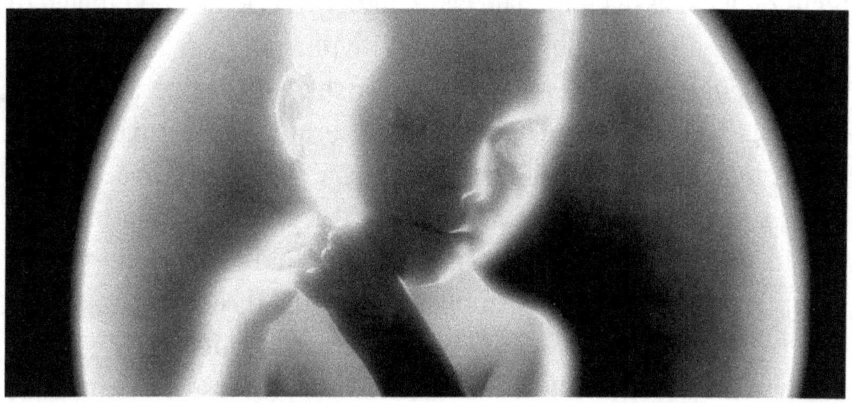

The making of this shot was, for a change, a troubled affair. After Kubrick and Clarke had decided that Bowman had to appear "transfigured" or "reborn" after his contact with the extraterrestrial beings in the conclusion of the movie, a first test version of the scene was carried out with a real baby shot against a black velvet background. The main contribution of Liz Moore in 2001 was definitely the beautiful and eerie Star Child that stares at us on the covers of books, CDs, DVDs, posters, and billboards, and has become one of the most powerful and recognizable symbols of the movie.

In September 1967, it was up to Liz Moore to create a clay sculpture, about two and a half feet tall, with facial features intentionally similar to Keir Dullea (the actor who played Dave Bowman). From this mold, the final fiberglass model was built.

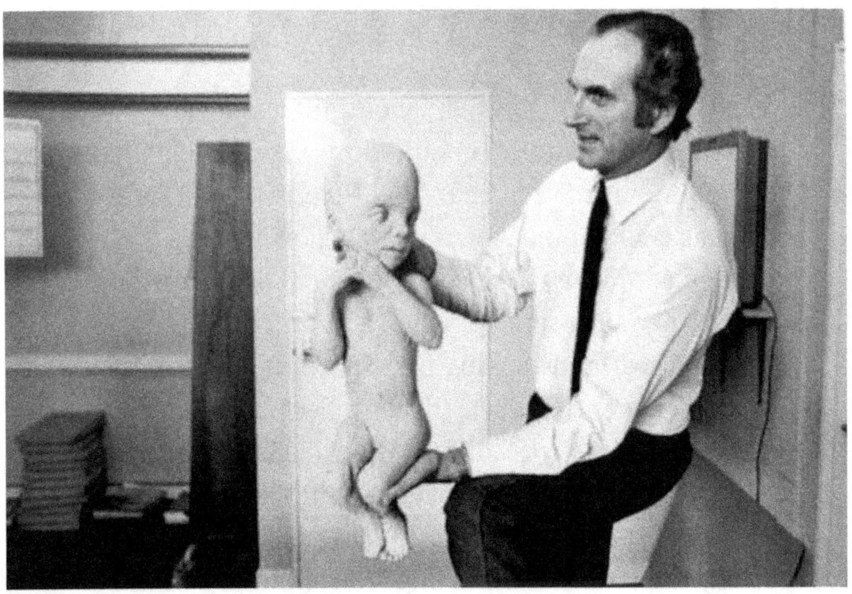

Production Designer Anthony Masters 2001 with Liz Moore's clay sculpture (*The Stanley Kubrick Archives*, p. 370)

Brian Johnson, in an interview in the magazine *Cinefex*, recalls:

> "Stanley did not want him to look like a normal human child, but to have a more 'evolved' look, with a slightly bigger head. In the beginning, it had to be a more complex puppet, with arms and fingers that could move, but then Stanley had the idea of surrounding it with a 'cocoon' of light, and finally decided that all he needed were eyes that could move. So I built glass eyes and

a small mechanism using drives and bearings, with some selsyn motors that made them move sideways and slightly up and down."

Douglas Trumbull recalls the making of the Star Child, again from *Cinefex*:

(Stanley) shot it through about fifteen layers of a special gauze, with about 40,000 watts of backlight—something like four big arc lights to rim-light it, and got this tremendous, overexposed glowing effect. This particular gauze—actually very rare, lady stockings from pre-war Europe—created a beautiful softening of the light, without making it unsharp. If you use a fog filter, it makes the image unsharp because it's actually a piece of glass with diffusion on it. But with gauze, part of the camera lens is seeing right through it, without interruption, so it tends to scatter the light without really stopping it from being sharp. Stanley filmed a number of different moves on the Star Child—shots of it entering frame and sliding through frame and so on. Then I airbrushed the envelope that surrounded it onto a piece of glossy black paper, which was photographed on the animation stand and matched in movement to the model, also with a lot of gauze and overexposure. The ten seconds of the shot were actually made with eight hours of exposure: to achieve the effect of large depth of field and sharpness of the image, the scene was filmed in stop-motion, three frames per second. The glowing effect was therefore obtained because of the long exposure time of each frame so that the backlight seemed to penetrate into the sculpture.

2001: A Space Odyssey (1968) depicts the fraught relationship between humanity and technology, the origin of man, and the possibility of alien intervention in his evolution within the bounds and realm of cosmic evolution. These themes were visually presented by the film using pioneering special effects. Made before the first moon landing, the film continues to exert widespread influence on cinema, design, painting, architecture, and advertising.

"Envisioning 2001: Stanley Kubrick's Space Odyssey" is on view at the Museum of the Moving Image in Queens, New York, through July 19, 2020.

The museum will present a major exhibition that explores Kubrick's influences, his obsessive research, and his innovative production process in envisioning a world of the future—the year 2001 from the viewpoint of the 1960s. The exhibition includes original artifacts from international collections and from the Stanley Kubrick Archive at the University of the Arts London, as well as from the museum's own collection.

Throughout its six-month run at MoMI, "Envisioning 2001: Stanley Kubrick's Space Odyssey" will be accompanied by a wide variety of screening series, public programs with guest speakers, and specialty themed workshops, tours, special events, and more.

Exhibition highlights include Special Photographic Effects Supervisor Douglas Trumbull's concept sketches for Clavius Base; from MoMI collection: costumes, including a spacesuit worn in the Clavius Base scene, Liz Moore's clay sculpture of the Star Child, and the Moonwatcher ape suit worn by Dan Richter in the "Dawn of Man" scene; and storyboards, contact sheets, test films, and photographs related to the Stargate special effects sequence.

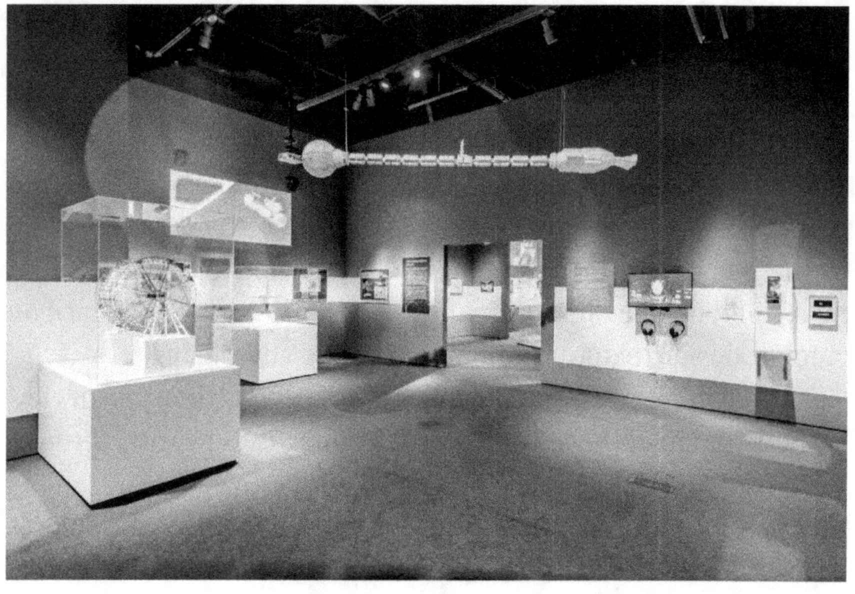

Planet of the Apes (1968)

Planet of the Apes is a revolutionary science-fiction film directed by Franklin J. Schaffner. It stars Charlton Heston, Roddy McDowall, Kim Hunter, and Maurice Evans. The screenplay by Michael Wilson and Rod Serling was loosely based on the 1963 French novel *La Planete des Singes* by Pierre Boulle.

The film tells the story of an astronaut crew who crash-lands on a strange planet in the distant future. Although the planet appears desolate at first, the surviving crew members stumble upon a society in which apes have evolved into creatures with human-like intelligence and speech. The apes have assumed the role of the dominant species, and humans are mute creatures wearing animal skins. In the course of the movie, remnants of a technologically advanced human society pre-dating simian history are discovered in a cave. George Taylor (Heston) identifies artifacts such as dentures, eyeglasses, a heart valve, and to the apes' astonishment, a talking children's doll. Taylor nonetheless thinks it best to search for answers despite being warned that he may not like what he finds. Heston then searches out answers to how the apes became the dominant species, and man became their slaves on an alien planet.

Scene: The Statue of Liberty

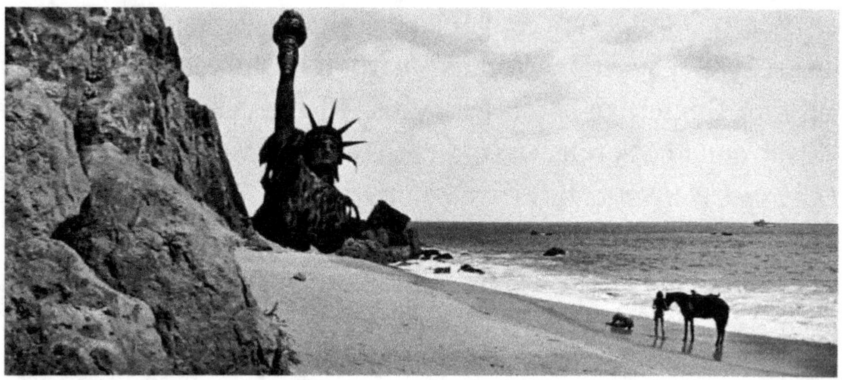

The ending scene of *Planet of the Apes* is one of the best "shock" moments in cinematic history. This is the moment when Heston discovers that the planet is actually Earth, drawing this conclusion purely from Lady Liberty's presence. The destroyed, sunken into the earth statue is a symbol that hope is lost. The days where the Statue of Liberty stood high on its pedestal are long gone, and mankind's time is over. In the film, it isn't just a symbol for America; it's a symbol for the human race.

We can only imagine the impact that this had on audiences back in the day when they had no idea what was coming. Even now, it stands up as a solid moment, and it truly is one of the most iconic scenes in science fiction movie history.

Riding along the seashore, Taylor notices the needle crown of the Statue of Liberty—all this time, he was already at home. Once here stood New York, but two thousand years of self-destructive wars and misunderstandings changed the geological and psychological landscape beyond recognition. Falling down on his knees and thrashing the sand with his hands, he yells:

"O God! I returned! I'm at home … you maniacs! You blew it up! Ah, damn you! God damn you all to hell!"

It was during the early script revisions that the idea for the famous ending to *Planet of the Apes* was devised.

Producer Arthur P. Jacobs said:

We were trying to make the audience believe it was another planet, which differs from (Pierre) Boulle's novel in which it WAS another planet. I thought that was rather predictable when we were doing the first screenplay. It's funny; I was having lunch with Blake Edwards, who at one point was going to direct it, at the Yugo Kosherarna Delicatessen in Burbank, across the street from Warner Bros. I said to him at the time. "It doesn't work; it's too predictable." Then I said, "What if he was on the earth the whole time and doesn't know it, and the audience doesn't know it." Blake said, "That's terrific. Let's get a hold of Rod." (Rod Serling was the screenwriter). As we walked out, after paying for the two ham sandwiches, we looked up, and there's this big Statue of Liberty on the wall of the delicatessen. We both looked at each other and said, "Rosebud" (the key to the plot of Citizen Kane). If we never had lunch in that delicatessen, I doubt that we would have had the Statue of Liberty as the end of the picture. I sent the finished script to Boulle, and he wrote back, saying he thought it was more inventive than his own ending, and wished that he had thought of it when he wrote the book.

There are two scenes where we see the Statue of Liberty, each scene having been done a different way.

The first is shot from above, down through the crown of the edifice, showing the hand holding the torch; art director William Creber built a half-scale model replica of the top of the head and the torch from cardboard and paper mâché, expertly positioned in the frame to look real. This shot looking down at Taylor required a seventy-foot high scaffold tower to be constructed. At sixty-six years of age, director of photography Leon Shamroy refused to climb the structure, while the assistant director had a phobia of heights. Instead, director Franklin J. Schaffner and William Creber lensed the perspective shot, filmed on a secluded cove named Westward Beach situated between Zuma Beach and Point Dume on the Malibu coast of California.

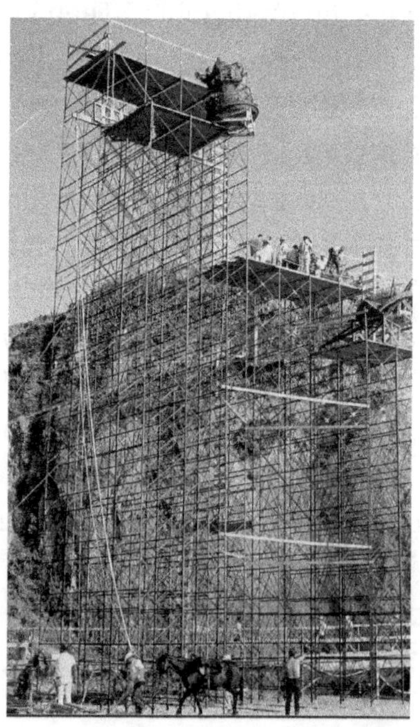

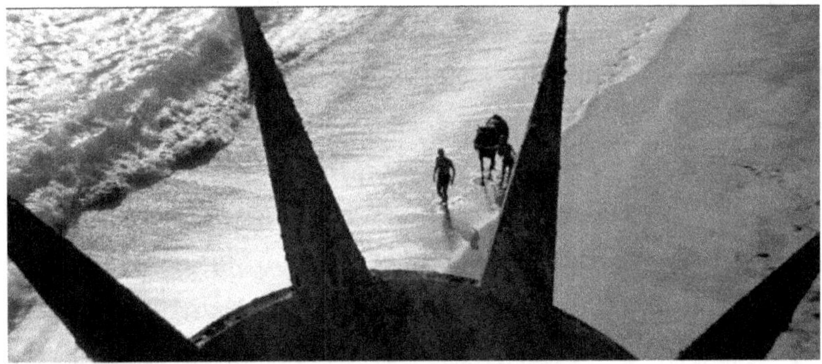

The second scene was a matte shot—a very detailed painting done on glass by Emil Kosa Jr., with transparent areas through which the live-action could appear. The extra-smooth surface permits the artist to be very detailed without the surface grain of canvas or paper.

This is a photograph of Zuma's Point Dume in Malibu, California, with an overlay of the partially buried Statue of Liberty.

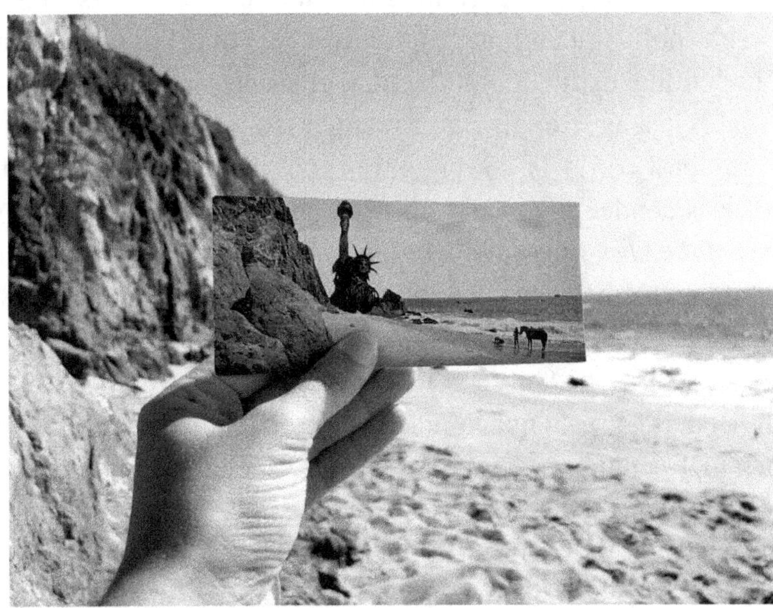

"Fifty years of *Planet of the Apes*: why the original series still holds a warning for us all" (Source: *BFI*, Jon Towlson, February 8, 2018)

The astonishing ending of *Planet of the Apes*, with Charlton Heston screaming in despair as the camera lingers on the shattered remains of the Statue of Liberty, is unremitting in its bleakness. And even watching it fifty years later, we can hardly rest easy.

Premiering on February 8, 1968, before US release in April (the same week as that other sci-fi milestone *2001: A Space Odyssey*), Franklin J. Schaffner's provocative allegory led to four sequels, which were no less downbeat. Indeed, it's difficult to imagine such a grimly apocalyptic movie series existing today. The modern reboots are decidedly less nihilistic.

For audiences, seeing civilization as we know it come to an end in the apes movies seemed to have a hypnotic effect. What's more, the franchise's commentary—on America's interracial conflict, the country's love-hate of immigrants, its violent protests, clashes between youth and authority, feminism, and (most pressing of all) the impending extinction of the human species in a nuclear war—resonates just as strongly now as it did then.

The apes' world is starkly authoritarian, operating on strict race/class/gender divisions, with humans designated to slavery. *Planet of the Apes*—like all the best science fiction—holds up a mirror to our world. We may have swapped places with them, but the apes are us. And we are doomed to blow ourselves up—the films tell us—just like the Statue of Liberty has been blown up.

Indeed, the great conceit of the series is its time-loop premise, which makes our extinction inescapable. The first sequel, *Beneath the Planet of the Apes* (1970), presented the ruins of human civilization buried underground and run by mutant survivors of a nuclear holocaust who continue to worship the doomsday machine.

Brent (James Franciscus), a fellow space traveler, is sent to investigate the disappearance of Taylor's ship. Like his predecessor, Brent is captured by apes and manages to escape, only to find himself stumbling into the clutches of the mutants. There he finally locates Taylor, who, driven insane by it all, proceeds to exact revenge on humanity by detonating the Alpha-Omega weapon himself, thereby bringing history (human and ape) to an end.

Scenes in *Beneath* depict anti-violence demonstrations held by the peace-loving chimpanzees wielding placards ("Wage Peace Not War"), while the war-mongering gorillas led by General Ursus (James Gregory) mount a campaign to storm the Forbidden Zone, and the progressive-minded Cornelius and Zira clash with the arch-conservative Dr. Zaius.

Beneath again reflects the mood of America in the Vietnam era when the younger generation rebelled, and police fired live bullets at student demonstrators on university campuses. It ends in a frenzy of machinegun fire, with Brent and Taylor mowed down, and even the mute flower-child Nova (Linda Harrison) shot dead by the rampaging guerrilla army.

The third entry in the series seemed to take a lighter tone in comparison, but even this proves to be deceiving. In *Escape from the Planet of the Apes* (1971), Cornelius and Zira manage to repair Taylor's spaceship and take a reverse trajectory back to Earth in 1973. There they are treated like celebrities by the media until the authorities begin to realize the implications of Zira's becoming pregnant. The two chimpanzees are forced into exile as the military tries to hunt them down before they can trigger the end of human civilization.

The film resonates as an allegory to America's own real immigration issues, especially the desperate influx of emigrants from Mexico and Central America. Cornelius and Zira are ultimately viewed as illegal immigrants and a threat to the American way. *Escape* also had much to say about the then-burgeoning second-wave feminist movement: Zira emerges as a strong, intelligent, and politicized female who puts the males around her to shame. In the end, though, the time-loop narrative of the series prevails; the conclusion of *Escape* is another despairing one, as the saga drives relentlessly toward the predestined cataclysm.

The race relations subtext would come to the fore in *Conquest of the Planet of the Apes* (1972), with critics of the time reading social comment into scenes of the enslaved apes taking to the streets. Set in 1991, Zira's baby has now fully grown and is named Caesar (Roddy McDowell). Emerging from his circus hideaway, Caesar is shocked to find America a police state, his fellow simians imported by the boatload to be used as slaves to the humans. He leads them in an uprising, the moment of ape revolution on Earth.

Conquest ends with Caesar's triumphant proclamation: "Tonight, we have seen the birth of the planet of the apes." Those words might perhaps have offered a salvation of sorts, the possibility of negating the saga's self-fulfilling prophecy, but the final film in the franchise, *Battle for the Planet of the Apes* (1973), dashes any such hope. Indeed, *Battle* sees the survivors of the apocalypse (it's revealed that humans eventually resorted to nuclear weapons to try to quell the ape uprising) engaged in a final—ultimately futile—war for control of the planet.

By its close, we are left with no doubt that the series has come full circle; we are back where we started, staring at the shattered remains of liberty.

This one has a message," Charlton Heston reputedly told nervous 20th Century-Fox executives about *Planet of the Apes*. Hollywood was doubtful that audiences would take such a message, one that spoke to revolution and history repeating, to the symbolic destruction of freedom and democracy, to madmen with their fingers on the doomsday button. Half a century later, however, that message remains as urgent as ever: "You maniacs! You blew it up! Damn you! Damn you all to hell!"

THE 1970s

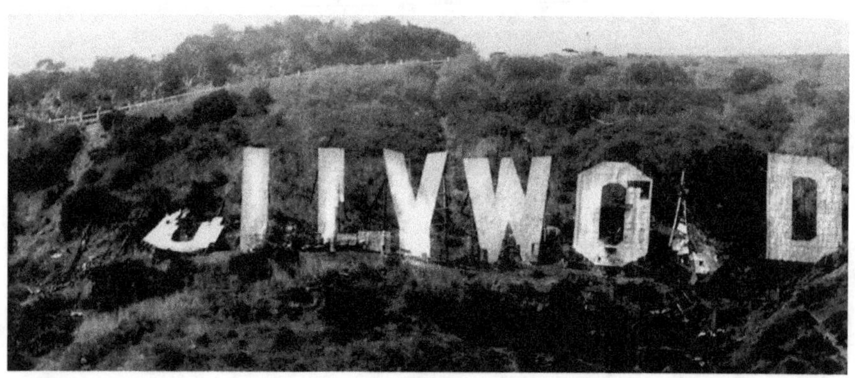

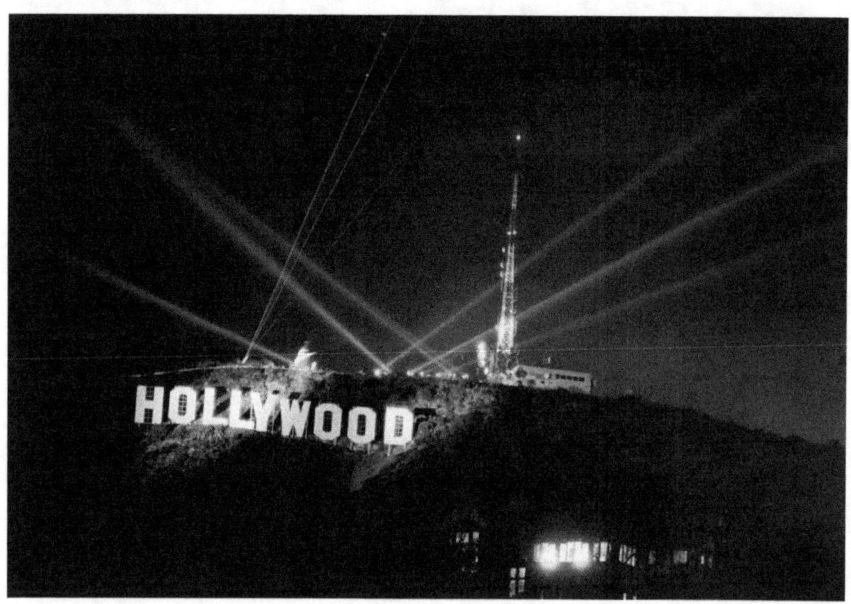

Patton (1970)

Patton is the epic film biography of the controversial, bombastic, multi-dimensional World War II General and hero George S. Patton. The larger-than-life, flamboyant, arrogant, self-righteous, maverick, pugnacious military figure was nicknamed "Old Blood and Guts." It was directed by Franklin J. Schaffner from a script by Francis Ford Coppola and Edmund H. North. The story was based on two books: *Patton: Ordeal and Triumph* (1963) by Ladislas Farago and *A Soldier's Story* (1951) by General Omar Bradley. Patton is played by George C. Scott, with a strong supporting cast including Karl Malden as Omar Bradley.

Scene: The Speech

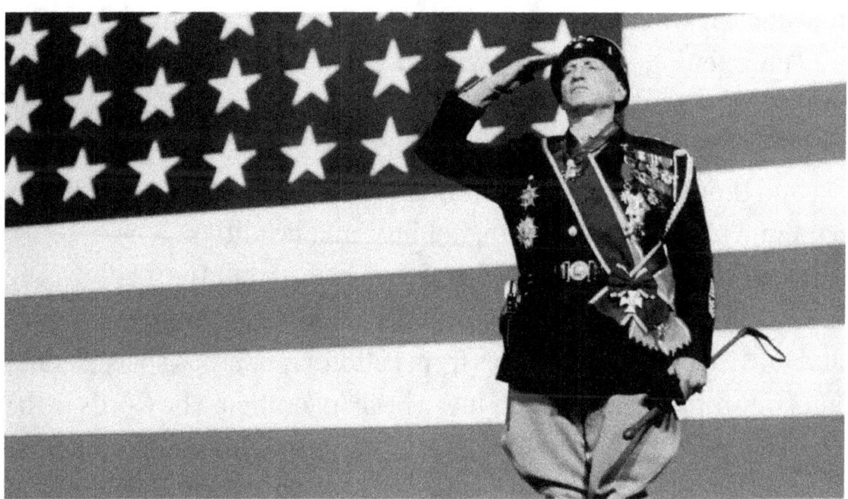

"The Speech" was, in actuality, a compilation of numerous orations the real General George S. Patton, Jr. delivered countless times to units of his 3rd Army before the invasion of France in June

1944. It remains one of the most recognizable opening scenes in modern cinema. If you ask any American born after World War II what immediately comes to mind when the name "Patton" is mentioned, chances are they will conjure an image of an empty stage dominated by an enormous American flag, when a tall, uniformed soldier with a chest full of medals and badges suddenly strides to its center and begins to address an unseen audience of soldiers. *Patton* was the perfect movie for its time, as 1970 was ripe for a movie that changed the game. *Patton* reinvigorated the war films because it brought in huge audiences and opened people's minds to a more realistic depiction of warfare and command in warfare. The movie cannily tapped into the country's Vietnam War psyche. The hawks saw Patton as the kind of general we needed to win a just cause. Doves could sneer at the type of mentality that had gotten us into the mess. You saw what you wanted to see. Even today, it is unclear whether Patton should be seen as a role model.

The opening scene was written by the screenwriters Francis Ford Coppola and Edmund H. North and was not intended to be in the final cut of the movie, but director Franklin J. Schaffer had second thoughts and fortunately left it in. The speech of Patton was a unique blend of patriotism, nobility, and crudities.

However, Patton never gave such a speech. It would be totally wrong to state that the speech was just a fabrication. Screenwriters Coppola and North cleverly took quotes from Patton's numerous speeches and interviews and coupled them into a brilliant oration. The words in the speech are Patton's apart from some lines used by the screenwriters to integrate the quotes into a coherent speech. The result was one of the most outstanding introductions in movie history.

Screenwriters Coppola and North had to tone down Patton's actual words and statements in the scene, as well as throughout the rest of the film, to avoid an R rating; in the opening monologue, the word "fornicating" replaced "fucking" when he was criticizing the *Saturday Evening Post*. Also, Scott's gravelly and scratchy voice is the opposite of Patton's high-pitched, nasally, and somewhat squeaky voice, a point noted by historian SLA Marshall. However, Marshall also points out that the film contains "too much cursing and obscenity [by Patton]. Patton was not habitually foul-mouthed. He used dirty words when he thought they were needed to impress."

When Scott learned that the speech would open the film, he refused to do it, as he believed that it would overshadow the rest of his performance. Director Schaffer assured him that it would be shown at the end. The scene was shot in one afternoon at Sevilla Studios in Madrid, with the flag having been painted on the back of the stage wall.

All the medals and decorations shown on Patton's uniform in the monologue are replicas of those actually awarded to Patton. However, the general never wore all of them in public and was, in any case, not a four-star general at the time he made the famous speeches on which the opening is based. He wore them all on only one occasion: in his backyard in Virginia at the request of his wife, who wanted a picture of him with all his medals. The producers used a copy of this photo to help recreate this "look" for the opening scene.

Some memorable quotes from the opening speech:

> "Now I want you to remember that no bastard ever won a war by dying for his country. He won it by making the other poor dumb bastard die for his country."

> "The Nazis are the enemy. Wade into them. Spill their blood. Shoot them in the belly. When you put your hand into a bunch of goo that a moment before was your best friend's face, you'll know what to do."

"Now there's another thing I want you to remember. I don't want to get any messages saying that we are holding our position. We're not holding anything. Let the Hun do that. We are advancing constantly, and we're not interested in holding onto anything except the enemy. We're going to hold onto him by the nose, and we're going to kick him in the ass. We're going to kick the hell out of him all the time, and we're going to go through him like crap through a goose."

"Thirty years from now, when you're sitting around your fireside with your grandson on your knee, and he asks you, 'What did you do in the great World War II,' you won't have to say, 'Well... I shoveled shit in Louisiana.'"

Dirty Harry (1971)

Dirty Harry is a neo-noir action-thriller film produced and directed by Don Siegel. It is the first in the *Dirty Harry* series. Actor Clint Eastwood plays the title role, in his first outing as San Francisco Police Department (SFPD) Inspector "Dirty" Harry Callahan. The film drew upon the real-life case of the Zodiac Killer as the Callahan character seeks out a similar vicious psychopath.

Dirty Harry was a critical and commercial success and set the style for a whole genre of police films. It was followed by four sequels: *Magnum Force* in 1973, *The Enforcer* in 1976, *Sudden Impact* in 1983 (directed by Eastwood himself), and *The Dead Pool* in 1988.

Eastwood's iconic portrayal of the blunt-speaking, slightly sadistic, unorthodox detective set the style for a number of his subsequent roles. The "alienated cop" motif was subsequently imitated by a number of television shows and Hollywood movies. Even more than the main Scorpio plot, *Dirty Harry* endures in large part because one incidental sequence, where an off-duty Harry—eating a hot dog at a greasy diner next to an adult bookstore—witnesses a bank robbery in progress and stops it with his .44 Magnum before pointing his gun at one of the criminals and asking, "You've got to ask yourself one question: 'Do I feel lucky?' Well, do ya, punk?" The language, attitude, and spectacular violence of that scene soon crept into the likes of Kojak, Baretta, and Starsky and Hutch, and into movies like *Walking Tall* (1973) and *Death Wish* (1974).

Scene: It's All About Feeling Lucky

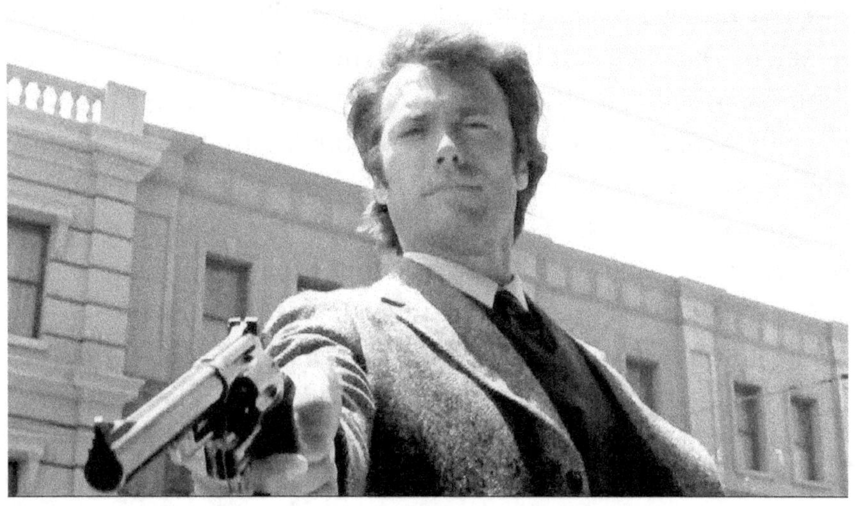

Early in the film, during his lunch break, Callahan foils a bank robbery. He shoots two robbers, and then he walks up to the wounded robber, whose shotgun is lying within grabbing distance. Does the guy dare reach for his shotgun? Harry plays dirty by taunting him and holds a third at gunpoint, bluffing him to surrender with an ultimatum:

> "I know what you're thinking: Did he fire six shots or only five? Well, to tell you the truth, in all this excitement, I've kinda lost track myself. But being this is a .44 Magnum, the most powerful handgun in the world, and would blow your head clean off, you've got to ask yourself one question: 'Do I feel lucky?' Well, do ya, punk?"

Although the robber initially taunted him with the idea of reaching for his nearby shotgun, Clint's description of the killing force of his gun dissuades him. With that, Clint picks up the gun and begins to walk away, but the injured robber's curiosity overtakes him, and he says to Clint, "I've got to know." In other words, did he still have one more bullet in his gun chamber? Instead of just saying yes or no, Clint boldly goes up to him, to the poor robber's horror, and sadistically cocks the gun and fires it at point-blank range. Fortunately, nothing happens for the gun is indeed empty. Clint laughs, and while he walks away, the robber utters, "You son of a bitch."

Although *Dirty Harry* is arguably Clint Eastwood's signature role, he was not a top contender for the part. The role of Harry Callahan was offered to John Wayne, Frank Sinatra, Robert Mitcham, Steve McQueen, Burt Lancaster, and George C. Scott.

The actor who was looking at the business end of Clint's imposing Magnum in this scene was Albert Popwell (July 15, 1926–April 9, 1999). Popwell was a talented and versatile African-American stage, television, and film actor whose acting career spanned six decades.

Born in New York City, Popwell started as a professional dancer before taking up a career in acting. Popwell made his professional debut on Broadway at the age of sixteen in *The Pirate*.

He appeared in the first four films of the *Dirty Harry* series. Popwell was, of course, the wounded bank robber at the receiving end of Eastwood's "Do you feel lucky?" monologue from *Dirty Harry*. Popwell was a murderous pimp in *Magnum Force*. He appeared as Big Ed Mustapha, a black militant leader, in *The Enforcer*, and as Harry's detective, colleague Horace King, in *Sudden Impact*. He did not appear in the last film in the series, *The Dead Pool*, due to a scheduling conflict.

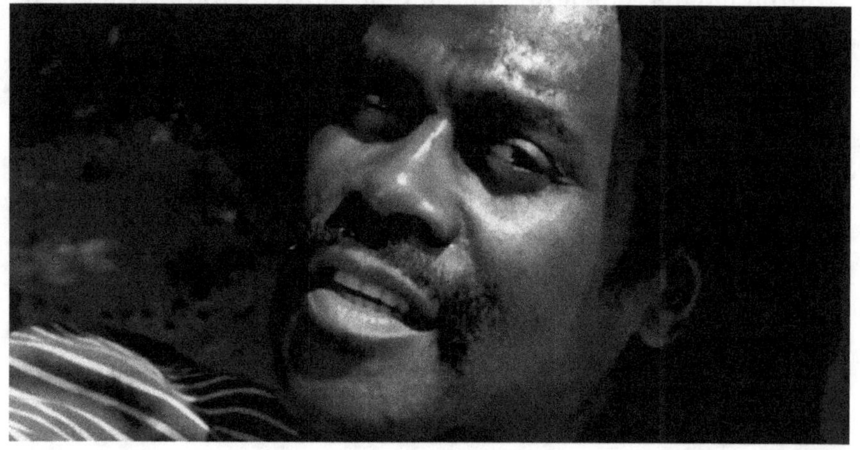

The Godfather (1972)

Francis Ford Coppola's epic, trail-blazing, award-winning film is part of a lush saga/trilogy that has earned its place in American culture as a modern-day iconic film about violence, power, corruption, family loyalty, and revenge. The Corleone crime "family" in Manhattan in the mid-1940s is dominated first by wise godfather/patriarch "Don" Vito Corleone (Marlon Brando in a tremendous, award-winning acting portrayal), the head of one of the five Italian-American "families" that operate a crime syndicate in New York City. Don effortlessly balances the vicious world of organized crime, the ethnic family values within it, and the deeply realized, tragic characteristics of those who share these values.

Scene: The Granting of Wishes

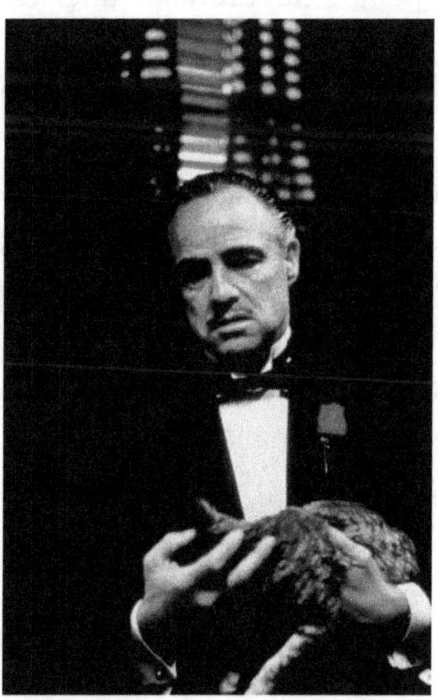

In the long opening scene of the film, Corleone is in his home's dark office, regally and ruthlessly carrying on business during his daughter Connie's (Talia Shire) wedding reception, held in the bright, sunshiny outdoor veranda. It is the custom of the father of the bride to grant favors to all petitioners and those who pay homage. Ostensibly, Don is a gentle, understated, restrained, sixty-two-year-old aging man, sitting behind his study's desk in an under-lit room. His face has a bulldog appearance with padded cheeks, and he speaks slowly with a high-pitched, hoarse, raspy, guttural mumbling accent. On his lap is a cat whose head he lovingly and gently strokes. Even though it was unplanned, the cat later came to represent the claws that hid beneath the otherwise warm exterior of the mob boss. Although he moves stiffly, he wields enormous lethal power as he determines the dispensation of justice—who will be punished and who will be favored. One by one, he listens to supplicants' requests for extra-legal help and determines how to make offers that people can't refuse. American justice has failed the undertaker Amerigo Bonasera (Salvatore Corsitto), and only now does he turn to the Godfather for real justice and revenge. Two men have severely beaten up his daughter after trying to rape her. Although duly arrested, they only received a suspended sentence in court. The Godfather first scolds him for not coming to him first and for his arrogant attitude toward him. Only after Bonasera asks the Godfather to be his friend bows and kisses his hand and calls him "Godfather" does Don agree to help him and then makes the necessary arrangements to make this happen.

From the screenplay by Mario Puzo and Francis Ford Coppola:

BONASERA
I'll give you anything you ask.

VITO CORLEONE
We've known each other many years, but
this is the first time you came to me for
counsel, for help. I can't remember the
last time that you invited me to your
house for a cup of coffee, even though my
wife is godmother to your only child. But
let's be frank here: you never wanted my
friendship. And uh, you were afraid to be
in my debt.

BONASERA
I didn't want to get into trouble.

VITO CORLEONE
I understand. You found paradise in
America, had a good trade, made a good
living. The police protected you; and
there were courts of law. And you didn't
need a friend of me. But uh, now you come
to me and you say "Don Corleone give me
justice." But you don't ask with respect.
You don't offer friendship. You don't even
think to call me Godfather. Instead, you
come into my house on the day my daughter
is to be married, and you uh ask me to do
murder, for money.

BONASERA
I ask you for justice.

VITO CORLEONE
That is not justice; your daughter is
still alive.

                    BONASERA
Be my friend...
          (after bowing and the Don
          shrugs)
Godfather?

                    VITO CORLEONE
          (after Bonasera kisses his
          hand)
Good.
          (then)
Some day, and that day may never come,
I'll call upon you to do a service for me.
But uh, until that day accept this justice
as a gift on my daughter's wedding day.

                    BONASERA
          (as he leaves the room)
Grazie, Godfather.

                    VITO CORLEONE
Prego.
          (to Tom Hagen, after
          Bonasera leaves the room)
Ah, give this to ah, Clemenza. I want
reliable people; people that aren't gonna
be carried away. I'm mean, we're not
murderers, despite of what this undertaker
says.

Each of the people who come to ask Don for favors on this day does eventually help him or his family members during the course of the movie. For instance, Bonasera is the undertaker who has the grisly task of preparing Sonny's bloodied body for his funeral.

Marlon Brando wanted to make Don Corleone "look like a bulldog," so he stuffed his cheeks with cotton wool for the audition. For the actual filming, he wore a mouthpiece made by a dentist. This appliance is on display in the American Museum of the Moving Image in Queens, New York.

Don Vito Corleone's distinctive voice was based on real-life mobster Frank Cosrello. Brando had seen him on television during the Estes Kefauver hearings in 1951 and imitated his husky whisper in the film.

The film's opening scene, a three-minute zoom-out of Amerigo Bonasera and Don Corleone, was achieved with a computer-controlled zoom lens, which had earlier been used in *Silent Running* (1972).

The cat held by Brando in the opening scene was a stray that Coppola found while on the lot at Paramount Pictures, and was not originally called for in the script. So content was the cat that its purring muffled some of Brando's dialogue and, as a result, most of his lines had to be looped. Looping is the process of fitting speech to film already shot, especially by making a closed loop of the film for one scene and projecting it repeatedly until a good synchronization of film and recorded speech is achieved.

Cinematographer Gordon Willis earned himself the nickname "the Prince of Darkness," since his sets were so underlit. Paramount Pictures executives initially thought that the footage was too dark until persuaded otherwise by Willis and Francis Ford Coppola that it was to emphasize the shadiness of the Corleone family's dealings.

Marlon Brando did not memorize most of his lines and read from cue cards during most of the film, sometimes held by his fellow cast members.

Scene: The Horse's Head in Bed

From the screenplay by Mario Puzo and Francis Ford Coppola:

```
                                              CUT TO:


PAN OF EXTERIOR OF WOLTZ' ESTATE - DAWN

Music is a variation of the Title Theme, then we see the interior
of Woltz' bedroom. Woltz awakens in a pool of blood, and finds
Khartoum's severed head in his bed; and SCREAMS
ah...ah...ah...ah...ah!
```

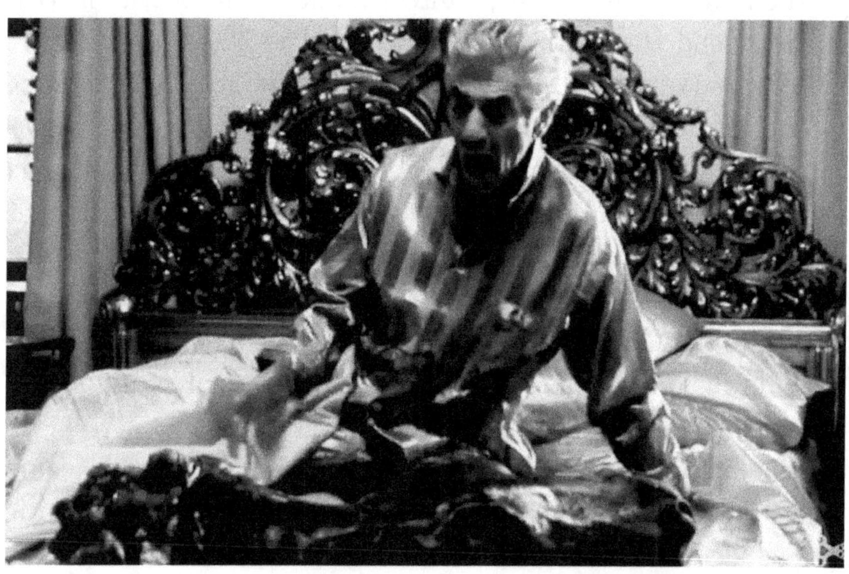

Francis Ford Coppola's crime drama *The Godfather* remains a hugely influential film decades after its release, and perhaps the one scene from that movie most often referenced in pop culture is one in which Hollywood producer Jack Woltz, who unwisely refused a request from the Corleone family to cast Johnny Fontane (Don Corleone's godson) in his new film, blaming him for deflowering and ruining the acting career of one of his best female prospects, awakes to find the severed and bloody head of his prize thoroughbred in his bed. In an earlier rendition of the scene, after Tom Hagen returns from Hollywood, he discusses with Don Vito Corleone his conversation and visit with the film producer, followed then by the horse head sequence. However, in the final film version, the scene where Tom Hagen leaves the house is immediately followed by the notorious "horse head in bed" sequence without the intermittent scene with Corleone.

The Godfather was shot about a decade before the Screen Actors Guild adopted the American Humane Society's "Guidelines for the Safe Use of Animals in Filmed Media," so it's reasonable to be concerned that at least one horse was diverted from being the ingredients in dog food in order to appear on the silver screen. It is true that the horse's head in *The Godfather* was genuine but completely untrue that the animal was killed specifically for that scene. The horse was already slated to be butchered.

This is the actual horse head used by Paramount Studios during the rehearsal scenes of the first Godfather movie. It is a taxidermy mount of an actual head and neck of a horse that had been mounted on a Styrofoam form.

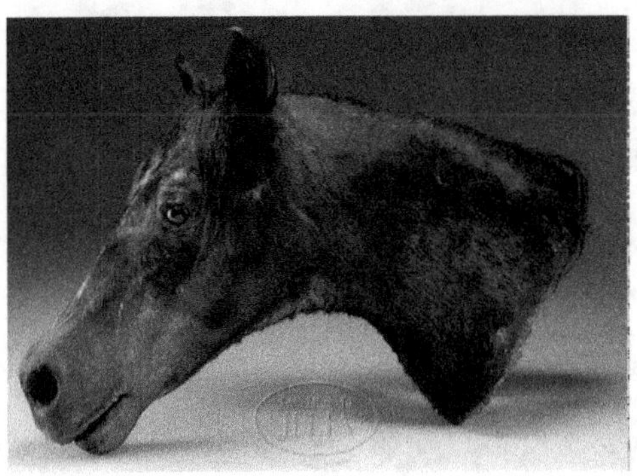

As a result of various correspondences with Paramount Studios, the consignor, and a former employee of Paramount, who originally owned the taxidermy mount, it was eventually sent to the set of the film. Despite the lifelike and grisly appearance of the taxidermy mount (the horse head was painted red and looked very realistically bloody), apparently, Coppola was still not satisfied with its realism. According to Producer Al Ruddy, this head was "unsuitable," one reason being that the seam/crack in the middle of the taxidermy horse's neck was too obvious. Coppola wanted no question of it being the real head and neck of a recently decapitated horse along with fresh blood for total realism.

In this rehearsal scene, using the taxidermy mount, veteran actor John Marley, who plays Jack Woltz in the film, is seen to the right of the bed while director Coppola is seen sitting on the bed describing how he wants the scene to develop.

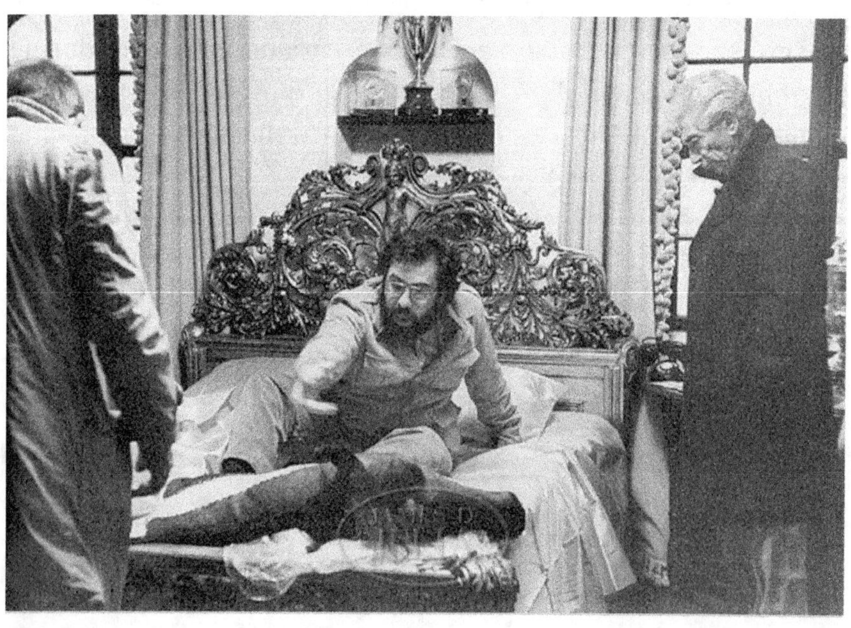

As a result, in the actual final filming, a real horse's bloody head was used. Coppola's scouts found a horse ready for slaughter at a dog-food plant in New Jersey. Warren Clymer, the art director, picked one that looked like the horse in the film and said, "When that one is slaughtered, send us the head."

Coppola later remembered, "One day, a crate with dry ice came with this horse's head in it." The crew had to scramble in order to film the scene before the head began to deteriorate once it was removed from the ice. But even before that, the horse's head had to be painted from white to brown in order to match the color of the horse previously filmed in a stable.

Actor John Marley was intentionally not told that the mount used in the rehearsal scene had been replaced by the head and neck of a real horse, so when he first saw it lying in a pool of real blood in his bed, his screams were quite authentic, just what the director wanted, filled with shock, horror, and utter fright emanating from the poor, unsuspecting actor.

Some incidental information surrounding this particular scene: The Triple-Crown winner Khartoum was bought for $600,000 ($15,073,980 in terms of 2019 dollars) by Woltz and who put his horse out to "stud." The horse had a fine stable built for him, the best vets and horse breeders that money could buy, and even a small team of private detectives to guard him "'round the clock." Obviously, Corleone's men were able to overcome this small contingency of guards in order to get at the horse. Woltz was very attached to the horse; his pride and affection for the animal clearly evident. As we know now, Khartoum was eventually killed and decapitated, and then Luca Brasi put his head in Woltz's bed to convince the director to grant Johnny Fontane the lead in the new war movie he was shooting. Upon discovering Khartoum's severed head, Woltz swore his staff to secrecy and had Khartoum quietly buried, and his stables all torn down.

This particular scene in the movie is filmed in a real-life grand Beverly Hills Mediterranean-style estate. It was built in 1927 and purchased by William Randolph Hearst. The estate has thirty bedrooms and, interestingly, forty bathrooms, as well as cascading waterfalls leading to an Olympic-size swimming pool, a two-story library, a lighted tennis court, two screening rooms, and a billiards room with herringbone parquet floors. In the film, the mansion is panned, in a serene morning shot, just before we enter the bedroom where Woltz is soundly sleeping.

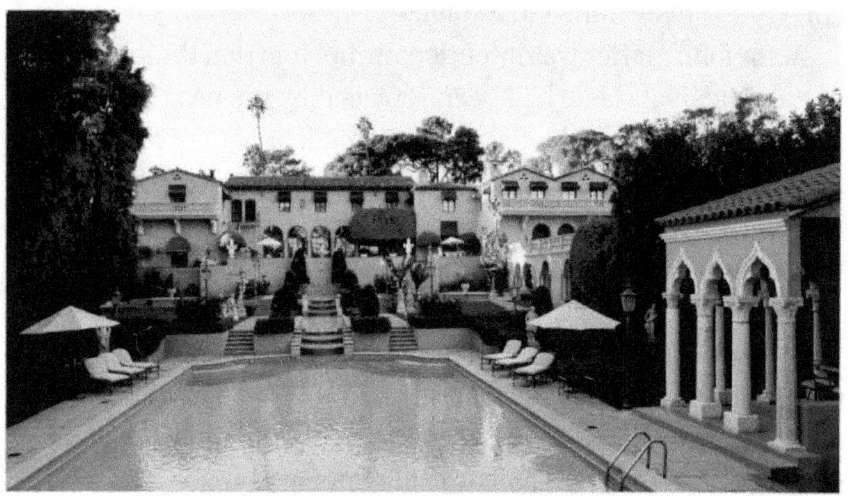

Francis Ford Coppola never shows or mentions in his interviews why he doesn't show the actual horse-killing process. The scene was intended for us to fathom the truly despicable and horrible acts of retribution and feats Don Corleone was capable of if his offer is refused.

Two main themes we identify in this scene are violence and punishment. The way Mr. Woltz is portrayed suggests to the audience that he is not a nice man, and we draw this from his incredible wealth and the fact that he sleeps alone and has no one to share it with. From this, we conclude that what is done to him is a punishment. And we know that those who punished have a violent ruthless nature from the extremity of the punishment. Other themes are Italy and rivalry. The Italian music is a giveaway, to those who haven't seen the whole film that the story may be based in or about Italian culture, and the severed horse's head suggests mafia involvement.

Woltz's character is hard to analyze in this short scene as we don't see much of his behind the scene action. However, from what we are told, we get the sense that he is a materialistic, money-obsessed man. He has an obscenely big house, which, from what we can tell, he doesn't share, based on the fact he sleeps alone. We draw from this the fact he is a cold-hearted businessman.

Legacy of *The Godfather*

Brando parodied his portrayal of Vito Corleone in *The Freshman*, a 1990 comedy film.

The film has been parodied several times on the animated television series *The Simpsons*. For instance, in the season three episode "Lisa's Pony," Lisa wakes up to find a horse in her bed and starts screaming, a reference to the horse's head scene in *The Godfather*.

Megan Gambino said in an article entitled "What is *The Godfather* Effect?" in the *Smithsonian* magazine (January 31, 2012):

> I feel it helped Italianize American culture. All of a sudden, everyone was talking about Don Corleone and making jokes about, "I am going to make you an offer you can't refuse." I think it helped people see that in this depiction of Italian-Americans was a reflection of their own immigrant experience, whether they were Irish or Jews from Eastern Europe. They found that common ground... I think it squashed the idea that Italians were uneducated

and that Italians all spoke with heavy accents.

On the sociological level, we had been facing the twin discouragements of the Vietnam War and Watergate, so it spoke to this sense of disillusionment that really started to permeate American life at that time. I think also the nostalgia factor with the Godfather cannot be underestimated, because in the early '70s [the first two films were in '72 and '74], it was such a changing world. It was the rise of feminism. It was the era of black power. And what The Godfather presented was this look at the vanishing white male patriarchal society. I think that struck a chord with a lot of people who felt so uncertain in this rapidly changing world. Don Corleone, a man of such certainty that he created his own laws and took them into his own hands, appealed to a lot of people.

Although many films about gangsters preceded *The Godfather*, Coppola steeped his film in Italian immigrant culture, and his portrayal of mobsters as persons of considerable psychological depth and complexity was unprecedented. Coppola took it further with his 1974 sequel *The Godfather, Part II*, and the success of those two films, critically, artistically, and financially, was a catalyst for the production of numerous other depictions of Italian-Americans as mobsters, including films such as Marin Scorsese's *Goodfellas* (1990) and TV series such as David Chase's *The Sopranos*. The highly acclaimed *The Sopranos* (1999-2007) is widely regarded as one of the greatest television series of all time. A comprehensive study of Italian-American culture on film, conducted from 1996 to 2001 by the Italic Institute of America, showed that nearly three hundred movies featuring Italian Americans as mobsters (mostly fictional) had been produced since *The Godfather*, an average of nine per year.

The Exorcist (1973)

The Exorcist is the sensational, shocking horror story about devil possession and the subsequent exorcism of the demonic spirit Pazuzu from a young, innocent girl of a divorced family. *The Exorcist* was directed by William Friedkin. The film's screenplay was faithfully based upon author William Peter Blatty's 1971 best-selling theological-horror novel of the same name.

This controversial film is the sensational, tawdry, shocking horror story about devil possession and the exorcism of the demonic spirits from a young, innocent, twelve-year-old Regan MacNeil (Linda Blair). Ghastly expressions of her possession were masterfully created with remarkable special effects to manipulate audiences into feeling dread, nausea, and fright.

The controversial nature of the film's content, exorcism (accompanied by blasphemies, obscenities, and graphic physical shocks), was supposedly based upon an authentic, nearly two-month-long exorcism performed in 1949 on a fourteen-year-old boy (with the pseudonym "Robbie Mannheim") in Mt. Rainier, Maryland by the Catholic Church (in the form of a fifty-two-year-old Jesuit priest named Father William S. Bowdern and Father Raymond Bishop). The official exorcism was reported in Thomas B. Allen's and Carl Brandt's 1993 book *Possessed: The True Story of an Exorcism.*

Scene: The Vomiting

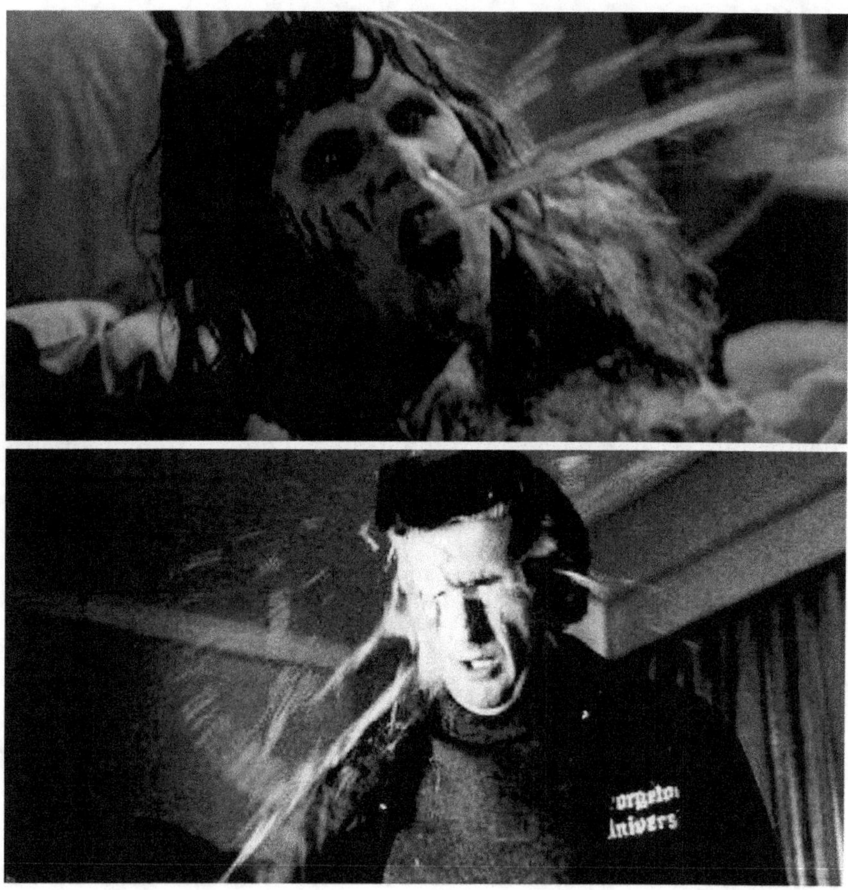

In the grossest scene of the film, and there are so many of them to enjoy while eating, occurs when Father Karras (Jason Miller) approaches closer, Regan lurches forward on the bed and spews bilious pea-green soup/green oatmeal vomit from her mouth in a single projectile stream directly into his face. The thick green slime sticks to his face and clothing. Vomit also dribbles down onto Regan's nightgown.

TCM reported that in an interview with *Cinefantastique* correspondent David Bartholomew, special effects artist Dick Smith revealed a few (but not all) of his tricks:

> The vomiting—by all means—was the most difficult ... it involved making flattened tubes that fitted across the cheeks of the actress. They were connected to a tube which went across the mouth from corner to corner—kind of like a horse's bridle—and it had in it a nozzle. Now, the rear part of this apparatus went back below her ears and was connected to rubber hoses, which went down her back. Now that's where the special effects man came in. He had the responsibility of having the pea soup at the proper temperature and properly seasoned. We never realized that people would tumble onto the fact that it was pea soup so rapidly. It was picked as a convenient item that seemed to be a color close to bile-like vomit... The final effect then, with the makeup and all, and a wig on top to cover the harness that held it all on, was a very good duplication of the demon makeup with the mouth open.

In this photograph, we see the special effects people getting Linda Blair's stunt double ready for the famous vomiting scene. The stunt double was initially used because the mouth apparatus, designed by Dick Smith, was found to be too uncomfortable for Linda Blair to wear.

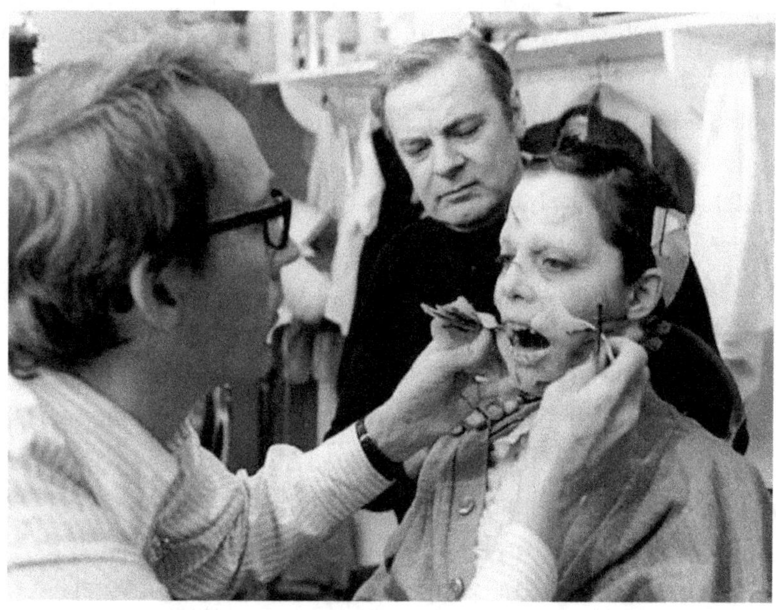

However, upon reviewing the dailies, director William Friedkin decided he was not satisfied with the effect and re-shot the scene with Blair miming the actions.

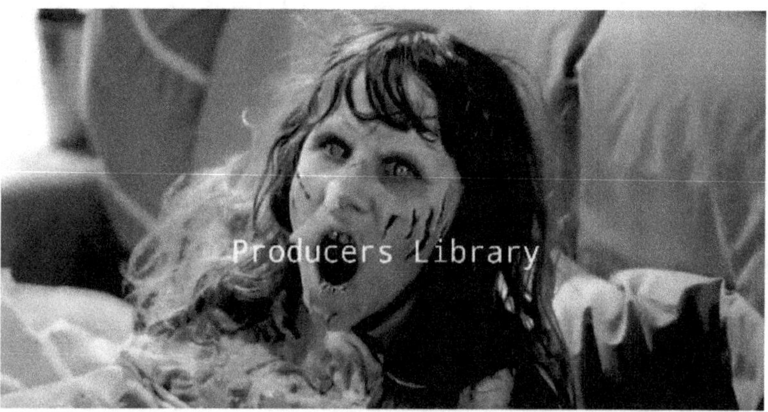

A thicker stream of vomit was then superimposed over the shot. Jason Miller's famous and spontaneous reaction to unexpectedly being shot in the face with the pea soup vomit is well known. The apparatus emitting the vomit malfunctioned and hit the actor directly in the face rather than in just in the chest. He was caught completely off guard, and it shows.

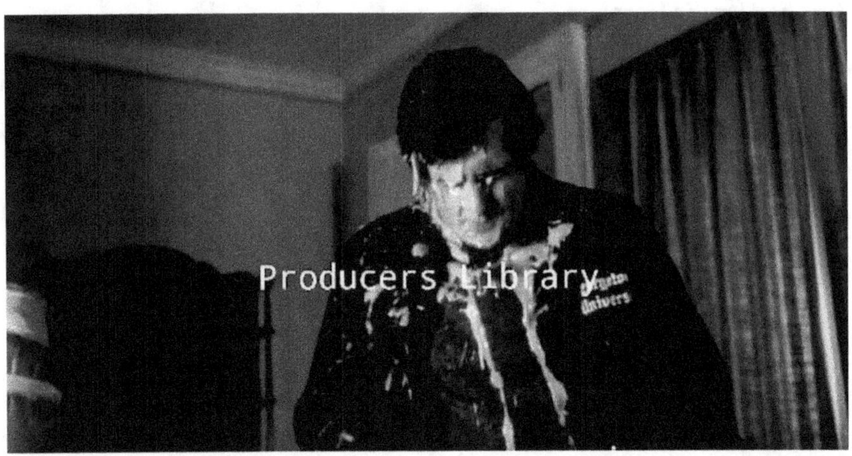

The original 1973 movie spawned a number of movies and two television series based directly on the original movie:

Exorcist II: The Heretic (1977)
The Exorcist III (1990)
Exorcist: The Beginning (2004)
Dominion: Prequel to the Exorcist (2005)
Television series:
The Exorcist (2016)
The Exorcist: The Next Chapter (2017)

Needless to say, *The Exorcist* was a smashing success and un-fortunately inspired numerous imitations that glutted the horror market for years. Titles like *Beyond the Door* (1975), *Abby* (1974), *The Tempter* (1974), and *The Devil Within Her* (1975), expanded on the demonic possession theme and took the genre to a new low. However, none of these films suffered the scorn and critical abuse heaped on John Boorman's ambitious and weirdly allegorical sequel, *Exorcist II: The Heretic* (1977).

Unfortunately, for the viewing public, the vomit scene in *The Exorcist* was not limited to this film alone. Such scenes, some even viler, if that is possible, appeared in the following:

Caddyshack (1980)
Monty Python: The Meaning of Life (1983)
Stand by Me (1986)
Matrix (1992)
Sandlot (1993)
Team America: World Peace (2004)
Superbad (2007)

One Flew Over the Cuckoo's Nest (1975)

One Flew Over the Cuckoo's Nest is one of the most American films of all time—a $4.4 million dollar effort directed by Czech Milos Forman. Its allegorical theme is set in the world of an authentic mental hospital (Oregon State Hospital in Salem, Oregon). It is a place of rebellion exhibited by an energetic, flamboyant, wise-guy anti-hero Jack Nicholson (Randle Patrick "RP" McMurphy) against the establishment, institutional authority, and status-quo attitudes personified by the patients' supervisory nurse Louise Fletcher (Mildred Ratched).

Expressing his basic human rights and impulses, the protagonist protests against heavy-handed rules about watching the World Series, and illegally stages both a fishing trip and a drinking party in the ward—leading to his own paralyzing lobotomy.

Scene: Take Me Out to the Ballgame

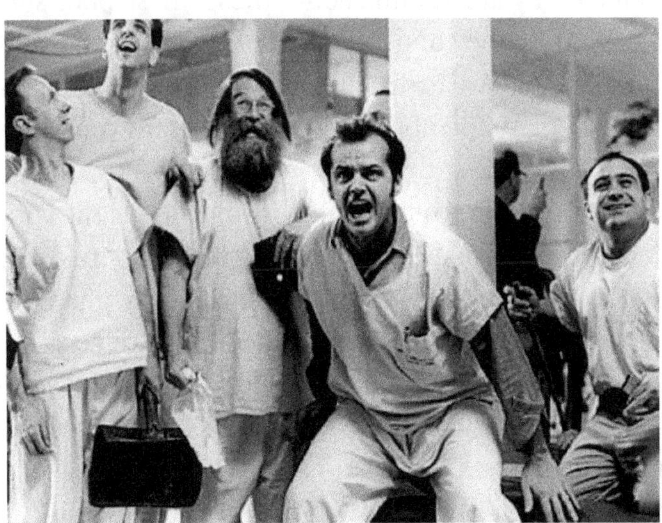

By controlling the patients, Nurse Ratched zealously serves her own ego needs rather than the therapeutic needs of the patients. Charlie Cheswick (Sydney Lassick), during a patient therapy session, proposes a vote about watching the second game of the World Series, thinking it would be a better therapeutic alternative. McMurphy encourages his usually compliant and spiritless fellow patients: "I wanna see the hands. Come on. Which one of you nuts has got the guts?"

Nine votes are counted in the therapy group, and McMurphy senses victory in this round over her. But Nurse Ratched refuses to have the other inmates won over to him and becomes the spoiler. She sadistically changes the rules with the sole purpose of defeating his proposal:

> Nurse: There are eighteen patients on this ward, Mr. McMurphy. And you have to have a majority to change ward policy. So you gentlemen can put your hands down now.
> McMurphy: (turning and gesturing toward other men out of hearing range on the ward floor) You're tryin' to tell me that you're gonna count these, these poor son-of-a-bitches, they don't know what we're talkin' about.
> Nurse: Well, I have to disagree with you, Mr. McMurphy. These men are members of the ward just as you are.

Nurse Ratched adjourns the meeting and closes the voting session as McMurphy struggles and fails to get the severely-disturbed patients to join in the vote. When the chief slowly raises his hand, McMurphy is elated, but the steely-willed nurse rejects the vote of ten to eight from behind the glass panel of the nurses' station and forbids them to watch television. She claims that the vote when the meeting adjourned was nine to nine:

McMurphy: The chief voted. Now, will you please turn on the television set?
Nurse: (she opens the glass panel) Mr. McMurphy, the meeting was adjourned, and the vote was closed.
McMurphy: But the vote was ten to eight. The chief, he's got his hand up! Look!
Nurse: No, Mr. McMurphy. When the meeting was adjourned, the vote was nine to nine.
McMurphy: (exasperated) Aw, come on, you're not gonna say that now. You're not gonna say that now. You're gonna pull that hen-house s—t now when the vote... The chief just voted—it was ten to 9nine Now I want that television set turned on, right now.
(The nurse slides the glass panel across the front of the nurses' station, shutting out his protest.)

In the most remembered sequence in the film, McMurphy subversively pretends to be enjoying the second World Series baseball game on television in a contest of wills with the nurse. He inventively re-creates the play-by-play excitement of the game. His excitement proves infectious—the other patients join him and look up at the dark television screen that reflects their faces—and they almost believe that the game is real.

The nurse glares wildly from behind her glassed room, knowing that she has been defeated. She gets on the microphone and demands through the speakers in the ward: "Gentlemen, stop this. Stop this immediately."

Producer Michael Douglas explained his attraction to Ken Kesey's novel about a strong-willed rebel fighting a domineering head nurse in a mental hospital. "Particularly in the sixties, people identified with this individual trying to overpower the system."

To start, one has to go back to the source material, Ken Kesey's best-selling novel of the same name. Although written in 1959 and published in 1962, this tale of oppression and rebellion within an Oregon psychiatric hospital became closely associated with the anti-authoritarian counter-culture of the latter part of the 1960s, containing what film critic Pauline Kael called "the prophetic essence of the whole Vietnam period of revolutionary politics going psychedelic."

One Flew Over the Cuckoo's Nest launched the producing careers of Michael Douglas (*The China Syndrome* [1979] and *Romancing the Stone* [1984]) and Saul Zaentz (who went on to win two more Best Picture awards with *Amadeus* [1984] and *The English Patient* [1996]), relaunched the careers of Milos Forman and Louise Fletcher, and established Jack Nicholson as a rebel superstar.

The cast of asylum inmates included several virtual unknowns who later made bigger names for themselves, including Danny DeVito (*Taxi*, 1978-1983 on TV,, the Penguin in *Batman Returns*, 1992), Christopher Lloyd (also *Taxi, Back to the Future*, 1985), Brad Dourif (*Dune*, 1984; *Alien: Resurrection*, 1997), and Native American actor Will Sampson (*The Outlaw Josey Wales*, 1976; the TV series *Vega$*) as Chief Bromden, the narrator of the book but silent here.

Jon Swaine wrote an essay "How *One Flew Over the Cuckoo's Nest* changed psychiatry," in *The Telegraph* (February 1, 2011):

> "Ken Kesey's 1962 book and the film version released thirteen years later, are both credited with irreparably tarnishing the image of electroconvulsive therapy, or ECT, and quickening its departure from mainstream mental health care."

Dr. Frank Pittman, the renowned American psychiatrist, has said the publication of the book "had an enormous effect" on his field. He told the Discovery Channel:

> "It gave voice, gave life, to a basic distrust of the way in which psychiatry was being used for society's purposes, rather than the purposes of the people who had mental illness. Back in my training in the early 60s, we gave shock treatment, particularly at that time, as a treatment for agitated depression. It worked more quickly than the drugs we had then—more quickly than the drugs we have now—but it left me squeamish. The brain is much too delicate, much too mysterious, for us to mess with."

The book's publication contributed to a backlash against the entire psychiatric treatment system in the US in the 1960s. Huge, spirit-crushing state institutions—like the Oregon facility later depicted in the film—began reducing their excessive resident numbers and granting patients more rights.

Amid a minor revival in ECT in the early 1990s, the *New York Times* noted that thanks to the film's memorable images, "in the public mind 'shock therapy' has retained the tarnished image given it by Ken Kesey's novel: dangerous, inhumane, and over-used."

Jaws (1975)

Jaws is a trendsetting thriller film directed by Steven Spielberg and based on Peter Benchley's1974 novel of the same name. In the film, a giant, man-eating, rogue great white shark attacks beachgoers at a New England summer resort town of Amity Island, prompting police chief Martin Brody (Roy Schneider) to hunt it with the help of a marine biologist Matt Hopper (Richard Dreyfus) and a professional shark hunter named Quint (Robert Shaw). Quint's hatred for sharks is based on his war-time experience aboard the USS *Indianapolis* (CL/CA-35), which was torpedoed by the Japanese after delivering the Hiroshima bomb. Most of the crew were systematically killed by sharks before they could be rescued out of the waters of the South Pacific. Quint's arrogance only exasperates their battle with the white shark that eventually sinks their vessel *Orca* and devours Quint before being killed by Brody.

The filming of the movie was done mostly at Martha's Vineyard in Massachusetts and was besieged by mechanical difficulties with the three full-size pneumatically powered prop sharks, the intrusion of sailboats in a number of scenes and going over budget and past schedule. Despite all of it, the film is considered one of the greatest films ever made. *Jaws* was the prototypical summer blockbuster, regarded as a watershed moment in motion picture history.

Scene: "You're gonna need a bigger boat"

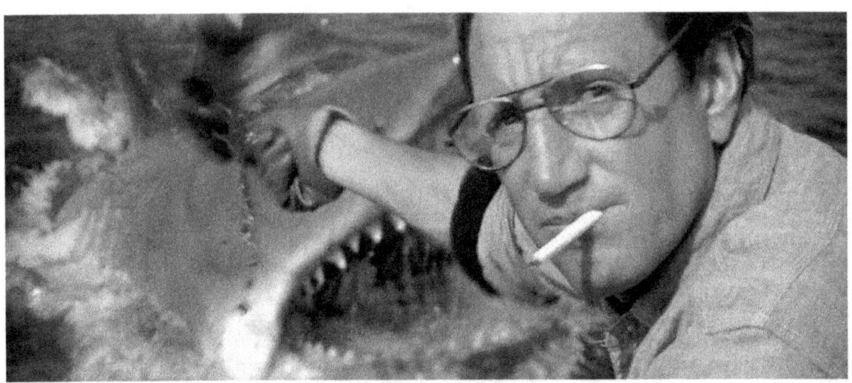

It was 1975, a time before *Raiders of the Lost Ark* (1981) and *Jurassic Park* (1993) and all the other movies that would make director Steven Spielberg a household name. While working on his breakout film *Jaws*, it seemed as though Spielberg and his crew were constantly at odds with the producers, who were described in an interview as being very "stingy."

Many people working on set would try and goad the producers into putting more money toward the film by saying, "You're going to need a bigger boat," every time something would go wrong. The line was so catchy that, during the scene where Brody, at last, comes face to face with that massive great white shark, actor Roy Schneider decided to ad-lib the inside joke as a line right then and there.

The now-famous words spoken by Brody, as he tries to bait the shark and it nearly bites off his arm, rings true for us even today. After seeing the enormous shark for the very first time, up close and personal, he quickly realizes that they are completely outmatched and need to quickly reassess their situation. How often do we venture out into something without really planning out all contingencies and consequences of our actions? We sometimes assume that we can manage all that will happen based on what we may or may not really know about a situation. Our own stupidly and arrogance blinds us to the realities of the situation. The brave crew of the *Orca* goes sharking without really thinking it out. Quint tries to initially catch it with a hook and line as he would a marlin, Brody shoots at it with his service revolver, and Hopper wants to inject it with a needle filled with poison into the shark's mouth underwater in a flimsy aluminum cage. Does this sound like a well laid out plan of attack against a twenty-five-foot, three-ton, man-eating shark?

In its initial screening of the film, the audience's screams had covered up Schneider's "bigger boat" one-liner, Brody's reaction after the shark jumps behind him was extended, and the volume of the line was raised.

Quint's demise is almost preordained from the very beginning. He has survived being eaten by sharks during World War II and still remembers all of his friends being butchered in the South Pacific waters; he refuses to listen to the other crew members aboard the vessel; he destroys the radio set when Brody tries to solicit the aid of others; he deliberately burns out the engines of his boat, knowing that it will set the stage for his face to face encounter with the shark. Like the equally deranged Captain Ahab in Moby Dick, he must kill the shark on his own terms or die doing so. Again, the story of how one man's obsession can spell the doom for many others.

Scene: Quint's Demise

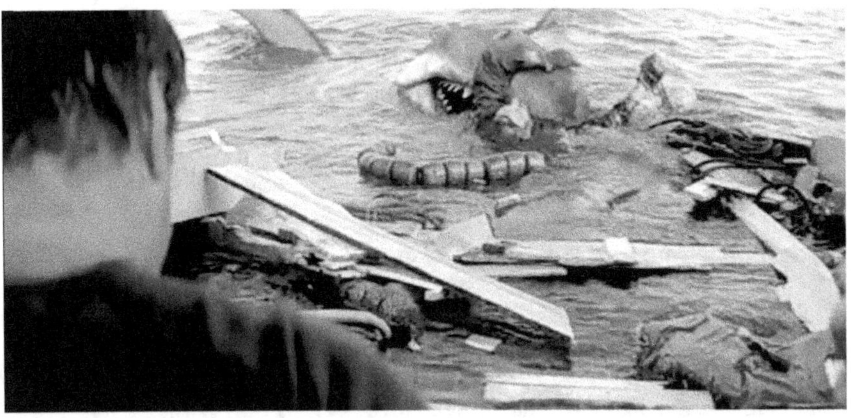

Quint's arrogance throughout the movie comes to pass near the end of the movie when he burns out the engines of his ship and the great white shark decides he has enough of being speared, laden with barrels and shot at and decides to come aboard and take matters into his own mouth.

The Peter Benchley script describes the scene:

```
The shark breaks water right beside the Orca, rising with a
great whooshing noise. It rises vertically, towering overhead,
blocking out the sun. The pectoral fins seem to reach forward.
The shark, in all of its monstrous glory, falls onto the
stern of the boat with a shattering crash, narrowly missing
Quint and Brody. It drives the stern underwater, the ocean
pours in over the transom. The jaws snap from side to side.
Brody flounders backwards away from it.
```

CLOSE - BRODY

```
He is clinging to the mast for dear life, as the ship begins
to tilt to stern, and everything starts to break loose around
him.
```

NIGHTMARE ANGLE - DECK OF THE ORCA

```
The giant jaws are snapping irresistibly at everything: great
chunks of wood torn out of the deck and superstructure.

Deck chair, irons, rope, gear, beercans, bottles, Brody's
bag, all are food for the insatiable maw blindly churning
away.

Quint is clinging next to a rack of lances: he is enraged at
this ultimate violation of his territory. He snatches up a
lance and hurls himself at the shark with a wordless bellow.

The great head weaves side to side, the deck is at a
treacherous incline, slippery with blood and seawater. Quint's
footing falters and slips, he stumbles at the Mouth of Hell,
the big teeth seize him and snap.

Quint's roar of rage and pain is choked off as his body is
clamped between the grinding, sawing teeth, and his head and
legs suddenly contort as the shark's teeth meet across his
torso. Blood gushes onto the deck. The remnants of his body
tumble from the shark's mouth.
```

The iconic music that penetrates the action of the film is noticeably absent as Quint calmly surveys the sea before him, a stern,
knowing expression planted on his face. The image cuts to the
shark moving fluidly through the water, its wide mouth agape. The
action culminates in a medium-wide shot of the two men, Quint
and Brody, standing against the cabin as the shark breaks the glassy
surface of the water and lands on their boat, mere feet away. The

creature then effortlessly begins chewing through the boat and the sea of items falling from the cabin into its open jowls. The dead-eyed, silent stare of the beast is made all the more haunting when one considers the thoughtless nature of its destructive tendencies.

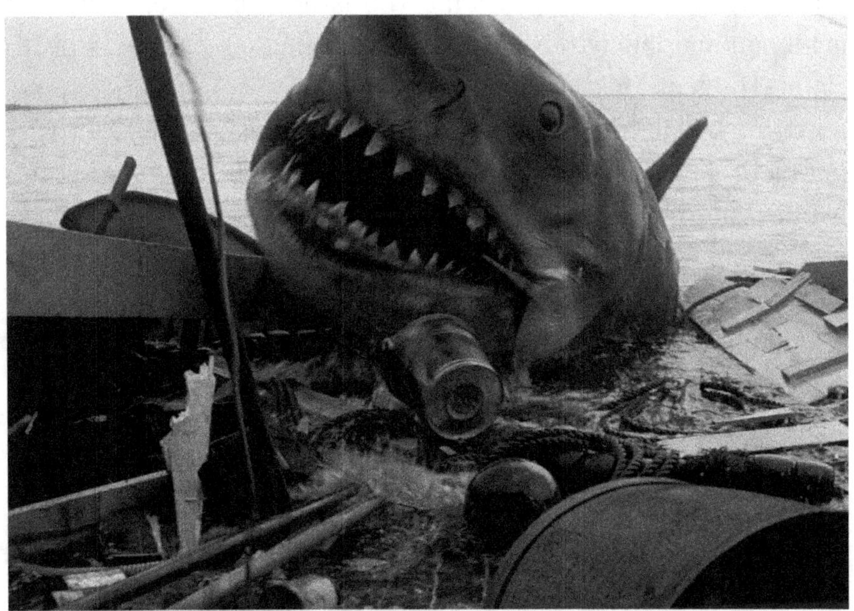

A medium-shot, over Quint's shoulder, tracks the shark's terrible visage through the doorway to the cabin that Quint is so desperately clinging to. His feet struggle and kick, slick against the wet deck, showing real terror and powerlessness.

In the screenplay, the heading to this sequence reads in bold text: NIGHTMARE ANGLE – DECK OF THE ORCA

The words "nightmare angle," by definition, speak to a sense of indescribable terror, meant to stimulate an alarming visual sensibility that, while indefinable on the page, is important for the eventual filmmaker to embody. The shark, in turn, is written as a gnashing, murderous machine:

In the film, Quint clings to the doorway, hanging tight as several items fall from the cabin into the creature's gaping mouth. His expression is pained and fearful, suddenly struck with mortality, recalling glimpses of his expression the night he told the story of the *Indianapolis.* This is a Quint who is not infallible; rather, he is human and facing the death that he ultimately knew was his to claim. His feet kick lamely against the wet wood, frantically attempting to halt himself from sliding into the path of those crushing teeth, but the worry in his eyes tells that even he knows the fruitless nature of his exploits.

The camera follows Quint as he slides into the massive monster's mouth: "The Mouth of Hell." The screenplay brings a sense of poeticism that again strikes a sense of abhorrent horror while providing the filmmaker with tone as opposed to direction. The shark is on full display, terrifying and driven, fulfilling the promise that the film had been making since the opening dread-filled moments where two teenagers met the shadowy creature in dark ocean waters. But the audience's eyes are less attached to the shark and more to the frantic, flailing efforts of Quint. The camera holds close as he kicks out his legs, fighting to prop himself against the sides of the tremendous creature's head.

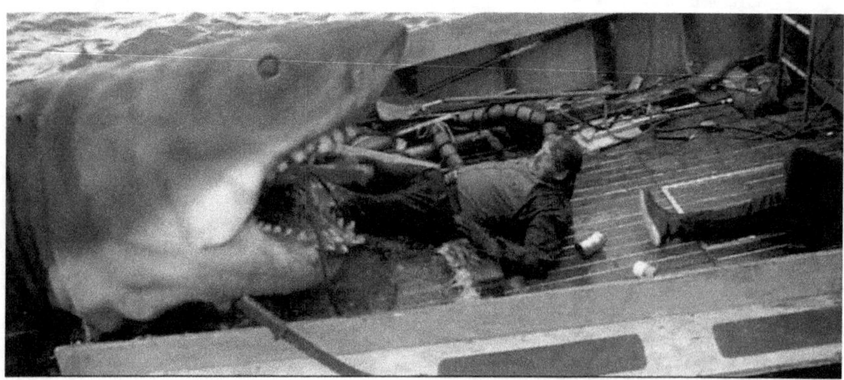

As Quint slides into the creature's mouth, he releases a guttural scream, haunting and real, infused with as much fear as it has pain. The screenplay describes this as well, continuing the idea that the shark is a grotesque machination of blind consumption, reading: "his body is clamped between the grinding, sawing teeth." When the shark finally does bite into Quint's torso, the camera holds on a close-up on Quint. Blood gushes from his clenched teeth, making the death far more personal and disturbing in a way that showing the gore of his meaty torso could never have achieved. The screenplay reads, "Blood gushes onto the deck," but the film shows blood in the water, which seems to dissipate quickly, focusing on the nature of life and death in the wild. Specifically, how fleeting and impersonal the act of eating for the animal truly is.

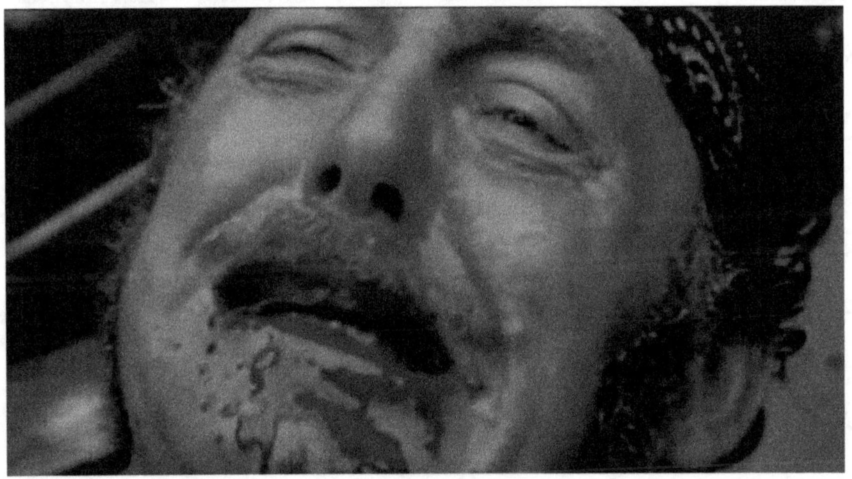

The screenplay completes the exchange somewhat unceremoniously:

"The remnants of his body tumble from the shark's mouth."

In the film, Quint strikes back in spite of the sounding of his death knell, stabbing the shark repeatedly as it shakes him back and forth, more blood pouring from his mouth.

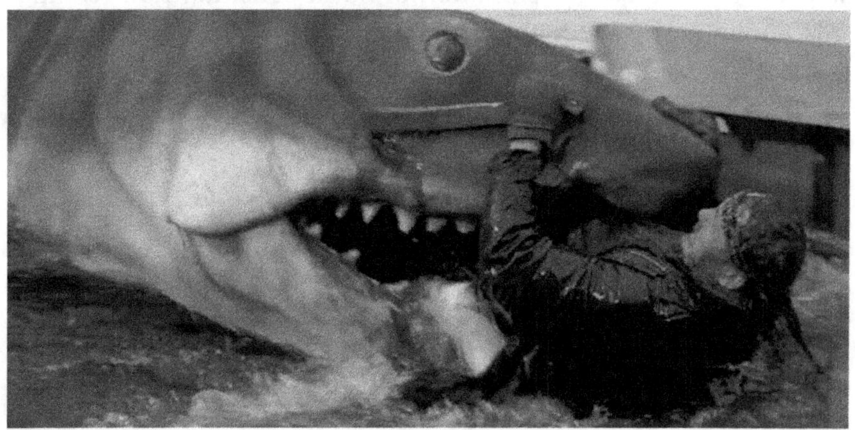

The audience watches from over Brody's shoulder in a medium-wide shot as Quint goes limp. The shark pulls him below the surface, and, as the ocean was less than two minutes before, all is calm.

No "remnants" of Quint tumble from the shark's mouth. He is simply swallowed whole by the shark, by the ocean, by the natural world he's always been so quick to want to tame, to hunt and to survive in, but deep down, so certain he would be consumed by it in the end.

Our discussion of *Jaws* will conclude with these two shots involving Robert Shaw as Quint. The first is a production shot, and the second is obviously after the graphic death scene.

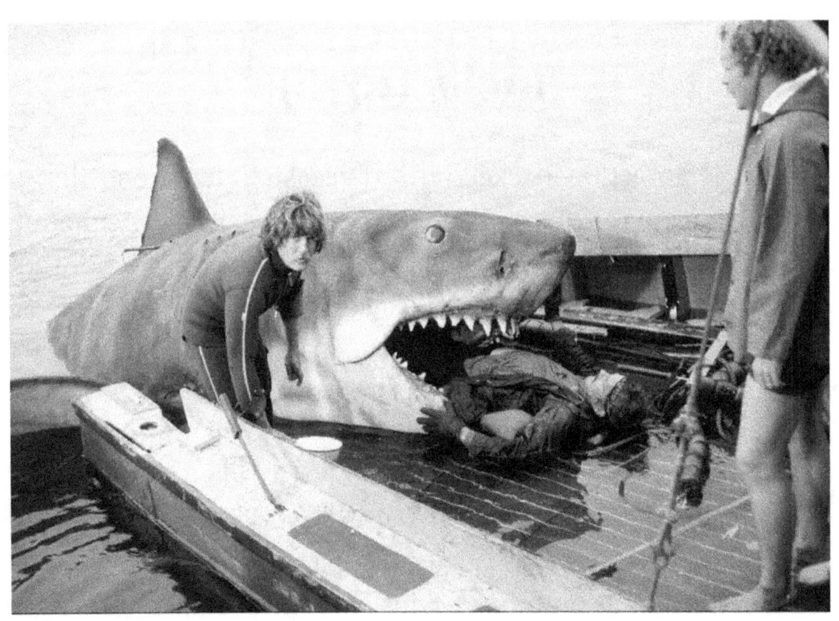

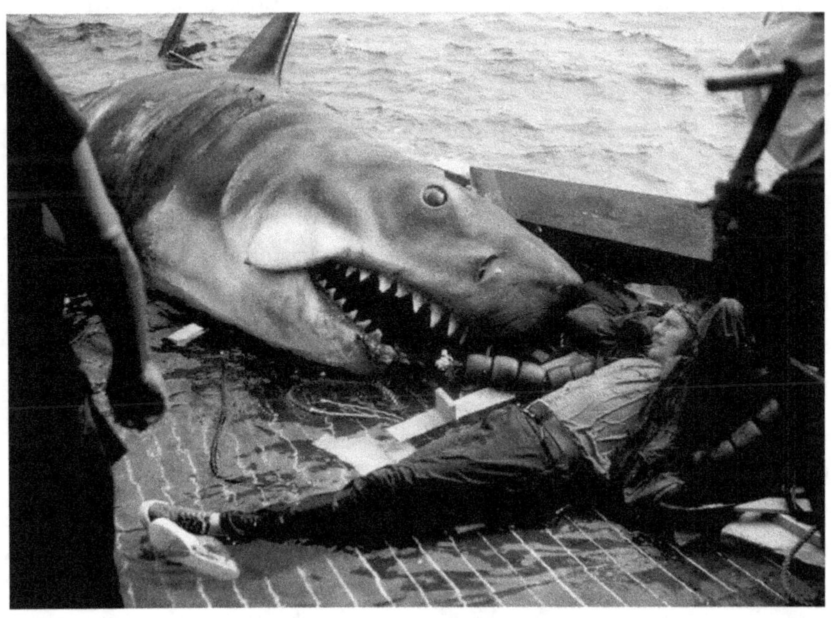

Rocky (1976)

Rocky is an action-packed, crowd-pleasing, feel-good film of the rise of a small-time Philadelphia boxer against insurmountable odds. It was directed by John G. Avildsen and written by and stars Sylvester Stallone. It tells the age-old rags-to-riches American Dream story of Rocky Balboa, an uneducated but kind-hearted working-class Italian-American boxer, working as a debt collector for a loan shark in the slums of Philadelphia. When the unknown Rocky is chosen to be boxing champ Apollo Creed's (Carl Weathers) opponent for the January 1 event, it is a world heavyweight title fight—a once-in-a-lifetime boxing opportunity.

Rocky's training program begins in earnest under weathered gym manager Mickey's (Burgess Meredith) rigid and arduous fight training and management. It transforms a flabby, lazy, and disinterested boxer into a lean taunt and focused contender for the crown. The message is clear. Hard work, persistence, the love and support of others, and sheer determination of will can conquer most adversity in life and overcome any hurdles placed in front of you.

In the most memorable sequence of the film, a montage, Rocky undergoes grueling training from Thanksgiving to New Years by doing one-armed pushups, pounding hanging slabs of raw meat in a slaughterhouse freezer where his buddy Paulie (Burt Young) works and makes a run through the Philadelphia streets, including the famed Italian Market (vegetable vendors, butchers, fresh seafood, and Italian goodies), located on South Street in Philly.

Scene: The Top of the "Rocky Steps"

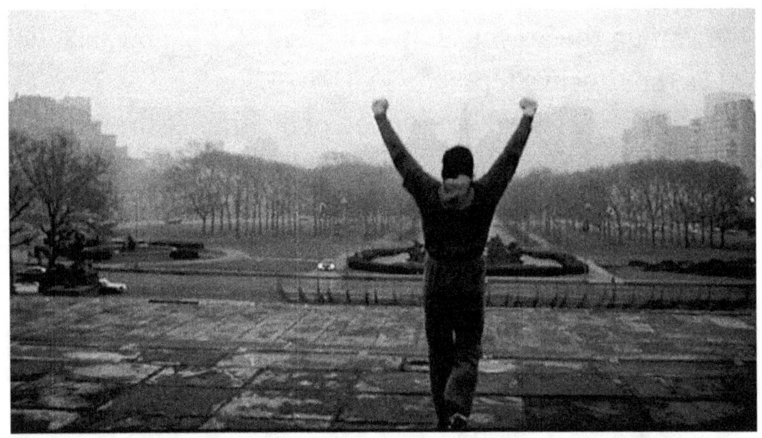

Now fit and trim and ready for bear, Rocky effortlessly runs up the seventy-two stone steps leading to the entrance of the Philadelphia Museum of Art and raises his arms in a victory pose accompanied by the rousing song, "Gonna Fly Now." The thirty-word song, also known as the "Theme from *Rocky*," was composed by Bill Conti with lyrics by Carol Connors and Ayn Robbins, and performed by DeEtta West and Nelson Pigford.

Trying hard now
It's so hard now
Trying hard now
Getting strong now
Won't be long now
Getting strong now
Gonna fly now
Flying high now
Gonna fly, fly, fly

Inventor/operator Garnett Brown's new Steadicam was used to accomplish smooth photography while running alongside Rocky during the film's Philadelphia street jogging/training sequences and the run up the art museum's flight of stairs, now colloquially known as the "Rocky Steps."

In the following actual production photographs, the famous run up the Rocky Steps is being set with Stallone and the camera crew (Brown and Richard Edesa), and then the actual filming.

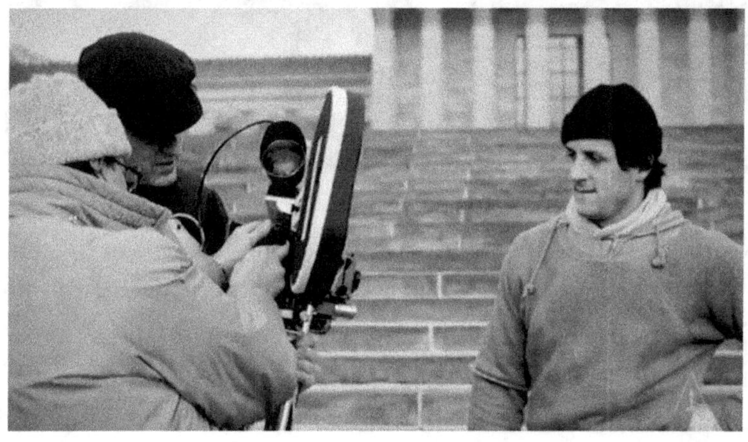

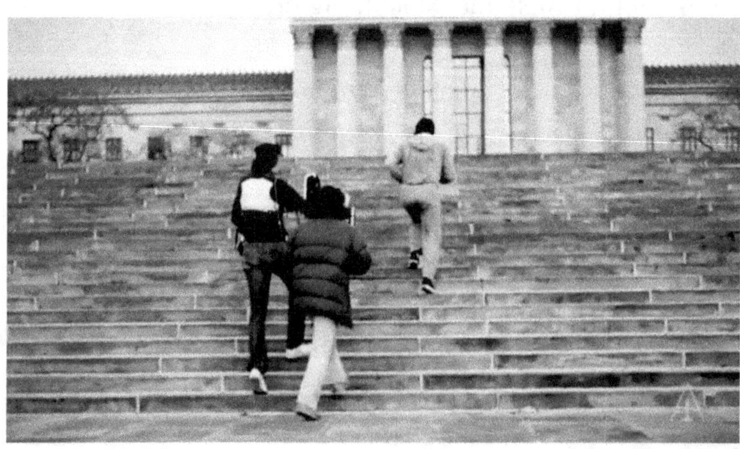

Alien (1979)

Alien is a thrilling science-fiction horror film directed by Ridley Scott and written by Dan O'Bannon. The film is based on a story by O'Bannon and Ronald Shusett. It follows the crew of the commercial space tug Nostromo, who encounters the eponymous alien, a deadly and aggressive extraterrestrial set loose on the ship. The film features Tom Skerritt (Captain Dallas), Sigourney Weaver (Warrant Officer Ripley), Veronica Cartwright (Navigator Lambert), and John Hurt (Executive Officer Kane).

Scene: The Chestburster

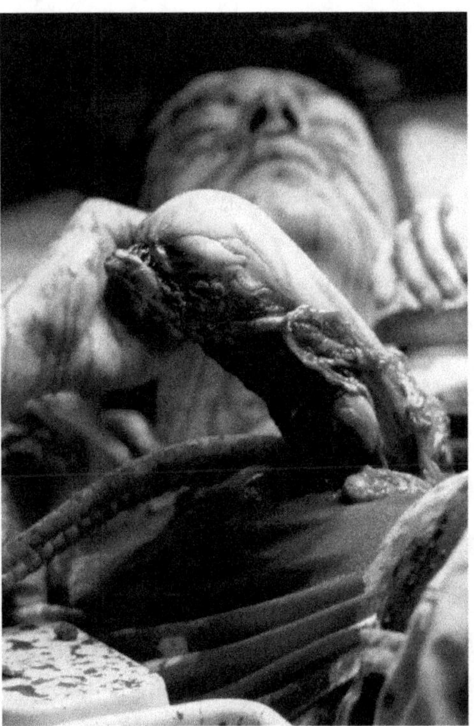

Paraphrased narration from the *Alien* Behind the Scenes 2014 documentary:

> "Prior to the actual filming of the chestburster scene, the cast members (Cartwright and Weaver) knew that the creature would be bursting out of Hurt, and had seen the chestburster puppet, but they had intentionally not been told by the director or the special effects team that fake blood would also be bursting out in every direction or anything else."

The overall direction of the special effects for *Alien* was done by Nick Adler with Alan Bryce as the floor effects supervisor. The first phase of the scene begins with actor John Hurt as Kane starts to have convulsions and falls onto the kitchen table. He is restrained by the other crew members. His white t-shirt has been pre-slit, and an air hose has been placed underneath it. The hose has been attached to a pump which forces up pinkish fake blood. Hurt's shirt pushes up as if something is trying to come out of his body while the fake blood oozes out of the slit in his shirt. At the same time, as Hurt says, he is undergoing what could be called "labor pains" as he cries out in pain, and his body shakes in sheer agony.

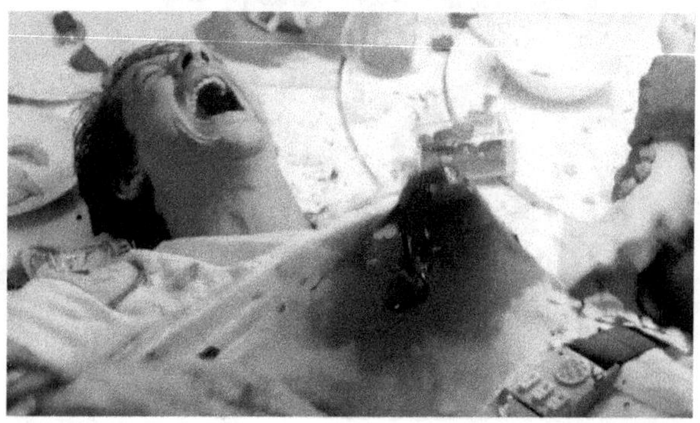

The director shouts, "Cut," and the room is cleared of the actors. Later, an artificial chest (John Hurt torso replicate) is screwed onto the kitchen table. Hurt's actual head and arms protrude through an opening in the table itself as well. Air lines are run through the artificial chest operated by high-pressure pumps. These pumps literally blasted fake blood and viscera out of the artificial chest all over the unsuspecting crew, especially Angela Cartwright, who is totally not ready to see this happen. In addition, squibs mounted on top of the artificial chest exploded, sending this fake blood out like projectiles across the entire room. A squib is a miniature explosive device used in a wide range of industries, including special effects. This shower of blood and viscera is intended to happen just as the creature emerges from the artificial chest.

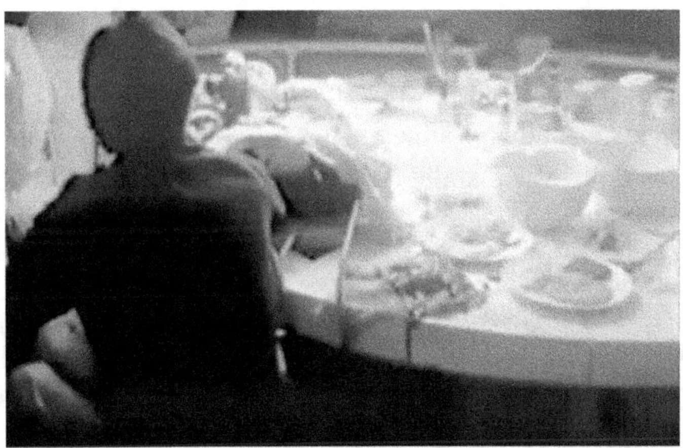

In order to make this happen, from under the kitchen table itself, Roger Dickens, the creator of the small alien form, had been assigned the "chest burst" technician. A hole had been cut in the table, lead through the artificial chest. At the right moment, Roger pushed through his puppet of the alien, mounted on a stick, amidst the volcano-like eruptions of fake blood, while Hurt's arms involuntarily fray widely in the air while his dead featureless face is covered with fake blood.

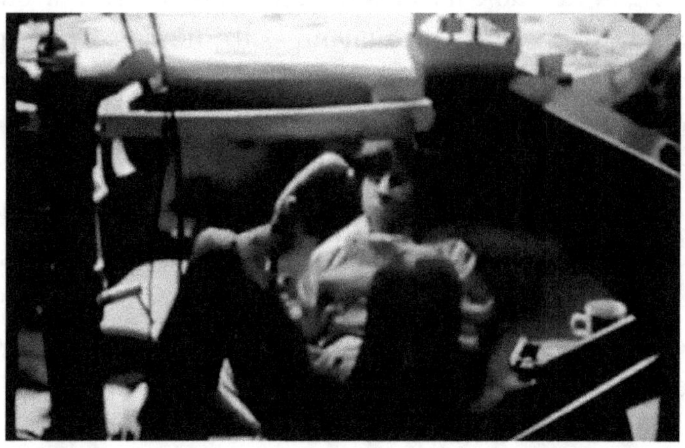

All of this creates a truly horrifying special effect. Once the alien greets the shocked crew, it sprints across the table and escapes. This effect was made possible using a six-inch slit in the table itself in which a dolly was installed. Once the alien was ready to move, a technician pulled a toll rope attached to the tail of the creature on its stick, causing it to fling forward across the kitchen table toward the camera. An air hose was attached to the tail to make it whip around as it flings forward. During this scene, after being sprayed directly in the face with fake blood, the shocked Cartwright literally fell to the floor, screaming in hysterics and had to get off the floor in order to get back into the scene which continued to "shoot" throughout her totally unscheduled fall and recovery.

According to actor Tom Skerritt, "What you saw on camera was the real response. She (Angela Cartwright) had no idea what the hell happened. All of a sudden, this thing just came up."

The real-life surprise of the actors gave the scene an intense sense of realism and made it one of the film's most memorable moments, and it was shot in one take.

The design of the "chestburster" was inspired by Francis Bacon's 1944 painting *Three Studies for Figures at the Base of a Crucifixion.* Giger's original design, which was refined, resembled a plucked chicken. Screenwriter Dan O'Bannon credits his experiences with Crohn's Disease for inspiring the chestbursting scene.

One of these figures, from Bacon's painting, really does resemble the hideous creature in *Alien* in the chestbursting scene.

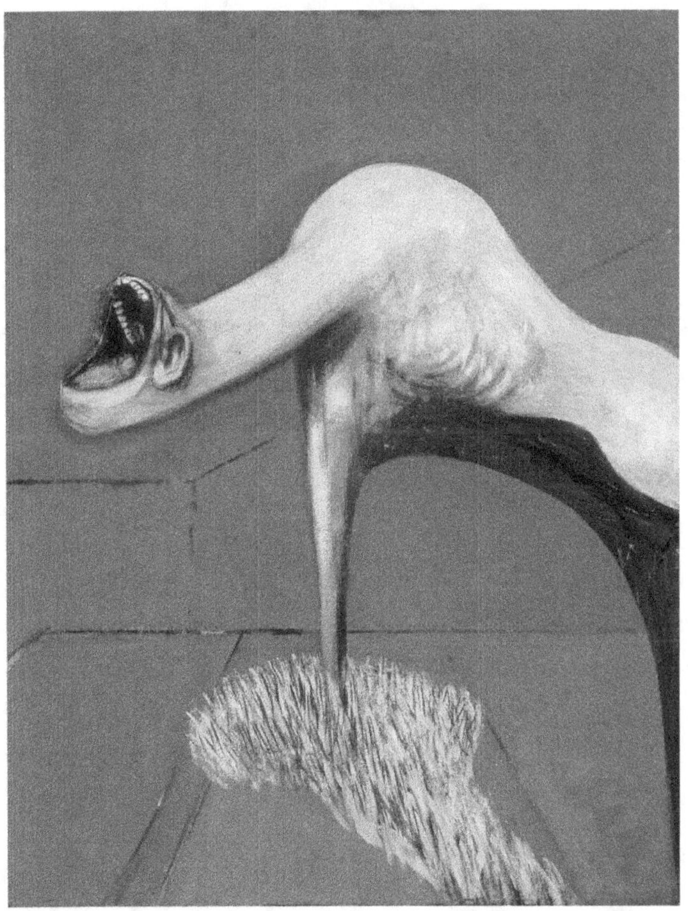

The scene reminds us all that sometimes it is best to leave well enough alone; don't venture into something until you know all of the facts (like an assumed distress message which is really a warning to stay away); be cognizant of the unknown until it becomes known; if something appears "bad," it probably is; and never ever break standard quarantine safety protocols or established regulations that might endanger you or others.

THE 1980s

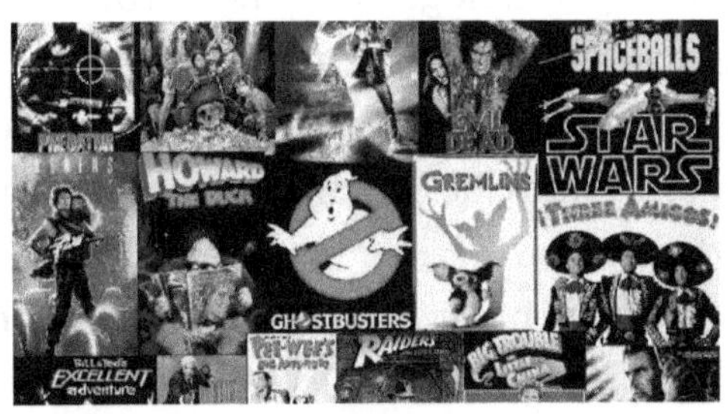

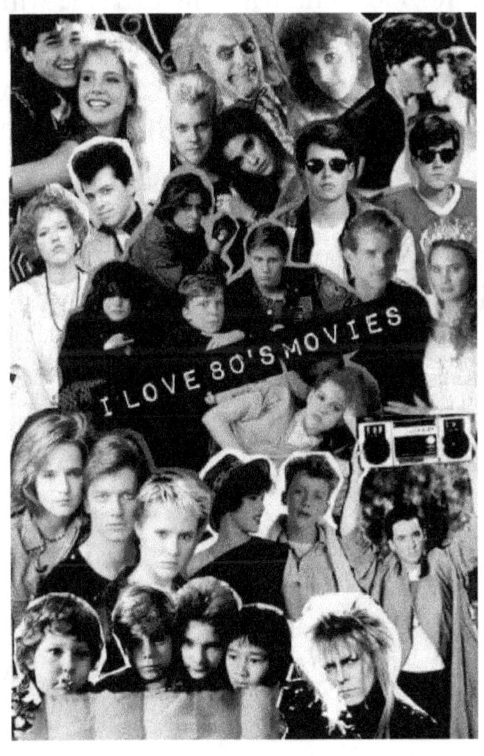

The Shining (1980)

The Shining is a psychological thriller produced and directed by Stanley Kubrick and co-written with novelist Diane Johnson. The film is based on the famed author Stephen King's 1977 novel of the same name. It stars Jack Nicholson, Shelley Duvall, Scatman Crothers, and Danny Lloyd.

The central character in *The Shining* is Jack Torrance (Nicholson), an aspiring writer and recovering alcoholic, who accepts a position as the off-season caretaker of the isolated historic Overlook Hotel in the Colorado Rockies. Enduring the extreme winter conditions at the hotel with Jack are his rather fragile wife, Wendy Torrance (Duvall) and young son, Danny Torrance (Lloyd). Danny possesses "the shining," psychic abilities that enable him to see into the hotel's horrific past. After a severe winter storm leaves the Torrances completely snowbound and isolated, Jack's sanity deteriorates due to the influence of the supernatural forces and beings that inhabit the hotel, placing his wife and son in imminent mortal danger.

Scene: Here's Johnny

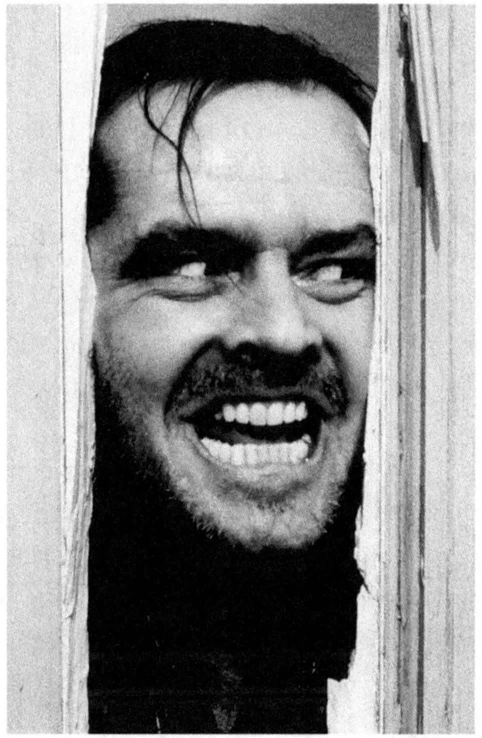

Some other interesting factoids from the articles found in the Turner Classic Movies (TCM):

Jack Nicholson supposedly ad-libbed the line "Here's Johnny!" in imitation of announcer Ed McMahon's famous introduction of Johnny Carson on U.S. network NBC-TV's long-running late-night television program *The Tonight Show Starring Johnny Carson* (1962-1992). Stanley Kubrick, who had been living in England since before Carson took over *The Tonight Show*, had no clue what "Here's Johnny!" meant. Carson once used the clip of Nicholson as the introduction to one of his annual anniversary specials. Monday, September 29, 1980, was the night of the eighteenth annual show. This was ten weeks after the release of *The Shining*, but most Americans had not seen the movie. They were aware that it was some sort of horror film starring Jack Nicholson and that it had received great reviews, but most had not yet seen the film and were not aware of any details. So, out of nowhere, there was Jack Nicholson running around the television set with an ax, Shelley Duvall screaming, the ax going through the door, then Nicholson saying his famous Johnny Carson line, at which time *The Tonight Show* theme played, and the show started. It was one of the funniest moments in the history of television. It also drove another couple of million people to see the movie, giving it an unexpected extended run.

Whether or not this line was actually improvised by Nicolson has become a minor source of debate in movie circles for years. While the line doesn't appear in Stephen King's source material, it does appear in transcripts of the film that can be found online. By this point in principal photography, Nicholson had reportedly given up on reading his pages for the day because they were constantly changing. It's likely that Nicholson did indeed improvise the line on the spot.

According to Shelley Duvall, the infamous "Here's Johnny!" scene took three days to film and the use of sixty doors until Kubrick was satisfied. This is no surprise, given director Kubrick's reputation for numerous retakes in all of his movies. This characteristic of his drove his cast and crew to tears. Shelley Duvall drew the worst of his ire. His methods pushed her to have a nervous breakdown; they constantly argued over the script; and she was so overwhelmed that she started losing her hair during the film's production.

For the scene in which Jack breaks down the bathroom door, the props department built a door that could be easily broken.

Nicholson was a former volunteer fire marshal and a firefighter in the California Air National Guard, and he already so pumped up for the scene that he tore through the fake door and a real, solid door had to be placed on the bathroom's hinges.

Stanley Kubrick personally panned the camera during the famous shot of Jack swinging the ax into the bathroom door. The camera was tripod-mounted, and Kubrick moved the panhandle in synchronization with each swing while keeping his eye on the monitor. The back-and-forth camera movement where Jack is breaking through the bathroom door mimics the pan-and-scan technique, used when widescreen formats are shown on a narrower screen, such as an older tube television.

The Legacy of *The Shining*:

Its influence on other filmmakers has also been immense, with David Lynch's *Twin Peaks: Fire Walk with Me* (1992), Ben Wheatley's *Kill List* (2011) and Paul Thomas Anderson's *There Will Be Blood* (2007) and *The Master* (2012), all owing a huge debt to the atonal and moody brilliance of Kubrick's work on *The Shining*.

Perhaps the highest-profile devotee of the film is *Toy Story 3* (2010) director Lee Unkrich. A seemingly unlikely candidate, Unkrich has been an obsessive fan of *The Shining* for many years, even going so far as to launch his own brilliantly detailed fansite, The Overlook Hotel.

Glory (1989)

Edward Zwick's *Glory* is a Civil War historical drama starring Matthew Broderick, Denzel Washington, and Morgan Freeman. It is especially memorable for its attention to physical detail; the cinematography and production design are both breathtaking. But Zwick's story, which is based on real events, also deals with the plight of African-American troops during the Civil War, a topic that, quite shamefully, is barely touched upon in this country's history books.

Broderick portrays Union General Robert Gould Shaw, a baby-faced Bostonian, who is assigned to lead the 54th Massachusetts Volunteer Army, the first black fighting regiment in the war. The men of the 54th are a scruffy collection of former and escaped slaves. We follow the men—including a rebellious, deeply embittered escaped slave portrayed as Private Silas Trip (Washington), and a wise, emotionally-measured gravedigger named Rawlins (Freeman) as they're turned into soldiers. But first, they have to be accepted as human beings by the often-brutal military officers that are training them. In addition, they must face the ridicule of white soldiers fighting under the same flag, as well as other white officers who still think of them as "little children" who must be kept underfoot. The men's inner and outward battles finally come to a head during a horrific suicide mission at the Second Battle of Fort Wagner on Morris Island, South Carolina, fought on July 18, 1863.

One of the most poignant scenes in the movie occurs when Tip is caught deserting his post in search of shoes. He is stripped of his shirt, revealing numerous wounds from previous whippings endured while he was still a slave. As he is whipped by actor John Finn as Sergeant Major Mulcahyhe, Trip sheds a single tear while he stares directly at the grimacing Colonel Shaw, who rendered the sentencing of flogging.

Scene: The Whipping

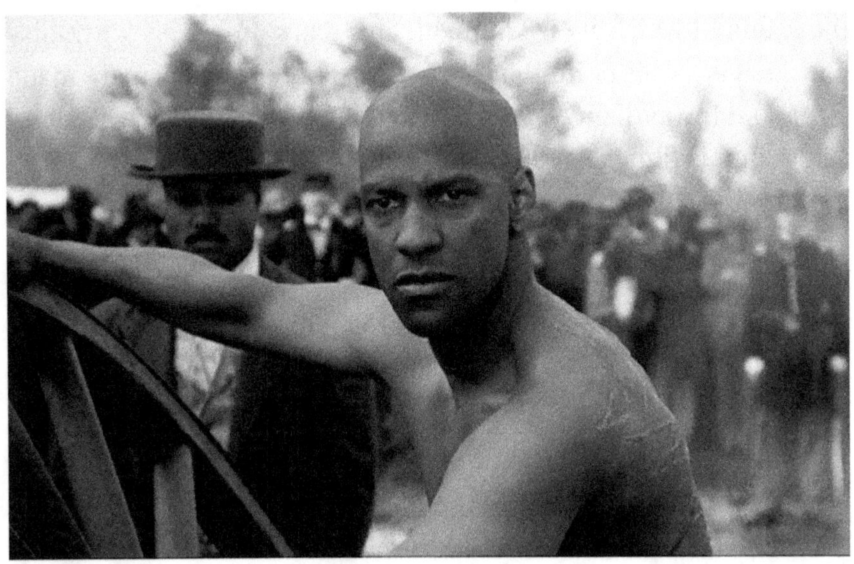

Zwick was careful when filming *Glory* not to turn it into a black story with a more commercially convenient white hero.

"We didn't want this film to fall under that shadow," Freeman said. "This is a picture about the 54th Regiment, not Colonel Shaw, but at the same time, the two are inseparable."

In order to assure accuracy, Zwick hired Shelby Foote, who would later become a semi-household name courtesy of Ken Burns' popular 1990 PBS nine-episode documentary *The Civil War*, as a technical advisor.

In the film *Glory*, Trip is one of the most complex, fascinating, and perhaps realistic characters. He was once a slave and carries a great deal of resentment about his country and is one of the only black characters that repeatedly speaks with bitterness. Although he is cynical and unhappy most of the time, he does offer the most sensible voice out of the group on issues of racial inequalities and leads the movement to reject the paychecks out of protest. It is difficult to not feel strongly about this character, especially during the scene in which he is whipped, and scars on his back are displayed. It is at this point that the reasons for his cynicism are made clear, and the audience can begin to understand him. All the characters in this film have depth, but none stand out quite like Denzel Washington's depiction of the character Trip in the film *Glory*.

It is interesting to note that Washington was reluctant to take on his role in *Glory*. "I had a lot of reservations about doing something like [*Glory*]," he said in a 1990 issue of *Ebony* magazine. "My father-in-law was a principal at one of the top black high schools in North Carolina, and he always told me the worst thing that ever happened was integration. In a lot of ways, I agree with him because we have gotten further and further away from (black) culture." But he finally recognized that *Glory* gave him a shot at "an honest portrayal, a fully realized character." He accepted the role, of course, and won an Oscar as a result.

That scene where Denzel has a tear run down his face is one of the most powerful in cinematic history! Absolutely brilliant, and it secured his Oscar!

The whipping scene was not true at the time the events of the movie actually occurred. At the beginning of the war, flogging was a legal punishment, but it was banned in the US Army in August 1861 and in the Confederate Army in August 1862. Colonel Shaw was also a staunch abolitionist and would have never approved such a punishment.

Edward Zwick claimed that, for the flogging scene, Denzel Washington was lashed at full contact, with a special whip, which would not cut his back, but still stung. For the final take of the scene, Zwick hesitated to call "Cut!" to signal the flogging to stop, and the result was Washington's spontaneous tear down his cheek.

The movie candidly portrays the trials and tribulations that men of color faced during the Civil War in being accepted as equals even by their own government and the other soldiers who served under the Union flag. Only when they were shown to be willing to make the ultimate sacrifice were they accepted as equals on the field of battle. Unfortunately, the bigotry, inequality, and hatred that these African-Americans faced during the Civil War are still with us today.

CHAPTER 8

THE 1990s

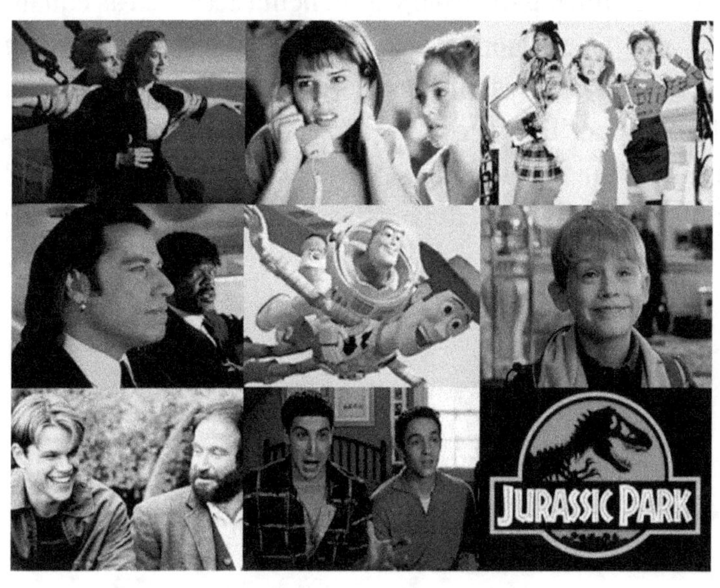

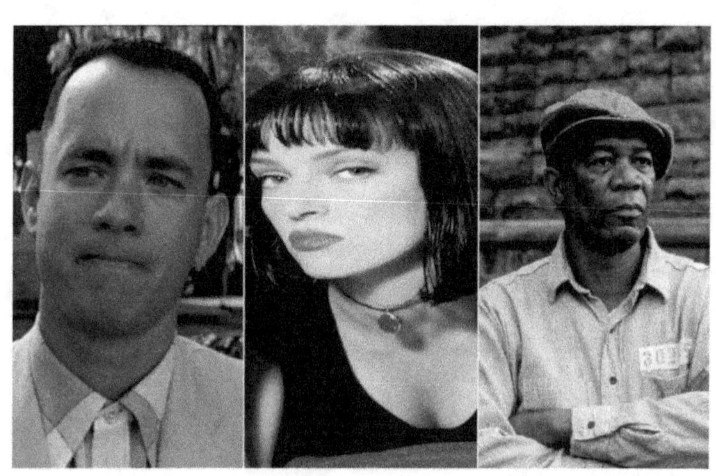

Rudy (1993)

Rudy is a biographical sports film directed by David Anspaugh. It is an account of the life of Daniel Ruettiger, who harbored dreams of playing collegiate football at the University of Notre Dame in South Bend, Indiana, despite significant physical, family, and emotional obstacles. It was the first film that the Notre Dame administration allowed to be shot on campus since *Knute Rockne, All American* in 1940, starring Pat O'Brien as the legendary famed football coach.

All his life, people told Rudy (Sean Austin) he's not good enough, not smart enough, and not big enough. But nothing can stop his impossible dream of playing football for Notre Dame. From the time he's a young boy, Rudy is determined to join the Fighting Irish. But his blue-collar family only laughs at his ambitions—they know Rudy will follow his father and brothers to the local steel mill. And, for four long years after high school, he does just that. But some dreams won't die, as Rudy proves when he goes to heroic lengths to win admission to Notre Dame. Once there, he becomes a walk-on player, serving as little more than a human tackling dummy against the starting players. Bloodied but unbeaten, Rudy wins the respect of legendary coach Ara Parseghian and the other Irish players, who give him one shot at gridiron glory.

When he tackles the quarterback of Georgia Tech, on the very last game of the season and the very last play of the game, he is triumphantly carried off the field in front of his once-doubting father and brother who now cry, cheer, and shout his name out loud for all to hear.

Scene: Being Carried Off the Field

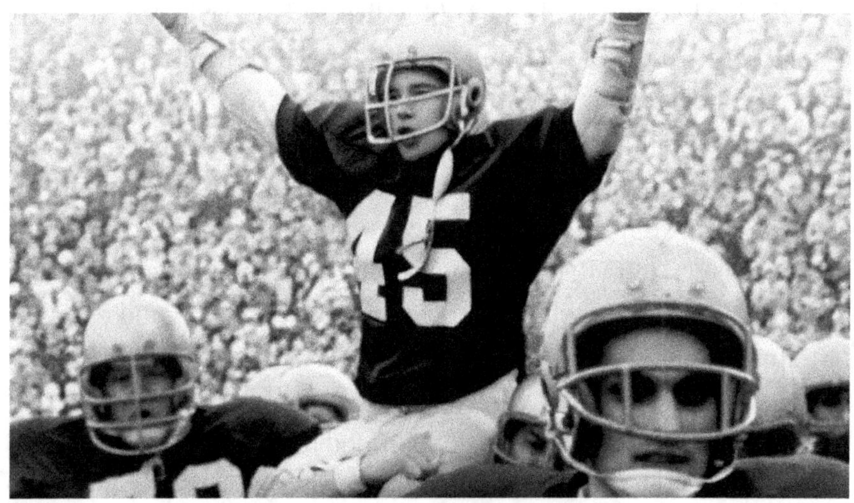

An epilogue states that after 1975, no other player for Notre Dame had been carried off the field to the time of the film's release in 1993.

This is the ultimate feel-good movie about how hard work, sheer determination, blood, sweat, and tears will, in the end, overcome all kinds of adversity and pitfalls. This ethic is a wonderful lesson for all of us to remember in life.

This is an actual photograph of the real "Rudy" Ruettiger being carried off the field at Notre Dame University on November 8, 1975.

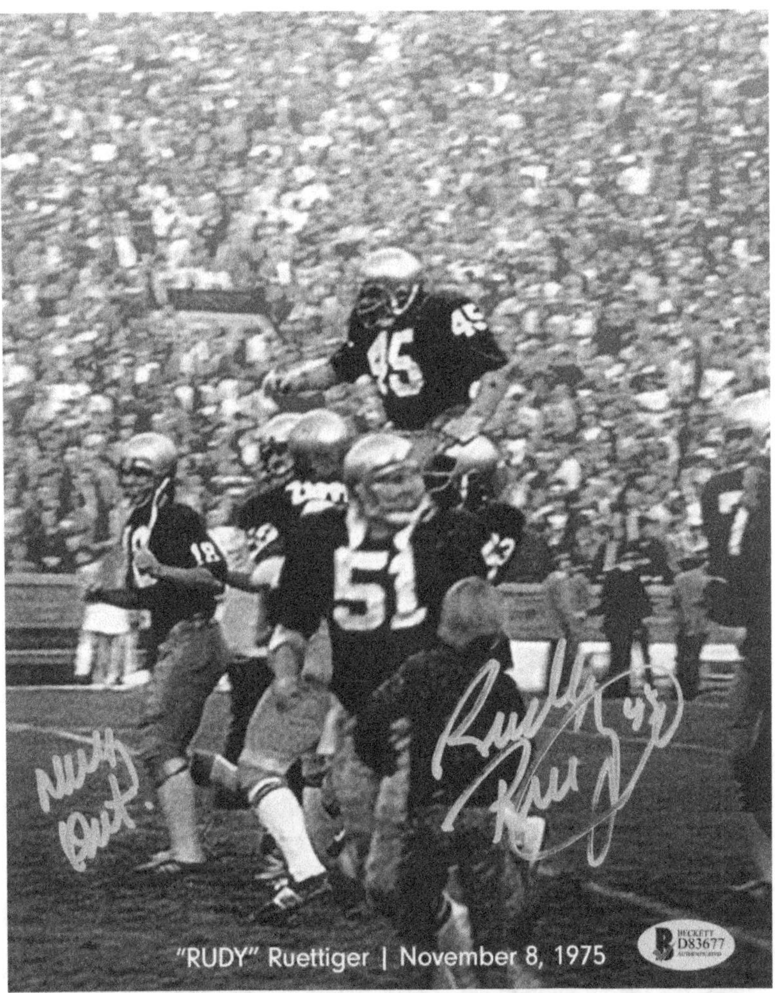

"RUDY" Ruettiger | November 8, 1975

This movie is essential for every sports fan. You may hate sports and curse the fact that we put so much stock in sports teams, but it is impossible for anyone to watch this movie and not feel, in the end, like they can conquer the world. Oh, and have a tissue handy for the end. Yes, this applies to all those "hard–hearted" people out there. I cry every time I see it. It is probably the most inspirational motion picture of all time.

Schindler's List (1993)

Schindler's List is a historical period drama film directed and co-produced by Steven Spielberg and written by Steven Zaillian. It is based on the 1992 novel *Schindler's Ark* by Australian novelist Thomas Keneally. The film follows Oskar Schindler, a Sudeten German businessman who saved more than a thousand mostly Polish-Jewish refugees from the Holocaust by employing them in his factories during World War II. It stars Liam Neeson as Schindler, Ralph Fiennes as SS officer Amon Göth, and Ben Kingsley as Schindler's Jewish accountant Itzhak Stern.

Scene: The Girl in Red

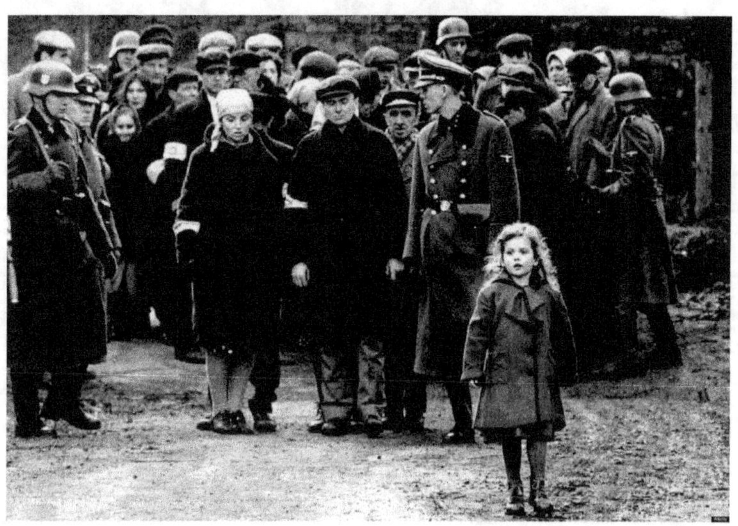

Perhaps the most moving image in Steven Spielberg's epic *Schindler's List* is the little girl in the red coat—one of only four color images in the three-hour, black-and-white film. Our attention is drawn to the little blonde tot, overlooked by the German troops, who wanders alone amid the horror and panic. She is wearing a red coat, which draws the viewer to her even when she is but one of a hundred people in a wide shot.

In the film, she was played by actress Oliwia Dabrowska, who was just three years old at the time. Spielberg made her promise not to watch the film until she was eighteen and old enough to understand it. This is a photograph of Spielberg directed her in preparation for her role in the movie.

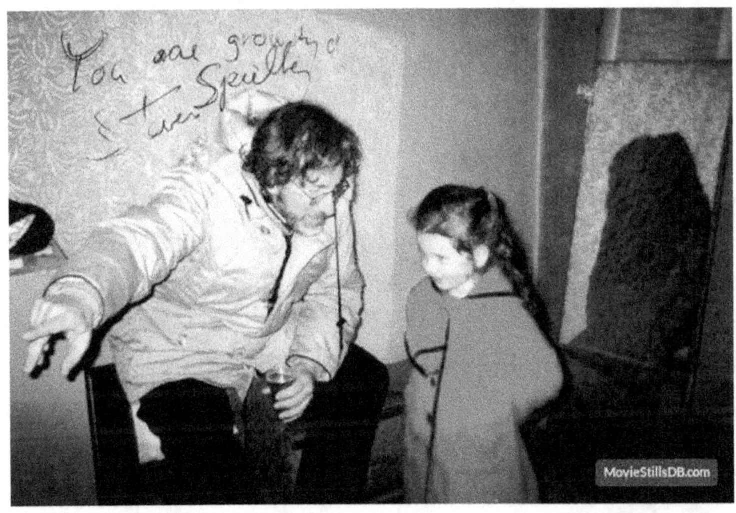

But she broke her promise when she was eleven. She now says that watching the movie at such a young age traumatized her; she vowed then that she'd never watch it again and was angry at her parents for allowing her to play the role. It was only when she grew up that she realized Spielberg was right; she had been part of something she could be truly proud of. The girl in red had a pivotal role in perhaps the greatest Holocaust movie in history.

Spielberg has said the role of "the girl in red" in the film was to symbolize how the West knew what was happening in Europe, yet failed to act. As one of the few splashes of color in a black-and-white film, the Holocaust was impossible to ignore—yet the Americans and British did nothing to help European Jewry until it was too late.

Other critics note that her appearance is the point at which Schindler actually sees the truth for the first time. At a primal level, she is the Red Riding Hood of fairytales, symbolizing innocence, pursued by the darkest predator of them all—other human beings.

In his book *Schindler's Ark*, Thomas Keneally tells about Oskar Schindler, on horseback, as he views the liquidation of the Cracow ghetto from atop an adjacent hill. The child in red compels Schindler's attention, and his mistress Ingrid comments that the child must be female, because little girls get obsessed by color, especially a bright shade of red like that. In the beginning, the SS guard corrects her drift and nudges her back into line. Schindler cannot see why he does not bludgeon her with his rifle butt since, at the other end of Krakusa Street, mercy has been canceled.

> "At last, Schindler slithered from his horse, tripped, and found himself on his knees, hugging the trunk of a pine tree. The urge to throw up his excellent breakfast was, he sensed, to be suppressed, for he suspected it meant that all his cunning body was doing was making room to digest the horrors of Krakusa Street.
>
> "Later in the day, after he had absorbed a ration of brandy, Oscar understood ... they permitted witnesses, such witnesses as the red toddler because they believed all the witnesses would perish too..."

Schindler had previously rationalized to himself that the reports of atrocities were just the isolated acts of individuals, but now realizes that if such atrocities are occurring in full view of this little girl, the Nazis must be acting with the full knowledge of their superiors, with the approval of the highest authority.

Schindler identifies with the little girl in red, as she makes her way, aimless and alone, past the madness and chaos in the street. A woman is machine-gunned behind her. Schindler loses sight of the small figure as she walks behind a building, but then he glimpses her again, walking by a file of Jews being herded down a sidewalk. During the roundup, a Nazi soldier fires at a single-file lineup of men, killing several with one bullet. Stricken by the nightmare below, Schindler sees the little girl in red entering one of the empty apartment buildings. There, she climbs the stairs and crawls under a bed for cover in a ransacked room. An individual victim, lost. Schindler's soul is touched by the child; he feels her pain and cries for her. The plight of the one little girl in red touches him in a way the sheer numbers make unreal; it is easy to get lost in numbers. He transforms the faceless mass around him into one real palpable human being. This one child is a symbol of all the 6 million victims exposed to ruthless slaughter. Each was an individual who had dreams, who had a life, who had a family.

It was at that moment that Oskar Schindler vowed that he would do everything within his power to destroy the Nazi Regime.

While the girl is strolling unscathed while murder and brutality happen all around her, we see other stories forming or ending, but even in a telephoto view, the viewer cannot take his eyes off the little red-tinted girl. She is the purity, the innocence, walking unnoticed through the Nazis, and witnessing their every crime. But the Nazis don't worry—in the end, there will be no witnesses.

We do not know what has happened to her until much later in the film itself. The Nazis are ordered to dig up all the Jewish corpses they have buried to incinerate the evidence of the slaughter of the Cracow ghetto. As the decomposing corpses are trundled in wagons to the fires, Oskar Schindler catches a glimpse of a red-tinted rag of a corpse.

The use of color to follow the little girl in her red coat has by now achieved the stature of legendary. However, most people do not know that this image is based upon a true story, told at the trial of Adolf Eichmann, one of the most feared and hated Nazi leaders of World War II, responsible for the deaths of millions of Jews.

In the 1997 PBS documentary *The Trial of Adolf Eichmann*, this image loses none of its impacts when the actual story is told by Assistant Prosecutor, later Supreme Court Judge, Gavriel Bach, in an interview which appears in the program. When asked if there was any moment in the trial that affected him more than any other, this is the moment he describes.

Bach was questioning Dr. Martin Földi, a survivor of Auschwitz, about the selection process at the train station in the shadows of the famous "Arbeit Macht Frei" sign at Auschwitz. Földi described how he and a son went to the right while a daughter and his wife went to the left. His little daughter wore the red coat. When an SS officer sent the son to join the mother and daughter, Földi describes his panic. How would the boy, only twelve, find them among the thousands of people there? But then he realized the red coat would be like a beacon for the boy to join his mother and sister.

He then ends his testimony with the chilling phrase, "I never saw them again."

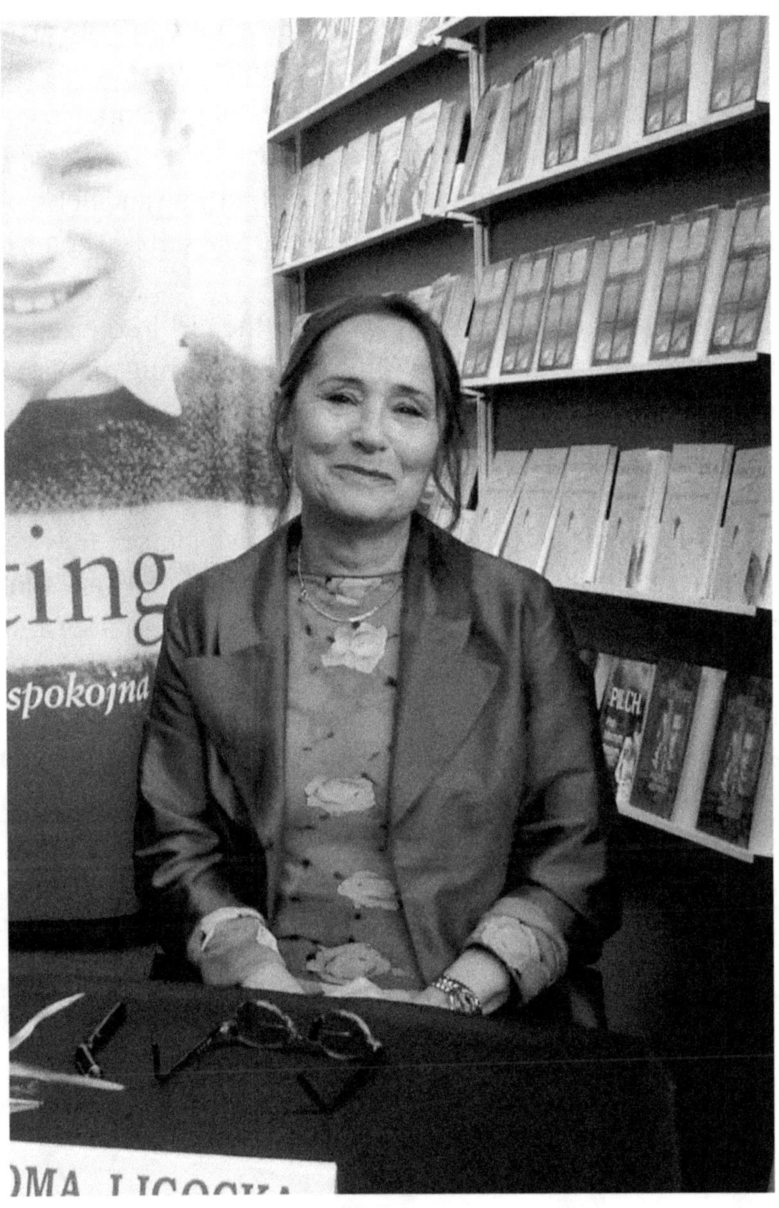

Roma Ligocka at The Krakow Book Fair in 2004.
Photo by Mgieuka CC BY-SA 3.0

The most striking image of the movie was more than an artistic decision. *Schindler's List* was shot in black and white, but one character, a little girl in a red coat, had her garment presented in color.

Roma Ligocka, artist, model, and author of *The Girl in the Red Coat* (2002), was a true-life version of the child. She and her mother fled the Krakow ghetto and hid from the Nazis in the home of a sympathetic family.

Ligocka said in a *Guardian* interview, "the girl in the red coat in the film is a symbol of all the children killed during the Nazi regime. In Poland alone, 1.5 million were murdered. The experiences of the film character and mine are identical, with one important difference—I survived."

There's an echo of the movie in her explanation of how color helped her in the ensuing years: she used bright colors and clothing—as bold as the red coat—to keep the darker memories at bay. "Because I never had toys as a child, I needed to paint a grey and hopeless world [into something] more beautiful in my mind," she says. "When times were bad, I felt clothing to be a kind of protection."

Saving Private Ryan (1998)

Saving Private Ryan was one of Stephen Spielberg's most acclaimed films. When General George Marshall learns that three of the four sons of the Ryan family were killed in action and that the fourth son, James, is with the 101st Airborne Division somewhere in Normandy, a small platoon of American soldiers is assigned the daunting task of locating and retrieving him from danger and sending him home. However, before those events can ever transpire, the successful invasion of Germany-held France must occur.

The script was inspired by a true story: the Niland family had lost three of their four sons to the war. The War Department, still remembering the five Sullivan brothers who all died while serving on the same battleship (which led to the policy of preventing siblings from serving together), was not going to let it happen again. They sent a platoon to pull the fourth Niland son out of harm's way; he was a young soldier who had parachuted in with the 101st on D-Day.

Robert Rodat's script fictionalizes the particulars but draws upon real history to tell the story of the soldiers who land on Omaha Beach on June 6, 1944. The real-life landing was a slaughter. The pre-invasion barrage had failed to knock out the dug-in German guns, and heavily-entrenched soldiers on the hills above the beach, and the Germans slaughtered the first wave of American soldiers.

After reading the script and liking the story, cinematographer Kaminski said, "I then imagine how I can enhance the storytelling through visuals."

According to the 1999 book *100 Years of Hollywood* produced by Time-Life Books, in the chapter entitled "Capturing the Story in the Camera's Eye," the filming of the Normandy landing in this epic film was related to the readers:

Janusz Kaminski had the challenge of making the camera translate filmmaker Steven Spielberg's vision into reality. For its first twenty-five minutes, this powerful World War II drama focuses unrelatedly on the carnage and chaos of the Allies' D-Day landing on the Omaha Beach sector of France's Normandy coast. After studying actual combat footage and photographs, especially the work of legendary *Life* magazine photojournalist Robert Capra, Spielberg and Kaminski decided the film should, as Kaminski put in, "look like it was shot in 16mm by a bunch of combat cameraman."

To achieve this sense of realism, Kaminski had his camera operators shot mostly with hand-held cameras. They simulated the frenetic quality of combat with deliberate out-of-sync shutters and special devices that shook the cameras. If water or artificial blood splattered the lenses, Kaminski said, "We kept shooting because that's what we assumed would happen in reality."

Kaminski also manipulated the lighting. Because he wanted a "kind of burned-out, bleary sky," he had protective coating stripped from lenses for flatter contrast. Overhead silk canopies and heavy black smoke helped diminish sunlight. And to enhance the documentary look, he extracted roughly 0 percent of the color from the final negative, creating muted tones.

For making the camera a real participant in the film, Kaminski received an Academy Award for Best Cinematography at the 1999 award presentation.

Scene: The Normandy Landing

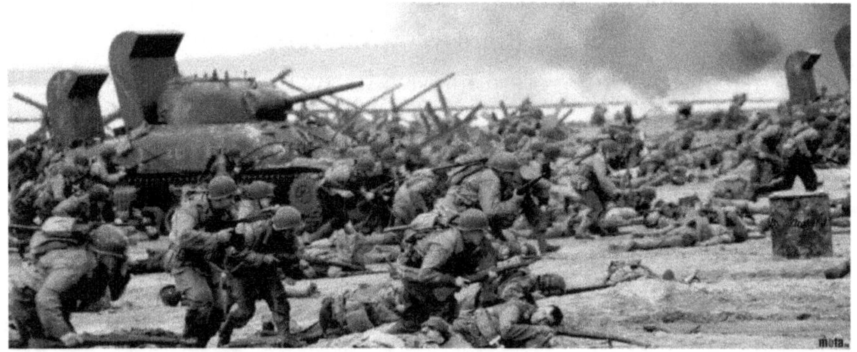

Spielberg transformed the scene into the film's most visceral and memorable accomplishment: the shell-shock of the brutal, bloody, in-your-face chaos of American soldiers hitting the beach on D-Day. The unrelenting barrage of exploding shells and pelting gunfire on a beach littered with the bodies and limbs of American soldiers hits the audience like an assault on the senses. "I tried to be as brutally honest as I could with what I had," explained Spielberg. Bullets tear through the air, water, flesh; men stagger about, lost and limbless; explosions shatter the dull scream of war; soldiers bleed, fall, and die, just so many bodies in the detritus of battle. Spielberg's razor-sharp images are charged with panic, and his camera is almost too alert as it takes in the shocking information overload. War has never been portrayed as so intimidating, so terrifying, so arbitrarily destructive. It may be the closest Hollywood has ever come to recreating the combat experience, thanks in large part to Spielberg's brilliant orchestration of the chaos. Visions such as portrayed in this scene must always be remembered in our subconscious, lest we forget that hatred, bigotry, suspicion, lust for power, and sheer human arrogance can all lead to such human horrors being repeated over and over again until we come to our senses.

The nearest match to stage the harrowing landing scenes was found on the southeast coast of the Republic of Ireland, at Balinesker Beach, Curracloe, just north of Wexford, about seventy miles south of Dublin. Vintage landing crafts were brought in from all over the world. It took fifteen days to film this sequence, using 1,500 extras with one thousand of them members of the Irish Army Reserve, and hundreds of guns were loaded with blanks for the actors and extras on the front lines of the film (the rest were issued rubber guns). The actors wore earplugs to protect them from the noise of the explosives and ordnance used to create the spectacle of the German assault on the landing. Computer effects were used to add background explosions and fill out long shots with more soldiers and chaos. For the film's other major location, a French village set, the company built its own village in a rural field in Hatfield, just north of London. They actually constructed real, functional buildings and then destroyed them to create an authentically war-scarred look.

Actual amputees were used in order to add realism to the scenes like the one showing a soldier supposedly retrieving a limb, which has been shot off from the beach.

The filming of this scene cost $12 million alone, and forty barrels of fake blood were used. Squibs were used to simulate bullets and artillery striking the beach, as well as individual soldiers. They were carefully coordinated and timed with shots of enemy rifles and artillery firing in order to give realism and authenticity to the action.

The editors (color coordinators) put the film's negatives through a process to extract color from the film in order that minute dirt and water particles would become quite clear to the audience.

In this production scene, Spielberg is seen giving instruction to the crew of one of the landing crafts which are about to hit the beach (left) and a soldier carrying his own limb after it was shot off by enemy fire (right) is a scene from the movie itself.

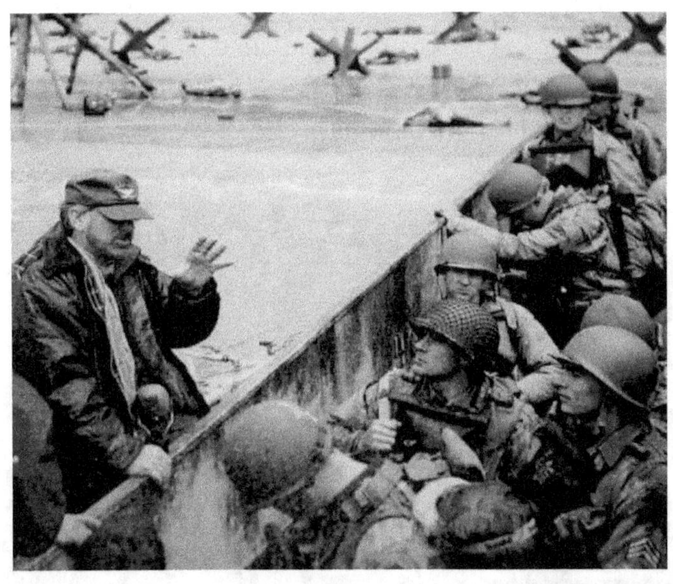

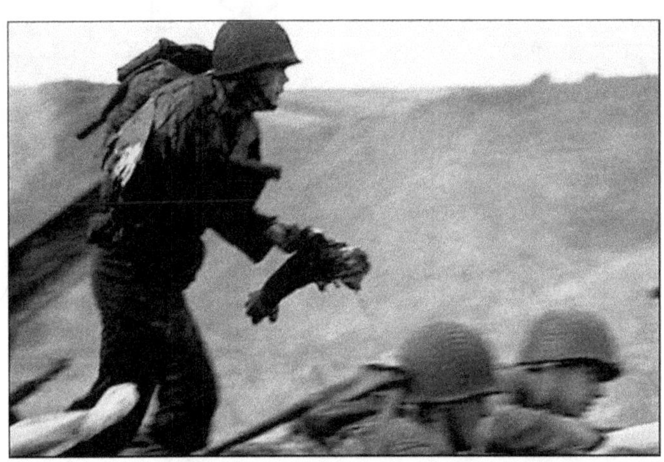

The experience of seeing such vivid and realistic images of the Normandy landing on the silver screen sent some World War II veterans reeling into vivid flashbacks of perhaps their own wartime experiences and stunned the viewing audiences into an awed, aghast, and humble silence. No other film depiction of the Normandy landing, either in earlier movies, such as *The Longest Day* (1962), or any other movie since *Saving Private Ryan*, such as *Storming Juno* (2010), has ever depicted this scene so vividly and realistically.

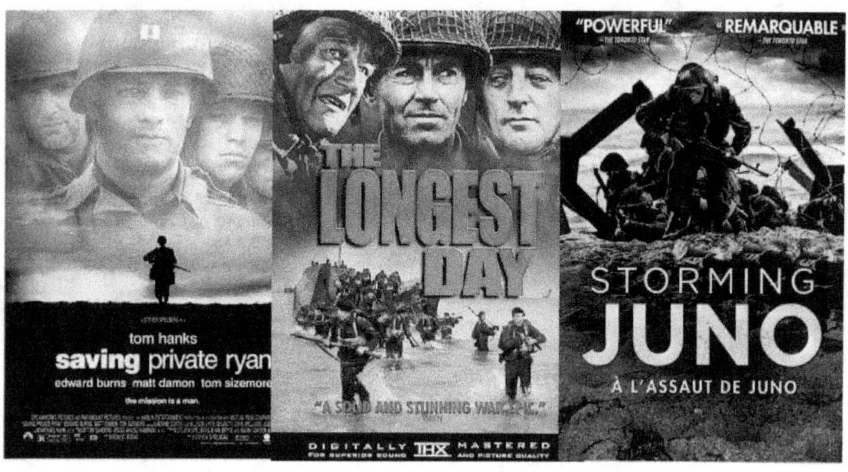

CHAPTER 9

THE HONORABLE - MENTION SCENES

The following motion picture scenes didn't quite make the cut of the top one hundred greatest movie scenes, but it is impossible to ignore the sheer impact they had on moviegoers and their significance within the context of the movie in which they appeared, as well as their relevance even today in the total spectrum of the movie genre or the socio-political realities that we face and witness in the world each and every day.

The Triumph of the Will (1935)

Triumph of the Will was commissioned by Adolf Hitler to glorify the Nazi Party rally in Nuremberg in 1934, where 700,000 supporters came to express support for the party. The rally's organizers arranged the supporters in massed rows that conveyed a sense of overwhelming size together with focus and discipline—a combination Riefenstahl worked to capture in the film. An undeniably brilliant filmmaker who broke new ground with pioneering techniques, Leni Riefenstahl nonetheless lived in infamy for her alleged friendship with Adolf Hitler during the reign of Nazi Germany. She was caught in a quandary. She wanted to be able to express her artistic abilities as a filmmaker but had to adhere to the direction of Hitler if she wanted to work in her craft. Her earlier work for him *Victory of Faith* (1933) was not initially well-received by him nor by her, as some Nazis didn't want her to get credit for the film because of her political beliefs. Finally, she agreed to redo the film, which set the stage for her to do *Triumph of the Will*, the filming of the Nazi Nuremberg party rally in 1934.

Scene: 1934 Nazi Party Congress in Nuremberg

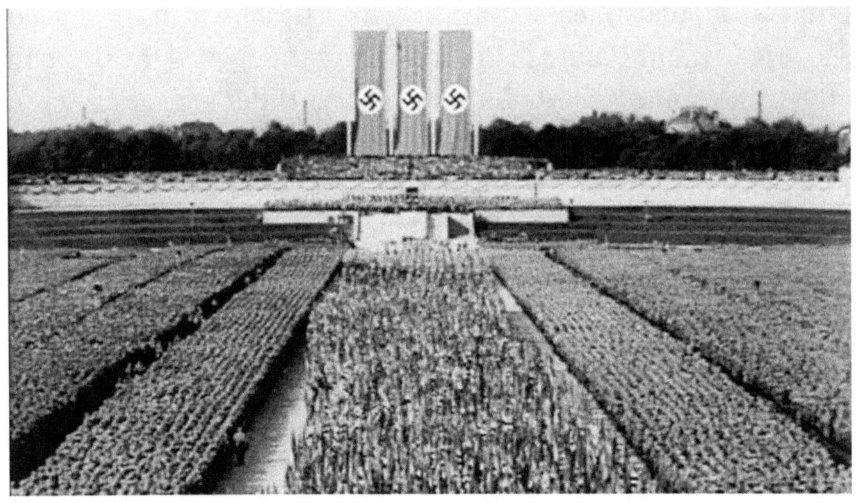

5–10 September 1934, Nuremberg
Reichsparteitag der Einheit und Stärke (Reich Party Congress
of Unity and Strength); documented in Triumph des Willens by
Leni Riefenstahl

The famed Nuremberg rally that portrayed the Fuehrer as a god who comes to Earth to save the German people. Though the film was hailed as a masterpiece, Riefenstahl was unable to live down her reputation for being a Nazi sympathizer—a label that dogged her for the rest of her life. The film follows a similar script as Victory of Faith, which is evident when one sees both films side by side. For example, the city of Nuremberg scenes, down to the shot of a cat that is included in a car-driving sequence in both films. There are panning shots across the roofs of the old town, showing the city awakening before the rally starts in earnest. The camera angles and editing that made Riefenstahl's *Triumph of the Will* a ground-breaking film already demonstrated in *The Victory of Faith.* Meanwhile, she kept Hitler in the background for her other documentary masterpiece, *Olympia* (1938), which chronicled the 1936 Olympic Games in Berlin. While she depicted the German athletes as somewhat godlike, keeping to Hitler's ideal of Aryan superiority, Riefenstahl did focus much of her attention on the American hero, Jesse Owens, an African-American who bested Germany's top athletes to take home four gold medals.

Famed film critic Roger Ebert wrote in 2008:

> There are also questions of spontaneity. During one Hitler speech, he is interrupted by sieg heil! exactly six times, as if there were an applause sign to prompt them when to begin and end, and we note that throughout the film, there are no scatterings of individual voices at the start or finish of sieg heil! Only a single massed voice, in unison. I found myself peering intently to observe other moments of the film revealing its mechanism. Although Riefenstahl used thirty cameras and a crew of 150, only one camera appears to be visible on screen; during the outdoor rally before three gigantic hanging swastika flags, you can see the camera on an elevator between the first and second, its shadow cast on the second.
>
> That Triumph of the Will is a great propaganda film, there is no doubt, and various surveys have named it so. But I doubt that anyone not already a Nazi could be swayed by it. Yet it must have had a persuasive effect in Germany at the time; although Hitler clearly spells out that the Nazis will be Germany's only party, and its leader Germany's only leader for 1,000 years to come.

At the end, there is a singing of the party anthem, the Horst Wessel Song; under Nazi law, the right-arm salute had to be given during the first and fourth verses.

Leni is seen filming *Triumph* in these photographs using some of her various cameras for different scenes.

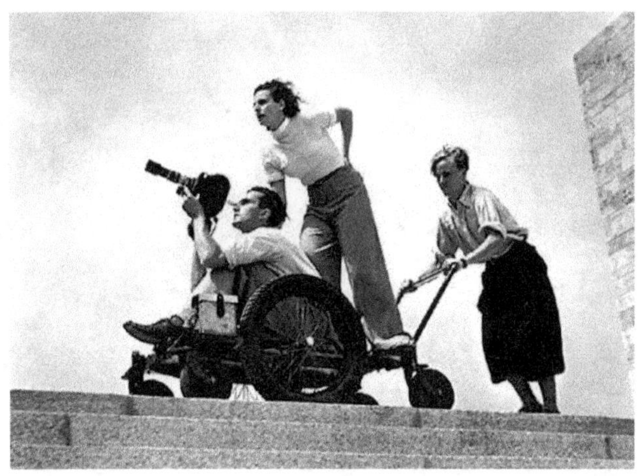

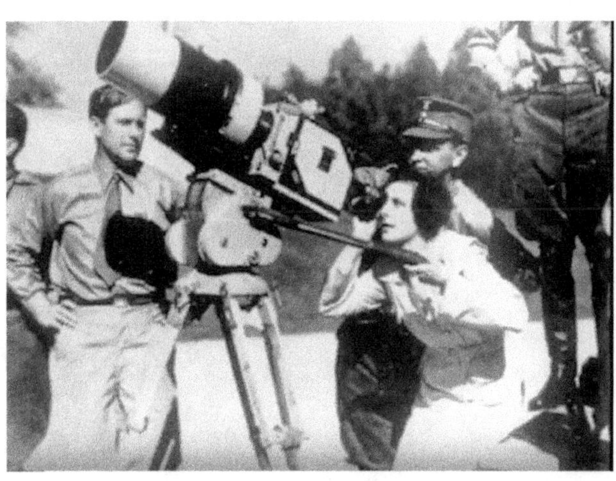

In the closing scene from *Star Wars* (1977), and so to the awarding of the medals, a scene of great ceremonial pomp which Lucas was brazen enough to crib, in its layout and shot choices, from the most famous Nazi propaganda film ever made. Luke, Han, and Chewbacca walk through the massed hordes of Rebel Alliance extras Hitler, Himmler, and Viktor Lutze, laying a wreath at the memorial for President Hindenburg, in *Triumph of the Will*'s equivalent sequence.

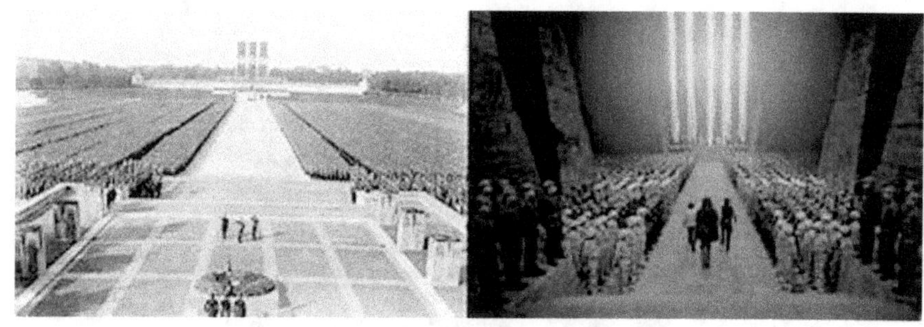

A Chump at Oxford (1940)

A Chump at Oxford was directed by Alfred J. Goulding and released on February 16, 1940, by United Artists. It was Stan and Ollie's second-to-last effort for Hal Roach. What makes this film distinctive is that it is the first and only time that we see and hear Stan Laurel play a dual role where the alternate character—cultured, intellectual, boorish, and combative—is the polar opposite of Stanley's trademark slow-witted, good-natured innocence. In turn, Laurel reveals another dimension of his comedic mastery. The story was written by Charley Rogers, Felix Adler, and Harry Laughlin.

Scene: Stan's Metamorphosis

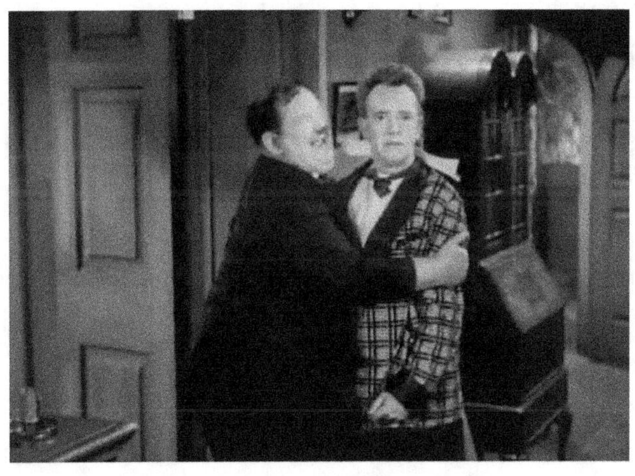

The movie follows the adventures and misadventures of the pair as they accidentally capture a robber, and as a reward by the bank president, they get to go the Oxford University in England as a means of furthering their education. At Oxford, they are met with pranks by the other students, including Peter Cushing, just because they are "Yanks." However, it's really the last ten minutes, as they try to escape the wrath of the other students, where the film transcends Laurel and Hardy's usual fun. A windowsill hits Stan on the head, and he "regains his memory," transforming into the brilliant but arrogant Lord Paddington. The surprise this creates is matched only by the relief felt by Ollie when Stan is knocked on the head once again to regress back to his old gentle, naive self. Stan's metamorphosis is truly magical, and it's a reminder that his talent had richness and depth that is often taken for granted. In this scene from the film, the audience feels the genuine love that Ollie has for his lifelong, devoted friend and reveals the true heart of the roles they played on the screen. It is a truly great movie memory. The film is one of my all-time Laurel and Hardy favorites, and this scene is one of the most touching and endearing in motion picture history.

Stan & Ollie is a 2018 biographical comedy-drama directed by Jon S. Baird and written by Jeff Pope. The film focuses on the later years of the lives of the famed comedy act of Laurel and Hardy. The film stars Steve Coogan and John C. Reilly as Stan Laurel and Oliver Hardy. *Stan & Ollie* is a sweet and charming movie about Laurel and Hardy, long after the comedy duo's careers have peaked. It's a love story of sorts, with all the complexity and resentments of a long marriage, its bickering and banter, but in the end, their true love for each other becomes apparent.

In 1937, while making *Way Out West*, Stan Laurel refused to renew his contract with Hal Roach because Stan believes the studio and Roach himself are failing to financially recognize the global fame the pair enjoyed at that time. Oliver Hardy remains tied to Roach on a different contract and isn't let go, with the studio attempting to pair him up with Harry Langdon in the film *Zenobia*, and while Laurel and Hardy would soon get back together, Ollie's absence during a meeting with Fox results in them not being signed on by the studio, leaving Stan feeling betrayed and bitter for years. Sixteen years passed, and in 1953, the comedy duo embarks on a grueling music hall tour of the United Kingdom and Ireland while struggling to get another film made: a comedic adaptation of *Robin Hood*. However, the tour is hampered by poor initial planning, unpleasantness between their wives, artistic differences, and Ollie's failing health.

In the end, the duo forgives each other and their past differences and has a most successful tour.

As the film ends, a written epilogue reveals that the tour was the last time they worked together. Ollie's health continued to deteriorate after the tour, leading to his death in 1957; Stan, devastated by his friend's death, refused to work without his partner and went into retirement, dying eight years later in 1965. Stan continued to write sketches for Laurel and Hardy in the last eight years of his life.

The screen actors said that they had to love each other off-screen before they could do the roles of Stan and Ollie on screen.

Here is a scene from the movie. Ollie has suffered a heart attack while judging a beauty contest. Ollie lovingly helps him back to his hotel room.

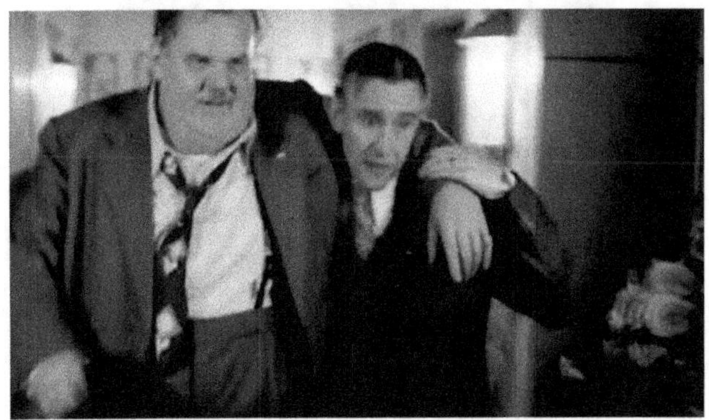

Broadway Melody of 1940 (1940)

Broadway Melody of 1940 is an MGM movie musical starring Fred Astaire, Eleanor Powell, George Murphy, and Frank Morgan. It was directed by Norman Taurog and produced by Jack Cummings. As photographed by Joseph Ruttenberg and Oliver T. Marsh, it is one of the most visually arresting of all black-and-white film musicals. The movie marks the first and only teaming of dancing legends Fred Astaire and Eleanor Powell, who were considered the finest movie musical dancers of their time. The story was written by Jack McGowan and Dore Schary. The story revolves around a case of mistaken identity, loyalty, and sustained friendship involving a Broadway show. It features music by Cole Porter, including "Begin the Beguine."

Scene: Begin the Beguine

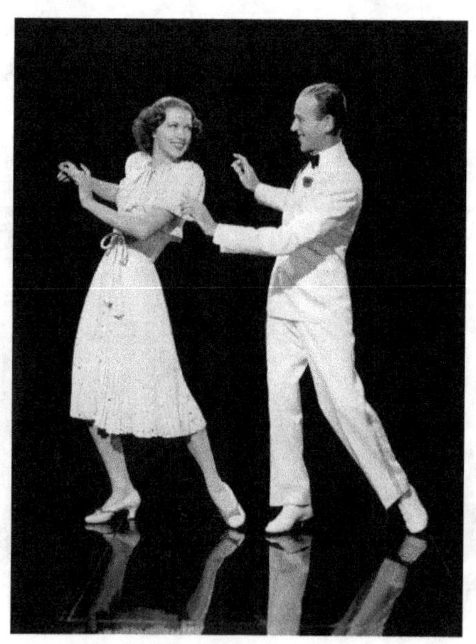

Fred Astaire and Eleanor Powell danced to Cole Porter's "Begin the Beguine," which is considered by many to be one of the greatest tap sequences in film history. According to accounts of the making of this film, Astaire was somewhat intimidated by Powell, who was considered the only female dancer ever capable of out-dancing Astaire.

In his 1959 autobiography *Steps in Time*, Astaire remarked, "She 'put 'em down like a man,' no ricky-ticky-sissy stuff with Ellie. She really knocked out a tap dance in a class by herself."

There was much publicity concerning his filming with a new partner, and some fans resented his being "unfaithful" to his former dancing partner Ginger Rogers, who had already achieved stardom as a top actress in her own right at RKO Studios. In addition, Astaire was reportedly a bit intimidated by Powell, as she was considered, at the time, one of the few female dancers capable of out-performing Astaire at his own craft. According to Powell, in the introduction to John Douglas Earnes' book *The MGM Story* (1985), the feeling was somewhat mutual. Powell recalled finally saying to Astaire, "Look, we can't go on like this. I'm Ellie; you're Fred. We're just two hoofers." That broke the ice because, after that, they got along well and rehearsed so much that they practically wore out their rehearsal pianist.

Broadway Melody of 1940 was in production from early September until late November 1939. Cole Porter's "Begin the Beguine" was written in 1935, and it became one of his biggest all-time hits. The set for the "Begin the Beguine" number cost $120,000 to construct. It utilized a sixty-foot multi-paneled mirror mounted on a revolving track to change backgrounds. The glittering cinematography reaches its peak in a climactic, three-part production number built around Porter's famous score and includes a female chorus, a jazz orchestra, and an elaborate mirrored set with a glass floor that had to be kept at temperatures near freezing to guard it against cracking under the lights. The numbers justly celebrated final passage, a competitive tap duet by Astaire and Powell, and forms a highlight of *That's Entertainment!* (1974). Film historian David Thomson, in his *Biographical Dictionary of Film* (2004), writes that he would choose this segment if he could "have only one film clip to watch while sentenced forever to solitary confinement for eternity."

The set has a black-and-white motif and a hard reflective floor that recedes into darkness. Fred is dressed in all white with a black bowtie. Eleanor Powell wears three-quarter heels and a dress that stops just below the knees. I know of nothing as exhilarating or unfailingly cheerful, and maybe the loveliest moment in films is the last second or so, as the dancers finish, and Powell's alive frock has another half-turn, like a spirit embracing the person.

In this photograph, Astaire and Powell are shown rehearsing the "Begin the Beguine" scene.

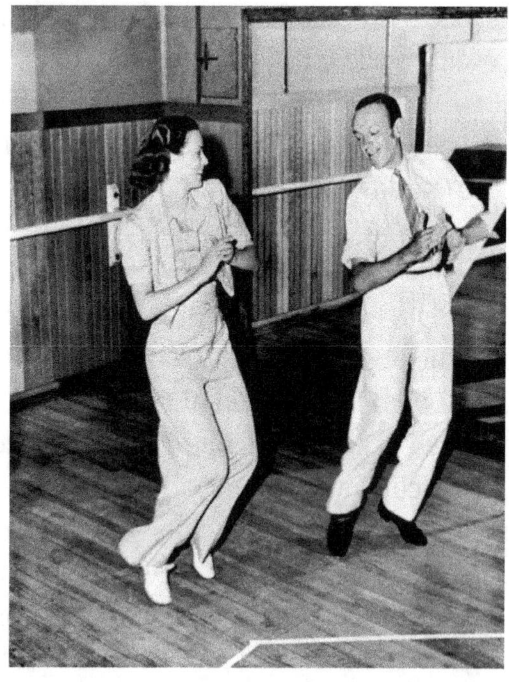

Knute Rockne, All American (1940)

Knute Rockne, All American, is the biographical film that tells the story of life and times of famed Knute Rockne, the famed Notre Dame Football coach. It stars Pat O'Brien, portraying the role of Rockne, and Ronald Reagan as player George Gipp, a.k.a. "The Gipper."

Scene: Return to South Bend

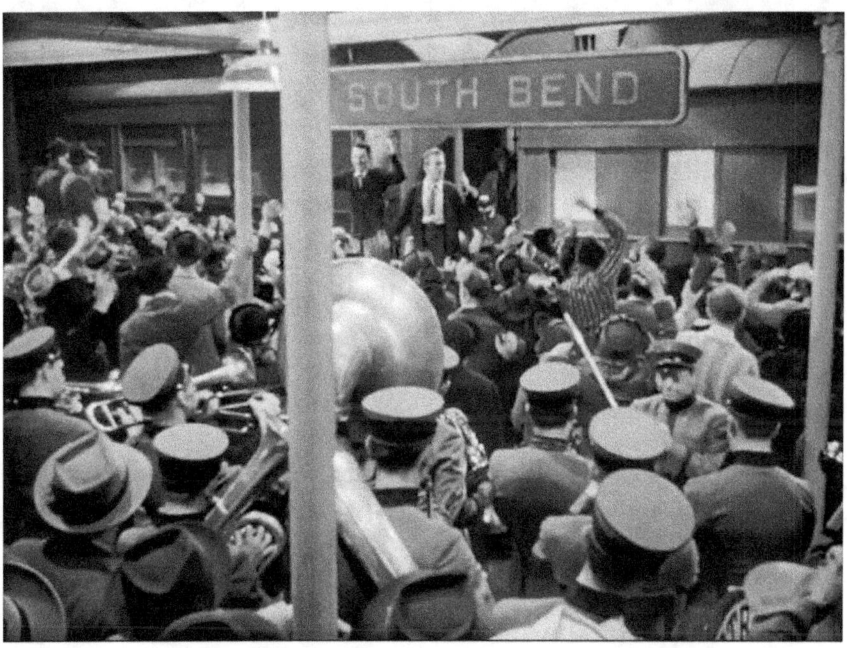

My own personal touching scene, in this movie, shows disheartened and dejected Coach Rockne getting a rousing and totally heartwarming reception at the train station in South Bend, despite losing the national championship to Army at Yankee Stadium in 1925.

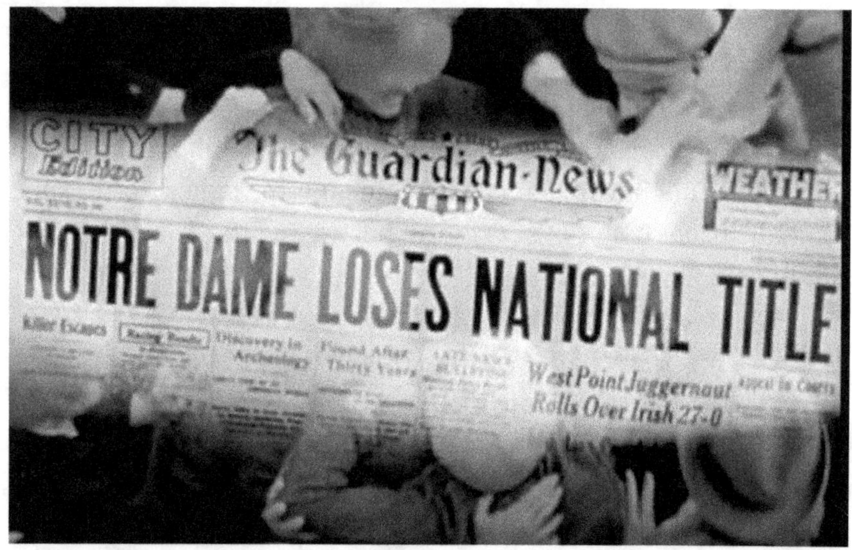

The Knute Rockne Legacy: Knute Rockne Memorial Society

Larger than Life

He changed how the game of football was played, coached, watched, and promoted.

He inspired a nation with an unyielding dedication to achieving excellence with honor.

He showed countless coaches on how to positively influence young lives.

Three National Titles

Rockne guided Notre Dame to its first consensus national championship in 1924, with a team featuring The Four Horsemen and The Seven Mules. His team went 9-0 during the regular season, then defeated Stanford, 27-10, in the January 1, 1925, Rose Bowl.

He guided the Fighting Irish to two more national titles, with undefeated teams in 1929 and 1930, before his shocking death in an airplane crash on March 31, 1931.

Coach of Coaches

Owing to their fame and success on the field, and Rockne's extensive contacts and personal magnetism, dozens of his Notre Dame players became football coaches at schools and colleges nationwide.

In addition, Rockne mentored hundreds of more young coaches through his summer coaching schools held on college campuses from coast to coast. In every corner of the nation, the Rockne influence guided the game.

Master Communicator

Rockne became one of the most oft-quoted Americans of his time. He connected with the masses through his speeches, newspaper and magazine articles, and later radio and newsreels. People would always want to know, "What does Rock have to say?"

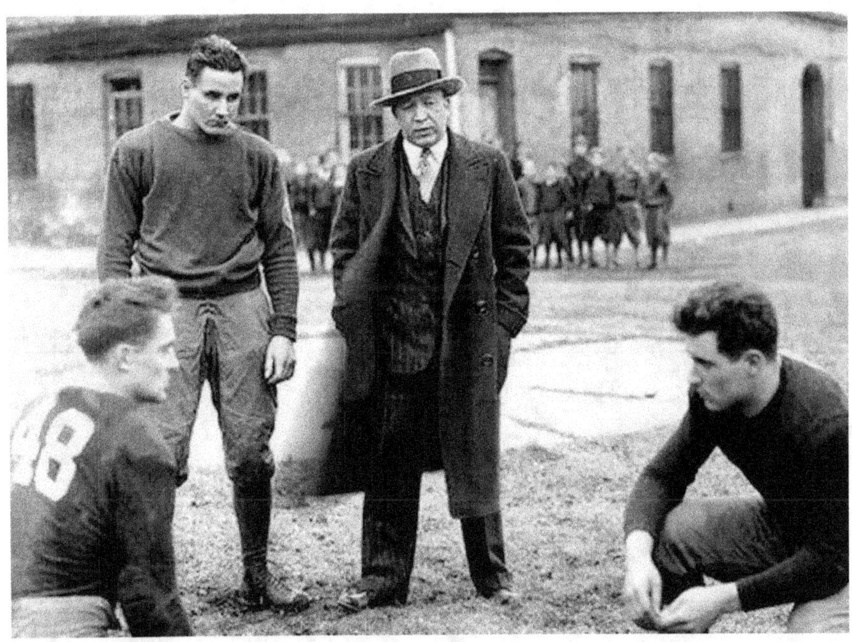

The Long Voyage Home (1940)

The Long Voyage Home is a drama film directed by John Ford and produced by Walter Wanger. It stars John Wayne, Thomas Mitchell, and Ian Hunter. The film tells the story of the crew aboard a British tramp steamer named the SS Glencairn on the long voyage home from the West Indies to Baltimore and then to England. The film covers their internal conflicts, partying, and being shanghaied as the crew tries to get Ole Olsen (John Wayne) back home to his aged mother and family back in Sweden.

Scene: Sultry Tropical Night

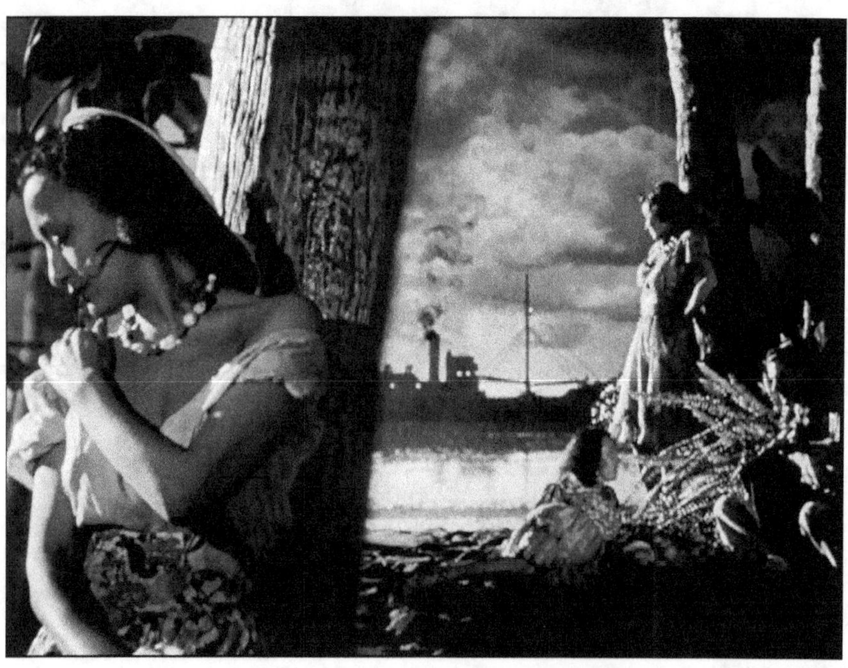

The film opens on a sultry night in a port in the West Indies where the crew has been confined to their ship by order of the captain, yet they yearn for an opportunity to drink and have fun with the ladies. It is a beautifully sultry and seductive opening scene where one can see the cinematic artistry of Greg Toland at work. Toland made the film among the most beautifully photographed black-and-white films of the era, its low-key lighting and deep focus photography contributing to the pessimistic atmosphere of the film and directly foreshadowing his work on *Citizen Kane* (1941).

Innovations in *The Long Voyage Home* and *Citizen Kane*:

Toland's techniques were revolutionary in the art of cinematography. Cinematographers before him used a shallow depth of field to separate the various planes on the screen, creating an impression of space as well as stressing what mattered in the frame by leaving the rest (the foreground or background) out of focus.

In Toland's lighting schemes, shadow became a much more compelling tool, both dramatically and pictorially, to separate the foreground from the background and so to create space within a two-dimensional frame while keeping all of the picture in focus. According to Toland, this visual style was more comparable with what the eyes see in real life since vision blurs what is not looked at rather than what is.

For *The Long Voyage Home*, Toland leaned more heavily on back-projection to create his deep focus compositions, such as the shot of the island women singing to entice the men of the SS *Glencairn*. He continued to develop the technologies that would allow him to create his images in *Citizen Kane*.

Similarities between *The Long Voyage Home* and *Citizen Kane:*

Toland had already had experience with heavy in-camera compositing, and many of the shots in Kane look similar in composition and dynamics to a number of shots in *The Long Voyage Home*.

For instance, both movies contain shots that create an artificial lighting situation such that a character is lit in the background and walks or run through dark areas to the foreground, where his arrival triggers, off-screen, a light not on before. The result is so visually dramatic because a character moves, only barely visible, through vast pools of shadow, only to exit the shadow very close to the camera, where his whole face is suddenly completely lit. This use of much more shadow than light, soon one of the main techniques of low-key lighting, heavily influenced film noir.

The Long Voyage Home and *Citizen Kane* share a number of other striking similarities:

Both films allowed lenses at times to distort faces in close-up, especially during low-key lighting sequences described above.

Sets, both interiors and exteriors, were lit mostly from the floor instead of from the rafters high above. A radical departure from Hollywood's traditional lighting, this technique also took much longer to execute, thus contributing significantly to production costs. However, the effect was strikingly more realistic, since light sources placed closer to the characters allowed softer lighting, which lights placed far above the set could not produce.

Both directors, Welles as well as Ford, put Toland's credit as cinematographer on screen at the same time as their own credit as director (director/producer in Welles's case), an unusual and conspicuously generous tribute; in both films, Toland's credit was also the same size as the director's.

In this production shot from *Citizen Kane*, Toland is "manning" his Mitchell camera while Welles is watching from a hospital chair since he had recently broken his leg.

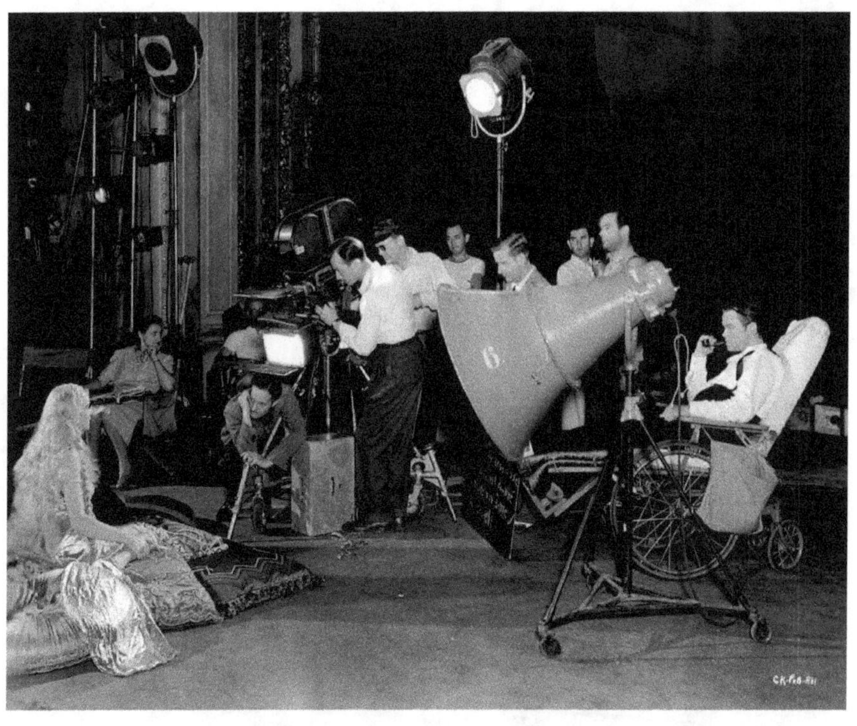

The Shop Around the Corner (1940)

The Shop Around the Corner is a romantic comedy film produced and directed by Ernst Lubitsch and starring Margaret Sullivan, James Stewart, and Frank Morgan. Eschewing regional politics in the years leading up to World War II, the film is about two employees at a leather goods shop in Budapest who can barely stand each other, not realizing they are falling in love as anonymous correspondents through their letters.

Scene: Christmas Dinner

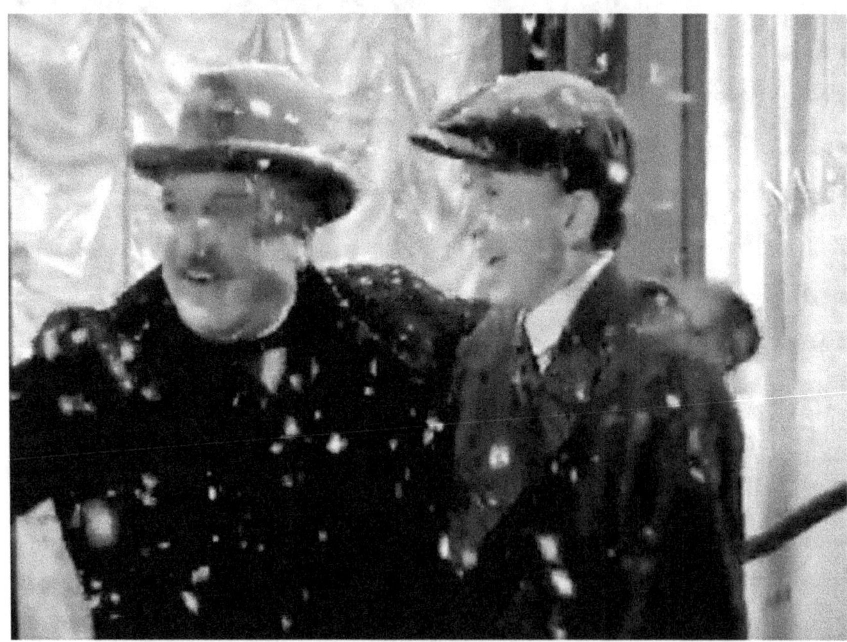

One scene in the movie lovingly touched my heart. Matuschek (Frank Morgan), having lost the love of his wife and then surviving an attempted suicide, is all alone on Christmas Eve. He is a decent employer, but he is also a stern man who has always maintained a certain distance from his employees. However, now faced with the prospect of spending the holiday alone, his facade crumbles. One by one, each employee graciously decline his invitation to a fancy restaurant, for one reason or another, until just he and the newly hired lowly delivery boy (Charles Smith) are left alone on the snowy streets. Matuschek swallows his pride and asks the boy to Christmas dinner with all the trimmings, and as they banter back and forth about their favorite dishes (stuffed goose, cucumber salad with sour cream) Matuschek's face lights up with the joy of finding a true friend and happiness for the first time in many years.

Legendary character actor Frank Morgan's best-remembered film performances are in *The Wizard of Oz* (1939): he played the Wizard and five other roles: the carnival huckster "Professor Marvel," the gatekeeper at the Emerald City, the coachman of the carriage drawn by "The Horse of a Different Color," the Emerald City guard (who initially refuses to let Dorothy and her friends in to see the Wizard), and the Wizard's scary face projection. An actor with a wide range, Morgan was equally effective playing seriously dramatic, comical, befuddled men, such as Jesse Kiffmeyer in *Saratoga* (1937) and Mr. Ferris in *Casanova Brown* (1944), as he was with more serious, troubled characters like Hugo Matuschek in *The Shop Around the Corner*, Professor Roth in *The Mortal Storm* (both released in 1940) and Willie Grogan in *The Human Comedy* (1943).

Saboteur (1942)

Saboteur is a film noir spy thriller movie ably directed by Alfred Hitchcock with a screenplay written by Peter Viertel and others. The film stars Robert Cummings, Pricilla Lane, and Norman Lloyd. Barry Kane (Cummings) is an average Joe plant worker, suddenly finds himself running from the law when he is falsely accused of sabotaging the airplane factory where he works and causing his best friend's death. Barry is fairly certain of the real culprit, a mysterious figure named Frye (Lloyd), and pursues him across the country, both to clear his own name and to stop a network of fascist sympathizers from carrying out even more destructive deeds. Along the way, he hooks up with a feisty model who at first believes him to be the villain but eventually trusts him. They fall in love, but time is running out, and they must join forces to stop the saboteur from striking again. The final confrontation between Frye and Kane takes place on the torch of the Statue of Liberty, symbolizing the never-ending battle of tyranny against democracy.

Scene: Statue of Liberty

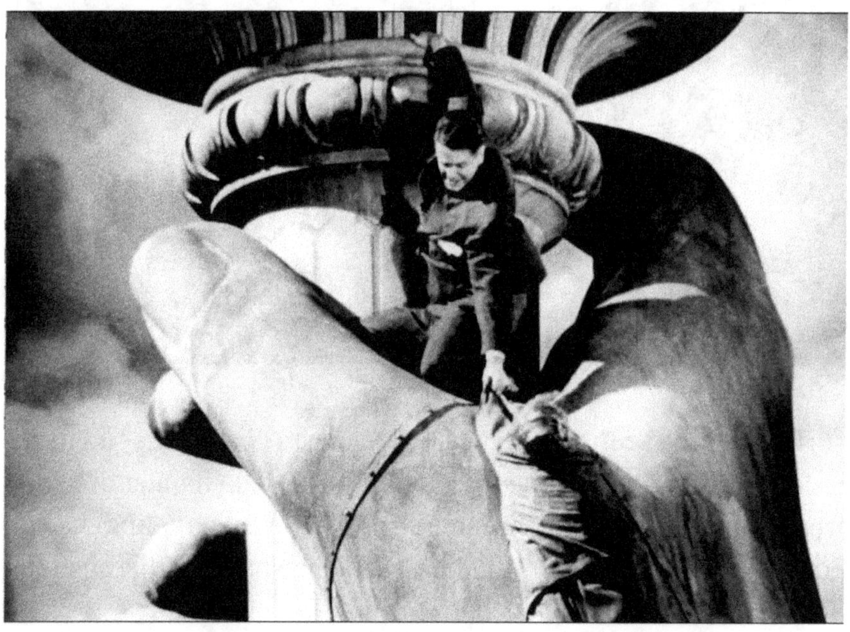

Saboteur is often seen as a forerunner to Hitchcock's *North by Northwest* (1959) with its story of an innocent man on the run from the law and in pursuit of the real criminals, taking him out of his element and across vast stretches of the country. The final Mount Rushmore (another National Monument) sequence in the latter movie is closely related to the Statue of Liberty sequence in *Saboteur*.

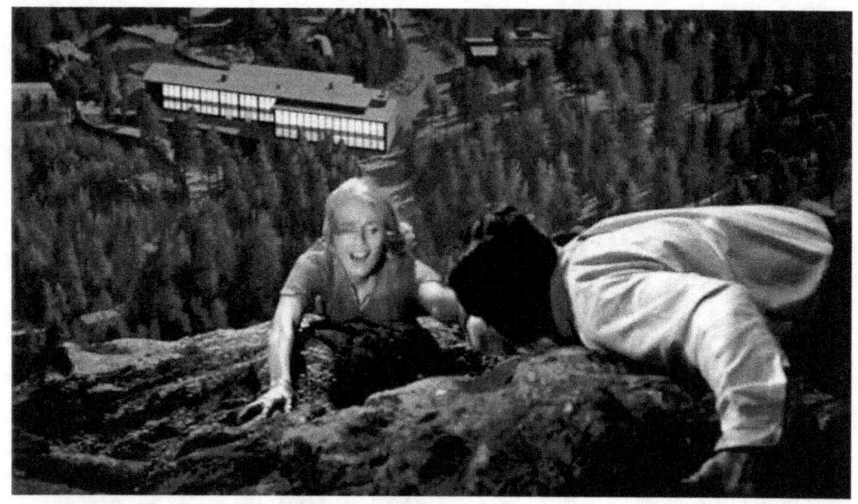

This may be seen as Hitchcock's chance to correct his "mistake" in *Saboteur*, i.e., having the villain, not the hero, in danger of falling from a great height. The director always believed dangling the bad guy was a miscalculation that lessened the suspense because the audience didn't care if he fell.

The premise of the wrong man fleeing the law and pursuing the true villain across the country, encountering either hostility or support from various everyday Americans along the way, was also used with great success in the truly classic and memorable television series *The Fugitive* (September 1963 to August 1967) which starred David Janssen and Barry Morse and its 1993 film version which featured Harrison Ford and Tommy Lee Jones as the respective hunted and hunter characters.

The special effects crew took stills of the statue's upraised hand, her torch, and the ledge beneath it. These were recreated to scale on the Universal soundstage.

The use of the Statue of Liberty, as a climactic finish to a movie or merely as a backdrop, may have begun in *Saboteur*, but it continued for years to come.

In fact, there are probably close to fifty movies, maybe more, in which the Statue of Liberty plays an uncredited (and probably unsalaried) role. I won't attempt to discuss them all. That is the subject of a book onto itself.

As in the movie *Saboteur*, the Statue of Liberty is often used as the backdrop of violence in the unending battle between good and evil in the world.

There is a sequence set on top of the Statue of Liberty in *Remo Williams: The Adventure Begins* (1985).

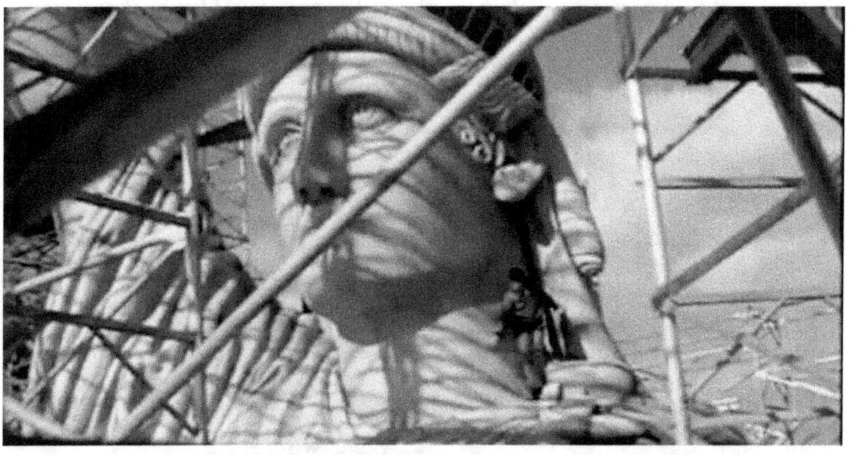

The 2000 movie *X-Men* used the Statue in its climactic finale between the X-men and the villain Magneto.

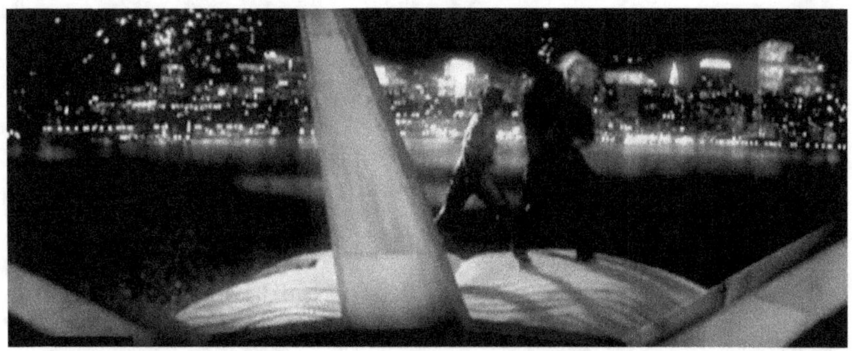

Fortunately, the Statue of Liberty is more commonly portrayed in movies as a symbol of hope and freedom.

In the 1984 movie *Splash*, a mermaid (portrayed by actress Daryl Hannah) turns herself into a human and views the statue as an icon of freedom and a fresh start.

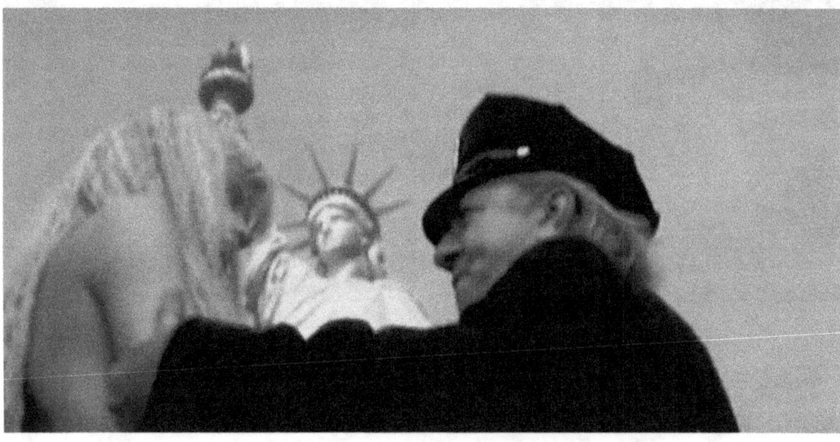

The Statue of Liberty plays a comedic and triumphal role in the 1989 movie *Ghostbuster 2*.

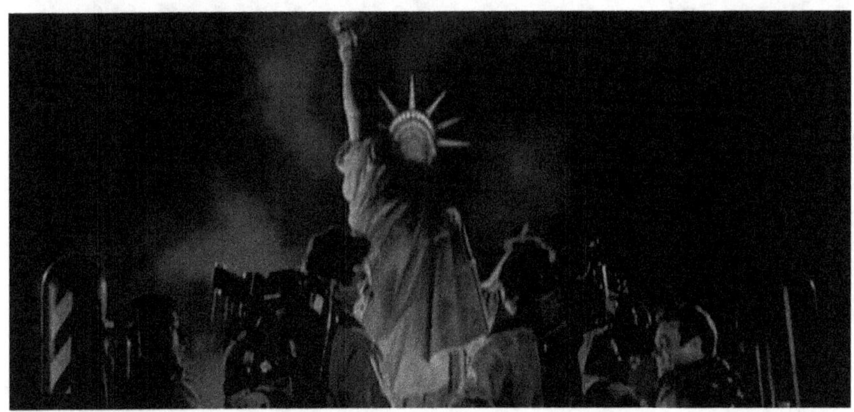

Rose, portrayed by actress Kate Winslet, cast as one of the survivors who appeared in the 1992 movie *Titanic*, views the Statue of Liberty as a sign of renewed hope and endurance after her traumatic experience and terrible loss.

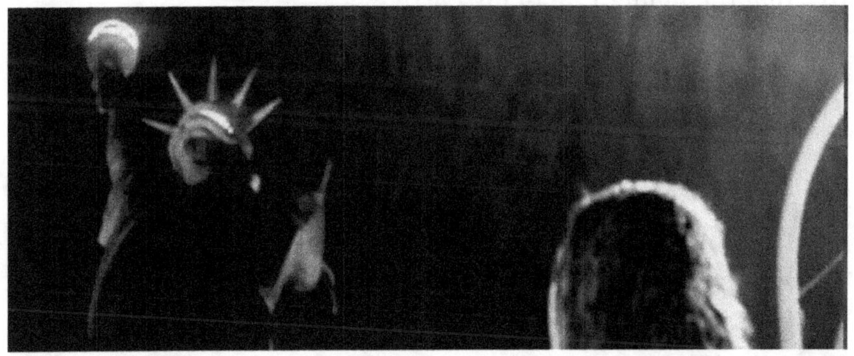

Although considered to be an icon of hope and freedom, the Statue is often associated with the four D's: despair, destruction, disaster, and doom.

The first of these four D movies is worth noting. A tsunami decapitates the Statue of Liberty in the 1933 disaster film *Deluge*.

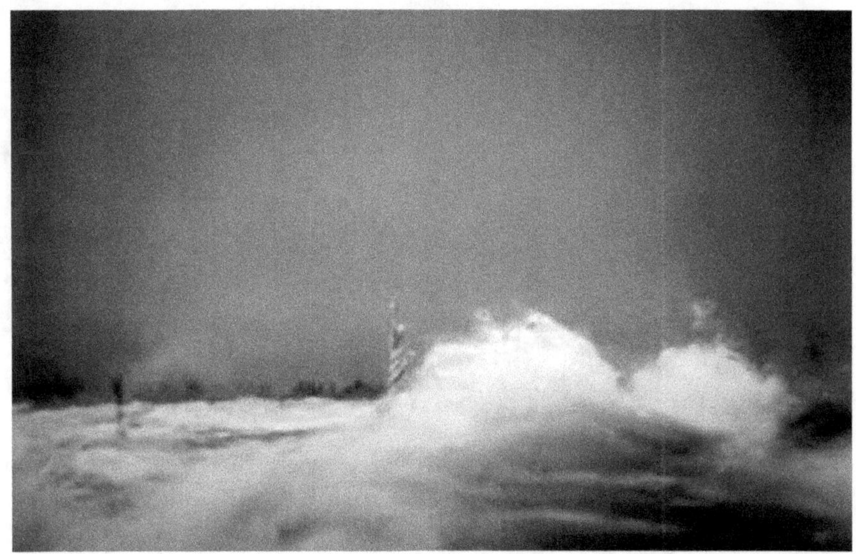

It played a pivotal role in the thrilling climax on the supposedly alien *Planet of the Apes* (1968) when the hero, in total despair, realizes that the planet is actually Earth.

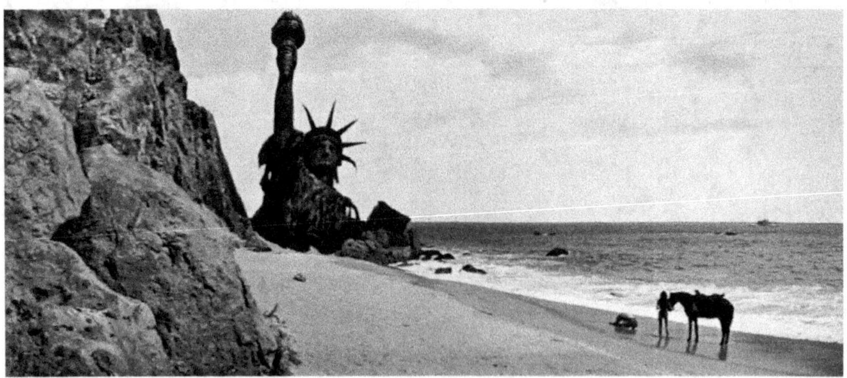

The poor statue is used as an actual weapon of destruction in the horrible 1987 *Superman IV: The Quest for Peace* by its villain Nuclear Man.

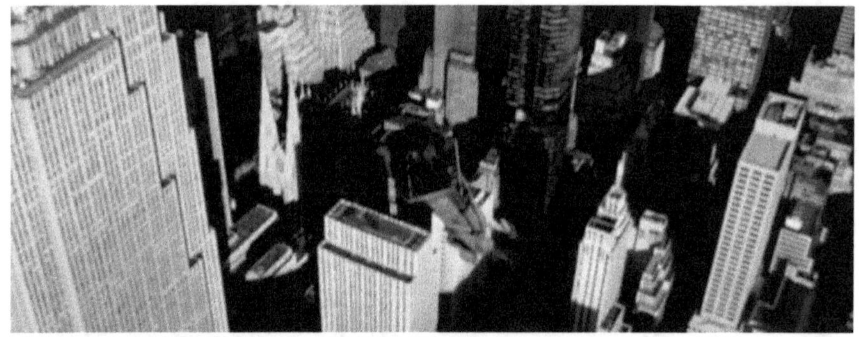

The poor lady is flattened in the thriller 1996 sci-fi thriller *Independence Day* by nasty aliens. Liberty is onscreen so briefly, most people probably don't remember she was even in it, part of a montage of other famous world sites busted under the black sky of the alien saucers.

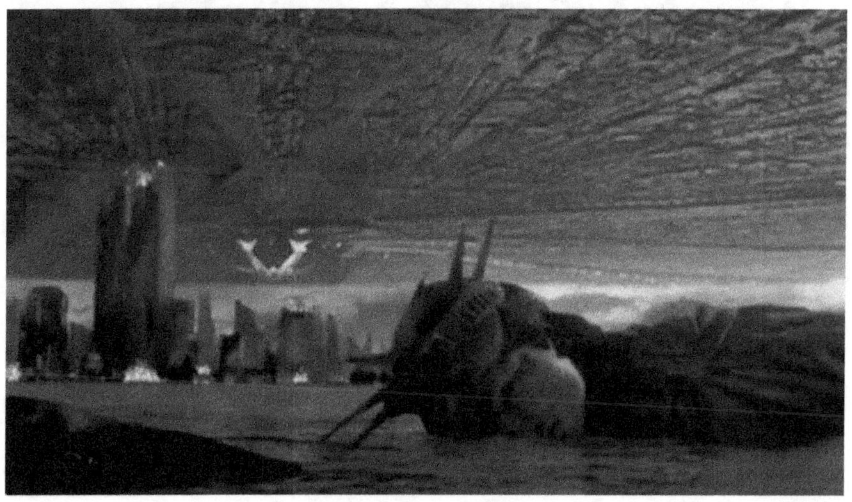

Another tsunami decapitates the Statue of Liberty in the 1998 disaster film *Deep Impact*.

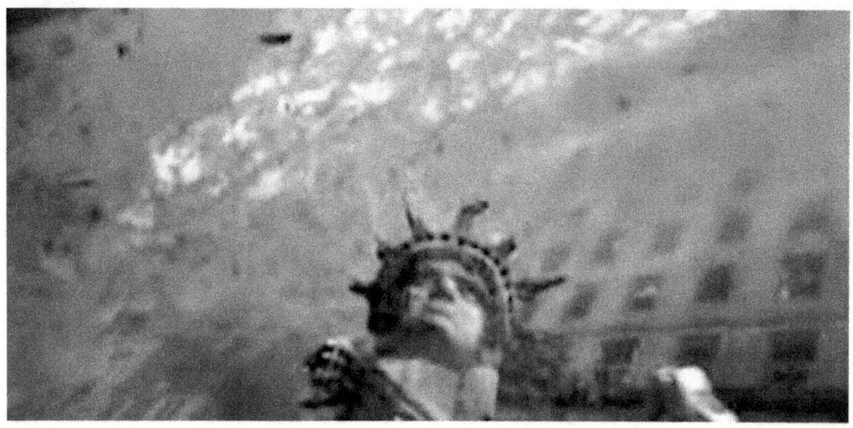

Still, another (whew) tsunami destroys the Statue in the 2004 disaster flick *The Day After Tomorrow*.

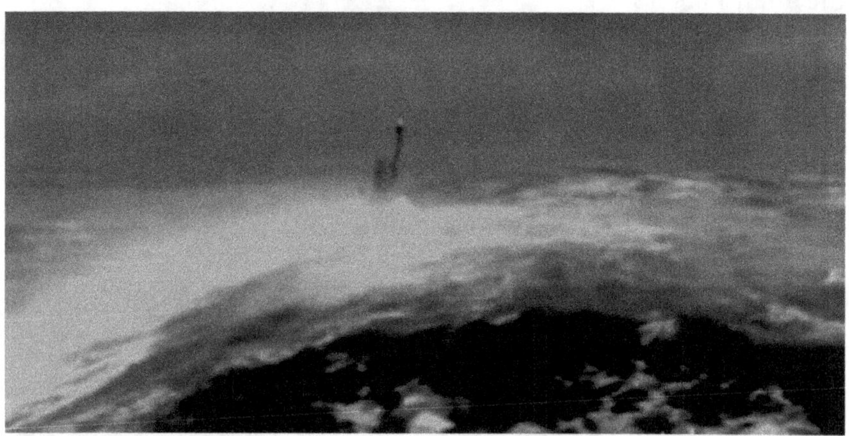

The decapitated head of the Statue suddenly appears in the 2008 disaster film *Cloverfield*.

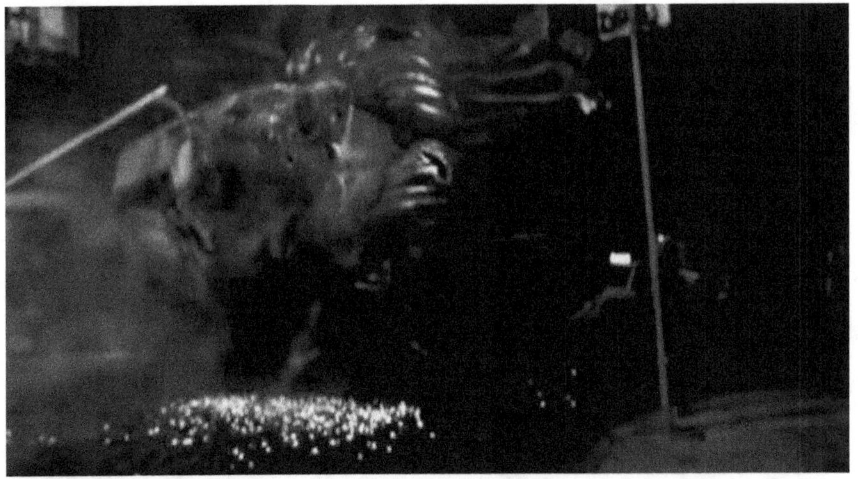

The Third Man (1949)

The Third Man is a visually-stylish film noir thriller directed by Carol Reed, written by Graham Greene and starring Joseph Cotten, Alida Valli, Orson Welles, and Trevor Howard. The film is set in post-World War II Vienna was an worldwide overnight hit and is often listed as the greatest British film of all time. American influence came from producer David O. Selznick and the stars Joseph Cotten and Orson Welles, but there is no mistaking the European flavor of the movie. Shot largely on location, it captures the darkness and decay of the formerly grand city that is now littered with rubble, just as it captures the corruption and decadence in the soul of people warped by World War. It centers on Holly Martins (Joseph Cotton), an American pulp writer, who is given a job in bombed-out, post-war Vienna by his friend Harry Lime (Orson Welles), but when Holly arrives in Vienna, he gets the news that Lime is dead. Martins then meets with Lime's unusually eccentric, and often contradictory acquaintances, in an attempt to investigate what he considers a suspicious traffic accident that killed Lime.

Scene: Harry Lime, I Presume

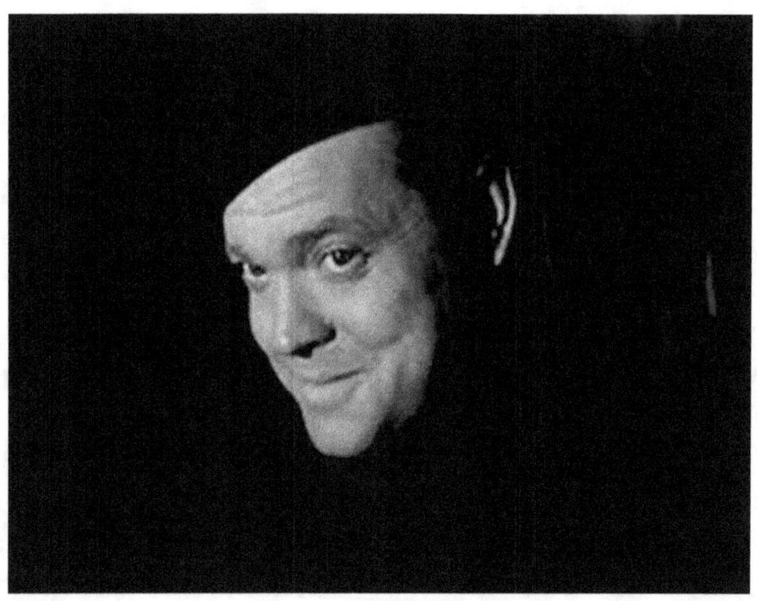

One night, Martins becomes aware of a figure in a doorway on the opposite side of the wet street from the apartment of Lime's Czechoslovakian girlfriend Anna Schmidt (Alida Valli) when he hears her cat meow loudly. The animal rubs itself at the feet of the silent, motionless figure. The figure's big shoes are illuminated— whose are they? Holly defiantly calls out to the figure to come out and reveal himself. Then, Holly momentarily and suddenly sees Harry, the "third man" himself. (The third man, whom he suspected was responsible for Harry's "accidental" death.)

Light from an upstairs window briefly illuminates the figure's face, shining straight across the street. Amazed to see Harry still alive, Holly is startled by the sight of the teasing, smiling face of his friend staring back at him. The light is extinguished, and before

Holly can reach his friend, a car approaches and blocks his path, coming between them. The figure makes off and vanishes to the sound of retreating footsteps in the dark as Holly finds the doorway empty by the time he crosses the street.

The atmospheric use of black-and-white expressionist cinematography by Robert Krasker, with harsh lighting and distorted "Dutch angle" camera technique, is a major feature of *The Third Man*. Combined with the iconic theme music, seedy locations, and acclaimed performances from the cast, the style evokes the atmosphere of an exhausted, cynical, post-war Vienna at the start of the Cold War.

Six weeks of principal photography was shot on location in Vienna, ending on 11 December 1948. The crew sprayed water on the cobbled streets to make them reflect light at night.

Robert Krasker shot the night scenes of the film, which present a brilliantly stylized world filled with wet streets, shining cobblestones, shafts of brilliant light illuminating running shadows—angled shots with stark contrasts, and deep-focus baroque detail. The flashy photography was not merely for show. It truly reflected the mindset of a city divided. The story, too, is served by the theatrics, and the corruption and decay of the city are also reflective of the corrupted morals to be found within. In a movie filled with wonderful performances, Orson Welles is truly unforgettable as Harry Lime. One of the great, complex villains of the cinema, Lime sets himself up in the Russian sector after being "killed" in an accident, and maneuvers about the city using the underground sewer system.

Some modern sources also credit Welles with the famous shot in which "Harry Lime" is suddenly revealed in a shaft of light, but this scene is as it appears in Graham Greene's novella.

Harry's initial appearance is punctuated with the wonderful zither score composed by Anton Karas. Composer and Zither-master Anton Karas had quite a career following the release of *The Third*

Man. His "3rd Man Theme" (as it was more commonly written out) was a worldwide hit. Consequently, the tune was covered by many artists and performers throughout the 1950s and beyond. The tune was adapted to almost every musical style and taste, from Big Band, calypso, space-age, cha-cha, Hawaiian, rock, and more.

The Third Man rewards repeated viewings because it goes far beyond being a witty and exciting mystery-thriller. It flips all expectations on their heads by featuring an attractive embodiment of villainy and ineffective heroism, an enjoyable sense of cynicism and a bleak view of romance, a calming sense of chaos, and a nostalgic vision of decadence. And when you meet Harry Lime, prepare yourself for a smiling justification for everyday corporate evil in the post-war modern world.

John M. Miller, writing for Turner Classic Movies, stated:

> The popularity of The Third Man, and especially the charm and allure of Harry Lime as a character, spawned spin-off series for both radio and television. Orson Welles had been a fixture on the radio since the late 1930s of course, through such series as Mercury Theatre on the Air, Campbell Playhouse, and Orson Welles Almanac. Beginning in 1951, he could be heard as the title character in the British series The Adventures of Harry Lime. A total of 52 half-hour episodes were recorded, several of which were also written by Welles. The premise was set up every week: After the audience hears Lime met his death in the sewers of Vienna in the opening, we hear Welles say, "Harry Lime had many lives. And I can recount all of them. How do I know? It's very simple. Because my name is Harry Lime."

The stories are flashbacks, then, of a less villainous but nevertheless roguish adventurer and opportunist hopping the globe in search of romance and easy riches. In one notable episode written by Welles, "Man of Mystery," Lime meets up with eccentric financer Gregory Arkadin. In this show, Welles was developing ideas he would later incorporate into his film Mr. Arkadin, released in 1955.

In 1959, the BBC and Twentieth-Century Fox co-produced a syndicated TV series called *The Third Man*, but it bore little resemblance to the film. Michael Rennie starred as a much more respectable Harry Lime, now an art dealer jet setting the world and solving crimes with a sidekick played by Jonathan Harris. Seventy-seven half-hour episodes were produced. Although this series did not follow the lead of the film, it did set a tone for subsequent TV jet-setters, such as those in the British mystery spy thriller *The Saint* (1962 to 1969) starring Roger Moore, and the NBC spy spoof comedy *I Spy* (September 15, 1965 to April 15, 1968), starring Robert Culp and Bill Cosby.

The Third Man wonderfully captures a time and a place unique in history; it is an early example of a cold-war intrigue that, while not depicting a single spy, can be seen as a prototype for spy thrillers to come. It also works as a study of post-WWII morality with Harry Lime viewing his victims not as humans but as far-removed dots that stop moving. It is also a character study featuring a hopeless love triangle.

Since Graham Greene is so associated with the Cold War spy mythos, both in fact and in his fiction, and since the spy genre was to become so important to the 1960s British film industry, it should be no surprise that there are connections between *The Third Man* and the later James Bond series of films. Reed's assistant director, Guy Hamilton, went on to a notable directing career of his own, most conspicuously at the helm of four James Bond films, including *Goldfinger* (1964), which many regard as the quintessential Bond movie. The others he directed were *Diamonds Are Forever* (1971), *Live and Let Die* (1973), and *The Man With the Golden Gun* (1974). Hamilton also directed the non-Bond spy thriller *Funeral in Berlin* (1966).

All About Eve (1950)

All About Eve is a riveting film written and directed by Joseph L. Mankiewicz and produced by Darryl F. Zanuck. The film stars Bette Davis as Margo Channing, a highly regarded but aging Broadway star. Anne Baxter plays Eve Harrington, an ambitious young fan who maneuvers herself into Channing's life, ultimately threatening Channing's career and her personal relationships. However, Bette Davis' famous eyes flash with mischief at every turn. She's not the type of gal to say "no drama" on her Tinder profile. She creates it.

This film has a realistic, dramatic depiction of show business and backstage life of Broadway and the New York theater. Thematically, it provides an insightful diatribe against crafty, aspiring, glib, autonomous female thespians who seek success and ambition at any cost without regard to scruples or feelings, When Margo's fiancée-to-be, theatrical director Bill Sampson (Gary Merrill), a show business veteran and one of Margo's inner circle, turns his attention toward Eve, her sympathy for Eve slowly turns into alienation and hostility. Paranoid and suspicious, Margo smells "disaster in the air" before a belated birthday (and welcome home from Hollywood) party for Bill. She is clearly plagued by jealousy, "age obsession," and "paranoiac insecurity," and she turns acerbic toward Eve—"she's a girl with so many interests."

Margo begins to get roaring drunk and feels "Macbethish" in mood—she snidely calls Eve "the kid" and "Junior," feeling menaced by the deceptive young actress. At the height of her bitchery, she warns some of the birthday party guests about what to expect in the film's most famous line—after finishing another martini, her slur is delivered as a lip-sneering, nasty admonition: "Fasten your seat belts; it's going to be a bumpy night."

Scene: "Fasten your seat belts"

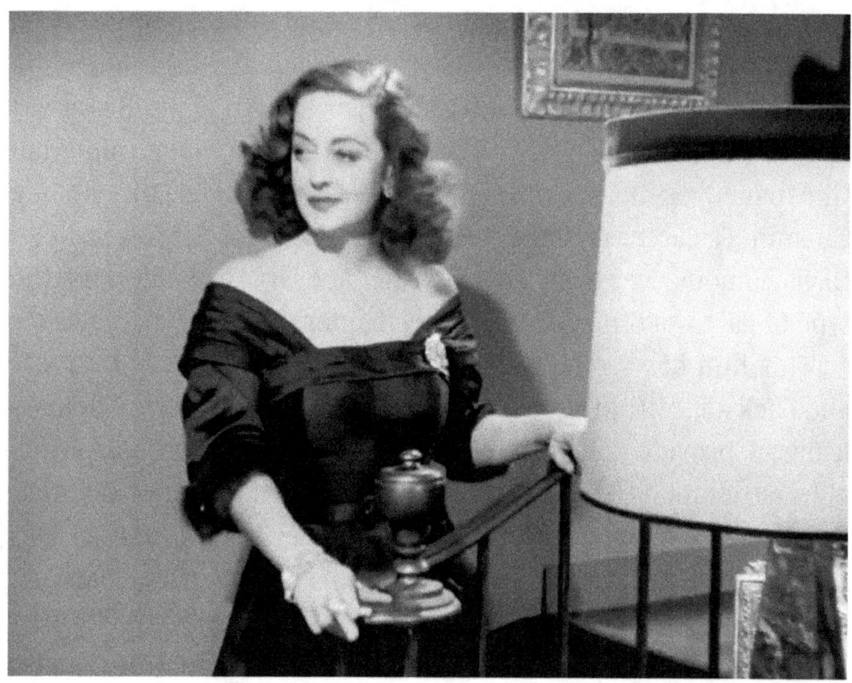

What Margo Channing is talking about here isn't airplane turbulence (the use of seat belts in automobiles did not begin in earnest until the mid- to late-1950s), it is life's turbulence, and she's the one who's going to be shaking things up.

The quote is often misquoted as "Fasten your seat belts; it's going to be a bumpy ride." The actual quote predicts only "a bumpy night," but anyone aware of how human beings behave when power is at stake knows the bumpy ride will last longer than one night. That may explain why the actual quote has been altered in its repetition over the years in order to suit the actual situation at hand by certain human beings over the course of time. The not-so-fictive Miss

Channing understood what vicious games could be played in genteel surroundings.

Film critic Roger Ebert, in his review in *The Great Movies*, says Eve Harrington is "a universal type," and focuses on the aging actress plotline, comparing the film to *Sunset Boulevard*. Similarly, Marc Lee's 2006 review of the film for the *Daily Telegraph* describes a subtext "into the darker corners of show business, exposing its inherent ageism, especially when it comes to female stars."

Kathleen Woodward's 1999 book *Figuring Age: Women, Bodies, Generations (Theories of Contemporary Culture)*, also discusses themes that appeared in many of the "aging actress" films of the 1950s and 1960s, including *All About Eve*. She reasons that Margo has three options:

> To continue to work, she can perform the role of a young woman, one she no longer seems that interested in. She can take up the position of the angry bitch, the drama queen who holds court. Or she can accept her culture's gendered discourse of aging which figures her as in her moment of fading. Margo ultimately chooses the latter option, accepting her position as one of loss.

The plot of the film has been used numerous times, frequently as an outright homage to the film, with one notable example being a 1974 episode of *The Mary Tyler Show* titled "A New Sue Ann." In the episode, the character of Sue Ann Nivens (Betty White), hostess of a popular local cooking show, hires a young, pretty, and very eager fan (Linda Kelsey) as her apprentice and assistant, but the neophyte quickly begins to sabotage her mentor, in an attempt to replace her as host of the show. Sue Ann, however, unlike Margo Channing, prevails in the end, countering the young woman's attempts to steal her success and sending her on her way.

The movie is based on Mary Orr's 1946 *Cosmopolitan* magazine short story, "The Wisdom of Eve." There is only one person to thank for *All About Eve*, and that is Elisabeth Bergner, the notable stage actress, who became the unfortunate victim of an aspiring young hopeful whose only motives were to destroy and take advantage of her newfound employment that was granted to her by Bergner. Years later, Bergner reflected back on the past and recalled the incident to Mary Orr about the young girl who she first met while performing in the stage play of *The Two Mrs. Carrolls*. Orr was that immersed in the story that it became the basis for a short story. The idea of a young ingénue upstaging and charting the territory of an already established actress was a worthy subject for a film. Previously, a similar premise had been generating in the minds of a few studio executives, especially Joseph L. Mankiewicz, who saw this sort of plot as great material. However, the thought quickly diminished until Mankiewicz read "The Wisdom of Eve" and suddenly realized that he could make movie magic with this type of story.

> "I can think of no project that from the outset was as rewarding from the first day to the last. It is easy to understand why. It was a great script, had a great director, and was a cast of professionals all with parts they liked. It was a charmed production from the word go."
> —Bette Davis on *All About Eve*

A Few Good Men (1992)

A Few Good Men is stirring legal drama film directed by Rob Reiner and starring Tom Cruise, Jack Nicholson, and Demi Moore in the lead roles. It was adapted for the screen by Aaron Sorkin from his play of the same name. The film revolves around the court-martial of two U.S. Marines charged with the murder of a fellow Marine and the tribulations of their lawyers as they prepare a case to defend them. In the heart of the nation's capital, in a courthouse of the U.S. government, one man will stop at nothing to keep his honor, and one will stop at nothing to find the truth.

Mention the 1992 film *A Few Good Men* in a conversation, and within a few minutes, you'll invariably hear someone's best Jack Nicholson impression as he snarls, "You can't handle the truth!" The role also landed Jack Nicholson a cool $5 million—not bad for four scenes of screen time and two weeks' work!

Tom Cruise portrays Lieutenant (junior grade) Daniel Alastair Kaffee, USN, JAG Corps, and Jack Nicholson as Colonel Nathan R. Jessup, USMC.

Scene: Jessup: You can't handle the truth!

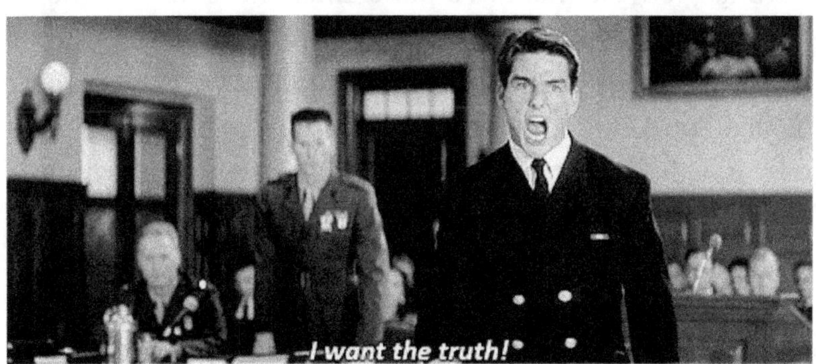

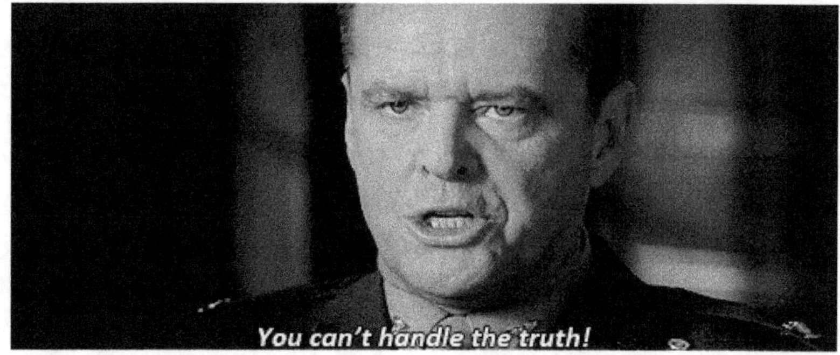

Son, we live in a world that has walls, and those walls have to be guarded by men with guns. Who's gonna do it? You? You, Lieutenant Weinberg? I have a greater responsibility than you can possibly fathom. You weep for Santiago and you curse the Marines. You have that luxury. You have the luxury of not knowing what I know: that Santiago's death, while tragic, probably saved lives. And my existence, while grotesque and incomprehensible to you, saves lives! You don't want the truth, because deep down in places you don't talk about at parties, you want me on that wall. You need me on that wall. We use words like "honor," "code," "loyalty." We use these words as the backbone of a life spent defending something. You use them as a punchline. I have neither the time nor the inclination to explain myself to a man who rises and sleeps under the blanket of the very freedom that I provide, and then questions the manner in which I provide it! I would rather you just said, "thank you," and went on your way. Otherwise, I suggest you pick up a weapon, and stand a post. Either way, I don't give a damn what you think you are entitled to!

According to Eleanor Quin writing in TCM:

> But Nicholson did not merely rest on his laurels: for the filming of the climactic courtroom scene, Reiner required several takes of Jack's monologue in order to film different characters' reactions. Reiner explained: "We have this eighteen-minute scene in the courtroom at the end, and he's got a speech that's, like, two pages long. And he gets all worked up. He comes in there and bangs it right off. He's there to work and do his job. And then we did coverage on all the other people, and he was off-camera. He must have done the thing fifty times, with the same amount of enthusiasm, with the same amount of energy every time. I was surprised, because you get ideas about a guy of his stature. And I said, 'Jack, it's amazing, you do your...' And he says to me simply, 'Raab, I love to act. I don't get a chance to play a part this good very often.' And that's it. He loves to act."

The film scored four Oscar nominations, including a Best Supporting Actor for Nicholson, but didn't win any Academy Awards. Still, the filmmakers think they got their $5 million worth for Nicholson's now-legendary performance. As he once explained, "Let me put it to you this way. They won't pay it to you if you ain't worth it. Period."

When Jack Nicholson uttered, "You can't handle the truth!" in the movie *A Few Good Men*, the line became an instant classic, permanently etched in American pop culture. There is great wisdom in this short quote, as it expresses an important reality: most people actually really can't "handle the truth" about many things, and that many of our problems in life spring from our insistence upon avoidance or denial of the more difficult realities of life.

I think the relevance of this is quite apparent when one looks at today's political reality in Washington, DC, and the seemingly unending tweet rants of "fake news" by President 45 and his "perfect" everything.

Sometimes unwavering allegiance to a fixation, whether it is true or not, can blind someone from accepting basic truths and norms and prevent them from accepting the clear and present danger that others clearly see.

MY TOP 5 MOVIE SCENES

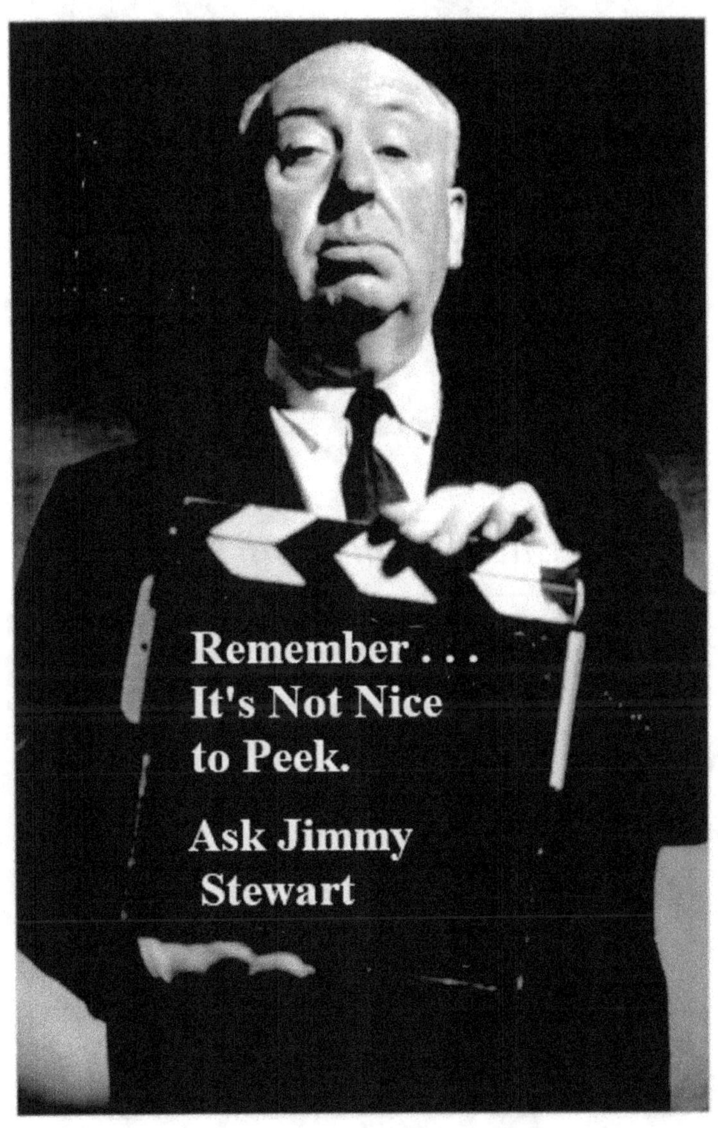

The Grapes of Wrath: I'll Be There

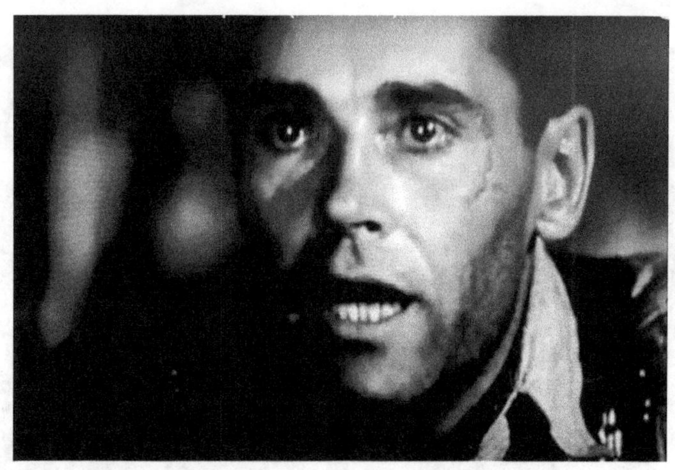

Citizen Kane: Rosebud

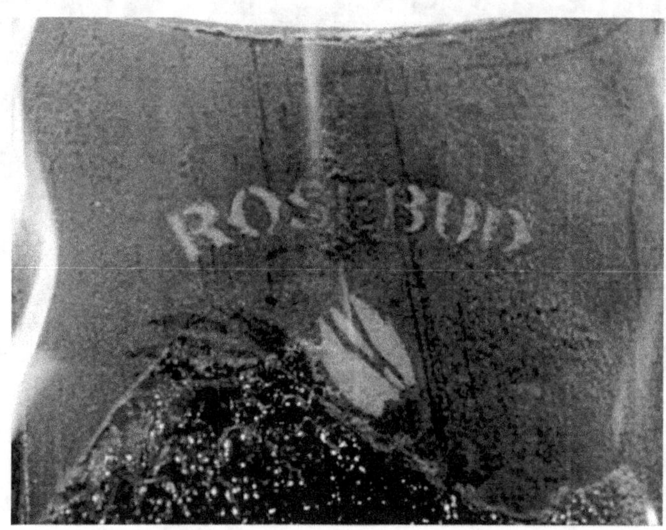

Psycho: The Shower

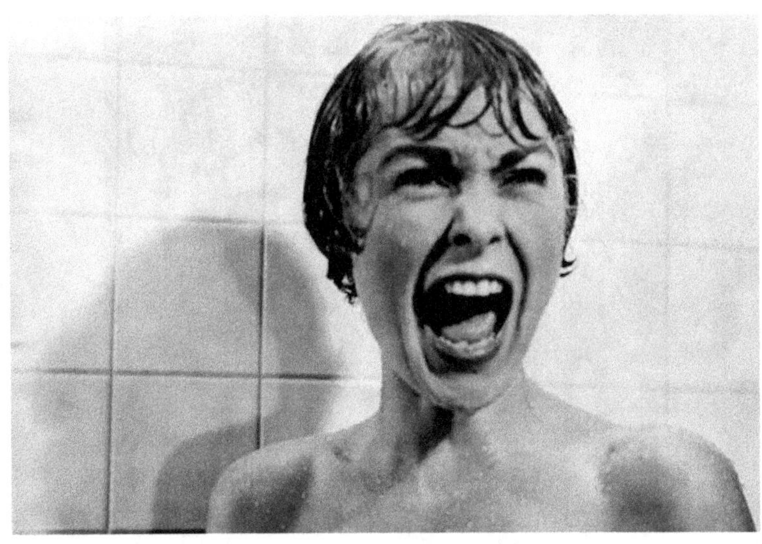

Rocky: Rocky Steps

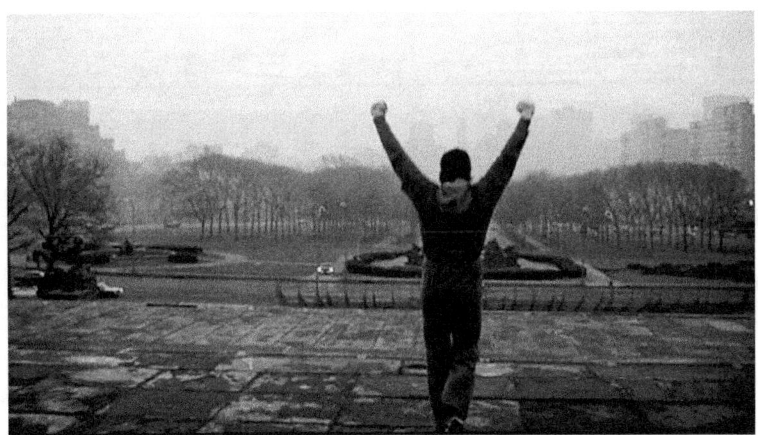

The Kid: Two Hearts United

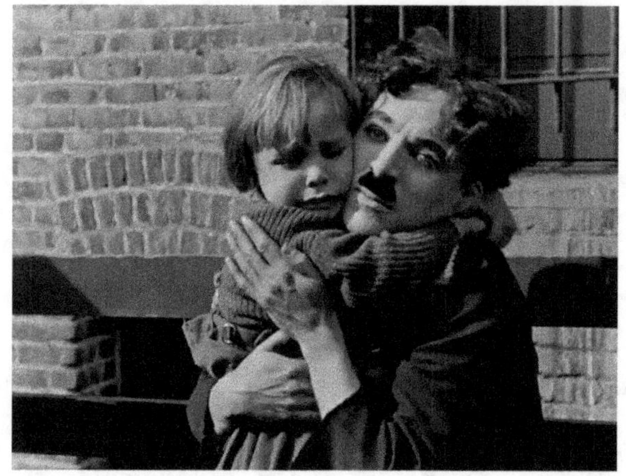

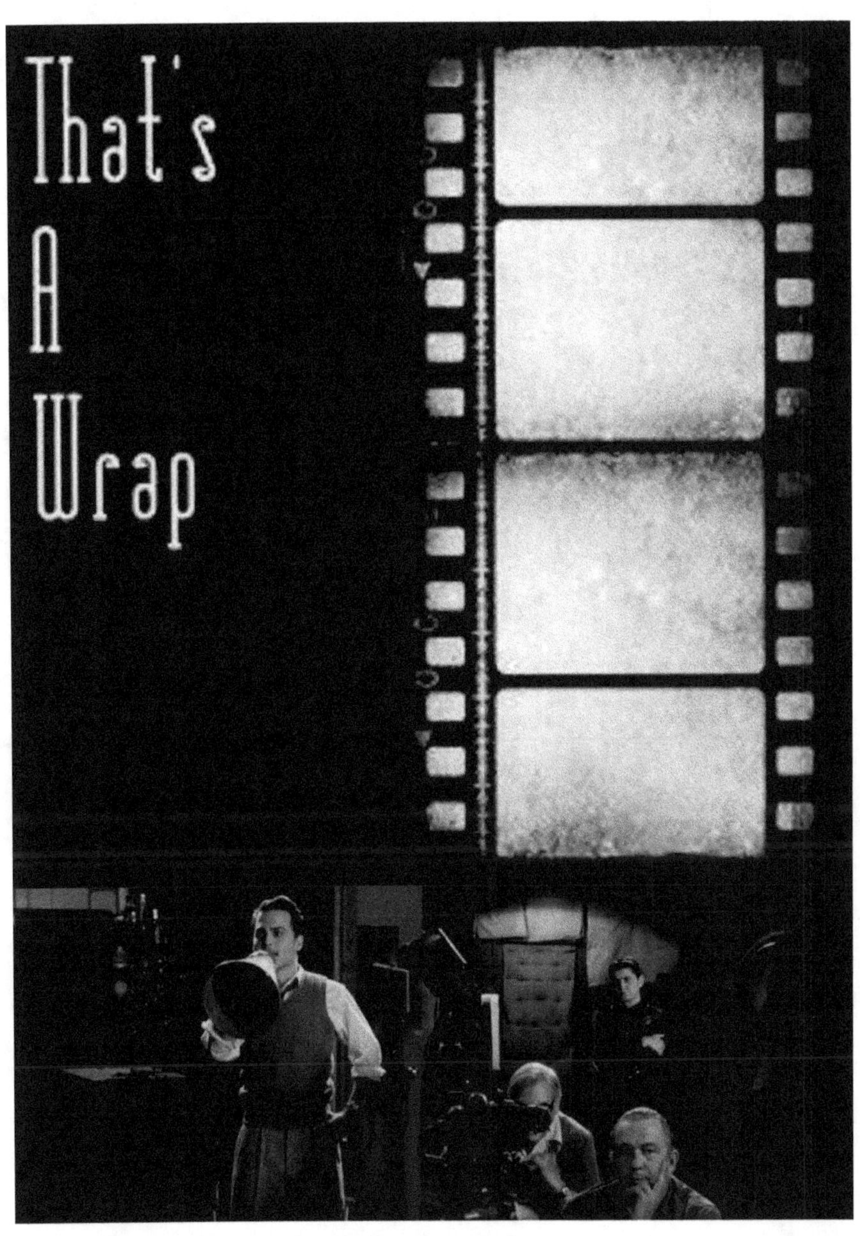
That's
A
Wrap